O Daughter of Babylon

Journey of an Iraqi Patriot
and
What Chilcot Didn't Say

Riad El-Taher

Edited by Francis Clark-Lowes

Published by New Generation Publishing in 2018

Copyright © Francis Clark-Lowes 2018

First Edition

The author asserts the moral right under the Copyright, Designs and Patents Act 1988 to be identified as the author of this work.

All Rights reserved. No part of this publication may be reproduced, stored in a retrieval system or transmitted, in any form or by any means without the prior consent of the author, nor be otherwise circulated in any form of binding or cover other than that which it is published and without a similar condition being imposed on the subsequent purchaser.

Every effort has been made to fulfil the requirements with regard to reproducing copyright material. The author, editor and publisher will be glad to rectify any omissions at the earliest opportunity.

www.newgeneration-publishing.com

O daughter of Babylon, doomed to be destroyed,
blessed shall he be who repays you
with what you have done to us!

Blessed shall he be who takes your little ones
and dashes them against the rock!

Psalm 137, verses 8 and 9 (English Standard Version)

Dedicated to the people of Iraq whose opposition to the draconian UN sanctions, and the occupation which followed, was such an inspiration.

For my children and grandchildren.

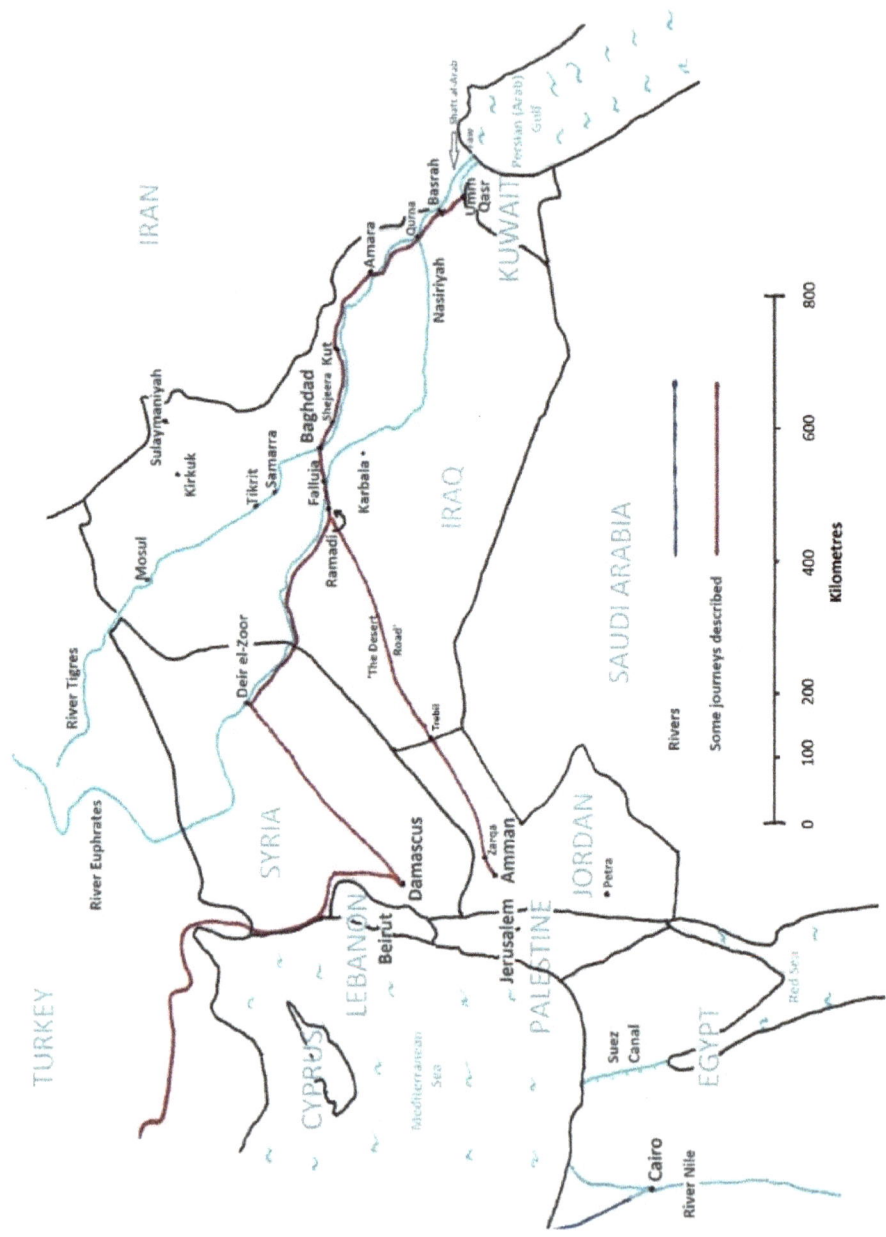

CONTENTS

Abbreviations	xii
Introduction by the late Tam Dalyell	xv
Editor's Foreword	xvii
Acknowledgements and Remarks	xxiii
Illustrations and Credits	xxvii
Chapter One: Crossing cultures	1

- Youth in Basrah
- College in Southend-on-Sea
- Holiday work, Politics, and College in Brighton
- Marriage, Honeymoon and Return to Iraq

Chapter Two: Engineering in the Oil Industry	15

- Entry into Iraq's oil industry
- Shell on Teesside
- The Kuwait Oil Company
- Short stay in Libya, and Coppas
- Pioneering North Sea development with McDermott

Chapter Three: Enterprise and idealism	30

- Establishing Petcon
- AREC: Enthusiasm and Disillusion
- Free-range poultry farming
- Petcon's Heyday

Chapter Four: Kuwait and the Arab Nation   43
- Kuwait and political engagement
- The enduring imperial legacy

Chapter Five: The Desert Road   57
- My country in ruins
- Tam Dalyell, George Galloway, Tim Llewellyn

Chapter Six: More on the Desert Road   79
- Sue Lloyd Roberts
- Albert Reynolds, Mick Lanigan et al
- Canon Andrew White
- A delegation of church leaders
- Rescued by Jany le Pen

Chapter Seven: Friendship across Frontiers   95
- Establishing FAF
- The Labour Victory of 1997

Chapter Eight: Paradise and the President   114
- My farm by the Tigris
- Saddam Hussein

Chapter Nine: Oil-for-Food and the Surcharge   131
- New opportunities for Petcon
- The oil-for-food programme
- The surcharge crisis

Chapter Ten: In the Juggernaut's Path   145
- 9/11 and Iraq
- Weapons of Mass Destruction
- The Iranian connection
- Shifting justifications

- The 'Dodgy Dossier'
- Lord Goldsmith's evolving advice
- The Atlantic Summit

Chapter Eleven: The Extra Mile for Peace   **161**
- Stop the War Coalition
- Acting as a go-between
- My last trip to Iraq
- Human shields
- Tony Benn's trip to Baghdad
- Protest marches across the globe
- Reaching out to the opposition
- What if?
- FAF vindicated

Chapter Twelve: Back under the Yoke   **174**
- The Second Gulf War
- Establishing the occupation
- Devilish details
- De-Ba'athification
- The aftermath

Chapter Thirteen: What to do now?   **195**
- FAF revises its strategy
- 'End the occupation!'
- Don't divide Iraq
- Black gold
- Demanding an inquiry

Chapter Fourteen: Political prisoners and assassinations   **214**
- Saddam Hussein
- Tariq Aziz
- Intellectual cleansing

Chapter Fifteen: A Tale of Two Trials: Part 1,   **231**
- The Chilcot Inquiry is announced
- Scepticism about the inquiry
- The Iraq Inquiry report
- What about oil and Palestine?
- Blair can't be charged

Chapter Sixteen: The Tale behind my Tale   **246**
- Levantine politics, British Style
- The Volcker Committee
- The Attorney General, Lord Goldsmith
- Investigating the investigators

Chapter Seventeen: A Tale of Two Trials: Part 2   **259**
- Arrested and bailed
- Charged
- Preliminary hearings
- Sentencing

Chapter Eighteen: At Her Majesty's Pleasure   **277**
- Wandsworth Prison
- Appeal upheld and re-categorisation
- Ford Open Prison
- Release on a tag

Chapter Nineteen: Aftershocks and Afterthoughts   292
- A £70,000 bill
- The Garda on my case
- Expulsion from the Labour Party
- The failure of our campaign
- My naivety
- Disillusion with democracy
- The so-called Arab Spring

Chapter Twenty: Towards Journey's End   311
- Winding up FAF
- The balance sheet of US-British intervention
- Thoughts of a free man
- What Chilcot didn't say
- Resolution through yoga

Appendix One: Timeline   326

Appendix Two: 'In the Footsteps of Sir Percy,'
                by Tim Llewellyn (1993)   329

Appendix Three: Tony Benn's Interview with
                Saddam Hussein (2003)   334

Appendix Four: Tam Dalyell's obituary of
                Tariq Aziz (2015)   341

Endpiece: 'From Pol Pot to ISIS,'
                by John Pilger (2015)   346

Annotated Index   353

ABBREVIATIONS USED IN THIS BOOK

ADNOC	Abu Dhabi National Oil Company
ARAMCO	Arabian-American Oil Company (now Saudi Arabian Oil Company)
AREC	Arab Engineering Company
AUC	American University of Cairo
BAE	BAE Systems plc, previously British Aerospace
BBC	British Broadcasting Corporation
BP	British Petroleum
BPC	Basrah Petroleum Company; subsidiary of IPC
CEO	Chief Executive Office
CND	The Campaign for Nuclear Disarmament
CPA	Coalition Provisional Authority
DFI	Development Fund for Iraq
DG	Director General
DTI	The Department of Trade and Industry (British Government)
EU	European Union
FAF	Friendship Across Frontiers
FCO	Foreign and Commonwealth Office (UK)
GEC	General Electric Company
GM	General Manager
HQ	Headquarters
IAMB	International Advisory and Monitoring Board (Iraq)

IMF	International Monetary Fund
INC	Iraqi National Congress
IPC	Iraq Petroleum Company
KOC	Kuwait Oil Company
MB	Muslim Brotherhood
ME	Middle East/ern
MD	Managing Director
MOD	Ministry of Defence (UK)
MP	Member of Parliament
MPC	Mosul Petroleum Company, a subsidiary of IPC
NATO	North Atlantic Treaty Organisation
NGO	Non-governmental organisation
PPE	Philosophy, Politics and Economics
OAPEC	Organisation of Arab Petroleum Exporting Countries
OECD	Organisation for Economic Cooperation and Development
OPEC	Organisation of the Petroleum Exporting Countries
PM	Prime Minister
QC	Queen's Counsel
RC	Roman Catholic
SCIRI	Supreme Council for the Islamic Revolution in Iraq
SFO	Serious Fraud Office (UK excluding Scotland)
SOMO	State Oil Marketing Organisation (Iraq)
TJP	Truth, Justice and Peace
UAE	United Arab Emirates
UK	United Kingdom

UN	United Nations Organisation
UNESCO	United Nations Educational, Scientific and Cultural Organization
UNGAR	United Nations General Assembly Resolution
UNICEF	United Nations Children's Fund
UNMOVIC	United Nations Monitoring, Verification and Inspection Commission (1999-2007)
UNSCOM	United Nations Special Commission (1991-1999)
UNSCR	United Nations Security Council Resolution
US/USA	United States of America
WCC	World Council of Churches
WFP	World Food Programme
WMD	Weapon of Mass Destruction

INTRODUCTION BY THE LATE TAM DALYELL

I first met Riad El Taher in the period leading up to the First Gulf War. As a former Chairman (1974-1976) of the Parliamentary Labour Party Foreign Affairs Group, and a continuously active member, I had developed an instinct as to which of our myriad of guests were the ones who were worth listening to carefully. My political nostrils told me that not only was Riad El Taher worth listening to, but that his many concerns derived from an un-self-seeking desire to protect the well-being of people in Iraq. My feeling was that El Taher did not have any of the self-interested personal agendas of so many Iraqi émigrés – people who we know now misled Western leaders into the folly of bombing Baghdad.

After I had raised with him the report of the Harvard Medical School on the conditions facing children in Iraq, El Taher suggested I should go and see for myself. How would I get permission? 'I'll get it,' said El Taher. Could I bring Tim Llewellyn, the [ex] Middle East Correspondent of the BBC? 'Yes.' Then my parliamentary colleague, George Galloway, at that point in time the fiercest critic of human rights in Iraq, asked me: 'Can I come?' I knew El Taher must be trusted by the Iraqi government when the answer came 'Yes.' Albeit being careful to pay my way myself, the fact is that I would not have been able to go and meet senior Iraqis without Riad El Taher.

The first thing Tariq Aziz said to us in his office was 'We were dining you; you were dining us. How did all this [the First Gulf War and the sanctions] happen?' On the second visit, going with the Irish Taoiseach, Albert Reynolds, Tariq invited Riad El Taher to bring us to supper at his home. Etched on my mind are his parting words. 'People in the West may think that Saddam and I are awful – but if you get rid of us, what will follow will be far, far worse.' Riad El Taher nodded. Their warnings have proved only too tragically correct.

That Riad El Taher should land up in Wandsworth gaol was, in my opinion, a process of nasty, political vengeance.

Tam Dalyell
Linlithgow, May 2016

Tam at Karbala during our 1993 trip.

EDITOR'S FOREWORD

'History is written by the victors.' This truth strikes me ever more forcibly. Iraq was conquered in 2003, and it has therefore effectively lost control of its own narrative. Even those who campaigned against the sanctions and the war retreat defensively into hyperbole when it comes to the Ba'athist regime. Is any description adequate, they ask, in condemning that government, its brutal killing of its own people, its corruption, its denial of human rights? None, you'd reply, if you were part of the so-called opposition to Saddam, and therefore darlings of the West.

But that old adage implies that there is always another story to be told. When my friend Riad showed me the account of his life drafted in prison, I knew instantly that I had found a unique Iraqi voice. A strong tendency among those who come to live in the West is the adoption of our chauvinist view of the world. It makes life much easier for them, but it comes at the cost of denying something in themselves. Riad, who has lived most of his life since the mid-fifties in Britain and is a British citizen, has nevertheless remained an Iraqi patriot. When he saw the devastation rained down upon his homeland after the First Gulf war, and the courage of his compatriots as they struggled to survive in appalling circumstances, he knew where his priorities lay.

I saw in Riad's account an authenticity which touched me, and I therefore offered to help him get it published. It's been a much longer journey than I expected, involving as it did the co-authorship of a greatly expanded text. In order to make it comprehensible to others I needed to grasp such complexities as the oil-for-food programme, the Iraqi government's rationale for the surcharge it imposed on oil exports, and the vagaries of the English legal system. It also required a lot of research.

Riad's childhood memories, his collaboration in running a farm in the New Forest producing free-range eggs, his purchase of a farm in Iraq and its management on ecological principles, his encounters with the most unlikely of people, his campaigning against the sanctions regime, his relationship with Saddam, his trial, his time in prison and his discovery of Yoga, all needed to be filled out to make a more readable narrative, and in some cases had to be written from scratch.

I would like to emphasise an important point. Some may say that Riad's account is one-sided, and that what he writes is therefore not to be trusted. But first-hand accounts are necessarily told from the narrator's point of view; indeed this is what makes them interesting. On the question of trustworthiness I found time and again, as I researched aspects of Riad's story in order to make it more comprehensible to the general reader, that his account was corroborated.

For example, you might feel that Riad's description of the UN sanctions regime as 'draconian' is overstating his case, particularly in view of his account of how Iraqis gradually found ways around them. The BBC's World Affairs Correspondent, Rageh Omaar, covered Iraq for nearly a decade from 1997, and remained in Baghdad during the coalition invasion. Unlike, Riad, he was a staunch and unambiguous critic of Saddam's regime. Yet criticising the phrase 'the march to war,' which was much-used in the months before the launch of the invasion, he wrote:

> The truth is that the people of Iraq had already been traumatised by a decade-long war. Its weapons were not smart bombs or laser-guided munitions, but the harsh and silent reality of economic privation, known euphemistically as sanctions. Even now [2004] I am stunned at the lack of public examination in Britain and the United States of the long-term economic and psychological damage that policy caused the Iraqi people in the 1990s.[1]

---

[1] Omaar, R., *Revolution Day: The Human Story of the Battle for Iraq*, London, Viking, 2004, p 24.

You may disagree with Riad's interpretation of the facts, but as a witness of the recent history of his country, he is, in Tam Dalyell's words, 'worth listening to.'

Riad was never a member of the Iraqi Ba'athist party, and was even a fugitive from its clutches at one stage. He remains strongly critical of Saddam's regime and its disastrous mistakes, such as the war which it made with Iran. But he is also a realist. Unlike armchair moralists, he understands that the real world is a complicated place, and that there is no 'one-size-fits-all' solution to the problems nations face. Seeing the suffering of his fellow-Iraqis following the 1991 war, he did what he could to help them without concerning himself over much about who he had to deal with, and the methods he saw as necessary. This was to cost him dear, but he bore his punishment courageously, and emerged to tell the tale.

A word about the title of this book may be helpful. Psalm 137 begins 'By the waters of Babylon, there we sat down and wept, when we remembered Zion,' and ends with these words: 'Oh daughter of Babylon, doomed to be destroyed, blessed shall he be who repays you with what you have done to us! Blessed shall he be who takes your little ones and dashes them against the rock!' This shockingly vengeful declaration came from a people for whom Babylon was a place of exile, and they wept for the loss of Zion. But their place of exile is now Riad's homeland. The happiness which the psalmist envisages will derive from its destruction, now so cruelly realised, is for him a matter of profound grief.

Most of this book was written before the Report of the Iraq Inquiry (otherwise known as the Chilcot report or simply Chilcot) was unveiled on 6th July 2016. It goes to press well after that momentous event. The report was a damning indictment of UK, as well as US, policy on Iraq between 2001 and 2009, and, despite its omissions, it places Riad's actions in their true perspective. Whatever the law may have said about his case, Riad's historic campaign now moves centre stage, rather than being out in the wings.

Because of the complexity of this book, and also because parts of it are controversial, we felt it appropriate to footnote sources and explanations, rather than cluttering up the text with such material. Most of the source material came from the internet and where this is the case webpage addresses are given as appropriate. But long addresses are difficult to type in accurately, and so readers may often find it easier to search for sources with key words or phrases.

The same consideration led me to compile an annotated index, in which some information is given about the entries. This will help those who have little idea, for example, about the geography of Iraq or its politics. Putting it together reminded me of the difficulties of, and consequent inconsistencies in, the transcription of Arabic into English. I first encountered these during my career as a civil servant, and then again during my ten years living in the Middle East. I explore this question further in my introductory remarks to the index. Suffice it to say here that readers shouldn't expect the spelling of Arab personal and place names to be consistent.

Where I have quoted text written by Riad and other non-native speakers, I've tidied up the grammar, phraseology and spelling, and have not thought it necessary to indicate this each time. My purpose has been to enhance, never to alter, the meaning. Where there was any doubt about Riad's purpose I have been able to check with him exactly what he intended to say. On another matter, in order to convey Riad's conversational style, I've retained contractions such as 'he's,' 'we've' and 'I'd.' However I found it went against the grain to use 'who' where 'whom' was indicated by old-fashioned grammar. When it came to choosing the most suitable noun and adjective for Shia-Shiite, I settled on the former as being more commonly used nowadays, even though linguistically it's awkward. Where the word 'Shiite' appears in quoted text it remains unchanged. In this connection it's worth remarking, because he only indicates it in passing himself, that Riad comes from mixed Shia-Sunni parentage.

Riad and I have known each other for twenty years, but through our work together on this project we have become closer friends. While we share many ideas, on some matters we see things quite differently. My job as editor was to represent Riad's outlook as faithfully as I could, not to express my own. That's not to say I didn't nudge him here or there. Usually he accepted my suggestions, but sometimes he didn't.

Anyone reading this book with a fair and open mind will recognise Riad's fundamental decency, just as the late Tam Dalyell did on their first encounter. His story is poignant and needs to be heard. In my correspondence with Tam Dalyell before he died, he wrote to me: 'Tell the publishers that I think this is an important book,' and he even offered to speak to them. Alas, the latter is no longer possible, and for whatever reason, the former didn't have the desired effect, which is why we decided to self-publish. This did have its advantages.

I should like to thank Riad for entrusting me with editing his book, and for being patient with my many suggestions and queries. I am also grateful to Karen Dabrowska, whom I have never met, for typing up and editing the original draft, and to New Generation Publishing for all their assistance in bringing this project to fruition. Lastly I wish to acknowledge the invaluable resource which Wikipedia has proved to be when I wanted to add some detail or other. By its nature, Wikipedia is not perfect, but on the whole I have found its articles in the area which I was researching well-written and, on double checking, they usually proved to be accurate. My gratitude to those who established and contributed to Wikipedia is expressed in a small annual financial contribution.

In March of this year Riad was diagnosed with inoperable cancer. In view of this sad news we agreed that the book should be published as soon as possible, which meant cutting some corners. I believe, however, that it is substantially as it would have been had time not been at a premium.

Dr Francis Clark-Lowes,
Brighton, August 2018

Postscript

On the morning of 9th November, 2018, Riad died peacefully at the Martlet's hospice in Hove. He lived just long enough to enjoy seeing a sample copy of his book which had been sent to us by the publisher.

ACKNOWLEDGEMENTS AND REMARKS

My special thanks go to Karen Dabrowska, a journalist, whom I have known for many years. She suggested this book to me during her visit on my first night at Wandsworth Prison and she typed up the first draft. Without Karen's encouragement I wouldn't have embarked on this project. She not only provided me with a lifeline, but gave me a task through which I could express my beliefs and utilise my time constructively. Writing had the additional advantage of distracting me from the mindless and non-stop TV watched by my cellmates.

The book thus began its existence as handwritten notes which I posted to Karen. After my release I dictated the remainder of the original manuscript onto a dictaphone from which she transcribed it. But the text was in need of considerable editing, for which I didn't have the ability. Then early in 2015 my long-time friend Francis Clark-Lowes expressed an interest in this project, and subsequently agreed to prepare the book for publication. I wish to express my gratitude to him for this, and for giving me the courage to publish. Many thanks also to Caroline O'Reilly who proof read the text several times and made many useful suggestions, and to Francis's brother, Danny Clark-Lowes, a geologist with considerable experience of oil exploration in the Middle East, who read through, and commented on an earlier draft of the book.

The late Tam Dalyell, whom I met in 1992 and who plays a central role in my story, was a true friend and an unfailing source of encouragement. I would have dedicated this book to him as a mark of my inestimable gratitude had he not rightly pointed out that that honour should be reserved for the ordinary people of Iraq who have suffered so much, and with such fortitude. I'm very grateful to Tam's widow, Kathleen Dalyell, for agreeing for me to use his draft introduction as it stood when he died. He had asked me to check back with him before publishing it, but he died before we could do so. I also thank Kathleen for permission to quote extensively from Tam's memoir, *The Importance of Being Awkward*.

I'm grateful to Channel 4 News for permission to reproduce Tony Benn's interview of Saddam Hussein, which appears at Appendix Three, to *The Independent* for permission to reproduce Tam's obituary of Tariq Aziz, which appears as Appendix Four, and to Central News and *The Times* for permission to reproduce the article about Riad's imprisonment, which appears as an image in the last group of illustrations. Likewise thanks to John Pilger for permission to reproduce his essay 'From Pol Pot to ISIS: The blood never dried' which is posted on his website (it appears here as the Endpiece). Many thanks also to Oliver Miles for permission to reproduce about a third of the ambassadorial letter to Tony Blair he initiated in April 2004 and his agreement to my quoting from his article in *The Independent on Sunday* dated 22nd November 2009.

Others in the House of Commons to whom I owe sincere thanks for supporting me in one way or another are the late Tony Benn, Alice Mahon, Harry Cohen, Alan Simpson, Mike Wood, Glenda Jackson, Robert Marshall-Andrews, Paul Marsden, Joan Ruddock, Alex Salmond, Paul Flynn, Mike Hancock, Michael Clapham, Ann Cryer, Jeremy Corbyn, Diane Abbott, Sir Menzies Campbell, Ian Taylor, Dr (now Baroness) Jenny Tonge, Dr Caroline Lucas, Sir Teddy Taylor, Douglas Hogg, Kenneth Clarke, John McDonnell and Dennis Skinner.

Many thanks also to all those Iraqi ministers and officials of the Ba'athist regime who, though I didn't always agree with their policies, were almost always courteous and helpful to me, and with whom in some cases I developed warm personal relations. The Deputy Prime Minister, Tariq Aziz, became a valued friend, and what happened to him subsequently was a disgrace. It's normal to lock up the leaders of a defeated country, but to show no mercy when they become ill and are clearly no longer a threat to the new regime is, in my view, unpardonable.

Thanks to all those of you who cared for me, especially through my darkest days and even when they didn't know me. My partners deserve a special mention, and I'm sorry if I wasn't always as appreciative as I should have been.

I'm particularly grateful to Zena Haddad and Rifat Chaudhury, the solicitors in my case, who worked tirelessly on my behalf. Zena researched my case in great detail, and in a better world her efforts would have saved me from a prison sentence. I owe the success of my appeal largely to Rifat.

I'm grateful to the copyright owners of the images in this book for their permission to reproduce them. Credits to them are included in the list of illustrations which follows these acknowledgements and remarks.

Some of those who knew me in the late nineties and early naughties may feel that I deceived them about my relationship with Saddam. It is true that I couldn't be as frank as I would like to have been, and I'm sorry about this. The Kuwaitis claimed that I was 'Saddam's man,' and though I don't accept this description, they were right that I formed a relationship with the President. As I'll describe later, the *Daily Mail* picked up on this phrase, and splashed it across their front page. If this hadn't happened the day Lady Di perished in a Paris tunnel my story might have been very different. For if I had been forced to admit openly that I was talking to Saddam this would have undermined my position in the eyes of many of those I was trying to persuade on the issue of sanctions. I was economical with the truth in the same way that any politician with an instinct for survival is bound to be.

It remains for me to thank those closest to me. My children, their partners and my grandchildren suffered as a result of my trial, conviction and imprisonment. It was difficult for them to witness what was happening in the media and being asked about it by friends. I don't in general regret what I did, but I'm very sorry for the pain it caused them and I understand their wish to regard it as water under the bridge. Two considerations have persuaded me that I should, nevertheless, publish this book.

Firstly I believe that my story needs to be told. Others, most prominent among them Tam Dalyell, have supported me in this view. It is, if I may put it so, a missing piece in the Iraqi jigsaw puzzle. Secondly, history very quickly becomes distorted and exaggerated if there is no first-hand account of events on the ground. I wish to spare my children and grandchildren the unnecessary embarrassment of hearing, for example, that I was a common criminal or even a terrorist. This book is my account, as honestly told as I can made it, of what I did, and I hope it will convince them, if they should become curious, of the sincerity of my motivation.

In the light of all this, I hope my readers will understand why I have refrained from naming my immediate family or affording them the part in my life-story which you might expect in a book of this kind.

Riad el-Taher, Hove
May 2018

ILLUSTRATIONS AND CREDITS

Note: Personal collection means personal collection of the author

Cover & initial pages
1. Baghdad sky-line design for front cover: *Shutterstock*.
2. Map: *Francis Clark-Lowes*
3. Tam Dalyell at Karbala: *Tim Llewellyn*
4. Reconstruction of Babylonian Gate: *iStock*

Group 1 (between pages 14 & 15)
1. Date Palms: *Shutterstock*
2. Southend Pier: *Unknown author, GNU Free Documentation Licence, Version 1.2*
3. Wedding photo: *Personal collection*
4. Father with children: *Personal collection*
5. Family group: *Personal collection*
6. Brighton Pavilion: *Shutterstock*.

Group 2 (between pages 78 & 79)
1. Oil industry: *iStock*.
2. Hinchley Wood house: *Personal collection*
   Hinchley Wood garden: *Personal collection*
3. Poultry farm: *Creative Commons*
4. Petra: *Shutterstock*
5. Parliament: *Shutterstock*
6. Amiriyah Shelter: *Public domain*
7. George and Tam with official: *Tim Llewellyn*

8. Author, Omeid Mubarak, Tam and George: *Tim Llewellyn*
9. Tim Llewellyn: *Tim Llewellyn.*
10. Tariq Aziz: *Tpbradbury Creative Commons, Share Alike 4.0 International licence*
11. Trebil border post: *Public domain*

Group 3 (between pages 130 & 131)
1. Shejeera/Tigris: *Personal collection*
2. Shejeera/Author: *Personal collection*
3. Shejeera/Farmer's children: *Personal collection*
4. Shejeera/Sabah Kamal & wife: *Personal collection*
5. Shejeera/Author on Tigris bank: *Personal collection*
6. Shejeera/Sheep: *Personal collection*
7. Shejeera/White camels: *Personal collection*
8. Saddam Hussein: *Iraqi TV (AP Archive). Public domain*

Group 4 (between pages 173 & 174)
1. Friends House, Euston: *Personal collection*
2. Tony Benn: *Author I, Isujosh, Creative Commons Attribution-Share Alike 3.0*
3. Douglas Feith: *Public domain*
4. Tony Blair: *Author Jing Ulrich, public domain*
5. Blair meets Bush: *Unknown author, public domain*
6. Dick Cheney. *Author Karen Ballard, White House, public domain*
7. Anti-war march. *Author Simon Rutherford, Creative Commons*
8. Bomber's-eye-view. *iStock*
9. Paul Bremer et al: *Creative Commons Attribution-Share Alike 3.0*

Group 5 (between pages 246 & 247)
1. Walking: *Personal collection*
2. Lands End: *Personal collection*
3. Paul Volcker: *Kenneth C. Zirkel, Creative Commons, Share Alike*
4. Lord Goldsmith: *Johnnyryan1 at English Wikipedia, Creative Commons Attribution-Share Alike 3.0*
5. Southwark Crown Court: *Author unknown, public domain*
6. The Iraq Inquiry: *Author unknown, public domain*

Group 6 (Between pages 291 & 292)
1. Wandsworth prison: *Author Robin Webster, Creative Commons*
2. Wandsworth prison interior: *Author unknown, public domain*
3. Times article: *Central News and The Times*'
4. Ford Open Prison: *Personal collection*
5. Outside Peter Kyle's office: *Greg Hadfield*
6. Victory Arch: *Jeremy Weate of Abuja, Nigeria, 'Swords of Qadisiya*

CHAPTER ONE

CROSSING CULTURES

On my last visit to my homeland in January 2003, immediately before the coalition invasion, I sensed that despite the draconian UN sanctions Iraq was beginning to recover from the disasters of the previous two decades. As long as people kept to the rules, life was relatively secure, a degree of self-reliance had been achieved in food production and power generation, one could see new cars and trucks on the roads, and morale was rising with the prospect of a better future.

Then came the destruction of 2003. It was as if Iraq had landed on a long snake in the famous board game; back to square one. Not surprisingly, it was the last straw for many, and those who had the means to do so left the country. None of my closest family now live in Iraq, and the same goes for most of my friends and colleagues. The Arab country with the highest standards in education has been stripped of its intelligentsia as well as its artists and musicians. Our cultural heritage has been plundered either as a deliberate policy by the occupiers, or at least because of their criminal carelessness. And I hear that the previous high standards in the educational and health sectors have collapsed following a recruitment policy guided by the selection of those of the correct denomination of Islam, rather than those with suitable qualifications.

The mass emigration, estimated at a figure of around 4.5 million, has been actively assisted by the US and UK occupiers, who were particularly keen to facilitate the departure of Christians and professionals. It has been reported that the majority of the teaching staff at the elite Saddam university has moved to the US; that is to say, those who were not assassinated in the chaos which followed the war. Power generation, water purification, and sewage treatment is now as bad as it was in the worst days of sanctions, thanks to precision bombing, civil unrest and neglect by the occupiers. The transport sector is equally degraded, and food production has fallen.

Ever since the occupation began, the government and foreign embassies have been confined to the Green Zone in Baghdad, the only part of the country in which its members feel safe. This ensures that they are largely out of touch with the population in the rest of the country. And since the Green Zone is also the furthest that foreign politicians and reporters go, the picture we receive of Iraq in this country is highly distorted. Corruption has escalated, according to the UN, and a shocking disparity in wealth has developed between politicians and officials, on the one hand, and the rest of the population on the other. Some of the former have used their positions to amass the means to buy property around the globe.

The effect of all this has been to encourage a reversion to out-dated religious practices in what was, and still purports to be, a secular country. The relative security of the pre-2003 years has been superseded by a murderous insecurity both internally and spreading beyond the borders of Iraq. Meanwhile the South and North Oil Companies (formerly the Basrah Petroleum and Mosul Petroleum Companies respectively) are, after more than forty years, back in the hands of foreign oil companies such as BP, EXXON, Mobil and Shell. No doubt there is a connection between this <u>re-imposition of imperial control</u> and the fact that the largest US embassy in the world is to be found in the Green Zone.

When I compare Iraq now with the country in which I grew up I find myself adopting two contradictory views. On the one hand the difference seems colossal; on the other there has been a reversion with a vengeance to the imperialism of my youth. This is the paradox which underlies my experience as a proud Iraqi patriot. So let me start at the beginning.

Youth in Basrah

I don't know when I was born. In the Middle East births have not, until comparatively recently, been recorded, nor traditionally have birthdays been celebrated. Accordingly, all I can say about my birth is that it occurred in Basrah sometime between 1939 and 1941 and that my family belonged to the Iraqi middle class. However, like the Queen, I do have an official birthday, which is recorded in my passport as 7th July 1939. My father, Hamza el-Taher, was also born in Basrah, and was a Shia Muslim. He worked for a London trading company called Gray Mackenzie, the main activities of which were shipping and exporting dates and wheat.

In my early youth I enjoyed the summer holidays packaging dates on a plantation on the Shatt al-Arab River.[1] Date palms thrive in southern Iraq as they require a high temperature and humidity as well as plenty of water. I was attracted to the lifestyle of the Marsh Arabs who came for seasonal work and created makeshift dwellings of reeds, returning to the marshes at the end of the summer season. Their food was simple, consisting of bread (made from ground rice), fresh milk, butter, eggs and fish. The last were caught in the river, gutted and barbecued on an open fire. The plantation, which lay just outside Basrah, could be reached either by the single winding road to Faw, which had been constructed by the British, or by motorboat, which was a more picturesque route, as well as being easier and safer.

My father was regarded as an expert on dates and he travelled to various plantations by boat, accompanied by a British manager who

---

[1] This is formed by the merger of the Tigris and Euphrates at Qurna, and flows down to the Arab Gulf (also known as the Persian Gulf) emerging alongside the Faw Peninsula.

seemed only interested in enjoying the boat ride while my father selected the dates and made the deals. A banquet of a whole sheep, chicken and fresh-baked bread was always laid on for us wherever we stopped.

As a result of these early summer holidays I developed a keen interest in dates and in the part they played in the life of the people. The Garden of Eden is said to have been in Qurna and the entire region was covered in date palms whose trunks can be used to build farm buildings and footbridges across creeks.

The pollination of date palms by insects and wind is an uncertain business because the former tend to stay away from the dates until they ripen and fall off the trees. And so in spring farmers transfer the pollen from male to female palms by hand. The process is labour intensive, tedious and dangerous because it involves climbing between twenty and forty trees a day, each averaging 15 metres in height, but some rising to as much as 100 metres. In Spain, Malta and some North African countries there is a shortage of manpower as well as a lack of know-how about transferring the pollen, and consequently the date palms in these countries bear less fruit.[2]

The locals depend on the date trees in many ways. The fronds of the palms can be woven into fans, mats, hats and so on, and the stems can be used to make chairs, tables and cots. The dry branches can be burned for fuel for cooking and heating. The pollen has medicinal value and it's reported that nomads can live on dates and camel or goat milk for at least a year if there's no other food available. In a sense the date palm is the tree of life for it supports an interdependent life-cycle of insects, birds, farm livestock and human beings. In its shade its own fruit, as well as vegetables, can thrive and in turn it is nourished by the manure which is the by-product of farm livestock.

---

[2] Mechanisation has now been introduced in California and the occupied West Bank of Palestine.

In the West we are only familiar with a small number of the very many varieties of dates. In Iraq there are more than a hundred and fifty varieties: some very high in sugar, some quite dry, some red and some dark. The rarest varieties are considered a great delicacy. The wide ranging health benefits of dates are still a largely unexplored area of research. I have little doubt that my own consumption of this fruit paid off in later years. I have fond childhood memories of winter meals consisting of bread spread with a mixture of date syrup and ground sesame, or more simply of dates pressed with ginger, fennel seeds and walnuts.

My mother, Rifaat Wahaib, who was illiterate, came from a Sunni family in Baghdad, though after her marriage to my father she practised as a Shia Muslim. I was the youngest of three brothers and three sisters. My oldest brother, Kamil, was an officer in the newly formed Iraqi army and while serving took part in the Tulkaram campaign in Palestine in 1948. He also oversaw the handover of Habbaniya airbase by the British to the Iraqis in 1958. Abdul-Karim, the second of my brothers, was the first graduate of the Iraqi Police Academy, and was later commended in *The Times* for his part in uncovering corruption and theft at the port of Basrah. My third brother, Fadhil, was a lawyer, but he only practised for a short while before becoming politically engaged as a Social Democrat, with leanings towards the Communist Party. Later he joined the Basrah Port Authority of which, by the time of his retirement, he was director. My eldest sister, Fawzia, married a port official. My second sister, Souad died at the age of only nineteen following a fire caused by a paraffin heater. And my third sister, Shawkya, lost her life in a traffic accident which resulted from the shocking state of the roads following the invasion and occupation of Iraq in 2003.

There was an age gap between me and my other brothers and sisters which meant that I was a child in a family of adults. At an early age Kamil arranged for me to go to the only kindergarten in Basrah, which was run by French nuns. The standard there was high, and this stood me in good stead when I was moved to the only primary school in Basrah, built originally by the Turks. It was here that all my older brothers had completed their primary education. The school was a huge purpose built two-storey building with a large grassy playing field. It was a well-run institution and also had a high standard of teaching and discipline. There were around thirty pupils in each class. The teachers both here and at my secondary school, likewise built by the Turks and the largest school in Basrah, were well respected and their authority extended beyond the classroom. We had a visiting American teacher who taught us English in the final years which was something of a novelty. He helped the students with sport before classes and gave us an insight into life in the United States. Thanks partly to him I came to enjoy playing football, volleyball and basketball.

Upon completing the final year at secondary school most students expected to go on to a college education in Baghdad or to study abroad. In my case I wanted to study in the UK because in the field of science and engineering the tuition there was regarded as superior to Baghdad's colleges, these being still in their infancy.

College in Southend-on-Sea

In September 1956 my family and friends gathered at the small post-World War II Basrah airport to see me off on my first ever flight. The hardest thing for me was saying goodbye to mother, and as fate would have it this was to be the last time I saw her. At that time there was only one flight a week from Basrah to Baghdad, operated by KLM. This took just over an hour, and once in the capital I checked in at the Khayam Hotel in the historic Rasheed Street. The next morning I flew on via Istanbul and Geneva, again with KLM, and will never forget seeing the snow-covered Alps and marvelling at the beauty of the universe beyond Basrah.

From Heathrow I took a taxi to a hotel in the centre of London where I spent some time working out that I was supposed to slide myself between the tightly wrapped sheets rather than untangle the bedclothes to sleep under a duvet. I was exhausted by the flight and the barrage of new experiences, but was also excited about making my way to my final destination, the college in Southend. As a result I slept fitfully. In the morning I washed and made my way to the breakfast room where I faced a carefully laid out assortment of knives, forks and spoons. I had no idea where to start. I had never seen breakfast cereal and didn't know how it was consumed. Petrified and shy, I decided to give this renowned English meal a miss and made my way instead, again by taxi, to Fenchurch Street Station. I was baffled on the way by the driver's cockney accent.

I asked for a ticket, and the clerk told me the price; on receipt of the sum he gave me a single. I was afraid of missing my station, and so sat in the compartment holding tightly onto my cases ready to jump out as soon as I saw the Southend station sign. At last there it was, Southend-on-Sea, and I scrambled out of the train. Bewildered, hungry and confused, I made my way to Southend Technical College. I was wearing a heavy overcoat while the students were sunbathing in the cool September sun. Imagine, then, my relief when Latief Jorephani, a friend from my secondary school days in Basrah, greeted me and told me the college had asked him to take me to my lodgings.

Jumping ahead for a moment, in the eighties Latief was the producer of a film made in Iraq called *Clash of Loyalties*, starring Oliver Reed, among others. This aimed to portray the Iraqi fight for independence from the British, but although it was completed, it never made it onto Western cinema screens, and disappeared in Iraq after the overthrow of Saddam. On 24th July 2016 Channel 4 showed a documentary called 'Saddam goes to Hollywood' about the making of the film, based on a stash of reels in Latief's garage in Surrey. Unfortunately this attempt to reconstruct the sorry story of the film's production was in certain respects inaccurate, not least in the assertion that Saddam commissioned the film. I know that it was the Ministry of Information, acting on their own initiative, who were responsible.

But returning to my arrival in Southend, I was absolutely famished, and so insisted we stop on the way for a meal in a Greek restaurant where I devoured a chicken dish. I was to stay with a family of four: a kind housewife, her husband who resembled Andy Capp, a plain-looking teenage girl, and a child. They spoke true Cockney, having come from London, so while I was reading the *Daily Telegraph* to improve my English, they were conversing in what seemed like a totally different language. Alas, there was no way this family would help me to learn English, let alone improve it.

My three years in Southend, where I pursued my studies and got a grip on the language and culture, shaped my life. The change of food, climate and landscape was daunting at first, and made me apprehensive, but it was also exciting to be experiencing broader horizons. By good fortune, the majority of the Iraqi students were from wealthy families and were consequently not as academically motivated as I was. This provided me with the opportunity of helping them with their studies while I benefited from their experience, comradeship and knowledge of living in Britain. It was a fair exchange which helped me to overcome my homesickness and helped them to get through their exams.

There is one particular Iraqi student I have good reason to remember. A few months after my arrival in Southend I heard through my family that my secondary school classmate, Fadhil Othman, had also been accepted at Southend Technical College. So together with others I met him at the airport and we agreed that he should share my lodgings. This was a big mistake for he was a loner and had peculiar habits. Being a vegetarian he ate quantities of eggs, and as these were cheaper than meat, the landlady insisted I follow the same diet. I couldn't stand it, and so I soon sought alternative lodgings. As luck would have it, my new landlady was an excellent cook and introduced me to good English food.

In 1961. after completing his degree in chemical engineering at London University, Fadhil returned to Iraq where he rose through the ranks of the oil industry to become Manager of the South Oil Company and eventually Acting President of the oil marketing organisation in the Ministry of Oil (SOMO). In 1994 he resigned before fully reaching the top job, one can imagine for political reasons, and moved to Istanbul. There, among other things, he established himself as an independent consultant, founding Rumaila Oil Services, a company which, as far as I know he still runs. This takes its name from the Rumaila Oilfield where Fadhil worked as a supervisor in the early seventies.

But to return to my studies, in 1959, after three years in Southend, I passed my Ordinary National Diploma with distinction, and this reduced from three years to two the amount of time I was required to spend in Brighton studying for my Diploma in Engineering.

Holiday work, Politics and College in Brighton

During my time in Southend I never used the summer holidays, as most of my compatriots did, to visit Iraq, but chose instead to take various kinds of employment. These included working in a factory called EKO,[3] making TVs and radios, and coach cleaning for British Railways (as it was then called). These experiences widened my contact with the British working class which had begun in my lodgings. I learnt about the trade union movement and witnessed the British work culture. There were lots of tea-breaks during which my colleagues talked endlessly about football, pool and the races.

Late in 1956 I encountered British democracy in action when I attended a demonstration against Anthony Eden's Suez policy

---

[3] I don't know what this stood for. I expect the first word was 'Electrical'.

organised by the Labour Party in Trafalgar Square. Among the speakers were Aneurin Bevan and my later friend and mentor, Tony Benn. Attending this protest meeting as a newly arrived young Iraqi opposed to the war and the occupation of the Suez Canal zone was a precursor to sharing the same platform with Tony on numerous anti-war demonstrations many years later.

In 1959 I moved to Brighton where I continued my studies at the Technical College.[4] My two years of study in this town, to which I returned (well, to Hove, actually) in 2013, were hard work and tedious. We were set a lot of homework and had projects to complete, leaving hardly any time for recreation. We even had lectures on Saturdays. I excelled in mathematics and physics and had no difficulty in passing the Institute of Electrical Engineers exams for my Diploma in Engineering, a qualification recognised as the equivalent of a university degree. I considered progressing to PhD studies, but the nuclear physics lecturer advised me to go into industry. This was wise and considerate advice as I'm not a researcher by nature and I discovered that leadership and engineering management was what I enjoyed most.

In 1960, my brother, Fadhil, came to Britain as part of a delegation which was to be trained at the British Ports Authority. He and his colleagues visited me in Brighton and I became their mentor, helping them to understand the British way of life, food and conduct. What a turnaround this was from the apprehensive and inexperienced young teenager who had arrived in Southend just four years earlier!

When I completed my studies in 1961 I didn't go back to Iraq but returned to Southend and started post-graduate training with the Central Electricity Generating Board (CEGB). My time with this body deflated my ego for I thought that once I graduated I'd soon be appointed to a managerial position. Far from it! My theoretical knowledge didn't prepare me for what I found in the practical engineering world. Hard

---

[4] This changed its name to Brighton College of Technology in 1984, to City College Brighton and Hove in 2001, and to Greater Brighton Metropolitan College in 2017.

experience taught me that an engineering degree is only the start of a long uphill struggle. I had to learn the practical aspects of the profession and how to deal with subordinates and peers, both those who were less and those who were more capable than me. It was, however, a lesson worth learning, and helped me through the remainder of my career, especially during my eight years with the Iraq Petroleum Company (IPC).

Marriage, honeymoon and return to Iraq

My future wife, Doreen Saunders, was a fellow-student at college in Southend, where she also lived, and I owe her a lot for her support during my studies there. After completing her secretarial course, she went on to work as a legal secretary in the City and so our courtship was limited to weekends. When I moved to Brighton Doreen used to visit me once a month, staying the weekend at my lodgings, and then returning to work on Mondays. We'd go to the cinema, or walk to Hove where it was rather strange finding myself surrounded by people who were recognisably Jewish. Hove felt like 'Little Israel.' Readers may find this remark offensive, but from an Arab perspective what is being done in the name of Jews in Palestine is an invasion of the Arab nation, and my reaction should be seen in this light.

Doreen and I got married in church in 1962. It seemed the natural thing to do, but I'd given little thought to what would be involved. My perception of marriage was still very much based on traditional Iraqi culture, and it didn't at that stage occur to me that we were very different from one another. We flew to Zermatt for our honeymoon, as the citizens of Southend learnt from a report in a local newspaper.

On our return my father visited us in Southend and met Doreen for the first time. There were mixed emotions during his stay. The previous year the whole family had been devastated by the loss of my mother from cancer. I had missed her greatly, but because she was illiterate and my parents didn't have a phone, I'd not been able to communicate with her directly after leaving Iraq. She was a kind, compassionate and caring person, and totally unassuming. On the other hand, it was good to see my father again for the first time since I had left Iraq in 1956.

In the summer of the following year a friend drove us to Stuttgart, where I had arranged to buy a second-hand Mercedes 220 for the drive to Iraq. I only had a provisional licence, but somehow managed to get an international one, while Doreen wasn't able to drive at all as she suffered from epilepsy. It was a nerve-racking experience as we set off along the autobahn but somehow we managed to drive through Austria, Yugoslavia, Bulgaria, Turkey and Syria. In some parts of Turkey we were at times travelling along treacherous unpaved roads.

In Syria we ran out of funds but I managed to borrow some money from the Iraqi embassy in Damascus which covered the cost of our hotel in the city, and our expenses on to Baghdad. In our hurry we left Damascus in the evening on the unlit desert road to Deir el-Zoor without water or spare petrol. After several hours of difficult driving disaster struck when we veered off the road and the car got bogged down in the sand. I noticed a dim light in the distance and walked towards it even though I was not sure how far away it was. Luckily there was a full moon, and the sky was a magnificent canopy of brightly-shining stars, so it was not difficult to see where I was going. At last I arrived at a small encampment where the dogs barked viciously and the bedouin came to see who the intruder was. I explained my difficult situation in rusty Arabic as best I could.

They offered to walk with me back to the car where my petrified wife was left sitting in total darkness. I told them she was a Muslim from Turkey and they made us welcome. Bread was baked for us and we were given water which we discovered the next morning had come from the muddy Euphrates. Nevertheless, the generosity of the bedouin, who saved our lives, made an unforgettable impression on me. There is humanity in all of us if we exercise tolerance.

The bedouin pulled our car out of the sand and we made our way to Ramadi in central Iraq, where I believed my brother, Abdul-Karim, to be the chief of police. I thought our ordeal would as a result be over, but it turned out he had been transferred to Baghdad. A policeman was called to assist and he agreed to accompany us to the capital. We went first to the police pound, and succeeded in turning over the car on the way there. But at last we set out on the remaining two-hour part of our journey and when we got there, the policeman directed us to my brother, who had by then been promoted to regional inspector.

We relaxed for a few days in Baghdad and my wife enjoyed meeting an Irish companion married to my sister-in-law's brother. Life took a positive turn as I started the formalities, as part of the Iraqisation programme, to join the staff of the Basrah Petroleum Company (BPC), a subsidiary of IPC. Both were British/US owned and had the concession to operate and manage Iraqi oil resources.

To help us financially until the employment formalities were completed, I took a temporary job as an electrical engineer in Basrah's new Russian-built power station. Fadhil, who was by now the director in the port authority, was residing in a part of Basrah called Marquil, which had largely been built by the British. It boasted wide roads lined with trees and gardens and being close to the power station where I worked was an appropriate place for my wife to live. The station had just been commissioned by the Russians and was operated mostly by UK graduates. I was placed as a shift engineer with a close old Iraqi friend from Southend called Noori Juwair, whom I had helped with his studies. This was most fortuitous, for in no time he had relieved me of boring and arduous operations responsibilities.

Mr Walker, the General Manager of Gray Mackenzie in Threadneedle Street, and a good friend of his opposite number, Mr Grimsley, at BPC, had known me since my visits to the date plantations in my childhood. His wife had taught me English as a way of relieving the boredom of expatriate life, and he had acted for my father *in loco parentis* during my years of study in England. He now took a keen interest in expediting the employment formalities, which was also most fortunate, for the power station's non-technical General Manager, an ex-army officer, was keen to hold together his little empire of UK-trained staff and made an unsuccessful attempt to hinder my transfer.

This was my first experience of politics in the work environment where self-promotion, rather than what is best for the organisation or the country, often prevails. In the end the confrontation went right up to the Minister of Oil who resolved the impasse by transferring me to his department on the grounds that I had been trained in microwave and telemetering, that is digital telecommunications. These skills were unknown to other Iraqi graduate staff; indeed, I was the first Iraqi to receive such training.

1. Date palms

2. Southend Pier, the longest of its kind in the world

3. On our wedding day

4. My father with my children and their cousins

5. Some of my family around 1992. Left to right, standing: Hani, Huda and Haifa (Abdul-Karim's children), Abdul-Karim (second brother), Fadhil (third brother), Kamil (eldest brother), Rafid (Fadhil's son), Nabieha (Abdul-Karim's wife). Crouching in front: Ahmed (youngest son of Abdul-Karim)

6. Brighton Pavilion: royal excess

CHAPTER TWO

ENGINEERING IN THE OIL INDUSTRY

Entry into Iraq's oil industry

Right from the formation of Iraq in the aftermath of the defeat of the Ottoman Empire in World War 1, the oil industry had been run by the British and the Americans who were the majority holders of IPC. British Petroleum (BP) was the major shareholder in association with Mobil and Exxon. Oil production in Iraq was the cheapest and in terms of sulphur presence, the cleanest in the world, particularly in the south where the oil wells had a high reservoir pressure and low sulphur. Countrywide, the production cost per barrel was less than $0.50 while in other states of the Gulf it was in excess of $1 per barrel.

This commercial advantage gave rise to a paradoxical situation. Far from exploiting its resource to the maximum to make a handsome profit, IPC and its subsidiaries in Mosul and Basrah maintained exploitation at a minimum. The motive was to keep the oil industry firmly in Western hands. By ensuring that the Iraqi government, which was entitled to a percentage of the oil profits, remained relatively poor, and therefore weak, it reduced the possibility that the foreign oil companies would be challenged. The Iraqi kingdom had been created primarily to ensure that the British could control the country through a section of Iraqi society loyal to them, and to safeguard their military bases at Habbaniya in Al-Anbar governorate and Shaibah in Basrah governorate.

In 1958 a coup d'état replaced the kingdom with a republic which soon issued Law No 80 restricting the British concession to 5% of Iraqi territory. This was the start of a long road to Iraqisation of the oil industry, but the British continued to consider Iraq within their sphere of influence, and sought by various means to maintain their hold. The experience of these staff was adequate, but their academic qualifications were generally inferior to those of young Iraqi graduates.

When in 1963 I joined BPC, thanks to the Iraqisation programme, we were housed outside Basrah in the British-built oil compound at Barjessieha. With its golf course, tennis and squash courts, cricket field, billiard tables, swimming pool, shops and bars, it resembled a British town. The accommodation for the British was in bungalows which were provided with servants' quarters. Most of the stock sold in the grocery store was imported from the UK or Cyprus rather than local produce, although Iraqi meat, fish and vegetables were readily available at much lower prices.

The British staff enjoyed higher rates of pay, free UK education for their children, generous home leave, free air passages and fully furnished accommodation. None of their expatriate privileges were offered to Iraqi graduates, though certainly our pay was high in comparison with that of Iraqi government employees. This disparity created tension between British staff, who wanted to prolong their stay, and Iraqis who usually wanted to act responsibly and serve their country. The company was overstaffed with British employees both because it increased costs, thereby reducing the profit share going to the Iraqi government, and because the remittances from British employees benefited the British economy.

I experienced considerable hardship, abuse and discrimination at the hands of the British staff. My wife was allowed to join the British club in Basrah while I was not, and my family needed permission to visit us in our home. Those of them who were in the armed forces resented this requirement so much that they never came to our compound. For two years my British engineering supervisor wrote my annual report without discussing it with me. This intolerable situation finally ended when the Ministry of Oil rejected his request to go on annual leave on the grounds that he had insisted I was not capable of replacing him. They demanded that a short assignment engineer must be found or his leave application would be rejected. This forced him to revise his assessment of me, thereby allowing me to assume responsibility under the supervision of the Telecom Superintendent, who, however, had no experience in telemetering.

During the supervisor's three months leave there was no disruption to oil production and consequently the Ministry insisted that I continue doing his job for a further three months. Upon his return he was reassigned to another post and I was rewarded with promotion. The tables were turned when my supervisor came back to become a member of my department. From then on he had to discuss *his* annual report with *me*, but I was careful to treat him with courtesy. Eventually he left Iraq in disgrace after being caught in the company compound with tools and equipment which he was charged with stealing. By a quirk of fate justice had prevailed.

Life in Barjessieha, the company's living compound, was enjoyable. In summer we relaxed around the swimming pool after a hard day's work, while in winter we played cards, watched films, went to parties and danced. I was the first Iraqi in the compound to excel in karate and squash.

Because of Doreen's epilepsy, she went to England for the birth of our son and daughter. Being left on my own for some time during Doreen's absence had unforeseen, and I can honestly say, unintended consequences. One aspect of compound life of which one couldn't fail to be aware was the frequency of extra-marital affairs. Men and women of similar ages and intelligence were living together in close contact without the usual social constraints and also without the financial and other pressures of everyday life in Britain. It resembled, in some ways, a holiday camp, with enjoyment the only off-duty occupation. This philandering resulted in real heart-ache, not to say dangerous jealousies, but at the time those who took advantage of the opportunities had their eyes firmly fixed on the present. I found myself in demand, and the temptation was too great to resist.

Professionally my career progressed quickly, and so six years passed comfortably. In early 1966, just after my son was born, I did my military service which consisted of an unusually short period of four months at the Army Reserve Officer College. Our Platoon Commander, Lieutenant Hamid, who had lost an eye during the northern campaign in the sixties, was a person I could get along with particularly well, and so the four months weren't arduous. I was discharged the same day I was commissioned as a lieutenant so that I could return to my job where my skills in digital communications were urgently required. Had it not been that I was indispensable in my job, I would have been obliged to serve the usual two years in the army.

Things began to change after 1968, when the Ba'athists, under Ahmad Hassan al-Bakr, took power.[1] The government insisted that foreign wives and the children of mixed marriages should take Iraqi nationality, and restrictions were imposed on the emigration of well-qualified personnel in the oil industry. Leaving the country without permission came to be seen by the Ministry as a betrayal of the national and economic interest in its time of need. The authorities were particularly keen to retain and fully utilise skills such as mine.

Doreen, who had delivered our daughter in 1969, had no wish to take Iraqi nationality, nor did I wish her or the children to do so. Both children had been born in England and so there were no difficulties in that direction. Moreover, I had got into a dangerous liaison from which I needed to escape. And so in 1970 my wife and children went on what was officially annual leave but was in fact their departure from Iraq.

---

[1] The Arab Socialist Ba'ath Party, Iraq Region, a branch of the Arab Ba'athist movement in Syria, was founded in 1951 by Fuad al-Rikabi. In 1940 the Syrian philosopher and sociologist, Michel Aflaq, together with his fellow Sorbonne student, Salah al-Din al-Bitar, had formed an Arab nationalist party which eventually became the Arab Socialist Ba'ath Party, Syrian Region. Ba'ath means 'renaissance' or 'renovation'.

Then one morning I arranged with my trusted driver, who had been with me for several years, to take me clandestinely to the Kuwaiti border. My passport was in order and the border officials had evidently not been alerted to refuse my exit, so I crossed the border easily, but I had no idea what the future held.

For the previous eight years I had lived in an environment where the company took care of everything, from passport formalities to transport; the garden was attended to, light bulbs were changed, the house was maintained and so on. I was cocooned in a secure well-paid job with a comfortable life-style. Having left the country without permission, I knew that I could not soon return for fear of reprisals. I was irrevocably leaving behind my ageing father, who was suffering from diabetes (he died in 1973 without my seeing him again), and all the rest of my family living in Basrah and Baghdad. It was a formidable step, a leap into the unknown.

I took a taxi, driven by a Palestinian, to Kuwait City, but as I was checking into a hotel I discovered I was one bag short, and realised with horror that it was the one in which I had packed all my savings in cash. Imagine my relief, in this desperate situation, when the driver, who had remembered where I was staying, returned half an hour later to deliver it to me. This unusual honesty when it was most needed felt like a good omen.

I stayed one day in Kuwait before flying on to London.

Shell on Teesside

The years between leaving Iraq and gaining employment in engineering design with McDermott in the North Sea were difficult financially and unsettling emotionally. It was hard not to long for the good old days in IPC. I applied endlessly for a variety of jobs advertised in the newspapers and was regularly disappointed.

Then at last, through sheer persistence, I managed to get a temporary job with Shell Group Teesside in anticipation that one of their contracting companies would be successful in its bid for a maintenance contract with the Kuwait Oil Company (KOC) refinery. In the event of this happening, it was expected that I would be sent back to Kuwait.

Daily life on Teesside was alien to me, and the work practices were very different from those I had experienced in Iraq, owing to the restrictive trade union practices. On my first day in Saltburn I was taken by the team to a pub and introduced to Newcastle Brown. Not being a drinker I was left considerably the worse for wear. This became a standing joke among my fellow engineers, particularly those who managed to drink many more pints than me. After only two I was on the floor. But all things considered it was a good opportunity to break the ice and meet the staff informally.

While I was with Shell a group of Kuwaiti senior supervisors came to London on a development training course with the ostensible aim of preparing them for promotion to section managers. I was called to make a series of presentations over a few days, it being thought that my Arab background would make communication easier for them. However, the second day I was told at lunch that there was no need for me to waste my time and effort lecturing to them as their promotion was guaranteed on their return. They were simply in England to have a good time. And indeed as it happened, when I went to Kuwait a few months later I found all of them in senior management positions sitting comfortably behind ornate desks in large offices staffed by European secretaries and supported by European and US under-managers.

I spent only a relatively short time on Teesside and hardly saw the area at all because the weather was so bad. I used to leave my lodgings when it was completely dark and return from the office after night had closed in. Even during the day the sun didn't come out very often. Meanwhile I was applying for other positions on field maintenance contracts in Kuwait, and so when the British Shell Teesside project failed in their contract bid, I accepted with alacrity an offer of the same job with a Palestinian owned concern called Consolidated Contractors Company. This did a considerable amount of business with the Kuwait Oil Company. How I looked forward to better weather.

But before taking up my post, Doreen, the children and I spent a beautiful few days staying with my wife's brother who was living in Milan. They remained there while I travelled on to Kuwait to make arrangements for our accommodation.

The Kuwait Oil Company

Ironically far from escaping the bad weather of Teesside, I found that it had followed me to Kuwait. Actually it was even worse. The whole country had been brought to a standstill by torrential rain. As I was driven into Kuwait City on my first night back in the Arab world it was astonishing to see so many beautiful cars abandoned by the roadside or washed into the adjoining desert. The road was slightly elevated above the surrounding land, but the floods had covered the road, so that many drivers attempting to negotiate it had inadvertently driven over the edge of the embankment.

Working in Kuwait was a complete contrast to working in Iraq where the Iraqisation programme had achieved its purpose. The environment was very commercial and corrupt, with the same paradoxical policy of overstaffing with expatriate workers as had been the case in Iraq before nationalisation of the oil industry. The aim was again to deny local staff access to the upper echelons of management, and thereby to perpetuate foreign dominance. The working practices were those of the colonial era; the British staff, who were generally poorly qualified, strutted around with gin-induced red faces, wearing shorts, full-length stockings and desert boots. They had been there for many years, they ruled the roost, and they had no desire to leave Kuwait or to train the Kuwaitis to replace them. Activities like turbine and pumping maintenance were undertaken exclusively by American or European contractors.

By increasing costs the British reduced the amount of money which needed to be paid to the Emir, thus maintaining financial control in their hands. The transfer of relatively high earnings to Britain was useful to the home economy, and the burden of British unemployment was reduced by ensuring that a substantial number of British people were employed in Kuwait and elsewhere around the world. They reproduced in Kuwait, as they did everywhere they lived, an opulent style of life which was typical of the better-off classes in Britain.

Nevertheless, I persevered and worked for almost one year in this environment, in part thanks to an Iraqi of Kuwaiti origin who held a senior position in the KOC production facilities. He had worked for BPC but, unlike me, had not been able to progress any further in that company. He had therefore moved back to Kuwait where he was, fortunately for me, able to make life slightly easier than it would otherwise have been.

As I had already realised with the senior supervisor group in London, the Kuwaitis themselves were not particularly interested in being trained or improving their qualifications. All they wanted was to occupy managerial positions and they were happy for British staff to do the real work. My position was quite unusual, in that I was an Arab managing a project which was staffed mostly by Dutch senior engineers and a multinational staff of third country nationals (TCNs).[2] The Kuwaitis liked to pretend they were running their own oil industry but they simply allocated the maintenance of the oil facilities to US and European contractors.

As a consequence of the British dominance of the oil industry, KOC's British staff were not used to Arabs in senior positions and this

---

[2] The term Third Country National (TCN) has come to be used to refer to workers from poorer countries, such as India, Pakistan and the Philippines, employed in large and often international companies or organisations in richer non-Western countries.

caused me some problems. There was one incident when a Dutch engineer had some trouble getting a fault rectified and the British supervisor, who was in charge of the pumping station, got very impatient, demanding that the fault should be dealt with before the end of the day. When he called I was the only engineer available and so I offered to pass by the pumping station on my way home and see what I could do.

The Dutch engineer informed the British supervisor that his manager, referring to me, was coming over to help. When I arrived the supervisor got the shock of his life. He had assumed that the person in charge would be a European and was quite unprepared to deal with an Arab manager. This was totally outside his experience, and he showed it by being rude and aggressive. I had to put my foot down and told him that if he wanted to get the problem resolved he had to speak respectfully and stop using foul language. I asked him to get to the point and explain what the problem was.

Luckily the fault was rectified and we managed to get the turbines and the pumping station running again. I thought this incident should not pass without informing the owner of the project management company, the Crown Prince of Kuwait, Sheikh Jaber al-Ahmad al-Jaber al-Sabah, no less. (He was later, as emir, to experience the invasion of Kuwait by Saddam Hussein's forces.[3]) I told him such incidents had to be stopped or I wouldn't be able to perform my duties effectively. He was sympathetic and told the British supervisor to pack his bags as this kind of behaviour could not be tolerated. My position was consequently strengthened and the British staff, most noticeably those who had been in Kuwait for many years, were thenceforth respectful, thus making my year in Kuwait to a degree tolerable. There was power behind this Iraqi,

---

[3] Sheikh Jaber became the Emir in 1977 and ruled until his death in 2006. Within hours of the start of the Coalition invasion of Iraq in 2003, he moved his government to Taif in Saudi Arabia.

they concluded, and realised they would have to cooperate with him if they wanted to keep their jobs.

All KOC employees lived in Ahmadi, an oasis district away from the city. The majority had never been to Kuwait City, which in 1972 was still underdeveloped. Most of the 'Brits' I came across were unaware of the marine facilities in Kuwait or of the abundance of sea food for which Kuwait is famous. They were not contracted to the Kuwaitis and knew nothing about their way of life. The country comprised two societies, British expatriates living in their own compounds away from the city, and Kuwaitis, who were tribal people keeping themselves to themselves, ruled over by a princely elite with the help of British administrators and KOC. At that time the only evidence in Kuwait City of the foreign presence within the emirate as a whole was the existence of a few expatriate traders.

KOC was completely independent of the Kuwaiti administration and was run by the British, for the British. But the directors envisaged that if Iraq succeeded in its Iraqisation programme, educated Kuwaitis would draw comparisons and become resentful. They therefore sub-contracted maintenance to non-British companies thus reducing the number of British employees. For the same reason, a number of British-trained Kuwaiti graduates were appointed, but they were not dynamic, had little power and made no impact on future policies.

Things came to a head for me when I objected to the inhumane treatment of technicians by the owner of the contracting company. The last straw came when he allowed my signature to be forged so that he could dismiss one such who had been injured in a car accident. When I found this out I tendered my resignation and in reprisal he made it difficult for me to leave Kuwait. But ultimately he gave me back my passport and in 1972 we returned to the UK where we again faced an unknown future.

Short stay in Libya, and Coppas

I was soon offered a consultancy at the Zawiyya refinery in Libya by the American engineering construction contractor, Parsons Corporation. I flew out to Tripoli but only stayed in the job for a month, primarily because of the very severe restrictions imposed on foreigners.

To work there you had, as in Kuwait, to surrender your passport but the formalities required to get it back were more stringent. I met a British engineer called Steve Nash who swam forty lengths every day in the pool at the Zawiyya Tourist Centre where I was staying, and when I asked him why he was doing this he replied that it wasn't for his health but rather because he was contemplating swimming to Malta! He had some marital problems which made it urgent for him to return to the UK, but his passport had been held back by the authorities. I therefore decided I would insist on keeping my passport with me as long as I stayed in Libya. The authorities tried to persuade me that because I was of Arab origin I would be treated differently, but I didn't trust them at all.

It was at the Zawiyya Tourist Centre that I met Idi Amin, who had the previous year become the third President of Uganda. He was visiting the refinery in the company of Abdessalam Jalloud, who became Muammar Gaddafi's Prime Minister at about that time. I think Amin saw me as a fellow Muslim in an otherwise entirely European environment, and consequently felt sorry for me. At any rate, he invited me to join him for a swim in the pool, and when I explained I couldn't swim, he offered to teach me. What a picture it would have made if I'd accepted!

The Libyans I encountered were extremely lazy and not interested in learning or improving themselves. So after a short while I decided to leave Libya and return to the UK. That was a good move as it eventually led to me having the chance to work on the first project for the development of North Sea oil. But before that I found work for a year with a company called Coppas Int. based in Mitcham, Surrey, and run by Jo Bryan who was particularly interested in the Middle East. They offered specialist advice on technical manpower for projects in Kuwait, Libya and Saudi Arabia (particularly for one project in Al-Khobar).

Funnily enough Coppas sent me back to Libya on a business trip with its GM, Ashley Armstrong. And who should we find in Tripoli but Anthony Quinn. He was staying, like our team, at the only international class hotel in town, while playing the leading role of Hamza in the shooting of the film *The Messenger of God*. The hotel manager told me that Quinn was looking for some whisky, and it happened that I had a bottle with me. And so I shared this with him, and thereafter we became good companions. We would sit at the same table for meals, where we were joined by his young and beautiful Tunisian girlfriend. Our circle was enlarged when I introduced them to an ex-IPC petroleum engineer colleague, who happened now to be working for Mobil in Tripoli, where he lived with his Welsh wife. Through the Tunisian woman we learnt to enjoy 'brik,' a Tunisian samosa-like dish consisting of a thin pastry wrap filled with egg, chopped onion, tuna, harissa and parsley, and fried briefly in hot oil.

I enjoyed my time with Coppas, but the opportunity to join McDermott was not to be missed.

Pioneering North Sea Development with McDermott

The American company, McDermott Engineering Inc., which had experience in shallow-water platform construction in the Gulf of Mexico, was then just starting operations in the UK. I was fortunate to join seven American engineers on the staff around 1973. The company offices were initially in Ealing and then moved to Wembley Park where they purchased a huge building and the staff grew to about 800 employees.

Up until this time all oilfields were onshore apart from some shallow water production in the Gulf of Mexico. Deepwater production was unheard of due to the large capital investment required, the uncertainty of accessibility, the hostile environment, the problem of storing volatile crude, and the difficulty of providing living and working facilities on man-made steel and concrete platforms anchored on the seabed 100 metres below the surface.

The seven years I worked on this project were extremely taxing, not least because of their effect on my family life. In the circumstances the incompatibility between Doreen and me became unbridgeable. I couldn't accept the idea of continuing in such an unhappy relationship for the rest of my life. Doreen had been very loyal, and for a while we had been quite content together. Moreover, she had been a very good mother to our children, for which I remain very grateful. But we were not made for each other. I therefore left her, and while she continued to live in the house in Hinchley Wood until 1982, I rented a flat in nearby Surbiton. My daily routine from then on involved leaving home at seven o'clock in the morning, driving to Wembley Park, doing a day's work, getting home at seven in the evening, and after that visiting the children in Hinchley Wood.

I now faced the prospect of taking my children on holiday by myself. By good fortune a Sudanese man called Yahya, whom I met while working for Coppas, provided a solution to this dilemma as he was working on the construction of a refinery near Lisbon. He was married to a Dutch lady called Annemarie, and their children were friendly with mine, and so he invited me to spend my holiday with them in Portugal. This was a godsend and I enthusiastically took up his offer.

He and his friend, Leslie, met me at Lisbon airport and we drove to a resort, curiously called Siena, half way down the Portuguese coast to the Algarve. Leslie and Pauline, his wife, were staying in my friend's villa while waiting to be moved to their own within a week or so.

Pauline was a beautiful woman who had no children of her own and so she was pleased to accompany me every day to the beach with mine. We enjoyed each other's company, and before long we realised we had a lot more in common than she had with her husband. The two-week holiday developed into something much more serious and before we left Portugal a very unpleasant encounter took place between Leslie and me, which brought the holiday romance to an uncomfortable end. However, Pauline and I remained in contact, of which more later.

Despite the difficulties of my daily routine, my work in Wembley was enjoyable as well as financially rewarding. The first deep sea oil production facilities were in Norwegian waters, the contractors being the French company Elf-Total, in conjunction with the Norwegian Ministry of Oil. Unlike my previous work in Kuwait and Libya, I was now involved in pioneering design engineering and saw the TCP2[4] project right through from conception to completion. I also made a lot of friends.

I never actually went out to the North Sea platforms because there was no need for me to do so. Not wishing to face the hostile North Sea environment, I stayed onshore in London doing basic design engineering and travelling. I visited Paris on a regular basis, sometimes as often as once a week, to finalise the approval of drawings and provide progress reports on the project. This work-experience had a very positive impact on my future involvement with Iraq for I now had experience, in addition to theoretical training, particularly in the field of design engineering, qualifications which were almost entirely lacking in the Iraqi engineering fraternity as well as in the Arab world as a whole.

My new environment gave me a unique and comprehensive understanding of the whole process of engineering. Unlike me, the majority of engineers and project associates did not have maintenance experience, and this wider overview helped me to appreciate what was

---

[4] TCP2 is the acronym for Treatment Compressing Platform 2.

expected in maintenance and construction projects. My salary was way above average and so I enjoyed a high standard of living, as well as being able to pay for the private schooling of my children and provide financial support to my wife.

Like other people on a similar income, I embraced a hedonistic lifestyle, discovered I required more than one car, ate in expensive restaurants, went shopping at Harrods and generally lived like an aristocrat. It was only later that I learnt that happiness and a materialistic lifestyle are not necessarily compatible.

After completing the North Sea project a totally unexpected opportunity came my way.

CHAPTER THREE

ENTERPRISE AND IDEALISM

Establishing Petcon

In 1975 the Iraqi Oil Minister, Abdul-Karim Tayih, visited BP with his deputy, Dr Hashim al-Khursan, the latter a close friend of mine from secondary school days. In addition to Hashim's position as Deputy Minister of Oil he served as Director General of Exploration. The Iraqis needed technical assistance with their design engineering requirements and were delighted to discover that I was working in that field, and had exactly the expertise they were looking for. Thereupon I started dealing with Iraq and contacted my old colleagues from BPC who were now working for the nationalised oil industry. The IPC had in the meantime been divided into two parts known as the North Oil Company and the South Oil Company, which were respectively equivalent to the old Mosul Petroleum Company plus the IPC operation in Kirkuk, on the one hand, and BPC, on the other.

In 1976 I launched Petcon together with Steve Nash, the friend who had talked of swimming from Libya to Malta, and who like me was involved in the McDermott North Sea oil project. We were at the tail end of the Frigg field development[1] and were looking for new opportunities. We could see that there was an unfulfilled need in the Middle East for engineering design expertise and decided to try our luck at catering for it.

Petcon International Ltd, as it was officially called, kicked off in earnest while I was still working for McDermott, and so I was able to

---

[1] This field lies off the Norwegian coast and is named after the goddess Frigg. King Olav V of Norway officially opened production on 8 May 1978.

benefit from the assistance provided by their procurement department. They weren't at that time particularly busy, and the company judged that there were potential benefits for them in helping me. I had just taken over McDermott's new contract with ARAMCO which was repetitive and very tedious and so I had plenty of time, while still enjoying a regular income. Petcon's main business was providing the Iraqi oil industry with parts and materials for its technical operations.

Within a year Petcon started to realise its potential with a £1 million contract to supply cables. As the volume of work increased it became impractical to continue travelling every day to work at Wembley Park, and so I had to leave McDermott. The Iraqi South Oil Company had expanded enormously since the old BPC days, providing a ready market for our materials and services, and this increased still further when we started serving the North Oil Company as well. We also moved into Kuwait and by September 1980, thanks to unstinting collective effort, we had a substantial turnover. But in that month the Iran-Iraq war broke out and Petcon's prospects were suddenly in jeopardy. Enquiries diminished and I was very concerned about what the future held in store.

I thought it might be best to seek new work elsewhere in the United Arab Emirates where a large number of the Iraqi ex-IPC staff had by now established themselves. Many of those who were not Ba'athists had left following nationalisation of the Iraqi oil industry and were now working for the Abu Dhabi National Oil Company (ADNOC). When I contacted some of these they were courteous enough to invite me to Abu Dhabi. I travelled via Kuwait to evaluate the business potential there, and then went on to Abu Dhabi where fate took a hand in mapping out my future life.

AREC: Enthusiasm and Disillusion

By sheer chance I met there the General Manager of the newly-formed Arab Engineering Company (AREC) which was sponsored and financed by the members of the Organisation of Arab Petroleum Exporting Countries (OAPEC). Aziz Qurba, an Algerian, had difficulty in finding an Arab recruit qualified in engineering design, and so when he came across me, with my unique and extensive off-shore engineering design experience, he snapped me up and offered me a post as his deputy. The package included a very high salary, free accommodation, travel and the payment of school fees for my children.

In view of the Iran-Iraq war and the effect this had had on Petcon, I accepted the offer without hesitation. With Aziz's agreement I returned to the UK to arrange my affairs and to await the expected early resolution of the conflict. Sadly, it soon became clear that there was unlikely to be a cessation of hostilities any time soon,[2] and so after a couple of weeks I travelled back to Abu Dhabi to take up my post. Meanwhile, my faithful colleagues kept Petcon running in my absence.

In the summer I arranged for my son and daughter to visit me in Abu Dhabi and Pauline, who had by now split up with her husband and with whom I'd remained in contact, decided to come as well. The children stayed for about a month but Pauline remained and asked me to find her a job. This was easy as there were several British companies which were eager to establish a working relationship with me in anticipation of developing mutual business interests. For Pauline the pay was good and the conditions were excellent. She had had an uninteresting job in London which involved travelling to work every day on the congested underground. The life style in Abu Dhabi was far more attractive. I had access to the exclusive Marina Club, with its squash and tennis courts, swimming pool and restaurant, facilities which were mostly frequented

---

[2] The war actually lasted eight years.

by local privileged nationals. After three months Pauline's visa ran out, and so I arranged an Islamic marriage which entitled her to a residence permit and enabled her to remain in Abu Dhabi.

During the first year I travelled widely on a recruitment drive for AREC but it was difficult to find Arabs with experience in engineering design, and so I was obliged to recruit other nationals as long as they had the necessary experience. Arab recruits could in the meantime be brought in to be trained so that in two to three years' time we would have a truly Arab engineering company. In the end I managed to convince the board of directors of OAPEC that this was the best policy, and my plan was accepted.

Aziz was obliged to give me a free hand, realising that I was the only one who had that experience and that he would reap the benefit of my contribution. I therefore travelled to the UK where, with the aid of the multinational professional services company, Ernst & Young, I interviewed around 300 applicants. Among them I managed to identify a number who had the required engineering experience and were willing to help with the challenges ahead.

Within a year I initiated AREC's first project with ADNOC. This was a joint venture with the local National Petroleum Construction Company for a number of offshore shallow water production platforms in The Gulf off Abu Dhabi. Within a year AREC accordingly grew from a company consisting of a handful of inexperienced Arab friends of the GM to a thriving engineering organisation with four hundred employees.

Despite my best efforts to establish an Arab engineering company, however, I was frustrated by the typical Arab mentality of Aziz Qurba. Knowing that the Arab world cared more about façade than substance, his concern was primarily to promote the company's image while paying scant regard to what it actually achieved. My experience of the Iraqisation programme and my work for McDermott had given me quite a different mind-set. Sadly in these circumstances my ambition to lay the foundation for a thriving Arab company with engineering capabilities to match those of Western enterprises turned out to be a recipe for conflict with my superior.

Aziz tried to marry our two very different concepts rather than seeing them as incompatible. To boost the image of AREC, he persuaded the board to establish its headquarters in a prestigious and expensive building which seemed to me more suitable for a bank or an insurance company. In the circumstances, however, I had no option but to accept this decision.

At last I managed to find the necessary staff and we got involved in serious engineering work. Unfortunately the majority of the people who were sent by the OAPEC member states couldn't speak English. The Algerians spoke French, most of the others only Arabic. The Syrians sent officials with no engineering experience. Iraq sent two senior managers to give orders rather than undertake the work which was required. They arrived regarding their appointment as an opportunity for high rewards rather than the beginning of a serious and hard-working career. Accordingly they were shocked by the reality on the ground and were humiliated to discover they didn't have the knowledge and experience required.

I worked very hard and managed to get many contracts for engineering projects. But my conflict with Aziz came to a head one day and I realised that our different philosophies made my position untenable. I had made an appointment to see him one afternoon but arrived at his office to be told that he was busy somewhere else in the building. When he finally returned he shouted in the presence of others that I was attacking him for not being fit to manage. The heated exchange which followed ended in him challenging me to a fist fight. I threw off my jacket, while he placed his jacket neatly on the back of the chair. Even in this situation he was concerned about his image, and his action made me laugh. We both then saw the funny side of our argument and hugged each other in reconciliation. But I insisted that it was best for me to leave as we were undermining each other's ability to manage.

When Pauline and I left Abu Dhabi and returned to the UK I thought this was the end of my association with AREC. But my resignation made Aziz realise that he couldn't continue to manage without doing any serious work. So he sought me out in London where I suggested to him that the best way forward was to operate from the UK as well as Abu Dhabi. He was agreeable, and so AREC opened an office in High Street, Kensington.

Once again, this was a prestigious but inappropriate location and so eventually I persuaded the board to transfer the management to Griffin House in Hammersmith. That move marked the true start of a respectable Arab engineering company. I brought in people with experience in procurement, planning and design engineering whom I knew from McDermott, and we soon had a staff of over two hundred.[3] AREC's turnover now rocketed to an annual $800 million.

AREC now had joint ventures with the American companies Fluor and Bechtel, undertaking projects in Tunisia, Libya and Abu Dhabi. We were ambitious to seek more opportunities, but again there was a conflict between serious work and grandiose façade. As I gained an insight into the mind-set of Arab ministers and high ranking officials who set the tone in enterprises under their jurisdiction, my disillusion increased. The majority were corrupt, especially in North Africa and the Gulf, with Iraq standing out as an exception. I realised that the ministers and officials in most Arab states were not planning for the future, and I took it very hard. I couldn't understand why there was such a lack of vision for the future.

The Arab board of AREC made sure that the London office was independent and active. Aziz had his glamorous headquarters in Abu Dhabi, but relied on the real work being done in London. I managed both offices, one directly, the other indirectly, and naturally this made

---

[3] The staff in Abu Dhabi now numbered three hundred.

him feel insecure and jealous of me, despite his having the upper hand as a political appointee. Meanwhile all the profits were squandered on prestigious cars, lavish hotels, expensive restaurants and the like so that when at last the budget started to be examined serious discrepancies were found. To justify his *raison d'être* the GM decided to close the Abu Dhabi office and come to London, thereby displacing me. This was the signal which finally convinced me to quit rather than face another year of struggle and infighting. And so after four years with AREC I resigned in a state of disillusionment about the ability of the Arab world to stand on its own two feet and claim its rightful position in the world.

Iraq was unrelenting in its war with Iran, the biggest mistake it, or indeed Iran, ever made. This pointless conflict was financed and encouraged by the Western world, Russia and China. It brought both countries to their knees economically and resulted in tremendous and needless loss of life. They were the saddest years for both Iraq and Iran. One of the main beneficiaries was the Zionist entity, as many Arabs prefer to call the illegal Jewish state in our midst. From its perspective it was very satisfactory that the military might of both countries was destroyed. As the years went by it became evident that this war marked a major stepping stone towards the total subjugation of the Arab and Islamic world. Another came in 2003. And at the time of writing we're moving towards a further item on that agenda, namely Iran.

Free-range poultry farming

Unable to get AREC out of my mind, I decided to give myself a complete break from the Arab world and its politics. While working with AREC I had met Stewart Martindall who had by 1984 retired to his estate at Linwood in the New Forest, and together we decided to start a poultry farm producing free-range eggs on his land. I continued to live in Surbiton, and commuted to the farm by car, though I would sometimes stay a couple of nights with Stewart.

At that time free range eggs were not widely available, most eggs being produced by the battery system. We therefore started a pioneering free-range production unit in the belief that there was a demand for eggs which were produced in a more humane way. Battery hens were variously mistreated, ranging from being confined to a very small space for their entire lives, being artificially fattened by the use of growth hormones, and having tranquilizers added to their feed which passed via the food chain to humans. They never experienced natural light, and chicks were segregated from birth by gender, the females being used to produce eggs, and the males going for meat production. The eggs were artificially fertilised and incubated, and the chickens, having outgrown their usefulness, had thereafter a miserably short life.

We were both engineers from the oil industry, so we brought a particular perspective to the project. It was refreshing and morale-boosting starting something totally new. The staff from the Ministry of Agriculture, whom we found extremely helpful, could not believe that we were embarking on a venture about which we knew nothing. But I believe that when you are prepared to admit you don't know something and are willing to learn, people will extend a helping hand. When ego and arrogance are set aside people behave reasonably towards you. It is only when people try to pretend they know more than they do that a barrier is built up.

Our engineering design skills helped us to establish housing for the chickens which was quite different from the norm. We examined the high mortality rates due to respiratory illness, which is very common in chicken houses, and overcame the problem by allowing air to circulate rather than remain stagnant. As a result the death rate dropped from 8% to 2%. We also made sure the area was not contaminated with chicken droppings, and we used this excreta to produce methane gas to generate power.

On our farm the hens were allowed to roam freely in the field from morning until dusk. Indoors they were provided with perches, laying boxes, food, water and wood shavings with which they made nests. Young chickens thought my wellington boots were cockerels, and they would lie waiting to be mounted. One farmer advised me to place a hand on their backs and squeeze, at which they would ruffle their feathers in ecstasy. It was, however, rather exhausting doing this with a few thousand chickens, and I had difficulty explaining to friends and family what was happening when they witnessed the sheer delight of the chickens.

Regretfully, in time I had to conclude that though free range is one step better than battery, it is not the answer. From an animal welfare point of view we discovered that the optimum flock should not exceed eighty, including cockerels, regardless of the space available. This was far below the level of 504 per acre indicated by the EU, and also well below what we had achieved. But as I gained greater awareness of food production I came to realise that the optimum was uneconomical. It was labour-intensive, and you were dependent on convincing the public that such small-scale production lessened the possibility of blood clots in the eggs and other abnormalities. Modern city dwellers were not interested in such solutions; in fact animal welfare was incompatible with modernity.

Nevertheless, this year away from engineering provided a completely different work experience. It didn't last very long, but while it did we were ambitious and wanted to expand. We aimed to reduce the price of free-range eggs sufficiently so that those on a low income could afford them. One interesting discovery we made was that handicapped people were more amenable to working with chickens than the able-bodied. They enjoyed the company of the birds and the birds found them kinder and more tolerant than able-bodied people. We thought the best approach was to involve organisations dealing with handicapped people as they had funds and could create job opportunities. We considered that the public would also be amenable to buying free-range eggs produced by the handicapped.

But unfortunately our declared intention to challenge battery egg production and reduce the cost was regarded as a threat to conventional producers. They could tolerate one farm but would not allow us to expand across the UK. Pressure was placed on the feed suppliers and in turn they made the unrealistic demand that the road to the farm be paved. We could not meet this expense and the whole project collapsed.

Today many farmers are using smaller flocks to produce eggs and are realising that the upper EU limit is unrealistically high. There are other problems with larger numbers such as dominating chickens which stop the remainder of the flock from going out and laying eggs. We also found that birds enjoy life as a family unit, which is what nature intended, and so segregation was not the answer.

It was customary among the chicken farmers to cull predators such as badgers and foxes. We found that this approach was counter-productive and so we fed dead fowl to the predators and they then gave up attacking our chickens. We realised that the predators are territorial and simply need to feed themselves and their young; if they are able to do this coexistence is possible. It is sad that the concept of selfishness rather than sharing and living together is largely absent in the rural environment.

We not only employed our engineering skills in the construction of the housing; fencing, feeders, watering systems and lighting also benefited from our expertise. But we could not have achieved what we did without the assistance of family, friends and local labour. This year of my life gave me a great deal of pleasure and enabled me to forget AREC, Arab politics, corruption and ministerial egos. I abandoned any intention of contributing my experience to the Arab world which I concluded was beyond redemption.

Petcon's Heyday

After we closed the farm in 1985 I re-engaged with Petcon which, despite the war, was flourishing. I soon stopped working from home and took an office in Kingston to handle the flood of contracts, again mostly with the South and North Oil companies in Iraq. After the Iran-Iraq war ended in 1988 Petcon experienced a short heyday. The Iraqi Ministry of Oil had embarked on a major project with Bechtel called PC2 (Petro-Chemical 2), and we were well placed to supply equipment for this development.

Senior managers from the Iraqi Oil Ministry kept on inviting me to visit but I was convinced that I was not forgiven for leaving Iraq without authorisation in 1970. And so my assistant and work confidant at that time, Charmaine, offered to go on my behalf and I agreed to this arrangement. She had never travelled to the Middle East before and had no technical background, but she conducted her visit courageously and effectively. The Ministry of Oil found Petcon more reliable than other companies, primarily because its mark-up was not excessive and the equipment provided was superior. My experience of North Sea engineering projects and design came in useful here.

At last in 1989 I visited Iraq in some trepidation for the first time in seventeen years and stayed two weeks. I didn't really believe I could find any further opportunities there, but as it turned out Iraq was very active commercially. The main hotels, Al Rasheed and the Sheraton, were full of foreigners representing multinationals seeking contracts. And so I came back with positive benefits, having signed large contracts related to the PC2 project and with the General Electric Company (GEC) for the supply of railway electrification equipment.

My last visit to Iraq before the First Gulf War was in July 1990. There was a general perception that something was going on, a feeling of tension and uncertainty. My nephew was in the Republican Guard and he was suddenly called up in the middle of the night. We anticipated the move into Kuwait but no one was sure what the outcome would be.

I visited Basrah where I stayed with my family and had a very enjoyable time getting reintegrated into the fold. But I found that the Kuwaitis were behaving in a very uncaring way in the city. The value of the Iraqi dinar had fallen. Ten Iraqi dinars were equivalent to one Kuwaiti dinar (previously they had been on a par), and so Kuwaitis were driving to Basrah to buy everything they wanted on the cheap – food, meat, and construction materials. The local Basrahwis were left with nothing because most of the good food and other provisions had been bought up by Kuwaitis.

Kuwaitis in Baghdad were also behaving arrogantly. They stayed in the Rasheed Hotel because for them it was cheap. Rightly or wrongly, they hadn't supported Iraq at all in the eight-year Iran-Iraq war, and were loathed by the Iraqi people for their behaviour. I believe, like many others, that the invasion of Kuwait was wrong, but one has to understand that Iraq had sacrificed up to half a million lives, as well as the potential development of the country, as a result of the war. When the Kuwaitis did not behave in a supportive manner, the people, both Ba'athists and non-Ba'athists, were antagonised.

On the business front this last visit before the war was as successful as that of the previous year. I left Iraq on 25th July, just a week and a day before Iraq entered Kuwait, full of optimism, particularly about the PC2 project. I had signed a £22 millon contract for the supply of engineering equipment for that project and many international companies were keen to be represented in Iraq by Petcon.

In the 1980s Petcon had built up a business in representing a number of British companies who didn't have access to the Iraqi market. They included UK companies manufacturing cables, electric switch gear and control valves. In addition to their railway electrification programme GEC approached Petcon to handle and promote their microwave telecommunications throughout Iraq. In return they agreed to pay 2% on the value of each contract.

The day I left most foreigners, fearing the worst, were scrambling to get out of Iraq. By contrast, I thought my life was about to change immeasurably for the better. For the first time I sensed I was moving into a completely different league and would achieve the peak of material well-being. It was not unreasonable to expect that Petcon would soon be earning millions a day.

CHAPTER FOUR

KUWAIT AND THE ARAB NATION

Kuwait and political engagement

The Iraqi invasion of Kuwait, starting on 2nd August 1990, marked a crucial turning point in my life. Up until then my primary objective had been material success. My wish to help establish an independent Arab engineering sector was certainly in part idealistic, but self-interest was also involved. From now on my business activities became subservient to campaigning.

Four days after the invasion, the UN Security Council passed resolution 661, which imposed a tough financial and trade embargo on Iraq. Its removal was made conditional on withdrawal from Kuwait, the payment of reparations, and the disclosure and elimination of weapons of mass destruction. The elated state in which I left the country soon evaporated, and I suddenly hit the ground with a thud. All my contracts were cancelled and materials which I had already shipped but were awaiting customs clearance could not now be paid for. As the UK had frozen all Iraqi assets about eight hundred thousand pounds of Petcon funds were forfeited. My only remaining asset was my house, and I even found myself compelled to work for a time as a cleaner. My depressed state wasn't helped by my relationship with Pauline coming to a definitive end with an Islamic divorce.

Luckily I had never used my house as collateral to borrow money from the bank. When the shutters came down I mistakenly thought that the crisis would be resolved within a couple of weeks and life would return to normal. I accordingly maintained my office in Kingston anticipating a change for the better. Most manufacturers shared my optimism and it was only when matters escalated to a war footing that we all became apprehensive. That is when we realised that disaster was looming.

Following the expulsion of Iraq from Kuwait, and the savage 'degrading' (that is mass slaughter) of the relatively defenceless Republican Guard in early 1991, the sanctions regime was extended by Security Council resolution 687, which established the United Nations Special Commission to organise inspections and required Iraq to observe the Nuclear Non-Proliferation Treaty. The Security Council stated that these measures 'represent steps towards the goal of establishing in the Middle East a zone free from weapons of mass destruction and all missiles for their delivery and the objective of a global ban on chemical weapons.' Given that the Zionist entity was the only country in the region with nuclear weapons, and that there was not the remotest possibility its leaders would agree to give up their WMDs, this last aspiration was pie in the sky.

My active involvement in politics came as a result of these reactions to Iraq's occupation of Kuwait. The BBC2 Newsnight programme organised a debate in which Mowaffak Al-Rubaie, a prominent member of the so-called Iraqi opposition and post-2003 a national security advisor to the Coalition Provisional Authority, presented the case in favour of intervention. I was joined by Palestinian Ghada Karmi in opposing this view.[1] We considered the crisis an internal Arab matter and believed that intervention was being promoted to ensure the continued flow of oil to the West. The Americans and the British were, in our view, only trumpeting human rights issues for cynical political

---

[1] I believe this programme went out on 31st October 1990, but have been unable to confirm the date. Jeremy Paxman was presiding. The BBC staff were very apprehensive about bringing people of such diverse views together for a debate. In one such programme they were therefore astonished that when we'd finished I shook the hand of the Kuwaiti ambassador, Khalid Al-Duwaisan. The Iraqi opposition had managed to convince people in England that those who did not support them were dangerous fanatics and Saddam apologists.

and economic gain. If the British government's real motivation had been to rid Iraq of dictators and if they had applied the same criteria throughout the Arab world, we might have been more sympathetic. But their selectivity in taking on one pariah and ignoring the rest betrayed their real motives.

That Newsnight programme was the start of my publicity offensive. Thereafter I participated in numerous other radio and television programmes, whether for the BBC (including its regional services), LBC,[2] Irish radio and television, Sky, CNN, Voice of America, or many other US broadcasters. My purpose was always the same; to inform the general public in the West about the effect of the draconian sanctions regime, and urging Western leaders to ask themselves about the likely long-term effects of this policy, both in humanitarian and political terms.

But before I go on with my story, this seems a good point to step back and look at the historical background to the crisis of 1990.

The enduring imperial legacy

The Western concern about the occupation of Kuwait sat strangely with their unending tolerance of the occupation of Palestine, whether we are talking of its entirety, or about the much reduced Palestinian areas of the West Bank, East Jerusalem and Gaza. Here a people quite foreign to the region had displaced or subjugated the native population, whereas in Kuwait the aim had simply been to change the sovereignty of the country from one Arab ruler to another. Moreover, the border between Iraq and Kuwait was quite artificial, having been created as recently as 1922 by Sir Percy Cox, the British High Commissioner in Iraq at that time.[3] Kuwait was not a country, but

---

[2] The acronym for Leading Britain's Conversation, a talk and phone-in radio station which started life in 1973 as the London Broadcasting Company, the first licensed commercial radio station in the UK.
[3] See Appendix Two.

rather an oil well with a flag, created and protected for political reasons by the British.

Iraq and Kuwait form part of the larger Al-Watan al-Arabi, the Arab Nation, and the divisions in this nation were created by imperial occupation. Starting before World War I, and confirmed in its immediate aftermath, the French, the Italians and the British carved up the Ottoman Empire in a divide-and-rule strategy. These artificially created countries were further weakened by imposing corrupt puppet leaders to rule over them. The legacy of colonial rule was division and corruption. Tam Dalyell (who would soon play crucial role in my life) saw Iraq's invasion of Kuwait just as I did:

> The world was outraged by the Iraqi attack on Kuwait in August 1990. I too was horrified, even though I'd inherited my father's prejudice against Kuwaitis, without knowing quite why he held them in such distaste.[4] I did know something of the history. Kuwait, like Iraq/Mesopotamia, had been part of the Ottoman Empire. On the creation of Iraq, a process led by the British, the state of Kuwait had been hived off, partly at the instance of, and benefit of, the Anglo-Persian Oil Company, as it was, long before it metamorphosed into British Petroleum or BP. I judged, therefore, that Baghdad's claims were not entirely bogus. Later I was to find in Baghdad, even among sensible officials, the belief that Kuwait ought to be the nineteenth province of Iraq. I was also aware of the very recent tensions between Iraq and Kuwait when the Iraqis, at the end of the war with Iran, asked the Kuwaitis for financial help on the grounds, not altogether spurious, that Iraq had protected Kuwait from the militant Islam of Ayatollah Khomeini. The ruling elite and Sheikhly

---

[4] Dalyell's father was on the staff of Sir Percy Cox, working under the direction of his famous oriental secretary, Gertrude Bell. He was also military secretary to William Willcocks, a water engineer who built the first dams on the Tigris.

family, however, replied with disdain. In particular, they suggested that Saddam Hussein should go back to the drains where his mother was a whore and that they would reduce the value of the Iraq currency, the dinar, to the value of lavatory paper. This infuriated the pathologically proud Saddam Hussein.

There was one other matter that inhibited me from going along with the outraged herd, and gave me confidence in opposing the war. The Iraqi embassy in London assured me that the US Ambassador in Baghdad, a senior career diplomat called April Glaspie, had given the Iraqi leadership tacit assurance that the Americans would acquiesce and take no military action, given Washington's appalling relations with Tehran. Later, there was talk of the folly of appointing a woman as ambassador to a Muslim state. This is nonsense. Saddam's regime was secular, quite unlike that in Riyadh. Furthermore, Glaspie was able and competent. I thought it was inconceivable that she should have conveyed such an impression without a green light from senior State Department figures, particularly Lawrence Eagleburger, back in Washington.[5]

Such a way of seeing things was very unpopular in the Labour Party, many having been swayed by the emotional account of an attractive Kuwaiti woman at their conference who spoke about the ravages inflicted on her country. Such atrocity propaganda was amplified by another woman's account of a purported incident during the invasion.

This was the appearance on coast-to-coast American television of a distraught Kuwaiti woman, who had claimed

---

[5] Dalyell, T, *The Importance of Being Awkward*, Birlinn, Edinburgh, 2012, pp 248-49.

to be a nurse in the paediatric ward of the Kuwait hospital and who had seen with her own eyes Kuwaiti babies being thrown out of the incubators by thuggish Iraqi invaders.

It was difficult to exaggerate the impact on American viewers. Some months later, it happened that two Filipino nurses, who worked in the babies' section of the hospital, saw a video repeat of the heart-rending appeal. 'Funny,' they said, 'we worked in those wards and no babies were thrown out of any incubators. What's more, we thought we knew all the nurses who worked with us in the wards. We do not recognise the nurse who appeared on American television.' On further investigation, it transpired that she was not a nurse at all. She turned out to be the actress daughter of the Kuwaiti Ambassador in Washington and her appearance had been arranged by Doulton's, the public relations firm. When challenged about why they had done it, their lame reply was that 'all's fair in love and war.'[6]

Tam's scepticism about imperialism sprang from a strand of British thinking which has deep roots. Wilfrid Scawen Blunt, for example, railed against the occupation of Egypt in 1882, and Lawrence of Arabia was shocked when he learnt that under the secret Sykes-Picot agreement an independent greater Syria, which he believed had been promised to Hussein bin Ali, Sharif of Mecca, was no longer to be permitted. Whatever the reality behind the myth, Lawrence appears to have felt that he personally, as well as the Arabs he had befriended, had been cheated into fighting a war against the Turks on false pretences. Having helped to drive the Turks out of the Hijaz and liberate Damascus, they had been betrayed.

This is considered a very controversial subject which most Westerners strive to skim over. They recognise the frontiers in the Arab

---

[6] Ibid pp 249-50.

world as if they were God-given. In reality none of them are sovereign. By drawing lines on the map to delineate Egypt, Libya, Tunisia, Algeria and Morocco the imperial powers created weak artificial countries which were intentionally dependent on the West. Iraq is the only Arab country with all the elements of nationhood, that is sufficient land, natural resources and an educated citizenry, all of which make it potentially self-sustainable. In this way it resembles the two non-Arab countries of the region, Turkey and Iran.

It is therefore not surprising that the West, and especially the Zionist entity, were particularly keen to set Iran and Iraq at each others' throats, and did so by backing both sides. The economic and military capabilities of its perceived enemies were thus downgraded. But though weakened, Iraq still posed a potential threat, and so the US lured Saddam into invading Kuwait, giving him the impression that they would not intervene if he did so. This was the opportunity for the West to replace Iraq's leadership with one more to its liking, and thereby once again to undermine its autonomy. Future generations, it was decided, would be brought up under the influence of the US and UK. When I later reflected on these events in my prison cell it became crystal clear to me that this had been the plan, and that it continued to be.

Egypt is a major country. It has water and population but it lacks sufficient additional natural resources to make it a fully sovereign state. If, on the other hand, Sudan, Egypt and Libya were amalgamated, with all their natural resources, there would be no need for such schemes as Gaddafi's Great Manmade River Project. This ambitious, but controversial scheme, involving the transfer by pipeline of large quantities of water from aquifers in the southern desert to the fertile country in the north, was only initiated because the frontier with Egypt made the waters of the Nile inaccessible to Libya. The $20 billion which were spent on this project in the 1980s was a complete waste of money. The main beneficiaries were the international contractors,

Bechtel and the Halliburton subsidiary, Brown & Root,[7] both parties to the Iraq invasion and occupation in 2003.

It was just such a sharing of Arab resources which Gamal Abdul Nasser dreamt of, and the long-term motive for the British, French and Zionist entity attack on Egypt in 1956 was to prevent its achievement. For the Arab world could only be controlled if it remained divided. If Arab countries had collaborated there would have been no need for the enormous migration to Europe from North Africa, especially from Morocco, Algeria and Tunisia. The combination of the land and natural resources of Algeria and Tunisia and the fertile land of Morocco could have provided a good standard of living to the people of these countries and thereby facilitated regional peace.

Tony Blair maintained that the Muslims were jealous of Western civilisation but this was, and remains, untrue. What they *do* dislike is the unfairness of Western policies. Though direct colonial occupation in the Middle East is now, with the exception of the Zionist entity, a thing of the past, the Americans, the British and the French continue to colonise in a different way. The world is looking for fairness and equality but the Western world, and the European countries in particular, haven't learned the lesson of past colonisation and are continuing to exploit without giving anything back.

This policy creates a chasm between pro-Western rulers and the people, who often remain backward. In 1972 Iraq stepped away from US/UK influence by nationalising their oil industry. Gamal Abdul Nasser had done something similar in 1956 when he nationalised the Suez Canal, but Egypt did not have the infrastructure to sustain its independence and so he had had to turn to the Soviet Union for help. The fact is that both the Soviets and the West shared common interests

---

[7] After Halliburton took over Dresser Industries in 1998, a subsidiary of Dresser, M. W. Kellogg, was merged with Brown and Root to form Kellogg Brown Root. In 2007 Halliburton sold this off after which its official title became the acronym KBR.

in the global economy, a vital consideration too long overlooked by Egypt's rulers.

The most blatant imperial legacy in the Middle East is the Zionist entity. This ruthless colonial enterprise, unflinchingly backed by the West, has made the remaining Palestinians captives in their own land, and those who have left it permanent exiles. While no Palestinians living outside historic Palestine are permitted to resume residence in their ancestral land, Jews anywhere in the world have a so-called right of return to what is considered their land. The Palestinians are branded as trouble-makers if not terrorists, while the Jewish state uses F16 fighter jets to bomb them. As some Palestinian wag wryly remarked, 'give us some F16s and we'll stop being terrorists.' Mind you, F16s are themselves weapons of terror.

In 1987 the first Intifada broke out in the occupied territories and over the next six years over 1000 Palestinians and around 160 on the Zionist side were killed. The number of wounded among the Palestinians ran into the tens of thousands, many of them children. The tactics used against the Palestinians changed over time because world public opinion was shocked by the use of live rounds and a policy of breaking the bones of protestors. Instead plastic bullets became the preferred weapon, but the aim was always the same; to deny that there was any justification for Palestinian protest.

Palestinians were overwhelmingly supportive of Saddam when he invaded Kuwait, and paid a heavy price after Kuwait was restored to the Sabah family. There was an exodus of Palestinians from the Gulf states, and yet support for the leader of Iraq, which had fired 39 scud missiles at the Zionist entity during the war, remained high. He was seen as the only Arab leader who was prepared to wage war against their oppressors. The missiles may not have been particularly effective in military terms, but they certainly put the wind up the Zionists.

The 1993 Oslo accords finally brought the uprising to an end, but however well-intentioned its Norwegian initiators and, indeed, Yasser

Arafat himself, were they turned out to be a poisoned chalice, tightening the noose still further around the necks of the Palestinians. Oslo even made their leaders, inadvertently or not, into their own jailors. The mistake of both the Norwegian and the Palestinian negotiators was to misconceive the nature of Zionism, and its power as an ideology. Palestine is a festering sore which the West wants to cover up and which the Muslim and Arab world will never forget. Those regional leaders who oppose Zionism and support the Palestinian resistance can expect to find themselves under attack and their countries on the list for regime change at a convenient point in the future. Saddam Hussein was one such, Muammar Gaddafi another, and next in line is the Iranian regime.

Zionist leaders are not only interested in replacing leaders who oppose them with compliant puppets. Given that the majority of Arabs and Muslims oppose Zionism, stirring up disorder among the countries where their enemies live is another tactic, and one which has caused untold harm to the peoples of the region.

Iraq learnt from the harsh lesson of its history, and consequently from 1970 the country was developed on the basis of technology transfer and self-dependence. In the first five years of unhindered development it progressed tremendously. By the time of my visit in 1989 I was amazed at what had been achieved. Illiteracy had been eradicated and the best free medical care and education systems in the region had been established. All Arab nationals were entitled to the benefits which Iraqis enjoyed, and if Iraqi nationals could not be treated in Iraq their treatment abroad was paid for by the government.

Petrodollars were ploughed into development to an extent that alarmed the West and especially the Zionists. They were determined to find a way to undermine Iraq's economic achievements. Unfortunately, Saddam Hussein walked into the noose being prepared for him. Because of his tribal background he adopted a dictatorial form of government. His opinion prevailed even though some of his closest associates were very well educated and could offer sound advice. Most ordinary people followed him and agreed with everything he said, which strengthened his hand. In the Iran-Iraq war he described himself as the Salah-uddin (Saladin) of the modern Arab world who would, like that illustrious historical figure, liberate Palestine. But this was a pipe-dream for the Zionist entity had been created, and was supported, by powerful forces across the globe. Anyone who threatened its existence could expect to be eliminated.

Saddam deluded himself that he was the supreme leader who could challenge and win against the regional power, Iran. He was duped by the US into attacking this neighbouring country, and the Iraqi people paid for the most stupid mistake of his life with eight years of carnage and impoverishment. But even at the end of it all, in 1988, the Iraqi leadership remained arrogant, believing they'd been victorious. This attitude was unwise on the international stage, for it made the West and the Zionist entity very jittery. Their concern was that Iraq's oil resources, known and as yet unknown, should remain available to the Western world and that the Zionists should remain safe.

While OPEC was in theory an independent cartel, it was in reality manipulated by the US through its close relationship with Saudi Arabia and was used to control most of the other oil producers. Iraq's evasion of this dependence through its takeover of the oil industry within its borders was therefore regarded with the greatest of unease. For if Iraq could do this with impunity a precedent would be set which might result in the West losing control in the region.

Consequently, from 1972 onwards, Iraq was the target of Western manoeuvring aimed at weakening the country. The Iran-Contra scandal was a prime example of murky imperialist dealings where leaders appeared to know nothing about them, and lower ranking officers were convicted when they came to light. The Iran-Iraq war was quite unnecessary, and Saddam must take much of the blame for its occurrence. Nevertheless, it could have been resolved much earlier, had the US not backed both sides, supplying each of them with weapons.

This was contrary to their own boycott of Iran as a supposed sponsor of terrorism.[8] It also contravened the US stated policy of not giving military support to either side.

In 1986 it emerged that the income from arms sales to Iran was being diverted to supporting the Contra rebels, fighting the Marxist Sandinista regime in Nicaragua, also in contravention of a congressional ban on such support. The monetary transfers were organised by a member of the US National Security Council, Oliver North, and were approved by his boss, John Poindexter. President Ronald Reagan and Vice-President George Bush both denied North's assertion that they knew about the covert operation, while he and Poindexter both lost their jobs and were convicted. However, both convictions were overturned a year later.

The assumption that Saudi Arabia has the largest oil reserves in the region may prove false. The entire territory of that country and the other Gulf emirates has been explored and their reserves are documented, but Iraqi territory remains largely unexplored and may possess the highest reserves in the world. As mentioned earlier Iraqi oil is cheaper to produce because, except for the oil in the north, it has high reservoir pressure and is free from water contamination and the presence of sulphur.

The Western world, Russia and China recognise their dependence on oil and gas and their foreign policies are shaped by their requirement for these vital energy sources. But they don't deal fairly with the oil producers, being interested in exploitation rather than co-operation. The international oil cartel, OPEC, tries to dupe the populations of oil-producing countries into believing that the operating companies have no agenda. But how can this be the case when the technicians who run the oil industry, whether in Egypt, Tunisia, Saudi Arabia or the Gulf, are foreigners? Though nationals of the countries concerned are usually

---

[8] The same *Realpolitik* was later to underlie the clandestine US-Iran pact during and after the Second Gulf War.

placed in some lower managerial posts they aren't at liberty to run their own industry independent of outside interference.

Iraq was the only oil-producing country where technology transfer occurred, particularly in the area of engineering design. While this aspect of engineering had before nationalisation been handled solely by IPC's London office, a strategy intended to limit Iraqi engineering capabilities and make Iraq dependent on outside help, after nationalisation in 1972 the Iraqi Ministry of Oil made strenuous and effective efforts to promote engineering design among its domestic employees and contractors. Elsewhere in the Arab world engineering design remained firmly out of reach for Arab nationals working in the oil industry. All graduates were assigned to operations and management, with engineering design confined to the international engineering contractors.

My opportunity to become the first Arab engineer to access this sector of engineering was probably unique. Already in 1962 my specialist training in digital engineering had paved the way to my being accepted by the Ministry of Oil. By contrast with others, my experience working for McDermott put me in a position to procure engineering manuals for the ministry's staff. The devotion of four years of my career to the Arab Engineering Company (AREC) was motivated by the dream of building the first Arab engineering company to break the shackles of the international engineering contractors. I was determined that we should stand on an equal footing with the rest of humanity, rather than being servants to the big internationals. As far as my own country was concerned, however, I was destined to make much of my contribution as an expatriate.

Iraq's development, exploration and drilling programme peaked in the decade 1970-80 prior to the Iran-Iraq war. In addition to using its oil revenue to finance infrastructure, education, healthcare, the eradication of illiteracy and the promotion of agriculture, the government promoted advanced technology and research. This resulted in Iraq having among the highest level of postgraduates per head of population in the world.

Travelling throughout the Arab world for AREC gave me the opportunity to compare other countries with Iraq, and this made it very clear to me that only my country had the indigenous capabilities to run its own oil industry and to free itself from foreign domination. Progress towards self-reliance was of necessity particularly pronounced during the sanctions of the 1990s. Before that Iraq had continued to be partly dependent on the West but now Iraqis ran the country efficiently and effectively. Even the French who visited Iraq at that time, and the British who accompanied me on trips which I organised to the country were impressed by the country's technical capability. Negotiations with the Ministry of Oil agencies were carried out professionally for, in contrast to Kuwait and the other Gulf states, there was little corruption in Iraq.

From 1990 the West used a number of tactics to wrest back Iraq's control of its own oilfields. These included engineering a reduction in the number of indigenous experts, applying sanctions and, not least, regime change, with an extremely bloody war to achieve it. A similar chain of events could be seen some years later with Libya. In 2009 Gaddafi announced that he intended to replace the US dollar as an oil currency with the gold-backed African dinar, a change which would have had a significant effect on global power relations. Two years later he was deposed.

CHAPTER FIVE

THE DESERT ROAD

My country in ruins

I was devastated when I saw the TV images of the bombing of Iraq in 1991. It was hard to imagine that anybody would be left alive in the country. Having received news that my close family members had survived, I felt compelled to go and see them. As I will relate later, a visit to Iraq would also be an opportunity to recoup some of my losses. However, getting to the country was not easy as air travel to Baghdad had been suspended and the only way to travel to the capital was by the 800-km desert road from Amman. Under normal circumstances, this took between six and twelve hours, but in the exceptional conditions of post-war Iraq, the journey might take double this time.

Fortuitously I was still in touch with my old school friend, Hashim al-Khursan, who had risen to become Director General of oil exploration in Iraq, but had now been seconded to work with the Jordanian Oil Ministry in Amman.[1] I wrote to him about my plan to drive from Amman to Baghdad and he invited me to stay with him in the Shimesiani quarter of the town while arrangements were made for the journey. Amman was then relatively small and in spring it was particularly attractive as you approached it from the airport, for the desert at that time bursts into a sea of green, dotted with a kaleidoscope of flowers. Another old Iraqi colleague, Ismail, with whom I'd worked in Kuwait and who was now obliged to live in Amman,[2] arranged for

---

[1] As I mentioned earlier, Hashim had visited the UK in 1975 with his boss, the Oil Minister, Abdul-Karim Tayih, and as a result of our meeting I set up Petcon.
[2] Following the First Gulf War, Kuwait expelled all its Iraqi and Palestinian residents.

us to travel in the car of his two brothers, and together we set out the next day on our long desert journey.

In the city much of the ground was covered with snow and this made the roads treacherous. Amman is situated on a cluster of hills and so the Baghdad road went up and down and we slid all over the place as if we were on an ice rink. Finally we managed to leave the snow-covered city and its immediate environs, and took the clear desert road to Baghdad. But my companions had no experience of long-distance desert driving, and therefore had little idea of what might lie ahead. Consequently, they hadn't checked the radiator coolant or ensured that there was an inflated tyre on the spare wheel.

We soon realised we had a slow puncture in one of the tyres and feared being stuck on this desolate highway, prey to any passing bandits. The driver of a huge lorry we stopped didn't have a pump, but he suggested we continue driving behind him on our half-deflated tyre until we found someone who had. At last we were able to inflate the spare tyre and replace the wheel. The lorry driver conscientiously stayed with us the whole way to Falluja in case of further problems, a service for which we were immensely grateful. There we ate grilled lamb kebab and flat bread, repaired our punctured tyre, and got safely back on the road to Baghdad.

When we arrived in the capital I was stunned by the disproportionate damage to infrastructure. The beautiful ministry buildings, designed by Iraqi architects and built by Iraqi engineers, had been smashed to smithereens. Still worse, they shared this fate with sewage plants, water works, power stations, bridges, roads and railways. Everywhere I looked I saw total destruction of the kind witnessed in WWII; everything which Iraq had built up over the previous fifty years had been destroyed. The targets were in most cases chosen for their infrastructural rather than their military significance. The purpose was to destroy Iraq as a viable independent country.

I was therefore astonished to find the people cheerful and held together by strong community ties. Seeing how they managed under such stressful conditions was very heartening. They seemed to get pleasure by laughing it off and being supportive of one another, reminding me of what I'd been told about the spirit of the blitz in London. Everywhere we went we received a warm and uncomplaining welcome, whether it was from complete strangers or from my own family.

Like everyone else, my relations had endured awful conditions, and seeing how they coped was especially uplifting. I made my way to the house of my brother, Abdul-Karim, who told us life was difficult but bearable; he said the survival instinct just kicked in. The people were forced to revert to traditional medical remedies because the sanctions imposed by UN resolution 661 in 1990 had prohibited the import of most medicines. Cars emitted pungent fumes because spare parts were unavailable to repair them. Hospitals were completely on their knees, with doctors working extremely long hours with inadequate equipment. But people accepted the challenges confronting them. Some even converted their garages into shops to make a living selling the bare necessities of life. Others who could find no regular employment started panning for gold in the waste water from the goldsmiths' quarter.

Innovation was the name of the game. Employees of the Ministry of Oil worked extremely long hours to repair the damage from the bombing. I visited both the South and North Oil Companies and was astonished at the extent of the damage both as a result of military action, and of the looting which followed in its aftermath, when the so-called uprising against the Ba'athist regime took place.

Another positive, though unplanned, outcome of the coalition invasion was to reinforce a change in the condition of women which had already begun during the Iran-Iraq war. So many men had died in the earlier war that many women were widowed, or if they were unmarried they had difficulty finding husbands. They had to manage on their own, and this had had the effect of making them more independent and assertive. Most of the employees in the ministries were women, for example. A similar scenario has been seen among Palestinian women whose husbands are routinely imprisoned, if not killed. And there is here again a parallel with Europe. Women in Britain, France, Germany and Russia were liberated due to their employment in munitions factories and the like during WWI, and because of the necessity, in many cases, to fend for themselves after their husbands had been killed.

I was astonished when I met the chairperson of the Women's Federation, Dr Manal Younis, to discover the measures her organisation had taken to advance women's emancipation. Women were by then playing a more pivotal role in Iraq's economy than anywhere else in the Arab world. I was, however, struck by their definition of women's equality. Dr Younis told me the West had got it wrong. Women were not *equal* to men, they were *complementary* to them. She disagreed with the Western emphasis on allowing women to undertake roles which were suitable for men, such as service in the armed forces. A women's role was that of a life giver, and it was therefore wrong to put her in the position of a life taker. This made me see the West's much vaunted women's liberation in a new light.

In Iraq women didn't wear the hijab and they drove cars; some became ministers, heads of departments, lawyers and doctors. They played every kind of role suitable to women and if they had a child their employment was protected with two years paid leave of absence. But unlike in the West, women were *obliged* to take this fully-paid maternity leave, for the Women's Federation had ruled that it was a woman's role to be their baby's constant carer. She was thereby doing her primary duty not only to her child, but also to the community and the country.

The looters of that 1991 uprising are now, in the aftermath of the 2003 war, ruling Iraq. They had no intention of serving the people then or now but rather were motivated by greed. Consequently when they managed to get rid of Saddam's government they replaced it with chaos, corruption, sectarianism and more looting. If their intention was to run the country, why did they destroy factories and children's playgrounds? Why did they have to loot the stores of oil companies and steal the beautiful old English furniture from the management offices in Kirkuk?

During the US-inspired uprising the insurgents had occupied Kirkuk and stripped everything there. Heavy earthmoving equipment, forklifts, cables, cars, even bathtubs, basins and sinks, vanished in next to no time. This was not the conduct of an uprising against a regime but chaotic, free-for-all anarchic looting. The looters and their collaborators in the US and UK, Iraqi opposition activists like Ahmad Chalabi, Mowaffak Al-Rubaie, Ayatollah M S al-Hakim and Bahr al-Ullum, lied to the BBC saying the uprising was in the interest of the country. It is no surprise, therefore, that they failed to restore the country to normality when they came to power in 2003, nor that the people turned against them. Iraqis who had not settled elsewhere in the world knew well that these puppets were not there to lead them on the road to democracy. On the contrary, they would simply pour acid into the wounds of war.

It was appalling hypocrisy on the part of the US and UK to impose a no-fly zone in order to protect the Kurds after their war lords, Masoud Barzani and Jalal Talabani, had systematically looted Kirkuk, Sulaymaniyah and Erbil. Effectively this ensured that these criminals were not brought to justice; on the contrary the first went on to become the president of the Kurdish region, and the second became the sixth president of Iraq. Meanwhile in the south a similar no-fly zone was imposed ensuring that the oil facilities there remained under western control.

What I had witnessed was so terrible, so much worse than almost anyone in my adopted country could imagine, that I decided I must redouble my efforts to tell the British people what they had been a party to. I thus underwent the same kind of politicisation which Edward Said experienced following the 1967 war in Palestine. His words echo my own feelings some twenty-four years later.

> Until the June 1967 war I was completely caught up in the life of a young professor of English and comparative literature at Colombia University. I was born in Jerusalem in late 1935, and I grew up there and in Egypt and Lebanon; most of my family – dispossessed and displaced from Palestine in 1947 and 1948 – had ended up mostly in Jordan and Lebanon. Sent to America as a schoolboy in 1951, I had completed my education here in 1963, and began teaching later that year. ... All that changed in mid-1967.
>
> For the first time since I had left to come to the United States, I was emotionally reclaimed by the Arab world generally and by Palestine in particular. This was a direct result of the war – which I experienced in New York – and of the severely damaged political, cultural, and, of course, military and geographical situation that it created.[3]

With this overload of impressions I travelled back to Jordan feeling the need for a mental rest. Charmaine, who had recently become my partner, flew out to meet me, and her presence was just what I needed. I liked her spontaneity, her fiery nature and above all her amazing get up and go which first struck me when she told me she was willing to travel on her own to Saddam's Iraq in 1988. Together we visited the ancient Nabataean city of Petra as well as the Nabataean remains 70 miles further south at Wadi Rum. Both were, to our astonishment, practically deserted. Seeing these famous remains of a previous civilisation helped to put recent events in a perspective which proved therapeutic.

---

[3] Said, E., *The Politics of Dispossession: The Struggle for Palestinian Self-Determination 1969-1994*, London, Vintage, 1995, pp xiii.

Charmaine and I went on to share a wonderful eighteen years together, our most enjoyable pastime being walking, whether in Surrey, Wiltshire, Somerset, Devon, Cornwall or even in the desert around Luxor in Upper Egypt. And though we eventually drifted apart she remained a good, solid and reliable friend, campaigning tirelessly on my behalf while I was in prison.

Tam Dalyell, George Galloway, Tim Llewellyn

Back in London, I entered a completely unfamiliar world of television appearances, radio interviews, writing for the press, making speeches in the House of Commons, attending conferences and demonstrations, networking with MPs, and publishing briefings. I also started on the long and frustrating task of looking for prominent people willing to come and see Iraq for themselves. I hoped that witnessing the stark reality of Iraq's situation would make them into advocates for the ordinary people of my homeland. I approached Tam Dalyell, the MP for Linlithgow, but he was wary of going unless he was part of a delegation. He did, however, seek my opinion on a matter pertaining to Iraq. As a *New Scientist* columnist, he had been sent a report by the University of Harvard Medical School on the condition of children in Iraq,[4] and had been appalled by its conclusions.

> A country that had been famous for its medicine – and Baghdad had recently been voted the cleanest city in the Middle East – had been reduced to a chronic shortage of drugs and sanctions were hitting the vulnerable, young and old. I had struck up a friendship with Basrah-born engineer

---

[4] The Harvard Study Team, 'The Effect of the Gulf Crisis on the Children of Iraq,' New England Journal of Medicine September 26th, 1991, online at http://www.nejm.org/doi/full/10.1056/NEJM199109263251330#t=article.

and oil trader,[5] Riad el-Taher, who [...] was a natural source to ask about the report. To my question, 'Do the Harvard team exaggerate the gravity of the medical situation?', Riad's reply was, 'Come and see for yourself. I can arrange it.' Indeed he was one of the comparatively few individuals in Britain who *could* arrange it.[6]

Tam was well aware that most Iraqis living in Britain were opponents of the Ba'athist regime, and therefore had no connections to it. Having checked with some 'reliable sources' he concluded, correctly, that I didn't have close links with, as he put it, 'the Tikriti gang,' and could therefore safely rely on my contacts in the government and the oil ministry, among whom was Tariq Aziz. All I had to do, therefore, to convince him to visit Iraq was to form a delegation and to get permission from the Iraqi authorities for each of its members.

I approached Diane Abbott, but she couldn't make it because of her commitment to her daughter. Then one day at a meeting in Conway Hall I found myself on the same platform as George Galloway, the MP for Glasgow Hillhead. I put it to him that Tam was willing to visit Iraq so long as I formed a parliamentary delegation, and he jumped at the opportunity. We discussed this further over tea at the House of Commons where he told me he was known as 'Gorgeous George.' I was a bit thrown, as it didn't seem to fit with the seriousness of the matter in hand, but there was no doubting George's astonishing eloquence on the Palestinian and Iraqi issues nor his keenness to visit my country.

Tam now agreed that he and George should form the first, albeit unofficial, parliamentary delegation to Iraq since the war, and asked me to invite the ex-BBC reporter, Tim Llewellyn, to join us. I later discovered that both Tam's parents had been Arabists, his father having

---

[5] In this detail, Tam was mistaken. I was not by profession an oil trader. I only lifted oil for a short period while engaged in campaigning against the sanctions.
[6] Dalyell, T., Ibid, p. 252.

been on the staff of Sir Percy Cox who, as I have already mentioned, was the High Commissioner of Iraq responsible for the artificial borders between Iraq and Kuwait. Cox ordered Tam's father to do what his secretary, the legendary Gertrude Bell, said he should do. So Tam had his own personal interest in seeing the situation on the ground. Nevertheless, his concern about the effect of the sanctions and bombing was indisputable.

Getting permission for Tam to visit Iraq was helped by Saddam's interest in farming:

> [...] I understood that my visit had to be personally approved by the president. This was made easier by a strange coincidence which was brought to his attention. A friend and constituent of mine, Brian Cadzow of Glendevon Farm, near Winchburgh in West Lothian, a pioneer sheep farmer and breeder, had been invited to Iraq in the early [1970s][7] when Saddam was vice-president and responsible for improving Iraqi agriculture production. Mercifully, the rams he sold had done their stuff to the satisfaction of Saddam and the ewes, and my association with Cadzow seems to have been a plus so the visit, at our own expense, went ahead.[8]

Curiously, it was through Saddam's interest in farming that I was also to come to meet him a few years later.

Getting a permit for George was less easy as he had been particularly outspoken in his condemnation of human rights abuses in Iraq. The fact that I managed it convinced Tam that I had the kind of connections in Iraq needed to organise a successful fact-finding mission.

---

[7] In Tam's book '1990s' appears here, but this is clearly an error, as by then Saddam Hussein was President. He was Vice-President in the early 1970s.
[8] Ibid, p. 252-53.

I contacted another school friend in Iraq, who was a member of the semi-governmental 'Solidarity, Friendship and Peace Organisation,'[9] asking him to organise our programme in Iraq. Within a short time we received an invitation, but being unsure about protocol, I visited the Iraqi Chargé d'Affaires in London, Zuheir Ibrahim, by then the only Iraqi diplomatic representative in London as all the other staff had been withdrawn. He was very unhappy about the visit seeing it as an encroachment on his preserve. I guess he wanted to give the impression he was the only active campaigner for Iraqi interests in the UK, and while he accepted that he had no power to prevent the trip, he told me I must take a secondary role in any meeting the MPs might have with the government. It seemed prudent to take his advice.

At last we set a date for our departure and in May 1993 we gathered at Heathrow for our flight to Amman. At the duty-free shop George wanted to buy some Gucci shoes with which to impress the people he met in Iraq. This struck me as ironic in view of the state of the country to which we were about to travel: 'You don't have to worry about fancy shoes,' I said. 'The people in Iraq have been impoverished, and the sanctions have added to their misery. People don't really care about appearances because they don't have enough money to buy new clothes.' I'd never met Tim before, but his reports on television for the BBC, where he had until recently been their Middle East correspondent, together with his published articles, had impressed me, and I was keen to have a journalist with us. As was his wont Tam arrived exactly at the appointed time.

Zuheir Ibrahim was at the airport to see us off and had arranged with the Royal Jordanian Airlines station manager to upgrade the politicians to first class. Tim and I remained in tourist class. This reinforced the distinction between my position and that of the MPs to which he had insisted I adhere. But it had the advantage of giving me the chance to get to know Tim one-to-one.

---

[9] Also referred to as the Iraqi Friendship Society.

We arrived in Amman and were met by an Iraqi embassy delegation who took us to the VIP lounge where we found two cars waiting for us, a Mercedes and a Chevrolet. George said he'd like to take the Mercedes but when I explained this to the delegation they were somewhat taken aback. What was I thinking? *Of course* the Mercedes was for the politicians. When Tam and I got to the cars we found George sitting in the front seat of the Mercedes, while Tim was sitting in the back. This was quite wrong in protocol terms, for distinguished guests always travel in the back and George, as an MP, certainly qualified for that privilege. But who were we to argue? Tam and I took our places in the back of the Chevrolet and so the two cars set out on the fifteen-hour journey to Baghdad.

After we'd passed the lunar landscape just beyond Zarqa,[10] with its black rocks scattered across the desert, there were many tedious hours of driving across the featureless desert, most of it in the dark, until at last we arrived at the Jordanian border post where the formalities were simple. Then came a short drive to the Iraqi post at Trebil, where we were met by the British educated Dr Mohammad al-Adhami of the solidarity organisation. After a short break and a snack bought for us by our hosts in the VIP lounge, we made our way along the impressive but empty eight-lane highway to Baghdad. We had to pass through numerous checkpoints, and we negotiated a number of bomb craters at points along the route.

In Baghdad we stayed at the magnificent Rasheed Hotel, originally built for a conference of Arab heads of state. and accordingly boasting luxurious rooms. But sanctions had had a disastrous effect on the hotel's business, and it was now solely maintained for official visitors. The menu was basic, there was no entertainment and the sports facilities were no longer in use.

---

[10] A town which owed its existence to Chechen refugees in the early twentieth century. It rose in importance when it became a major station on the Hijaz Railway. This German-built line ceased to operate after the exploits of Lawrence of Arabia during the Arab Revolt.

This visit by British parliamentarians to Iraq was historic in being the first to break the prohibition, under the sanctions regime, on visits by politicians. They could only ignore the ruling because of their parliamentary immunity. Neither Tam nor George had the blessing of their own Labour party whip in coming to Iraq, and the right-wing press reflected this negative attitude. In an article in the *Daily Express* on 14th May 1993 entitled 'MPs taking in the sights of Saddam' Peter Hitchens wrote: '… it is one thing to criticise your own government, and quite another to become the "useful idiots" of another. How do they imagine their presence will be portrayed on Iraqi TV and in Saddam's Press?' Nevertheless there was considerable support in the House of Commons for our trip.

Our time in Baghdad was well organised. At breakfast the first morning we met with an 18-member delegation from the solidarity organisation, and discussed, over an omelette (there was nothing else), who we wanted to see. George prefaced his remarks by saying: 'I seem to be the only one here in this room who has not been to a British university!' As Tam commented, this was true, for 'there were graduates from the universities of Aberdeen, Birmingham, Cambridge, Dundee, Edinburgh, Imperial, Leeds, Loughborough, the LSE and Strathclyde. Some of them regarded London as their second home.'[11]

And so we set out. Tam and I travelled in one car, Tim and George in another and the officials in a third. Our first visits were to the Saddam Children's Hospital and the Amiriyah air-raid shelter. The former had been a model institution before the war and was top of the list for visits by foreign dignitaries. What we experienced was extremely distressing. Distraught mothers, assuming that Tam and I were doctors, begged us to help their dying children. Some of them had terrible malformations resulting from the use of radioactive armour-piercing shells in 1991. There was no medication for the babies and it was only a matter of time

---

[11] Ibid, p. 253.

before they died. These desperate pleas for help had a profound effect on us all.

From then on Tam became fully committed to the Iraqi cause and sent a very powerful message to the world. He shed tears on television when he said that if the British and American leaders could see what he had seen they would have a different view about the war and the impact of sanctions. In a letter to the *London Review of Books* he pointed out that far from undermining Saddam, sanctions were 'fostering a real loathing of the British and the Americans.' They were particularly upset about the British, whom they felt should as a result of their history understand the Arab World better.

He graphically described our visit to the Saddam Children's hospital, and his horror at the conditions there. He quoted the figures given by a Canadian epidemiologist, Dr Eric Hoskins, for the manifold increase in the incidence of various diseases among its patients since the introduction of the sanctions regime three years earlier. Malaria, which had been eradicated had returned, dysentery was rampant and a drug-resistant form of cholera had appeared. He held the Americans and the British responsible for this disaster through their manipulation of the UN, and questioned whether they were flouting the 1989 UN Convention on the Rights of the Child. 100,000 children above the average had died since the First Gulf War.[12]

The infamous Amiriyah air-raid shelter, built during the Iran-Iraq war, was in its different way just as shocking. For some reason the coalition forces believed the Iraqi leadership was hiding there and so the Americans dropped two bunker busting uranium tipped bombs on it. This resulted in the horrifying death of over 400 civilians, but no members of the Iraqi leadership. The shelter, which had been preserved as a museum to show the atrocities the Americans and British had inflicted on the Iraqi people, was cared for by a woman who lost her

---

[12] Dalyell, T., letter to *London Review of Books*, Vol 15 No 12, 24th June 1993. See https://www.lrb.co.uk/v15/n12/letters.

whole family in the bombing and was determined to show the world how much she had endured. In that horrible shrine she told visitors about the holocaust in which whole families, the people from that neighbourhood, had perished, and pointed out a shadow where a mother and child had melted into the wall.

We visited various government ministers on our second day in Baghdad. Tam commented that these people more resembled civil servants than politicians.

> They gave me the impression of being extremely able people. Nor were they chosen on ethnic grounds, or exclusively from the Sunni power brokers. One absolutely key position, that of minister of health, was headed by a Kurd, Dr [Omeid] Mubarak from Sulaymaniyah. The ethos was secular.[13]

Both Omeid Mubarak and the Minister of Trade, Dr Mohammed Saleh Mahdi, were UK graduates and spoke very good English. I should mention, however, that the Governor of Baghdad, Jasim Nesaif, who was Chairman of the solidarity organisation, didn't speak English and his arrogant attitude towards us was not impressive.

The majority of the doctors were also UK graduates, they all spoke English and they eloquently described the lack of medicines which devastated people's lives. The hospitals were very well built but even the most basic medical equipment was absent. Because sewage treatment plants had been bombed raw effluent was pumped directly into the river and this caused a rash of diseases which were now virtually uncontrollable.

There was no end to this tale of woe, and as on my first trip after the war, we felt the need to escape from it all. So we visited the holy shrines in Kadhimiyah, a district of Baghdad, and Tam, Tim and I went to Karbala. But even there we saw the evidence of the carnage which took

---

[13] Dalyell, T., *The Importance* ..., p. 254.

place when the Iraqi troops retreated from Kuwait. There was blood on the walls of the shrines which had been used for torturing Ba'athist officials. We were confronted with a completely different picture from that presented in the media, which based its accounts on what it garnered from the so-called Iraqi opposition.

Our journey to Basrah in a hired car with a government approved driver reminded Tam of his parents' involvement with Iraq.

> I thought of my dad as we drove through Kut, where he and his generation had been hugely exercised by the massacre of British forces in 1917[14] and, when we stopped in Amara, we were reminded of what the RAF had done, dropping bombs and killing civilians not in the recent First Gulf War but during World War I.[15]

---

[14] Tam is referring to the siege of Kut by the Turks, under the German Field Marshal Baron Colmar von der Goltz, which actually took place in 1915-16. Around 23,000 British and Indian troops, under the command of General Charles Vere Ferrers Townshend, died defending the town, which was eventually surrendered at the end of April 2016, ten days after von der Goltz died of cholera. The losses there were among the worst suffered by the British army in WWI outside the European theatre of war.

[15] Ibid, p 256. It is unclear what incident Tam is referring to in Amara. It was not until 1st April 1918 that the RAF was formed from the Royal Flying Corps and the Royal Naval Air Service, and no engagement could be found involving Amara between then and the end of WWI. The Royal Flying Corps played a significant role in the Mesopotamian campaign, but again no engagement could be found in which Amara was bombed. It seems more likely that such an incident would have occurred during the Great Iraqi Revolution of 1920. In 1919 Winston Churchill was appointed Secretary of State for War and Secretary of State for Air, positions he held in the Lib-Con coalition of Lloyd George until 1921. Churchill was of the opinion that the most efficient way of controlling the natives was to scare them into submission by bombing from the air. He was happy to authorise the use of chemical weapons both by the army and the RAF, and mocked those who were squeamish about this strategy. During the uprising the RAF flew missions totalling 4,008 hours, dropped 97 tons of bombs and fired 183,861 rounds. See Glancey, Jonathan, 'Our last occupation – Gas, chemicals, bombs: Britain has used them all before in Iraq' in *The Guardian*, 19th April 2003, online at https://www.theguardian.com/world/2003/apr/19/iraq.arts. Niall Ferguson wrote in his book *The War of the World: History's Age of Hatred* (London/New York:

Tam recalled that his parents had described Basrah as a truly lovely city, and on our arrival there was struck with how inappropriate that description now was. We met the Governor, General Latif Mahal Hamoud, who spoke to us courteously about the effects of the sanctions.[16] The atrocities and carnage were equally evident in the barely functioning hospitals which we visited. The schools were also ill-equipped, unemployment was rising and the value of the dinar spiralled downwards day by day until it became worthless. It was a relief for all of us to visit my extended family who, as Tam remarked, 'could trace their ancestry back with certainty for 800 years – twice the time since my ancestor Thomas Dalyell had first settled at The Binns.'[17]

We drove out to the Iraq-Kuwait border and visited the headquarters in no-mans-land of the United Nations peacekeepers, a beautifully designed building which had previously housed an Iraqi military hospital. From their side of the border the Kuwaitis had scrutinised the United Nations observers for any signs of what might be happening in Iraq before the invasion itself took place. We also visited Umm Qasr, as Tam recalls:

> The devastating effect of sanctions was brought home to us by a visit to the hospital at Umm Qasr on the Iraq-Kuwait border. The chief superintendent, trained at Imperial College Medical School, in London, opened his nearly bare cupboards, which, before sanctions, had been well stocked

---

Allen Lane, 2006): 'To end the Iraqi Insurgency of 1920 . . . the British relied on a combination of aerial bombardment and punitive village burning expeditions. Indeed, they even contemplated using mustard gas too, though supplies proved unavailable.'

[16] Ibid, 256. Tam comments that this governor 'was the nearest I ever got to Saddam Hussein's innermost group. Governors of major cities and provinces were men (they were all men) of huge power, personally handpicked by the president himself. They were always from a part of Iraq that was far from the area over which they governed.'

[17] Ibid, p. 256.

> with medicines produced by the great pharmaceutical companies of the world. The bitterness being bred amongst a population that once looked to Britain made me very sad and angry at the folly of sanctions. ….[18]
>
> [Here] I saw the first cases of rickets, a disease I have not observed since Glasgow in the Fifties. ...[19]

Of particular interest to Tim Llewellyn at Umm Qasr was the issue of the border, about which he wrote an article on our return to the UK. During the Iran-Iraq war a blind eye had been turned by the Kuwaitis to the expansion of the town half a mile across its border. Kuwait, after all, was in particular danger from Iran, and Iraq was its ally defending the Arab world. But now a UN body had reinstated the old border, so that it ran through the middle of Umm Qasr. Tam had remarked that this action was 'a recipe for future disaster.'[20]

On our return journey from Basrah, we made an unscheduled stop for a few hours to visit some Marsh Arabs. Tam chose at random a village house to visit and was struck by the 'warm goodwill' shown to the Ba'athist councillor accompanying them.

> [T]hey self-evidently regarded [him] as a friend in the same way that a popular local councillor would be received in West Lothian. Much has been made of the alleged persecution of the Marsh Arabs by the Saddam regime and, indeed, of the draining of the marshes. Doubtless the programme was an ecological disaster and robbed some people of a way of life that their ancestors had 'enjoyed', if that is quite the right word for such a hard existence, for millennia. But the uncomfortable fact for me was that the

---

[18] Ibid, p. 256.
[19] Dalyell, T., same letter to *LRB* at https://www.lrb.co.uk/v15/n12/letters.
[20] Llewellyn, T., 'In the Footsteps of Sir Percy,' *The Spectator*, 4th June 1993, p. 14. The article is reproduced in full at Appendix Two.

> detailed plans for drainage had been drawn up by a distinguished firm of consulting engineers in Glasgow. I thought that the plight of some Marsh Arabs had more to do with a mistaken idea about economic progress than political vengeance and persecution.[21]

Tam pointed out that these people were not expecting us, yet in their reed constructed *mudiff* (guest house) we noticed a picture of Saddam in a prominent place. We took a short ride in one of their reed and tar boats and I relived the days of my youth when I would visit the marshes to shoot duck with my brothers.

Back in Baghdad, we visited the Deputy Prime Minister, Tariq Aziz, who was fluent in English. Here is how Tam recalls that encounter:

> The Iraqi Foreign Minister, Tariq Aziz [was] the international spokesman for the regime but, interestingly [he was] a Chaldean Christian. ... The first thing Aziz said to us was, 'You were dining us and we were dining you – and then all this happened.' The 'all this' he referred to was, of course, the First Gulf War. He was deeply hurt, personally. Like many Iraqis, by no means all sympathetic to the regime, Aziz passionately believed that the West ought to be grateful to Iraq for having been its shield against militant Islam in the form of Ayatollah Khomeini.[22]

Our ten-day visit had been a great success. Although Zuheir Ibrahim had advised me to stay in the background, Iraqi officials correctly regarded me as the UK organiser, and therefore an important member

---

[21] *The Importance* ..., p 255-56. It is worth listening to a somewhat different view of the draining of the marshes, put forward by Falih al-Khayat in 2009 and to be found at https://www.youtube.com/watch?v=J7xg2bKsSIY. The full version of this interview, which is advertised at the end of this thee-and-a-half minute clip, appears no longer to be available.

[22] Ibid, pp. 256-57.

of the team. When we visited the Iraqi National Assembly the Speaker addressed me as a friend of the Iraqi people. He selected his words carefully knowing that to claim me as an ally of the government would undermine my credibility in the UK. He accepted me as an expatriate who had studied and remained in the UK and had now come back to help his people. It's a pity most of Her Britannic Majesty's ministers and government officials, together with sections of the press, didn't see it that way.

The people we met never emphasised that they were Ba'athists or government ministers. They firmly believed that the government was committed to serving the people. We were all impressed by Dr Omeid Mubarak, the Minister of Health, who held a weekly session at which he answered questions from the public. Tam and George remarked that none of our ministers had this kind of direct interaction with the people. At every meeting we held we encountered Iraqis from all walks of life, many of them UK graduates. This highlighted the strong link between Britain and Iraq. But the high regard and affection the Iraqi people had for Britain has unfortunately been damaged by the British government's slavish toeing of the American line in pursuing the blinkered goal of controlling the country's oil resources.

During our stay in Iraq George asked me to arrange a meeting with Saddam. I told him I was not a Ba'athist, and therefore had no influence, but rather reluctantly I said I would relay his request. Tam shared my scepticism about meeting the President at this point, believing that it might well have a negative impact on our aim of highlighting the effect of the sanctions. Tariq Aziz had emphasised on a number of occasions that the sanctions had had little effect on the leadership, but that it was the ordinary people who were suffering. It was therefore this which we should be investigating. Tam did concede, however, that if it would help gain the release of three British citizens, Paul Ride, Michael Wainwright and Simon Dunn, who had inadvertently strayed into Iraqi territory from Kuwait (Ride and Dunn) and Turkey (Wainwright), a meeting with Saddam would be justified. We had visited all three in Abu Ghraib prison, and so there was no doubt that the leadership was aware of our concern on this matter.

Although we hadn't met the President, our visit set the ball rolling for the prisoners' release. On our return to Britain, Tam requested former Prime Minster, Edward Heath, to visit Iraq, as he had done in 1990, in order to talk to the President about the matter, and the outcome was as desired. Heath travelled to Iraq to meet Saddam in December 1993, and explained the success of his mission in the following words:

> He [Saddam] realises I told him the truth about the war three years ago, that the Americans and British would go to war against him if he didn't get out of Kuwait. He's always trusted me since. He made it known that if I wanted to go to [him] and discuss the prisoners, I was welcome at any time. I must make it absolutely clear that I made no 'appeal' to Saddam. We had two and a half hours together and he said 'I know what you want, and I will make arrangements accordingly'.[23]

There was a curious footnote to Heath's visit. He had bought an oriental rug while in Iraq which, on his way back to Amman by road, he had forgotten at the border. I was told about this, and on a subsequent visit was able to pick it up. I brought it back to the UK, and travelled down to Salisbury where I delivered it to the ex-PM at his home in the Cloisters. Heath knew about my campaigning and congratulated me on the team I had put together. Incidentally, a few weeks after Heath's visit to Baghdad, George appeared on television, together with a Greek

---

[23] Savill, A., 'Saddam trusts me and knows I tell the truth, says Heath,' *The Independent*, 12th December 1993. The whole article can be viewed at http://www.independent.co.uk/news/uk/saddam-trusts-me-and-knows-i-tell-the-truth-says-heath-1466989.html.

delegation, meeting with Saddam. Neither Tam nor I had any idea that he was intending to travel to Iraq again.[24]

But to return to the end of our own visit to Iraq, Tam, George and Tim departed by road for Amman, while I stayed with my family for a few days before returning to the UK by the same route. Meanwhile George had telephoned a report on our visit to the *Daily Mail* which was duly published,[25] and Tam had taken up the effect of sanctions with the Foreign Secretary.

> When I saw Douglas Hurd[26] on my return, he expressed disbelief, and said that medicines were exempt from sanctions. The fact is that neither Saddam Hussein's government, nor, in my view, any conceivable government of Iraq could possibly accept the UN conditions. The first and overwhelming call on funds from unfrozen assets goes to reparations for Kuwait. Little is left, it seems to Iraqis, for them, and what is left is partly swallowed up in paying the UN's administrative costs. As George Galloway put it, 'We expect them to pay their own gaoler.'[27]

The memory of my first official visit to Iraq stayed with me for a long time. I had witnessed the suffering and deprivation of so many people, whether they were begging in the street, using their cars as taxis because they had lost their jobs as lecturers and scientists, or simply grieving the loss of loved ones. But in spite of everything the people

---

[24] During his visit George made a speech on 19th January addressed to Saddam in which he said, among other things: 'Sir, I salute your courage, your strength, your indefatigability, and I want you to know that we are with you, *hatta al-nasr, hatta al-nasr, hatta al-Quds* [until victory, until victory, until Jerusalem].' See *The Times*, 20th January, 1994, 'I greet you in the name of thousands of Britons,' citing the BBC monitoring service. More of his speech can be read on Wikiquotes at https://en.wikiquote.org/wiki/George_Galloway.
[25] This article could not be found online.
[26] At that time Foreign Secretary in the Conservative government of John Major.
[27] Dalyell, T., same letter to *LRB* at https://www.lrb.co.uk/v15/n12/letters.

remained resolute and relatively cheerful and were able to carry on living in these extraordinarily difficult circumstances.

On my return to the UK, Tam and other activists asked me to set up an organisation opposing British policies in Iraq, and in particular the sanctions regime, and this is how Friendship Across Frontiers came into being. But of that more in Chapter Seven. Suffice it to say here that the further trips I made to Iraq mentioned below all came under the aegis of FAF.

1. The oil industry

2. My house and garden at Hinchley Wood

3. Free-range poultry farming in the New Forest

4. Petra 1991

5. I entered an unfamiliar world

6. The hole in the roof of the Amiriyah shelter made by a bunker-buster bomb

7. George, Tam and an unidentified official in 1993: the President looks out from a portrait on the table

8. Left to right: Myself, Omeid Mubarak (Minister of Health), Tam and George.

9. A recent picture of Tim Llewellyn

10. Tariq Aziz, patriotic and loyal

11. The Trebil border post in 2009; much as it was pre-2003, except for the US soldier

CHAPTER SIX

MORE ON THE DESERT ROAD

Sue Lloyd Roberts

Iraq held a yearly oil conference in Baghdad to entice international oil companies to explore and develop its oilfields on a profit-sharing basis. The potential of the existing fields, if properly developed, was tremendous, while the Western desert had unexplored blocks which, it was predicted, contained huge reserves. Foreign cash was required not only for development but equally to stop the alarming and destabilising decline in the value of the Iraqi dinar. One US dollar stood at 2,000 dinars, sometimes 3,000. When people went shopping they had to carry large bundles of virtually worthless paper, recalling earlier times in Germany. The West, America in particular, played on this hyperinflation to destroy the Iraqi economy. The well-to-do migrated *en masse* to Syria, Lebanon and Jordan taking as much of their capital with them as they could. The less well-off, if they could manage it, went to Libya.

In March 1995 I arranged for a BBC undercover journalist, Sue Lloyd-Roberts, to visit one of the oil conferences which I attended. She had approached me because she wanted to visit Iraq and though I didn't know much about her, I gambled that she would report on the work of the Iraqi Women's Federation and the impact of sanctions on Iraqi women. The oil conference was a convenient expedient for her trip. During her stay, however, she seemed more concerned about inequality in Iraqi society, while disregarding its root cause. The reality was that sanctions and war had created these disparities between those who amassed large fortunes through smuggling, and the majority of the population. Naturally, a section of the economy was diverted into catering for the very rich.

On her return, and at the time unknown to me, Sue interviewed the Iraqi-American, Ahmad Chalabi, whom I mentioned earlier. He was one of the renegade Iraqis who made a name for himself as part of the opposition and who was renowned for his close association with America, Iran and the illegitimate Zionist entity. He made no secret of his close association with the CIA and openly promoted its policies. He was being used by the Americans as an Iraqi opponent of the regime in Iraq, and therefore a potential leader-in-waiting. But the Americans never stopped to ask if he had any popular support within Iraq. Or rather, more cynically, many of them knew that he had none, but it suited their objectives and agenda to promote him.

That the Americans thought in this way was confirmed to me at an early stage when in 1992 I wrote a rather naïve letter to George Bush Sr to explain the reality of the situation in Iraq. I was thereupon invited to the American embassy in London where I met Frank J. Ricciardone Jr, an Arabist fluent in our language, who was clearly a 'kingmaker' promoting the Iraqi opposition. We had several meetings at which he tried to cajole me into the fold of the Iraqi opposition, but I wasn't interested in their politics and saw no advantage in playing such a political role. My primary aim was humanitarian to which my business interests were subservient. I was in no way affiliated to Saddam's regime, but nor did I wish to join its opponents. FAF had to remain non-political.

It was clear from these contacts that Ricciardone himself, as well as the US administration, had no faith in the expatriate Iraqi opposition, but used it to further their own regional interests. They gave no support to resident opposition activists who sincerely wished to serve their country. What mattered was to find Iraqis abroad who were corruptible; these were the right people for the job of promoting and extending American interests in Iraq as became obvious in 2003.

I organised a second visit for Sue Lloyd-Roberts so that she could report on the Presidential election in 2002, and during her stay she managed to get an interview with Tariq Aziz. I liked Sue, and was very sad when I heard that she had died at the age of only 64.[1] But I have to say that I found she was not the kind of journalist who was interested in unearthing the truth in the way, for example, Robert Fisk did, and I was forced to conclude that she, like many other journalists, were mainly interested in making a name for themselves.

Albert Reynolds, Mick Lanigan et al

Through a connection I had with an oil company called Bula I came to meet Albert Reynolds, the ex-Taoiseach who through the Downing Street Declaration of 1994, became a major player in the Irish peace process. He showed great interest in the situation in Iraq, and I therefore invited him to form a fact-finding delegation, and suggested we invited Tam as well. Others who joined us were Fianna Fáil senator Mick Lanigan, and Bill Griffin of Bula.[2] Tam comments:

> When, with the advent of the Labour government in 1997, it became clear that my incessant nagging of parliamentary colleagues was achieving little, Riad suggested that I join a group of Irish politicians, for whom he had arranged a visit to Iraq. They were to be led by Albert Reynolds, the former Taoiseach and famous as the father of the peace process. Once again, no planes being allowed into Baghdad airport, we made that horrendous journey from Amman across the desert. Reynolds and I shared one huge quality that is useful for any politician – the ability to go to sleep at will in the

---

[1] Sue Lloyd-Roberts died of leukaemia on 13 October 2015.
[2] A drinking friend of Bill's managed to get himself invited as well on the basis of a phoney story about being Albert Reynold's secretary.

most uncomfortable of places. For 12 out of the 15 hours it took, the former Irish prime minister was curled up in the back of a truck. Facing difficulties with sleepy and surly immigration officials at the Jordan/Iraq frontier in the early hours of the morning, I was exposed to the persuasive charm of the Irish. Indeed, part of the reason I was so pleased to go with Irish colleagues was that I reckoned they would cut more ice with the American leadership than any of my British Labour friends, who might have been willing to come to Baghdad. Reynolds, in particular, had excellent contacts on Capitol Hill.[3]

Our main purpose was to investigate humanitarian issues. My companions were appalled by what they saw. They met the Coordinator of the UN oil-for-food programme and most of the ministers. Tam takes up the story again:

We deemed it sensible not to ask to see Saddam himself. Had he taken the initiative, we could not have refused to see the president of a country to which we had gone. Years later, when George Galloway went to Iraq and was given an interview with Saddam, he received a pasting from the British press that was counter-productive to our cause.[4] And then we were due to see Tariq Aziz for half an hour. It was cancelled early in the morning, on the grounds that Mr Aziz wanted to talk to us properly and, with that in mind, we were to go to his house for an evening meal.[5]

---

[3] Dalyell, op cit, p. 257-58.
[4] Tam is referring to George's second meeting with Saddam in early August 2002. See Galloway, G., 'Exclusive Interview with Saddam Hussein: Why have you turned against us?', *Mail on Sunday* 11th August 2002, online at http://www.dailymail.co.uk/news/article-132779/Exclusive-interview-Saddam-Hussein-Why-turned-us.html.
[5] Ibid, p 258.

Inviting people to his home was not something Tariq Aziz did lightly. But he was keen to renew his acquaintance with Tam and to meet Albert Reynolds for this gave him the opportunity to explain to them at length what Iraq's intentions were, and what role America and Britain could play in alleviating the suffering of the Iraqi people.

> Instead of a half-hour meeting in an office, we spent five and a half hours in his home. In view of all that has been written, doubtless accurately, about Saddam's palaces and sundry extravagances, I should record that Tariq's home was a pleasant but modest stand-alone house, in a well-ordered residential area of modern Baghdad. Our meal was cooked by Mrs Aziz, who seemed to be helped by just one woman working in the kitchen, and was a delightful and simple Iraqi meal of Tigris fish that we all enjoyed. Saddam's sons may have earned a dreadful reputation for excess but there was little to suggest that his ministers led a 'high life'. Indeed there were a number of indications that the president's son, Uday, was the source of considerable complaints by officials.[6]

After the meal we smoked Havana cigars, courtesy of the Cuban government, drank Blue Label Johnny Walker whisky, and enjoyed an informal political discussion. There was no security on the door, and the relaxed atmosphere was enhanced by our agreement that no notes were to be taken.

> Most of our evening was naturally devoted to discussion of the current relations between Iraq and the West and, in particular, to the comings and goings at the United Nations in New York, a city Tariq Aziz knew well. I was moved and

---

[6] Ibid, p 258.

I acquit myself of naivety, by Tariq's pleas to Reynolds to use his friendships with Irish-American politicians to gain their understanding of Iraq's position in the US Congress. Tariq Aziz obviously did feel fervently about a renewed threat from Iran, answering my question about the gassing of the Kurds at Halabja by saying, 'Dreadful things were done by both sides in the eight-year Iran/Iraq war. But the fact, substantiated by a report in the *Wall Street Journal*, was that the toxic [substances][7] which caused the deaths were only possessed by Iran; Iraq had none of that particular awful weaponry. What could very well have happened was that Iraqi gunfire led to the explosion of chemical weapons in the possession of Iran.' The Irish and, I later concluded, our hosts genuinely believed this explanation.

Telling Tariq Aziz about my father working in Mesopotamia for Sir Percy Cox and Gertrude Bell[8] [...] uncorked a fascinating reminiscence of his own childhood, teenage years and early adulthood. His parents had opposed the Ottoman Turks and he had opposed the British and the French. He is, above all else, an Arab Nationalist, with a vast knowledge of modern Middle Eastern and, indeed European history – a decent man who wanted peace.[9]

As we took our leave that evening, Tariq Aziz remarked: 'You may think that Saddam and I are extremists; we are as nothing to what will come if these sanctions and this bombing do not stop. I hope you

---

[7] The original has the word 'subjects' in this position, but clearly 'substances' is what was meant.
[8] Dalyell mentions here that 'this is the subject of an extremely interesting book by the late H.V.F. Winstone.' The book is *Gertrude Bell* published originally by Quartet Books in 1980 and reissued by Barzan in a new edition as *Gertrude Bell: A Biography* in 2004.
[9] Ibid, pp. 259.

realise that by your actions of sanctions and bombing you are creating a whole generation of young Arabs who will grow up hating you.'[10] How right he has proved to be. Muammar Gaddafi expressed it perhaps more parochially: 'If Saddam goes, all of us will be in danger.'

The way the deputy Prime Minister invited us to dinner led me to suspect that the intention had been to use the opportunity afforded by this gathering to introduce Tam, Albert and myself to the President himself. In conversations with officials reference had from time to time been made to a 'minister without name' whom I was to meet, and I believe this referred to Saddam, or at least one of his close advisors. This impression was strengthened by another consideration, and here I must slightly correct Tam's account. Reynolds, Tam and I, together a couple of other Irish politicians, *did* actually go to Tariq Aziz's office for a short meeting that morning. As we left the Deputy Prime Minister signalled to me to remain behind. He then told me he'd like to invite just us to dinner that evening. I failed to realise the significance of that word 'just' and now realise he meant only Albert Reynolds, Tam and myself. I mistakenly understood that he was inviting the whole delegation, and when I re-joined them at the lift, I informed everyone that they were invited. In the event, only the three of us attended, but the possibility that the others might do so was probably sufficient to deter the President. Nevertheless, it was a fruitful evening.

Iraq had no intention of undermining reasonable US/UK interests. Tariq Aziz was trying to promote dialogue and the reestablishment of the strong relationship which Iraq had had with America, especially during the time of the Iran-Iraq war. Albert Reynolds took it upon himself to help Iraq in its dire situation. He was profoundly affected by the suffering he witnessed, especially the devastating conditions in the

---

[10] Dalyell, T., obituary of Tariq Aziz, *The Independent*, 6th June 2015. The full obituary is reproduced as Appendix Four.

hospitals, and reported this to his government and to Irish Americans. From early 1999 he spoke as Chair of Bula.[11]

Canon Andrew White

In 1998 Hans-Christoph von Sponeck[12] was appointed UN Humanitarian Coordinator for Iraq following the resignation of his predecessor, Denis Halliday. But he himself resigned in 2000, and for the same reason, that is to say his opposition to the UN sanctions on Iraq. Here is what he wrote about the worldwide ecclesiastical view of this policy.

> The World Council of Churches repeatedly called on the United Nations 'to lift immediately all sanctions that have direct and indiscriminate effects on the civilian population of Iraq'. The General Secretary of the WCC, Dr Konrad Raiser, referring to statements made by the [World Food Programme] representative in Iraq, Jutta Burckhardt, and myself on conditions in Iraq in a letter to the Secretary General Kofi Annan, wrote in early 2000: '[Iraq] sanctions are tantamount to violations by the United Nations itself of the fundamental rights inscribed in international law'. Pope John Paul II, throughout the years of sanctions, spoke in strong language about the Iraqi situation: 'I must call upon the consciences of those who, in Iraq and elsewhere, put political, economic or strategic considerations before the

---

[11] Oliver, E., 'Reynolds to chair Bula Resources,' *Irish Times*, 3rd March 1999, online at https://www.irishtimes.com/business/reynolds-to-chair-bula-resources-1.158855.

[12] Von Sponek's father, Hans Graf von Sponeck was a Lieutenant General in the German army during the Third Reich. He was imprisoned for disobeying an order not to retreat and in 1944 he was executed as an example following the failed attempt on Hitler's life.

fundamental good of the people, and ask them to show compassion. The weak and the innocent can not [sic] pay for mistakes for which they are not responsible.[13]

In Britain the Archbishop of Canterbury, Dr George Carey, who had all along opposed the sanctions, remarked: 'there is no doubt that [the sanctions] bite. Unfortunately, they have bitten the wrong people ... ordinary Iraqis.'[14] Cardinal Hume, the Roman Catholic Archbishop of Westminster, was also a strong opponent, and most other religious leaders took the same line when they learned of the damage being inflicted on the Iraqi population. They were naturally especially sensitive about the plight of the Christian community.

These considerations prompted me in the autumn of 1998 to offer to accompany Canon Andrew White, Director of International Ministry at Coventry Cathedral, on his first visit to Iraq. I made it clear to him from the start that I believed a church delegation would be the best way to raise awareness of the suffering of the Iraqi people, and so this initial visit by Andrew alone would be, as I saw it, an opportunity for him to familiarise himself with the situation prior to approaching clerical colleagues with a proposal to join a delegation.

It wasn't until March the following year that we undertook the trip on which we met, among others, the Deputy Prime Minister, Tariq Aziz, and the Minister of Health, Dr Omeid Mubarak. Andrew was keen to promote his pet scheme, which was a flying hospital, but this never materialised and I soon discovered that unlike other churchmen, Canon White was unreliable and elusive. I have since learnt that White is a staunch admirer of the Zionist entity,[15] and have come to believe

---

[13] Von Sponek, H.C., *A Different Kind of War: The UN Sanctions Regime in Iraq*, Oxford & New York, Berghahn Books, 2006, pp 128-29.
[14] Von Sponek, Ibid.
[15] Wakefield, Mary, 'The Vicar of Baghdad: 'I've looked through the Quran trying to find forgiveness ... there isn't any,' The Spectator, November 2015.

that he was working to a different agenda from his Church of England colleagues.

Andrew came out in favour of the 2003 invasion of Iraq and his position is made abundantly clear in a booklet he published in conjunction with Hope Jones in 2008. By then he was the so-called Vicar of Baghdad, as well as CEO and President of the Foundation for Relief and Reconciliation in the Middle East. According to White, 'the fact is that the biggest group of peacemakers today is the military.' He admits that a 'large amount of our support does come from the Pentagon and so we sustain particularly close ties with the US military both on the ground in Iraq and at the Department of Defence in Washington DC'. And he reveals: 'some of the politicians who we are very close to are real friends like the Iraqi National Security Advisor Dr Mowaffak Al-Rubaie.'[16]

On the subject of Islam, which you would have expected to be a specialist area for a clergyman working in a Muslim country, he has shown woeful lack of understanding. In an interview published in the Spectator he expressed the opinion that the root of the problem with ISIS was the Quran itself: 'The trouble is a lack of forgiveness in Islam. I have looked through the Quran trying to find forgiveness ... there isn't any.'[17] How about one of the most uttered phrases in the Muslim world, Mr White: 'Bism Illah al-Rahman al-Rahim,' that is 'In the name of God, the merciful and compassionate'? And then there are all the other names of God indicating forgiveness, Al-Ghafoor (The Forgiving – found more than seventy times in the Quran), Al-`Afuw (The Pardoner), Al-Tawwab (The Acceptor of Repentance) and Al-Haleem (The Clement).[18] Comparing Christian and Muslim attitudes to forgiveness might be an interesting exercise, but denying its existence in Islam is a travesty.

---

[16] Jones, Hope, and White, Andrew, *By the Rivers of Babylon*, 2008, pp. 38-40.
[17] Wakefield, Ibid.
[18] See a discussion of this question at
https://www.islamicity.org/11211/forgiveness-and-repentance-in-islam/.

One wonders also what kind of Christian charity underlies his statement that 'In the wake of applying democracy, Iran has elected an evil President, a terrorist government now rules Gaza and Iraq has suffered enormously because of its failure to form a government promptly.'[19] Does White believe that such intemperate language is appropriate for his mission of peace and reconciliation?

Well, I wouldn't want to be held up as an example of someone of Muslim heritage who can't be charitable. And so let me concede that Andrew has said some sensible things, for which I give him credit. He wrote, for instance: 'It is ... important to revise the idea that imposing western-style democracy in the Middle East will bring peace. When democratic systems have been introduced to the region in the recent past, the outcomes have often been destructive.'[20] Moreover, he had the contacts to get together the church delegation, for which I'm very grateful. And I'm sorry that Andrew has had to battle with multiple sclerosis and am pleased to hear that he has been successfully treated with stem cell therapy. It's just a pity we can't see the world, and in particular my homeland, through the same eyes.

A delegation of church leaders

My uneasiness about Andrew at that time has now been corroborated, but I was then still prepared to give him the benefit of the doubt. Following our return from Baghdad he got to work remarkably quickly to form a delegation consisting of the Bishop of Coventry, Colin Bennetts (the leader of the group), the Bishop of Kingston, Peter Price, Canon Patrick Sookhdeo of the Barnabas Fund, Dr Charles Reed from the Board of Social Responsibility, and himself. The group was joined in the Middle East by the Bishop of Cyprus and the Gulf, Clive Handford and Canon Ian Young from Qatar. These clerics were

---

[19] Jones and White, Ibid, p 35.
[20] Ibid, p 35.

all clearly interested in the Iraqi cause but I didn't know anything else about them. We gathered in Amman, and travelled on together by road to Baghdad for three days of intensive meetings on 6th, 7th and 8th May.

On arrival at the Al Rasheed Hotel I was surprised and disappointed that the bishops reacted negatively when they were introduced to Iraqi government officials. They believed these to be tainted by association with the regime and so were not interested in meeting them. They maintained that their mission was simply to witness how the Iraqi people were living under the sanctions.

The Apostolic Papal Nuncio to Iraq, the Most Rev Giuseppe Lazzarotto, whom we met as part of our programme, was more pragmatic and told the bishops categorically that they couldn't 'just sit on the fence when you see misery and suffering. You have to make up your mind and do what you can.'[21] After that meeting the bishops eased up and agreed to meet Tariq Aziz, Dr Omeid Mubarak and Hans. They also visited hospitals where they were visibly shaken by what they witnessed, and this changed their position as I suspected it would. After that they adopted a different attitude to my role during their visits and also to what was happening in Iraq.

It seems that Andrew, contrary to what he told me at the time, had minimised my role and inflated his own. His promotion of a flying hospital, clearly a figment of his imagination, was, in my view, designed to indicate his primary role. The bishops became aware that the situation was rather different when we were visiting the Minister of Health. It disturbed me, and perhaps them as well, that during our time in Baghdad, Andrew seemed more interested in visiting the Shia clerics in Kadhimiya and Sadr City (suburbs of Baghdad) than in attending to the dire situation of the whole country.

---

[21] It says something about the Holy See's outlook that during the 2003 war the only foreign diplomatic representative to remain in Baghdad was Fernando Filoni, Giuseppe Lazzarotto's successor as Papal Nuncio.

Hans did not mince his words with the delegation. He was absolutely appalled at what he had witnessed and expressed his outrage at the kind of game the British and Americans were playing with Iraqi lives. He insisted that the bishops must speak about what they had seen and should do what they could to help the Iraqi people as their suffering was dire. He stood accused of failing in his job as UN Humanitarian Coordinator, but in reality it was the US and UK governments who were responsible for the carnage of the ordinary Iraqi people. Hans was not a supporter of the Ba'athists, nor close to the regime, but he accepted that the Iraqi government was doing its best to help the Iraqi people.

Later Hans would write of this delegation of church leaders:

> The Church of England, in May 1999, sent a delegation of Anglican Bishops to Iraq with the full support of the Archbishop of Canterbury. [They] came to Baghdad well prepared. They had studied the documentation, had met, prior to their visit, with British government officials and Church groups as well as the public. Their time in Iraq with UN agencies, NGOs and their site visits merely heightened their awareness of the humanitarian crisis and how wrong Britain's Iraq sanctions were.[22]

The bishops took the opportunity to ask Tariq Aziz if they could bring in funds for the renovation of St George's, the Church of England's only place of worship in Baghdad. It had been neglected because of the sanctions and what they were asking would be an infringement of the UN resolution on the matter. Not surprisingly, the Deputy Prime Minister was agreeable, no doubt seeing it as a prudent gesture since it would open a crack in the sanctions regime. The Church of England didn't actually have many followers in Iraq, most of the Christians there being Roman Catholics, but as the established church

---

[22] Von Sponek, Ibid.

in England it had some moral influence in a country which, unlike the Holy See, was engaged in a form of warfare against the Iraqi people.

A similar breach in the sanctions regime which was tolerated because it was seen as a British interest, related to the neglected WWI cemeteries. The MP and future patron of FAF, Harry Cohen, took up this issue with the Ministry of Defence and a mission was sent to Iraq to renovate the graves and arrange for them to be guarded. It is likely that the Treasury authorised the transfer of funds for St George's and the cemeteries, but the fact that Britain permitted this while calmly enforcing the regime against the ordinary Iraqi people, thereby causing immeasurable suffering and countless deaths, starkly revealed the government's inhumane policy towards my homeland.

During our time in Baghdad I had been staying with a Roman Catholic couple, Sabah Kamal, whom I'd originally met in Southend, and his wife, Mary Rose. On the last day of our visit the bishops included my hosts in an invitation to Hans and me to attend a mass at which they blessed the Iraqi government for doing its best to help their people. As Hans recalls, apart from us, the only other member of the congregation was an old Iraqi caretaker.[23]

Leaving aside this gesture and the parochial matter of renovating the Church of England's building, what benefit derived from the church delegation to Iraq? Back in England, the Suffragan Bishop of Kingston, Peter Price, did what he could to highlight the suffering of the Iraqi people, in particular speaking at anti-war demonstrations. And the Board for Social Responsibility of the General Synod issued a statement dated 17th May 1999 which read:

> The delegation [of the bishops to Iraq] agreed that while it is important not to absolve the Iraqi Government of its responsibilities for creating the current situation, the evidence suggests that while sanctions are a legitimate tool

---

[23] Ibid.

of international relations, they are, in their present form, ethically untenable because they are hitting the weakest and the most vulnerable within society.[24]

Whether these initiatives made any material difference seems doubtful in the light of what subsequently happened. But they at least demonstrated that a significant moral and spiritual force underpinned our efforts.

Rescued by Jany Le Pen

My visits to Iraq grew in number as the political temperature increased, and by the turn of the century were averaging six a year, most of them on my own. It was incredibly tedious making that long trek across the desert, hence my relief when Tony Benn found someone else to accompany him on his trip to interview Saddam in February 2003. Nevertheless, those on the road enjoyed a certain camaraderie, and there was an awareness that we depended on each other if anything went wrong. On one trip my car broke down at the Trebil border crossing, and who should rescue me from my plight but Jany Le Pen, wife of Jean-Marie Le Pen, President at that time of the *Front National* in France. She was on the way to a meeting with Saddam, and gladly offered me a lift to Baghdad.

Jany's political orientation, like that of her husband, was not exactly close to my heart, but we had a fascinating conversation on the long drive to the capital. In 1995 she had founded a laudable organisation called *SOS Enfants* in collaboration with Michel Dubois, a member of the political bureau of the *Front National*, and Bernard Antony, President of *Chrétienté-Solidarité* (roughly Christian Solidarity), which campaigns on behalf of persecuted Christians. They undertook the

---

[24] See https://publications.parliament.uk/pa/cm199900/cmselect/cmintdev/67/67ap13.htm.

delivery of medicines to sick Iraqi children, and aimed to protect Iraqi children generally by providing the youngest with shelter and by educating the illiterate. I guessed, however, that a second strand of her motivation was similar to mine, that is to provide a conduit for communication, in her case between the French government and the Iraqi regime.

I reported the relevant details of all these trips to my parliamentary contacts in Britain, and in reverse conveyed back to my political contacts in Iraq what I was hearing in England. I hoped thus to increase understanding between the two sides, thereby paving the way to a peaceful resolution of the developing conflict. If politics were a reasonable business, it should have worked. That it didn't is evidence that international relations are something else.

CHAPTER SEVEN

FRIENDSHIP ACROSS FRONTIERS

Establishing FAF

As I mentioned earlier, in 1993 I set up Friendship Across Frontiers, primarily at Tam's suggestion. His reasoning was as follows:

> I returned to Britain believing that the policy of sanctions against Iraq was both immoral – because those who suffered most grievously were the children and old people – and unwise – because it engendered burning resentment against Britain and the United States, not only among the friends of the Iraqi regime, but in swathes of the Arab world, which did not like to see an Arab country humiliated. George Galloway and I did the rounds of both ministers and Shadow Cabinet ministers to endeavour to persuade them that sanctions should be lifted. Impact made we little: distaste for Saddam prevailed. One Shadow Cabinet member insulted me by suggesting that I was one of Lenin's 'useful idiots' […]
>
> There was a lacuna of understanding about the Arab world. Also I detected a feeling among ministers and shadow ministers that, gratuitously, they did not want to irritate the many friends of Israel by being too lenient towards Iraq.[1]

---

[1] Dalyell, T., *The Importance* ..., p 257. Tam continued: 'Where I detected this, I reminded them that there was an ancient, if small, Jewish community, allowed all the rights of Iraqi citizens, in Baghdad. Tariq Aziz was only one of those who observed correctly, "We do not think that your friends in Saudi Arabia tolerate, let alone make welcome, a Jewish community and it was in Riyadh, not this city of Baghdad, that a princess was dragged through the streets to the scaffold for being

The name 'Friendship Across Frontiers' came from a Cambridge artist involved with Cambridge Against Sanctions on Iraq. Our aim was to highlight the suffering of the Iraqi people and we conducted our campaign by holding meetings in the Houses of Parliament and arranging speaking engagements on Iraq in London and other British cities. It was a loose kind of organisation without formal membership, subscriptions or constitution. This unstructured gathering of people of like mind on Iraq, and especially of Members of Parliament, seemed to work best. If we had moved towards a more formal set-up, with a tightly defined objective, I suspect that half of those on our mailing list would have unsubscribed.

Tam, who was by now Father of the House of Commons, became our first patron, and gave us a caché which we would not otherwise have enjoyed. He was indefatigable in trying to persuade colleagues and the Conservative government to adopt a saner policy on Iraq, in part by drawing their attention to the efforts of FAF and myself. For example, on 20th July 1994 he addressed the House of Commons:

> I quote from Riad El Taher of Friendship Across Frontiers, with whom I went to Baghdad and to the valleys of the Tigris and Euphrates last year. He has learned from independent travellers that the health situation there is diabolical due primarily to extra shortages of medicine and the desperate situation concerning water pumps and filters. The Leader of the House will know that I saw the Prime Minister about that matter. In the sweltering heat of this summer, I told him that there is a humanitarian aspect that ought to be resolved.[2]

---

found to be an adulteress!'" This refers to Princess Mishaal bint Fahd, a member of House of Saud, who in 1977, at the age of 19, was executed for alleged adultery.
[2] Hansard 20th July 1994. See
http://hansard.millbanksystems.com/commons/1994/jul/20/adjournment-summer#S6CV0247P0_19940720_HOC_184.

On 12th January 1995, in a business session at the House of Commons, Tam referred to a report outlining the 'starvation situation in Iraq' written by Claude Cheysson, former French Foreign Minister and European Commissioner:

> [...] in view of the report of Riad El Taher outlining the medical situation in Iraq, which is in the possession of the Foreign Office, could we have a debate on what amounts to the manipulation of the United Nations by the United States and Britain, and on the continuation of these counter-productive, indeed wicked, sanctions?[3]

On 10th February 1995 Tam received a written reply from the Prime Minister, John Major, to his enquiry about his response to a report sent to him by me. It was hardly encouraging: 'The recent communication has been noted by my right hon. Friend the Foreign Secretary.'[4]

And then in a Hansard report on an adjournment debate[5] about 'Libya and Iraq (Sanctions)' on 29th November 1995, we read the following, the paragraphs in inverted commas coming from a FAF report written by me:

> **Mr. Tam Dalyell (Linlithgow)**: This is a debate about sanctions against two countries with which the United Kingdom has, historically, enjoyed excellent relations. Many

---

[3] Hansard 12th January 1995. See
http://hansard.millbanksystems.com/commons/1995/jan/12/business-of-the-house#S6CV0252P0_19950112_HOC_189.
[4] Hansard, 10th February 1995. See
http://hansard.millbanksystems.com/written_answers/1995/feb/10/iraq#S6CV0254P0_19950210_CWA_69.
[5] Half-hour adjournment debates come at the end of each day's business in the House of Commons. They are an opportunity for backbench members (i.e. those who are part of the government) to raise matters about which they are concerned. Slots must be applied for to the Speaker's office, and there is a ballot to choose who is successful. Notice also has to be given to the relevant government Minister who may reply him or herself, or many ask someone else to do so.

of the decision makers in Libya and Iraq were educated in this country. As we debate the issue of sanctions, we also debate our country's long-term relations with two very important areas of the Arab world.

Anyone who visits Iraq must be dismayed that a once sophisticated society should be reduced to grinding poverty in many areas. Every recent visitor to that country--including the right hon. Members for Old Bexley and Sidcup (Sir E. Heath) and for Tweeddale, Ettrick and Lauderdale (Sir D. Steel), the former leader of the Liberal party, and many others--is appalled, as I was, by the terrible conditions in the children's hospital in Baghdad or the conditions in another hospital at Um-Kasr on the Kuwaiti border. Infants, who cannot conceivably be responsible for any of the horrors of the past 10 years, expired in my presence--and I do not exaggerate.

The most recent visitor to Iraq with whom I have been in contact is Riad El-Taher, an Iraqi-born British subject. He is concerned about the British Government's entrenched support for United Nations Security Council resolution 986.[6] He writes:

"Can I bring to your attention . . . the long term erosion of trust and historical ties taking root among the upcoming generation".

I sensed that during my visit.

"The majority of UK educated Iraqis are reaching retirement age and are being replaced by a generation fed on suspicion of the West and particularly Britain's continued support of sanctions."

I mentioned that issue at Question Time, and I say as gently as I can, and I hope without giving offence, that I

---

[6] The oil-for-food resolutions, of which more in Chapter Nine.

wonder whether the Minister, his colleagues and his civil service advisers really realise the extent to which a generation is growing up about to hate the west – people who have been trading partners and friends. It is tragic.

"UNSCR 986 is heavily biased, being intrusive, divisive and certainly not addressing the chronic humanitarian shortages of food and medicine. These shortages are felt most strongly among the young generation ... and the salaried sector in general. The financial benefit, if Iraq manages to sell the allocated oil, after deduction of the heavy burden of reparations, administration and allocation to the Northern [Kurdish] Governorate under UN supervision, will be in the region of 7-8 US$ per person per month (outside Iraq)."

That places seriously in question the assertions that it is simply up to Saddam Hussein to change policy, and all will be well. I fear that the detail of what is happening shows that that certainly would not be the outcome.

One is forced to take the view that UNSCR 986 was not intended to provide humanitarian aid to the Iraqi people […]. Both the UK and USA hold substantial Iraqi frozen assets, which could be controlled effectively for the sole purchases of badly needed food and medicine from their respective countries and for immediate release. Even if Iraq were prepared to agree to UNSCR 986, there are no guarantees that funds would be available from the sale of oil or for the purchase of humanitarian requirements, due to the complexity of the contractual demands. The reparations burden should be set aside at this stage, as Iraq can tackle that issue when sanctions are lifted. The rest of the argument is well known to the Foreign Office.

I simply say to the Minister, and through him to the Foreign Secretary, that the right hon. and learned Gentleman the Foreign Secretary should go to some of his constituents, the Church and Nation Committee of the Church of Scotland – he represents many of the leading members of the Church of Scotland in the Pentlands constituency of Edinburgh – and speak to them about their detailed knowledge and their knowledge of the humanitarian position.[7]

On many occasions I attended meetings in the House of Commons, including some where my reception was decidedly cool. For example, I went to a meeting hosted by Ann Clwyd who strongly supported Tony Blair on Iraq. She had invited the Kurdish warlord, Jalal Talabani, to speak, and I wanted to hear what he would say and had in mind to ask him awkward questions. I got there early, but found the committee room empty. At last Ann Clwyd and others, including my friend Karen Dabrowska, arrived and were somewhat taken aback to find me there, sitting alone in the room. Karen told me afterwards that she'd overheard a discussion about whether to throw me out, but they evidently thought better of it.

Emma Nicholson also professed an interest in Iraq. She, Lord Avebury and other politicians wanted me to criticise Saddam Hussein, but my concern was with the effects of sanctions on the Iraqi people, not the leadership of the country. What good would it do to publicly undermine the President of Iraq? If I started to insult him would he walk away from his position, would it change things? Of course not. Moreover, I had a family in Iraq and was not prepared to put them in danger because of my actions.

These responsible politicians must either have been blinkered or obsessed in believing you had to be either with or against them. They seemed unable to respect people with a different opinions and to engage

---

[7] Hansard 29th November 1995. See
https://publications.parliament.uk/pa/cm199596/cmhansrd/vo951129/debtext/51129-42.htm.

with them in a dialogue, two principles central to the thinking of Friendship Across Frontiers. In the Middle East dialogue was less well established, but for British politicians, who are so proud of their democratic traditions, to go down this road was surprising, to put it mildly.

During those years of sanctions the media successfully manipulated people's opinion of Saddam Hussein. If you objected to the sanctions you were labelled Saddam's apologist. Were Tam Dalyell, or Tony Benn, or many other MPs who spoke against sanctions really apologists? Were they Ba'athists? Were they financially motivated? Labels are used to undermine people and make their views unacceptable to the public. This was what eventually happened to me when I was accused of using my humanitarian work as an excuse for financial gain.

On several occasions I met Dr Salah Al Shaikhly, who was to become one of the post-occupation Iraqi Ambassadors to Britain, and we appeared to achieve a cordial relationship. I was therefore disappointed to discover that he considered me to be Saddam's representative in Europe and an accomplice of Iraqi intelligence. What basis did he have to support such malicious allegations?

It came to the ears of the Kuwaiti embassy that I was persuading MPs and journalists to visit Iraq, and so they invited me to go and talk to them. I guessed that their intention was to persuade me to stop my campaign. I accepted, but took Tam with me. We met someone from the ruling Al Sabah family and he asked me sharply in Arabic: 'Why have you come with this MP?' I told them Tam was a patron of FAF and I understood I had been invited as chair of this organisation and not as a private individual. It was common courtesy to ask him to join me.

Another incident indicated the Kuwaiti attitude. While in Dublin I was invited by Brendon Johnstone, Chair of the Kuwait-Ireland Trade Association and prominent investor in Bula plc, to a fundraising evening for Palestine. Among the many Arab diplomats invited was the

Kuwaiti ambassador to Britain, Khalid Al-Duwaisan. Like Dr Salah al-Shaikly, he warned those sitting at the same table as me that I was Saddam's man in the EU. While I rejected categorically such a description, it alerted me to the probability that their secret service had picked up some clues about my contacts with the Iraqi President.

The Kuwaitis assumed that those who were against the sanctions were motivated by money. Undoubtedly some were. We all need money to provide security and comfort, but not at any price. My lifestyle was comfortable and I had come to realise that there was more to life than money, and I was determined that it shouldn't control me.

I accepted every invitation to speak and to reflect on the situation as this gave me the opportunity to counteract the lies of governments as well as those of most journalists. I did this in whatever public forums I could find and I received invaluable support from a number of sympathetic MPs in correcting the bias in the media. Through Tam, and as a result of my visits to parliament and the many letters I wrote when Labour was in opposition, I got to know a number of key personalities, among them George Robertson, Clare Short, Robin Cook, Derek Fatchett, John Smith and Gordon Brown, all of them supportive of FAF's efforts. They assured me that working with Tam was the best way to highlight the plight of the Iraqi people. The sad and unexpected death of John Smith in 1994 was a loss not only to the Labour Party but also to those who sympathised with FAF. He was familiar with Iraq and opposed the continuation of the sanctions because of the needless suffering it caused. Things would have been very different if he'd lived to become Prime Minister.

I saw it as an important part of FAF's work to encourage non-diplomatic contacts between Iraqi and British organisations with the aim of creating cracks in the sanctions regime. For example we were keen that the British Council should continue to maintain contact with Iraq and a visit by a British performing arts group was firmly on the cards; this was only prevented by the outbreak of the 2003 war. The

British Council had been popular among educated classes in Iraq since 1940 because it was one of the best channels for semi-official organisations in Britain to come to Iraq. The Chairperson of the British Council at that time was Baroness Kennedy, and Oona King, MP, who was on the board, was quite close to Clare Short, who held the Overseas Development portfolio in the shadow cabinet. I anticipated that such connections could be effective in easing the sanctions.

The Labour Victory 1997

Together with my many contacts in the Labour Party, I had high hopes that a Labour government, with its internationalist and anti-imperial traditions, augured well for Iraq.[8] Gordon Brown, the new Chancellor of the Exchequer, was sympathetic to our cause in the early days of the new government. I had several meetings with Derek Fatchett, the new Minister of State at the Foreign and Commonwealth Office and found him keen to learn about what was happening in Iraq. His department was also supportive of what I was trying to achieve, and I felt that I had allies there. But Fatchett's equally untimely death in May 1999, like that of John Smith, was another loss for FAF and the Iraqi people.

Meanwhile, at a more personal level, I got a nasty shock only four months into the new government which made me reflect that my position was no less precarious now than it had been before. As I said earlier, the Kuwaitis described me as Saddam's man, and I suspected they had picked up on something. I didn't agree with everything that Saddam did, far from it, but it's true that I supported his efforts to protect the Iraqi people from the terrible effects of the sanctions. Nevertheless, in order to maintain any kind of credibility in the atmosphere of hysteria which had been pumped up, I had to deny that I had anything to do with him.

---

[8] Labour won the general election which took place on 31st May 1997.

Alphabetical list of some MPs who supported the aims of FAF

Diane Abbott, Lab
Tony Benn, Lab +
Gordon Brown, Lab
Sir Menzies Campbell, Lib Dem
Michael Clapham, Lab
Kenneth Clarke, Con
Harry Cohen, Lab
Robin Cook, Lab +
Jeremy Corbyn, Lab
Ann Cryer, Lab
Tam Dalyell, Lab +
Derek Fatchett, Lab +
Paul Flynn, Lab
Mike Hancock, Lib Dem, later Independent
Douglas Hogg, Con
Douglas Hurd, Con
Glenda Jackson, Lab
Dr Caroline Lucas, Green
Alice Mahon, Lab
Paul Marsden, Lab - Lib Dem - Lab
Robert Marshall-Andrews, Lab
John McDonnell, Lab
George (now Lord) Robertson, Lab
Joan Ruddock, Lab
Alex Salmond, SNP
Clare Short, Lab
Alan Simpson, Lab
Dennis Skinner, Lab
John Smith, Lab +
Ian Taylor, Con
Sir Teddy Taylor, Con
Dr (now Baroness) Jenny Tonge, Lib Dem
Mike Wood, Lab

22 Labour
5 Conservative
3 Lib Dem (+ 1 temporary defector from Lab, Paul Marsden)
1 Green
1 SNP
Total 32 (at the time of writing those whom I know to have died are marked +)

In addition, Field Marshal the Lord Bramall, who had served as Chief of the General Staff, professional head of the British Army, between 1979 and 1982, and as Chief of the Defence Staff, professional head of the British Armed Forces, from 1982 to 1985 showed a keen interest in my work and was, I believe, sympathetic to it.

Imagine, therefore, my horror when one day, on my way home, I went to pay for some petrol and saw a picture of myself staring out from the *Daily Mail*. The headline read: 'Saddam's man in leafy Surrey.' I could hardly drive the car home I was so terrified, but it was to get worse. There, standing outside my house, were two police cars; they must be waiting for me, I concluded. So I drove away again, going through every option I could think of, some of them quite extreme. But in the end I realised that if they wanted to interrogate me, I'd be found, and so I drove home. It was only then that I learnt that my next-door neighbour had committed suicide. Moreover, that same day Lady Di was killed in a car accident in Paris, and the news about me therefore vanished from people's minds as if it had never appeared. It's a terrible thing to say, but I couldn't have been more relieved by these sad coincidences.

Disillusion with Tony Blair's government was not long in coming. He soon revealed himself to be an ardent supporter of US policy, and also of the Zionist entity. And gradually I found that Clare Short, Secretary of State for International Development, George Robertson, Secretary of State for Defence, and even Gordon Brown, the Chancellor, started to line up behind Blair's belligerent position. Tam comments on the last of these:

> Several times I went to see the Chancellor of the Exchequer, Gordon Brown, my parliamentary neighbour across the Forth. I had known him since he was a student leader and rector of the University of Edinburgh. I would come out of his office convinced that he was deeply unhappy with Blair's belligerent attitude on Iraq, not least on account of the consequences for the Exchequer. However, what I felt was – he was too cautious to explicitly say so – that he placed his relationship with the Prime Minister higher in his priorities than an objective assessment of action against Iraq. Indeed, I

am pretty well sure that he judged that, if he kicked over the proverbial traces over Iraq, Blair would sack him or demote him from the Treasury. In this, he may not have been wrong. And if Brown felt vulnerable, no other Cabinet minister, other than John Prescott, the elected deputy leader of the Labour Party and Deputy Prime Minister, could imagine that they were secure.[1]

In 1998, the US Congress passed the Iraq Liberation Act which stated that 'It should be the policy of the United States to support efforts to remove the regime headed by Saddam Hussein from power in Iraq and to promote the emergence of a democratic government to replace that regime.'[2] The main pressure for the act came from Ahmad Chalabi of the Iraqi National Congress, described by Aram Roston as 'not the only influence on Capitol Hill pushing to do something about Saddam Hussein, but he was the strongest.'[3] He had a remarkable 'knack for telling people what they wanted to hear'[4] and thereby building up a following in the US. But not everyone was convinced. An editorial in the *New York Times* commented on one provision of the act in these terms:

> This month Congress authorized the Pentagon and State Department to transfer up to $97 million in American military equipment to Iraq's unreliable opposition groups in the hope that they can somehow overthrow the Iraqi dictator and replace him with a democratic government. The White

---

[1] Dalyell, *The Importance* ..., p 261-62.
[2] Government Publishing Office (US) Pub.L. 105–338, 112 Stat. 3178, enacted October 31, 1998. See https://www.gpo.gov/fdsys/pkg/PLAW-105publ338/html/PLAW-105publ338.htm.
[3] Roston, A., *The Man who Pushed America to War*, New York, Nation Books, 2008, p. 150.
[4] Ibid, p 226.

House must firmly resist any temptation to arm these discredited organizations.[5]

The bill's sponsor was Benjamin A. Gilman, a staunch Zionist who contended that the Clinton administration had a 'lethargic approach' toward helping Iraqis who wanted to overthrow President Saddam Hussein. He also accused the administration of bullying the so-called Jewish state into accepting unfavourable terms in talks with the Palestinians. While having lunch with Benjamin Netanyahu around this time he declared: 'We want you to know that you're not only among friends, but among mishpocheh [family in Yiddish].'[6]

There was no indication that Blair demurred from this hard-line view. On our return from our 1998 trip, Tam, together with 'kindred spirits' Alice Mahon and Robert Marshal-Andrews, went to see him about the sanctions and made a strong case for them to be lifted. Tam records their reaction as they left:

> Coming out of the sofa discussion in the Prime Minister's room, we said to each other that we had had a courteous enough hearing but that there had been no meeting of minds. One curious, well-meant jocular remark illuminated what we saw as Tony Blair's lack of understanding of the situation in the Middle East at that early moment in his premiership. When I referred to my father's experience of working with Arabs in the Gulf he quipped, 'So all this trouble in Iraq is your fault, Tam!' At one level, it was a harmless enough remark but at another level, Alice and I thought it betrayed a

---

[5] 'Expensive Fantasies on Iraq,' opinion piece in the *New York Times*, 19th October 1998. See http://www.nytimes.com/1998/10/19/opinion/expensive-fantasies-on-iraq.html.

[6] Fried, J.P., 'Benjamin Gilman, a New York Congressman for 30 years, Dies at 94, *NYT*, 17 Dec 2016, online at https://www.nytimes.com/2016/12/17/nyregion/ben-gilman-dead.html.

basically flippant attitude and encapsulated a dangerously cavalier approach to the situation in the region.

Blair was in what the philosopher John Stuart Mill picturesquely called 'the deep slumber of a decided opinion.' Interviewed on his *Desert Island Discs* on 13 December 2010, I was interested that Robert Harris, the former political editor of *The Observer* and distinguished author, told listeners that, at Blair's invitation, he had spent a lot of time shadowing him and had come to realise how readily Blair was prepared to engage in war.[7]

Another ominous sign was his appointment the same year of Lord Levy as his Special Envoy to the Middle East. Levy was another staunch Zionist whom Blair had raised to the peerage shortly after the general election and who had been a major fund-raiser for the Labour Party since 1994. None of this suggested the new Prime Minister would regard Iraq in a sympathetic or objective way.

Then came Operation Desert Fox, ostensibly an attack designed to teach Saddam a lesson for supposedly expelling the weapons inspectors and to 'degrade' Iraqi military installations. President Clinton didn't even bother to obtain congressional approval for this US/UK bombing campaign which started with a four-day attack between 16th and 19th December 1998, but continued sporadically until the following May. It involved 36,000 sorties, in which half of the casualties were civilian.

I had a conversation with Tony Benn about Desert Fox, after which he recorded these remarkably perceptive words in his diary:

> *16th January [1999]:* I did have a very interesting phone call from Riad Al-Tahir [sic], an Iraqi businessman who said that the bombing had frightened people terribly because of the noise and the explosions, and that the hatred of Britain was

---

[7] Dalyell, *The Importance* ..., pp. 259-60.

now very evident – before, if you came from Britain, people were nice to you, but not now. Saddam Hussein is absolutely the super-hero of the Middle East – the new Saladin, who was the great Muslim leader at the time of the Crusades. We are going to have to pay a very heavy price for that policy in the future.[8]

Tam secured an adjournment debate on Iraq on 24th March 2000, and invited me to observe the proceedings from the Distinguished Strangers' Gallery. Tam began by quoting a number of Reuters reports from the Vatican expressing deep concern over the effect of sanctions. He went on to explain that this unease was shared by experienced UN officials on the spot, namely Denis Halliday, Hans von Sponek and Jutta Burghardt. Quoting a report from Mark Hillier he also drew attention to the lack of essential spare parts to maintain production of the Kirkuk oilfield. He said that he and George Joffé had visited the Secretary of State for Defence, Geoff Hoon, and had urged him to adopt two sets of proposals 'to try to counter the very adverse physical and intellectual consequences of the sanctions regime amongst the Iraqi population.'

Harry Cohen pointed out that there was 'a lack of transparency and accountability concerning the decisions of the sanctions committee and what this country's representatives are doing on the committee.' But Tony Benn, to whom Tam offered the last five minutes of his allotted time, was the star of the debate. He had a particularly clear-headed view of the Iraqi regime. He in no way approved of some of its methods, but he saw them in context. He accordingly addressed these hard-hitting but wise words to the one-time firebrand anti-Apartheid reformer, Peter Hain, Minister of State for Foreign & Commonwealth Affairs:

---

[8] Benn, A., *Free at Last: Diaries 1991-2001*, ed. Ruth Winstone, London, Arrow Books, 2003, p 523.

I rise briefly to support the remarks of my hon. Friend the Member for Linlithgow (Mr. Dalyell) because he has been a persistent and principled critic of this [sanctions] policy. I rise only because I have heard the Foreign Office reply many times and, if the Minister is to deliver the same answer, I must tell him in advance that it is wholly incredible and untrue.

We are told, for example, that the policy is necessary because one country has invaded another and has weapons of mass destruction. Israel has weapons of mass destruction and has occupied the southern Lebanon. Indonesia has weapons of mass destruction, which we supplied, and killed 200,000 people in East Timor. Turkey has weapons of mass destruction and occupies northern Cyprus, and the Government's policy is that Turkey should be admitted to the European Union. There is no credibility whatever in that argument.

The second argument, which I know that we shall hear because the Minister and the Prime Minister have given it before, is that the entire responsibility for the terrible health crisis and the tragedy in Iraq lies with Saddam Hussein. As my hon. Friend the Member for Linlithgow said, that is not the view of senior United Nations officials who have no connection with Saddam Hussein but who were in Iraq to do a job that they were denied the opportunity to do because they knew that the policy was wrong.

I hope that the Minister understands that the charge against the British and American Governments is that they are applying sanctions that amount to genocide. I use that word advisedly and with great gravity and regret. I repeat: the policy of the British and American Governments amounts to genocide. It is no good talking about the international community because it shares the view that my hon. Friend has put forward with such strength.⁹

Hain replied to the debate, saying, in essence, that although the sanctions regime could be improved, the blame for its shortcomings rested largely with Saddam. And referring to a new inspection regime he boldly stated: 'The new arrangements are designed specifically to determine whether the Iraqis are developing weapons of mass destruction – as we know they are doing.' That word 'know' now has a rather hollow ring to it.

I had written a letter to the FCO about the problems of distribution under the oil-for-food programme, and Tam referred to this: 'On delivery, will my hon. Friend get his office to give him the letter of 9 March from Riad El-Taher of Friendship Across Frontiers, which goes into detail on the matter of distribution?'[10]

During the debate, Peter Hain drew attention to a television programme on Iraq. 'The recent documentary produced by John Pilger tried to show that sanctions are responsible for the suffering of the Iraqi people. That argument has been repeated in the debate. It is a lie propagated by Saddam Hussein and his apologists.'[11] He was referring to 'Paying the Price: Killing the Children of Iraq' which was broadcast on ITV on 6th March, just a couple of weeks earlier. The hour-and-a-quarter long documentary was a devastating indictment of US/UK policy, and should be compulsory viewing for anyone who wishes to understand recent Iraqi history.[12]

---

[9] Hansard 24th March 2000. See http://hansard.millbanksystems.com/commons/2000/mar/24/iraq#S6CV0346P0_20000324_HOC_171.
[10] Ibid.
[11] Ibid.
[12] John Pilger's 'Paying the Price: Killing the Children of Iraq' can be viewed at https://www.youtube.com/watch?v=j55oZNp5-j0. The Iraq researcher for this documentary was Felicity Arbuthnot, who was to interview me for 'Global Research' four-and-a-half years later.

In the nature of things, such documentaries are polemical and therefore one-sided. But 'Paying the Price' told the side of the story which, despite all our efforts, was underrepresented. As its title indicated, it told of the disastrous effect of the sanctions on medical services, and the disproportionate harm this caused to children. It highlighted the little reported Desert Fox campaign, referred to earlier, and pointed out the almost certain link between the use of depleted uranium coated weapons during the First Gulf War and a massive rise in cases of cancer in the Basrah area. For this it held the US/UK governments responsible, for by their stringent application of the sanctions they impeded, rather than assisted, the safe removal of the radioactive battlefield wreckage north of Kuwait. Pilger also drew attention to the blatant hypocrisy and inconsistency of US/UK policy in its attitude to Saddam over the years. And there was much more.

Tam addressed a number of written questions to Peter Hain arising out of the debate on 24th March, and on 3rd April he received written replies. Here is the record from Hansard, worded in the prescribed fashion:

> **Mr Dalyell**: To ask the Secretary of State for Foreign and Commonwealth Affairs, pursuant to the oral statement of the Minister of State of 24 March 2000, Official Report, columns 1292–93 on Iraq, what assessment he has made of the letter of 9 March from Riad El-Taher of Friendship Across Frontiers. [116875]
>
> **Mr. Hain**: FCO officials replied to Mr. El-Taher's letter of 9 March on 29 March addressing his comments on the humanitarian situation in Iraq.
>
> **Mr. Dalyell**: To ask the Secretary of State for Foreign and Commonwealth Affairs, pursuant to the oral statement of the Minister of State of 24 March 2000, Official Report, columns

1292–93 on Iraq, what evidence he has received that Iraq is manufacturing chlorine-based mustard gas. [116871] 282W

Mr. Hain: To reiterate the point in my statement of 24 March 2000, Official Report, columns 1292–93, chlorine is a constituent of mustard gas which was used by Iraq in the attack on Halabja in 1988. It is therefore clearly important that we are sure that chlorine imported into Iraq under the 'oil for food' programme is used for the purposes for which it was approved.

Mr. Dalyell: To ask the Secretary of State for Foreign and Commonwealth Affairs, pursuant to his letter to the hon. Member for Linlithgow, concerning his willingness to debate Government policy on Iraq, if he will do so at Kensington Town Hall on 6 May with Denis Halliday and Hans von Sponeck. [117247]

Mr. Hain: As my right hon. Friend the Secretary of State said in his letter, he is happy to debate Government policy on Iraq, as am I. Indeed I debated our policy with my hon. Friend in the House most recently on 24 March.[13]

It will be noticed that Hain sidestepped the issue of what evidence he might have for asserting that Iraq was manufacturing chlorine-based mustard gas. Needless to say, he didn't attend the debate in Kensington Town Hall, to which Tam referred.

---

[13] Hansard 3rd April 2000. See
http://hansard.millbanksystems.com/written_answers/2000/apr/03/iraq#S6CV0347P0_20000403_CWA_35.

CHAPTER EIGHT

PARADISE AND THE PRESIDENT

Going back to live in Iraq was never in question for me; I had been away far too long and was always happy to return to my home and to visit my family in England. But I enjoyed meeting old friends, talking politics, conducting negotiations and taking advantage of the sunny weather in Iraq. And when things got too much for me a little project I started in the countryside provided me with a peaceful retreat from the hurly-burly of my political, business and social activities. Curiously enough, as I have indicated, it also afforded me the opportunity of getting to know Saddam Hussein.

My farm by the Tigris

I had made some money supplying sugar to Iraq from Jordan, but due to currency restrictions. couldn't transfer this out of the country. In 1995 Petcon's representative in Iraq, Mohammed Qimaishi, suggested a solution to this problem which, he persuaded me, would also benefit the Iraqi people. Accordingly, I acquired some farmland roughly 100 kilometres south of Baghdad near the ancient ruins of Sassifon and Suwaira,[1] and built a house there for myself and another for the farmer.

---

[1] Brigadier Abdul-Karim Qasim, leader of the 1958 revolution, was from the age of six brought up in Suwaira.

Next to the small village of Shejeera, the 100 metre wide strip of land extended around seven kilometres away from the river and was crossed by the minor road from Baghdad to Suwaira. There was a main irrigation channel up the strip from the Tigris and small subsidiary channels from it across the strip. As it was when I acquired it, the farm consisted of some barren land near the river, a few date trees, an olive grove and an orange orchard, with mud huts for the farmers across the road. The proximity of this property to Baghdad, but also its relative isolation from the capital, were persuasive factors in acquiring the farm.

The Roman Catholic couple I mentioned earlier, Sabah Kamal and Mary Rose, together with their daughter, Ghada, were the most frequent visitors. Being of independent means, they were in a position to spend a good amount of time at Shejeera, and also had the expertise to help with aspects of the project. Ghada. who had experience in landscaping, did a fantastic job managing the garden and making it into the paradise of my dreams.

I was keen to revive ancient construction methods in building the new house, as I was convinced that this would ensure it withstood the heat without the use of air-conditioning. My thought in doing this had nothing to do with financial gain, though in post-2003 conditions this would without doubt have been helpful. My motivation was rather that I remembered living very close to nature in my youth and growing up without either air-conditioning or refrigeration and I wanted to see if I could reproduce the arrangements which made that possible. In the summer my family used to place 'camel thorn,' packed into frames made from date tree stems, outside the windows. Water was then thrown onto the thorn thereby ensuring air-circulation in the rooms and relief from the scorching midday heat.

I planted the front garden, which ran the twenty or so metres from the river bank up to an arched wall, with gardenia. Also in this area were an incinerator, the rubbish bin and a perfumed garden. The arched wall, trained with creepers, stood five metres back from three sides of the house, and was designed to reduce direct sunlight. A walkway ran all the way round the house, the part between the arched wall and the house being covered. On the left of the house, looking from the river, there was a pump house, a treatment plant and a water tank, as well as a herb garden and grape vines. You approached the house by a drive from the public road to the rear. An orange and lemon orchard lay between the road and the house, but I later replanted this with grape vines, jasmine and gardenia. Beyond the road was the new brick-built house which I had provided for the farmer in place of the previous mud-houses.

The cavity walls of the house were packed with mud and straw, as in the ancient buildings in Samarra and Najaf,[2] in order to absorb the heat hitting the house. To enable the air to circulate properly the rooms needed to be fitted with funnel-type copper chimneys which could be closed in winter. Wooden shutters were fitted in recesses beside the windows, and these could be closed in summer to further reduce the heat.

You entered the house through an old recycled door. No cement was used in the construction and all the floors were finished with terracotta tiles. The outside of the house was covered with white gypsum to reflect away the heat of the sun's rays. In the winter heating was provided by an open fire in the middle of the house, the smoke from which passed through a chimney in the roof of the kind just described. In addition there was underfloor heating supplied by a wood-burning boiler. In the bathroom this had the effect of replicating the traditional Arab hammam. All the windows and the outside door were covered with insect netting to keep the flies and mosquitos out. The lamps were mostly enclosed inside perforated copper shades of a kind commonly found in the Baghdad souq. The only concession to modern building

---

[2] Two historic cities in Iraq. Najaf is considered the third holiest city of Shi'a Islam. Samarra was once the Abbasid capital and is famous for its distinctive surviving architecture.

techniques was the use of steel girders in the roof instead of the traditional wooden joists.

The garden furniture was hand-made from traditional date palms preserved with linseed oil and for shade I planted several fig trees as well as indigenous nubik trees. With their enormous evergreen leaves, the latter were ideal for this purpose, and in addition this indigenous species had the advantage of growing quickly and requiring little water. Its small apple-like fruit was much favoured by birds, humans and goats, in that order. Planting these trees in areas away from the river helped to improve the soil for cultivation, and reduced the temperature by a few degrees. Initially the surface soil was covered with salt and needed to be washed before being planted with cotton to sweeten the soil. Later the land was used for barley, wheat and sunflower production on an annual rotational basis. The wheat was ground in the mill with which I'd provided the farm, and the farmer's wife made beautiful bread in the oven which I'd also had built for the purpose.

The garden was a sea of colours, a perfumery of herbal and orange scents. I will never forget the sight of a field of yellow sunflowers dotted red with wild poppies, while the tranquillity was broken only by the restful song of the babbler bird. I re-organised the farm on a fair and ethical basis, which brought its rewards, though as I will relate, it also had its disadvantages. The farmer's house was plumbed with running water, wired with electric light, and had a bath and a septic tank, amenities to which he was unaccustomed. Although the added expenditure of a septic tank could not seriously improve the quality of the river water, I didn't wish to contribute still further to the pollution of the Tigris. Due to the sanctions regime there was by then no waste collection and so I encouraged the farmers to burn all waste in the incinerators I had built for the purpose. The farmer had a cow for his milk requirements and I added further milking cows, sheep and goats housed in brick-built sheds fitted with feeding and watering troughs and sheltered by reed covering. Their waste was used as organic fertiliser. No shooting of wild life was allowed.

The land further away from the river needed to be totally rethought. In the early years I followed the advice of the locals and used the cultivated soil mostly to grow crops. But in later years I decided to plant it with pomegranate shrubs, as well as date, pear, apricot and avocado trees, leaving some land beyond for arable farming. Thousands of olive trees, which are particularly hardy and grow quickly, lined the boundary of the farm. These methods became a model for others to follow, and many of the local farmers adopted them in order to improve the soil as well as the micro-climate away from the river.

This phase of development was difficult and expensive. Although I was born in Iraq I lacked an understanding of the rural Iraqi mentality, or at least the mentality of the Mesopotamian farmers. In country areas tribal loyalities prevailed and religion had a primitive hold. Education, although it was compulsory prior to sanctions, had become optional because of the need to survive. Children helped their families in the fields, while women had a secondary role to men, despite the fact that many were also teachers, doctors or even engineers in the ministries.

I unwisely ignored the advice of many not to provide the farmer with welfare and housing. They were right in as far as he considered my attention to his needs as a weakness and took advantage by claiming phantom expenditure and expenses. As far as he was concerned he had a right to benefit from my relative wealth. On one occasion he claimed for a fruit shrubbery he had planted, but while I was out of the country he dug out the trees and returned them to the nursery. When three or four months later I noticed that they were not there, he claimed the trees had all perished due to the bad soil. This made no sense to me, for at least some of the trees could have been expected to survive. Such conduct, as well as his starving of the livestock and guard dogs for whose food I was paying, made me suspicious of his expense claims and so I was compelled to replace him.

This behaviour is far from unique in Iraq and I fear is a deeply ingrained mentality. It explains Iraqi forms of government and sends a warning to those from outside who attempt to apply their own perspective to a country they don't understand. If even I, as an Iraqi, had failed to get the full measure of my own countrymen, what chance had outsiders of making useful judgements about my native land. Of course not all Iraqis are like my farmer, but enough of them are to make Iraq difficult to govern, even compared with other Arab countries. This made me less censorious of the Iraqi Government and its leadership at that time, for whatever its methods, it succeeded in holding this ethnically diverse country under effective control. Moreover it managed to withstand eight years of destructive war against Iran and thirteen years of draconian sanctions. The fact is that the majority of Iraqis were glad to have firm government, and placed the blame for their suffering firmly on US/UK policy rather than on the regime.

Post-2003 my farm was occupied by US forces in their drive against the resistance. I maintained contact with the new farmer, but around a year into the occupation his son telephoned me in Britain to inform me that he had been murdered. This was shocking enough news, but there was also something sinister about the call itself. Someone was clearly standing beside the farmer's son directing him what to say. I was pressed to come to Iraq immediately to deal with the situation which had arisen. Alarm bells rang, and I replied that I would need to consider the matter carefully. I have little doubt that this was a ruse to lure me to the farm, where I could have been dispatched as easily as his father. Ahmad Chalabi, the most prominent member of the Iraqi opposition between the wars, called me around that time and jokingly remarked that for just $100 a driver could easily be found to kill me.

I continued for a couple of years to give directions on the management of the farm from afar, insisting that the same ecological principles which I'd established should be maintained. But eventually all the livestock was stolen, and I had to accept that I could no longer control events on the ground, nor could I permit my family to put themselves in mortal danger by taking over in my place. My intention remained to sell up rather than return to what was for a while a little paradise; this way I would retain my memory of its beauty, tranquillity and peace.

As an aside, it is worth mentioning that neither the Americans nor the quisling Iraqi army, who took over the farm after the Americans left, paid me a penny for the use of my land, nor did they compensate me for the damage they did to it. There has been no acknowledgement, either, that they should do. In Basrah, by contrast, I'm told my right to financial compensation for the use of our family's property by the British army is recognised. Among the British there is at least some respect for the property rights of indigenous peoples. Those they got into bed with in this senseless adventure seem to have no such scruples.

Saddam Hussein

'Those whom the gods wish to destroy they first make mad.'[3] This seems apposite in a couple of ways with regard to the Iraqi President. Firstly, Saddam was certainly made 'mad,' in the American sense of 'angry,' by Western policy towards his country, and this caused him to become reckless in a way which led to his downfall. But the West also wanted to depict Saddam as crazy, a mad ogre, and therefore someone who must be destroyed. This demonization may have been good propaganda, but it was a poor description.

Through my frequent visits to Iraq I had come to know Hamid Yussef Hamadi, the Minister of Culture and previous personal secretary to Saddam Hussein. From him, Saddam was informed about my

---

[3] *Antigone* by Sophocles (verses 620-623) is probably where this proverb originated: 'evil appears as good in the minds of those whom gods lead to destruction.' In Longfellow's poem, 'The Masque of Pandora' (1875) it appears as 'Whom the gods would destroy they first make mad.' Enoch Powell also famously made use of this saying.

humanitarian and agricultural activities and expressed the wish to see me. My initial reaction was one of extreme caution, for I had no illusions about his ruthlessness. Indeed I frankly admit I was terrified before our first meeting. He evidently sensed this and made no attempt to push me beyond my comfort zone. Accordingly at the beginning of our acquaintance he arranged for us to see each other in the formal surroundings of government buildings. But I discovered his manner was not at all intimidating and, moreover, I found he was well-informed, widely read and interested in matters as diverse as dress, etiquette, history, art, literature and ecology. I came to believe that, whatever his methods, he loved his country and its people, and wished only the best for them.

And so with time we developed a more relaxed relationship, and he would sometimes invite me into the desert to visit his herd of white camels, a breed protected by a conservation programme he supported. He also visited me at my farm. He liked Blue Label whisky, and so I obtained bottles for him from England. Once he asked me to bring him the complete works of Shakespeare, which was easily done, and on another occasion his request was for an officer's black beret of the Royal Tank Regiment, which proved a more difficult assignment. Other commissions were a Lock & Co Panama hat, and Carrera sunglasses.

But I guess my main use, as far as he was concerned, was the information with which I could provide him about the British government's thinking, and in particular about those British MPs who supported FAF, and who, if not his friends, were at least opposed to the war-fever being developed by Tony Blair. In return he was attentive to my needs, and in particular conscious of the complications of my situation as an expatriate Iraqi. He insisted that no officials should expect me to exceed the limits which I believed it prudent to impose on my statements and activities.

In January 2003 Saddam presented me with two young white camels in appreciation of my creating a model farm and my concern to protect the river and its environment. He was particularly impressed that I had adopted the use of traditional copper art, for he supported the copper industry, and decorated all his palaces with its products. He also favoured my choice of architecture and in particular liked my traditional studded door. As I have made clear, I personally did not approve of Saddam's regime, but I could understand why many of my fellow countrymen regarded him with respect. After all, he managed so much better to hold Iraq together than his Iraqi and foreign enemies.

In other words I am ambivalent. I believe Saddam was intelligent, modest, down-to-earth, committed to the future of his country, unsectarian and shrewd in his delegation of governmental powers. This is saying something in a region where the leaders are often self-serving and corrupt. If he was not universally loved as a leader, he was, as Tam Dalyell discovered at a celebration in Bahrain in 1995, respected by many in the region for what he had achieved.

> After the pleasantries were over and presents were exchanged, we made to leave. I said that I had just one question on which I would value their opinion – Iraq. They immediately invited me to resume my seat and called for more coffee. They were very worried. The impression had been created in Britain and the United States that the Gulf Sheikhdoms and Emirates were thankful to the West for having protected them from Saddam Hussein. This was not the case. Kuwait was a special case, and had brought a lot of trouble on themselves. Saddam had many admirers in the bazaars of the Sheikhdoms. There was mounting antagonism to the use of Bahrain as a base against fellow Arabs. The Sheikh nodded his agreement when his brother said that the Iraqi/Kuwaiti problem could have been sorted out at a specially convened conference of the Arab states in Cairo.

> Six years later, I learned that the bombing of Baghdad in 2003 absolutely appalled them. To the Gulf Arabs, Baghdad was a special place. And, for them, the damage to the ancient sites of Iraq was an insult and injury to Arab cultural heritage and history.[4]

Yes, Saddam and his political party did a lot of harm, but equally they contributed to many popular measures. The successful development of the oil industry and maintaining it in the public sector contributed to the creation of jobs. Medical care and education, extending from nursery provision to university, were provided across the country in both urban and rural districts, and were the best in the region prior to the imposition of sanctions. Moreover, these services were provided free to all Iraqis and other Arab nationals working and living in the country. Before the wars Iraq had had a very high per capita income and this facilitated social mobility and the realisation of individual potential. The elimination of illiteracy had enabled its citizens to make informed choices about their lives, and this in turn provided a firm base for democratic government.

I found Iraqi ministers, as well as most Ba'ath party officials, well educated, hardworking and eager to serve. As we've seen, Tam formed the same opinion. He also remarked on a matter I touched on earlier.

> George Galloway and I were invited to address a session of the Iraqi parliament, which I felt to be less of a rubber stamp organisation than was portrayed in the West. Both at the parliamentary session and the reception [laid on for us after the formalities] there were numerous women in headscarves, indistinguishable from those one might encounter in the

---

[4] Dalyell, *The Importance* ..., p. 251.

streets of Athens or of Rome. One quarter of the members of the Iraqi parliament were women ...[5]

As I have indicated, the loyalty of ministers and officials went right to the top. Following Saddam's example, they were accountable to themselves and to the people. Corruption was largely eliminated. In fact I never paid a penny in a clandestine way to anyone in Iraq. When the Iraqi government decided to impose a surcharge on oil exports I complied for a number of reasons which I explain in Chapter Nine. But it's important to realise that this payment was not, as is often alleged, a backhander, that is a secret arrangement with a government official or politician, but was open and was applied to all legal oil exports at that time.

It can't be denied that there is a culture of corruption throughout the Arab world. It was for this reason that the Iraqi leadership dealt harshly with any financial irregularities. Saddam concluded that the only way to stamp out bribery was to adopt a policy of zero tolerance and severe penalties. People needed to fear the consequences of corrupt practices and to realise that whatever the financial gain the risk was not worthwhile.

In the eighties a Deputy Oil Minister, Mun'im Samerahi, was hanged because it was assumed that he took a bribe. Later it was revealed that he was not involved and the government apologised. It was a harsh lesson for ministers and officials, but as far as I could see it had in general the desired effect. Unlike other governments Saddam's regime refused to tolerate most cases of corruption. There were some elements among the Tikriti clan, to which the president belonged, who abused this connection, particularly his sons. But there is no evidence that this was supported by the President. Even Tariq Aziz's son, Ziad, was jailed in the belief that he took bribes, and his father couldn't do much to influence the process.

---

[5] Ibid, p. 254.

Some will say that Saddam's anti-corruption campaign was the pot calling the kettle black. It was often asserted during the sanction years that Saddam squandered the county's resources on palaces and expensive homes for himself and family. There is, however, as so often, another side to this story. The buildings which were indeed constructed provided much-needed employment for builders, architects and artists, they remained the property of the state and, most importantly, they used local resources. Schools and hospitals would have required the import of the kind of equipment regularly banned by the 661 Committee; and so desirable though it would have been to divert the country's energies in this direction, it was not a viable option.

One can't in all cases apply Western values when dealing with different cultures, and Arab culture is no exception. Western officials don't fully understand the Arab world or specifically the Iraqi mentality. If Iraqis know you they can be very cooperative, but if they don't know you, or don't like you, they can be obstinate and obstructive. Iraq can only be ruled by a government which understands its people and has a vested interest in serving the country as well as a patriotic desire to promote its interests.

Palestine

Saddam's support for the Palestinians was, unlike that of other Arab leaders, consistent and generous, and inspired admiration across the Arab and Muslim world. For to anyone who didn't bury his head in the sand, what had happened in Palestine was a clear signal of what the West had in store for the whole region. The fate of the Palestinians was therefore regarded as pivotal to the future of the Arab and Muslim world.

In September 2000 Zionist opposition leader and butcher of Sabra and Shatila, Ariel Sharon, provocatively visited the Haram al-Sharif in Jerusalem, causing a riot. Following on years of fruitless negotiation on the formation of a Palestinian state, the unrest widened into the Second (or Al-Aqsa) Intifada. In support of the resistance, Saddam paid $10,000 compensation to the families of suicide bombers, and between $1,000 or $500 to the wounded, depending on the severity of their injuries. I don't endorse this policy. Indeed it would be illegal to do so, though I note in passing that it's not illegal to express regret, as the revised revisionist Zionist Benny Morris has done, that the Jewish terrorist gangs of 1947-49 didn't complete the ethnic cleansing of Palestine. He thereby provided the justification for a future Zionist government to 'finish the job.'[6] What you're allowed to say apparently depends, even in democratic societies, on whose side you're on!

No wonder Saddam was so popular in the Middle East at that time, a status which was further elevated following the American and British air strikes on targets south of Baghdad on 18th February 2001. Many Palestinians believed that the real purpose of the raids was not enforcement of the no-fly zones, but punishment for the Iraqi leader's policy on Palestine. They compared his support with the largely empty promise of $1 billion from the other Arab leaders. At a time when sanctions were biting hard in Iraq, Saddam was criticised for sending money abroad, but his view, which is also mine, is that Palestine and Iraq stand and fall together; if they stand together against Western oppression they will not, in the long run, fail. Meanwhile, the deputy defence minister of the Zionist entity, Ephraim Sneh, threatened darkly that Saddam's 'stance on our conflict with the Palestinians is extreme, and could have influence in the near term.' What the Zionists predict usually comes to pass, and this was no exception.[7]

---

[6] Shavit, A., 'Survival of the Fittest,' *Ha'aretz*, 4th January 2004. See https://www.haaretz.com/1.5262454, also available at *Counterpunch*, 8th January 2004, see https://www.counterpunch.org/2004/01/16/an-interview-with-benny-morris/.

[7] Philps, A., *Daily Telegraph*, 19th Febuary 2001, 'Palestinians Hail their Local Hero Saddam.' See http://www.telegraph.co.uk/news/worldnews/middleeast/iraq/1323284/Palestinians-hail-their-local-hero-Saddam.html.

But what about Halabja?

No one can be indifferent to what happened in 1988, during the Iran-Iraq war, to the Kurdish-Iraqi [Iranian] town of Halabja. This was undoubtedly a terrible disaster, and quite possibly a crime against humanity. If so, I in no way condone it. Whether Saddam was himself directly implicated I'm unable to judge. Sadly, though, Halabja is only one of many massacres across the globe in modern times. How such events are judged seems to have more to do with political expediency than cool assessment.

Thus when Halabja happened, the CIA, which then favoured Saddam, firmly maintained that Iran was responsible. Saddam was known to be 'a bastard' or 'a son of a bitch' (take your pick), but as F.D. Roosevelt is supposed to have said of the Nicaraguan dictator Somoza, 'Yes, but he's our bastard,' and of General Patton, 'Yes, but he's our son of a bitch.' Winston Churchill is also supposed to have used the latter expression of General Montgomery. Sadly, this hypocritical and unethical thinking hasn't got any better. In the late nineties, as Saddam moved out of US and Zionist favour, the Halabja disaster became a major stick with which to beat him. This demonization was to get even worse once Iraq was defeated.

There is much evidence that the US government at the time turned a blind eye to the supply and use of chemical weapons in Iraq. Since US companies were providing the materials required for their manufacture, should American leaders not have stood alongside Saddam in the dock of public opinion when accusations of using chemical weapons were made? The fact that in 1983 Ronald Reagan signed a secret order instructing the administration to do 'whatever was necessary and legal' to prevent Iraq losing the war, and that shortly after Donald Rumsfeld, who had been Secretary for Defence under President Ford, was sent as his Middle East troubleshooter to convey to Saddam the US's willingness to restore full diplomatic relations, certainly suggests US complicity in the use of chemical weapons.[8]

Moreover, while chemical weapons may be horrible, so are nuclear weapons, and Iraqis remain especially conscious of those possessed by the relatively close Zionist entity. And if the Zionists say they would only use such weapons in self-defence, that is the argument usually advanced by any side when committing atrocities. Tariq Aziz spoke of the 'dreadful things' unleashed by the Iran-Iraq war, but history is a catalogue of atrocities across the globe, whether the victims were Vietnamese women and children, or Afghani wedding guests, or Jews, or Palestinians, or German and Japanese city dwellers, or Armenians, or Sikhs in Amritsar, or native Americans, Australians and New Zealanders. And this is not to mention the suffering of my fellow Iraqis as a result of Western policies. What about all of these 'dreadful things'?

Instead of cherry-picking atrocities, it might be better to make sure we avoid war altogether.

Some further thoughts

Saddam's war with Iran was wrong, but all five permanent members of the Security Council bear a heavy responsibility for encouraging him to start it, and once under way, urging him to resist efforts to mediate a resolution. As Tam pointed out, Saddam was probably also given the nod by the US to invade Kuwait, thereby putting his head into the noose prepared for him. If the West had wished for a peaceful resolution of that conflict, they would have given more time to Yasser Arafat, Chair of the Palestine Liberation Organisation (PLO), and Muammar Gaddafi, who were seeking to persuade Saddam to withdraw from Kuwait.

---

[8] Borger, J., 'Rumsfeld "offered help to Saddam,"' *The Guardian*, 31st December 2002 following the release of classified documents in the US. The article can be read at: https://www.theguardian.com/world/2002/dec/31/iraq.politics.

I deduced from my various visits to Iraq that if the country had not been invaded it could just possibly have emerged as a model society of harmony and self-dependence, and one in which the government served its people diligently. This model might even have united the Arab world beyond Iraq's borders and brought lasting peace and prosperity to the region. Perhaps that's precisely what the West, guided by the Zionist entity, wished to avoid.

Conspiracy theories aren't necessarily false. On May 26th 2010 Avi Dichter, one-time Minister of Internal Security to the Zionist entity and former head of Shin Bet, made a speech to the Israeli National Security Research Centre in which he is reported to have said:

> We have achieved in Iraq more than we expected and planned. Iraq has vanished as a military force and as a unified country. Our strategic option is to keep it divided. Our strategic goal is to not allow Iraq to take its regional and Arabic role back. Iraq must stay divided and isolated from its regional environment. Nobody can ignore what we have achieved in this field. Iraq can never be the same Iraq [as it was] before 2003.[9]

Fate decreed that I should have a relationship with Saddam as a human being. No doubt he was a man with many faults; I came to see his strengths as well. If he had continued as a friend of the West I could have been open about my association with him from the beginning. Now that he has entered the West's demonology I find myself under pressure to explain myself. In all my dealings with him I didn't sense that he was motivated by vindictiveness or war-mongering, but rather by the desire to defend and develop his country. His hard-line attitude was a reaction to the intransigence of US and UK foreign policy in Iraq and Palestine.

---

[9] See: http://gmmuk.com/chilcot/.

History doesn't always condemn hard men, or women, unreservedly, and once the dust has settled, I daresay people will adopt a more nuanced view of Saddam and Ba'athism.

1. Shejeera: my paradise on the banks of the Tigris

2. Shejeera: time off from the hurly-burly of Baghdad

3. Shejeera: The farmer's children, and my land stretching into the distance'

4. Shejeera: Sabah Kamal, my Roman Catholic friend from Southend days, and his wife, Mary Rose

5. Shejeera: in the garden between the river and the house

6. Shejeera: Saying hello to one of my sheep

7. Shejeera: Saddam's gift of two white camels

8. Saddam at his trial in 2004

CHAPTER NINE

OIL-FOR-FOOD AND THE SURCHARGE

New opportunities for Petcon

As I described earlier, the Iraqi invasion of Kuwait on 2nd August 1990 and the imposition four days later of sanctions caused me considerable financial loss. But I find in life that sometimes when one door closes another may open. Before I travelled to Iraq to see my family in 1991 I obtained a letter from the Department of Trade and Industry (DTI) giving me, as MD of Petcon, permission to talk to the Iraqi government about 'humanitarian' supplies under the sanctions regime. And so, by good fortune, my losses were recovered through supplying products for various projects in Iraq.

In order to repair its war-ravaged infrastructure, Iraq badly needed new investment. The returns on this would be paid in US dollars which were earned from Iraqi oil exports to Jordan under a special UN-supervised protocol agreement. The US and UK had been obliged to grant this exception to the sanctions regime because Jordan's economy was dependent on its trade with Iraq. The protocol was a way for the West to buy Jordan's support for sanctions and ensure its remaining stability.

The Deputy Oil Minister, Dr Falih al-Khayat, whom I'd interviewed when he applied for a post with BPC and who had meanwhile risen to become the Director General of the Ministry of Oil, reached an agreement with a Jordanian company, Elba House, managed by three Palestinian brothers from the Khouri family, to source and deliver badly needed materials such as bodywork parts for buses, equipment for the oil industry and a baby milk factory. However, the Khouri brothers were inexperienced in such matters, and Falih suggested that Petcon might assist. In this he proved himself one of my most loyal friends. A Manchester graduate, he was not a Ba'athist, but was sincerely committed to the diligent service of his ministry and the Iraqi people.

My agreement with the DTI recognised that the required equipment would need to be supplied through Jordan. This gave Petcon the opportunity to by-pass the sanctions with the clear knowledge and approval of the DTI. The money Iraq was allowed under the special protocol to earn by exporting oil to Jordan at a discounted rate was paid into an account in Amman, from which the exports to Iraq could be paid.

Although I had a monopoly in the supply of engineering equipment, I didn't abuse it, submitting my offers for consideration as if there were no sanctions. This ungrasping approach raised the reputation of Petcon and myself for reliability and fair-dealing within the Oil Ministry. The Minister issued a directive that all other foreign contractors were to be met in the lobby of the building; only I was allowed beyond that. No bribes were asked for, nor were any paid, in the whole course of my dealings in Iraq. Compare this with post-2003 Iraq, which has become the most corrupt country in the world by the UN's own standards.

Despite this upturn in my fortunes, I didn't return to the lavish lifestyle which I enjoyed while I was working on the North Sea projects with McDermott. My period of poverty and near nervous breakdown after Saddam occupied Kuwait had widened my outlook, and I now found more pleasure in the spiritual side of life, a sense of being connected to the universe and to people. It was the thought of helping my fellow countrymen which now dominated my life. That's what the Kuwaitis couldn't understand; I was not for sale.

In view of what had happened, moreover, I felt it prudent to reduce my overheads. So in 1992 I closed the Kingston office, and from then on, until I wound up Petcon in 2012,[1] the company was run from the garage at the bottom of my garden. And I hired a secretary who worked from home.

The oil-for-food programme

The 1995 conference which I attended with Sue Lloyd-Roberts took place in an atmosphere of anticipation that the sanctions regime would soon be relaxed. A month later, in April 1995, following considerable pressure from humanitarian organisations and Western public opinion, the Security Council passed resolution 986 which allowed Iraq to sell oil on the world market in exchange for food, medicines and other essentials. It was administered by the 661 Committee, so named because Security Council Resolution 661 had established the sanctions regime back in 1990. The committee was charged with ensuring that this concession did not enable Iraq to expand its military capability, but it was the strict interpretation of this assignment which ensured that the programme was only partially effective in eliminating the suffering of the people.

In 1996 a golden opportunity for advancing the anti-sanctions campaign arose when I was approached by a French company called Perenco. Their experience was in developing marginal fields in Africa and in the USA. The owner, Hubert Perrodo, had worked in Iraq as a tool pusher on a drilling rig in the boom years prior to the Iran-Iraq war. He was keen to acquire an allocation in the Rafidain oilfield development plan, and as he had an affection for Iraq and its people I was very willing to help him with my contacts in the Ministry of Oil and SOMO. In return I was given shares in the company, became a director, and in order to operate in Iraq set up a subsidiary company,

---

[1] Effectively the company ceased trading in 2003, but was not dissolved until 1st May 2012.

Perenco Iraq. I met Perenco's London representatives Paddy Spink and their lawyer, Roland Fox, and worked out the details with them.

Protracted negotiations ensued lasting around two and a half years. The DG in the Economics Department of the Ministry of Oil, who was of the opinion that only major oil companies should enter into negotiations, was not keen on Perenco's participation. Moreover, while the French team of Perenco was very cooperative, the English director dragged his feet because he didn't trust Arabs. This complicated situation needed the intervention of the minister to finally bring matters to a conclusion.

At last we put forward our definitive proposal, which was favoured, and the Rafidain field near Kut, with an estimated production potential of 100,000 barrels a day, was assigned to Perenco. But of course no one could carry out any work or investment while Iraq was under sanctions. The Deputy Oil Minister, the late Taha Hamoud, did not fully understand this and encouraged Perenco to openly break the sanctions. We didn't agree with the United Nations policy, but this was naïve and unacceptable. No company was willing to risk jeopardising its global interests for the sake of Iraq, but for some reason this logic eluded Hamoud.

While I was involved in these negotiations, I was approached by an Irish company, the publicly owned Bula Resources Holdings, with which it was easier to work. I had soon negotiated similar arrangements with them to those arranged with Perenco. I met the managers, found them desperate for involvement in Iraq, and in the light of their experience in oil exploration, Bula was allocated Block 4 in the Western Desert. The negotiations did not last long because the Irish were open and honest, and so was the Iraqi side, led by the DG of Exploration, Dr Radwan al-Saadi, another UK graduate and a brilliant engineer who served his sector and the country with the utmost loyalty. It was an honour to have known him. Both Radwan and the Irish were keen to establish a proper and fair partnership which is how lasting contracts should be negotiated. This way the parties can reach ethical arrangements to work together for ten or fifteen years, and if the contract is subsequently completed without problems, it can easily be extended.

The proceeds from the oil lift[2] were assigned to Bula Iraq and Perenco Iraq respectively. Bula in Ireland, that is the parent-company, received 30% for administration, and the remaining 70% was paid to Bula Iraq whose account was controlled by two signatories, myself and another member of the board. The funds in the Iraq account were to be used exclusively to promote awareness in Ireland of the situation in my homeland. A public relations company was engaged to highlight the plight of the Iraqi people and to lobby members of the Dail in support of the removal of the sanctions. This division of the proceeds was popular with the board with the exception of Albert Reynolds, who was to become Chair in 1999. He insisted that the parent company should get 100% of the proceeds, but was in this respect overruled.

The same split was agreed between Perenco Iraq, which received 70%, and the parent company in France, which got 30 %. The funds that I thereby had access to, with the agreement of my fellow signatories, allowed me to engage public relations consultants with the brief of promoting the Iraqi case in the media and among MPs and members of the House of Lords.

The funds from the oil lift were also used to help the poor people in Iraq. For example, there were children's charities which needed money and I organised funds for schools in the rural area adjacent to my farm outside Baghdad. But supporting such institutions in Iraq presented its own challenges, for once the word got about that we were supporting charitable work we found ourselves inundated with requests for help. The tragedies and needs were endless and how was one to decide between them? After a while I therefore pulled out of such charitable

---

[2] 'Lift' is the word used in the business for an oil consignment. Those allocated consignments are called 'lifters' and the process is called 'lifting'.

work deeming it more effective to use the funds to promote Iraq's case abroad.

The oil-for-food programme had been organised in haste and had many shortcomings. The funds from Iraqi oil sales were paid into an escrow account controlled by the United Nations, but run by the French-Dutch bank, BNP Paribas. Iraq was to have no direct control over the use of this money. Instead Iraqi officials would negotiate prices with international manufacturers and suppliers of essential goods, and the government would then submit their proposals for approval to the United Nations 661 Committee, which comprised representatives of the fifteen members of the Security Council.

Our oil allocation under the oil-for-food programme was known to the DTI, the FCO and the UK Mission to the UN through the list of lifters published by the last of these. It was no secret. Approval was given to the companies in which I was a shareholder, Perenco and Bula, these companies having coordinated all their dealings with those bodies. Moreover, my name appeared in all the documentation of these companies.

This arrangement was better than nothing. It could even have been fair, but in practice both Britain and America had the power of veto even if a majority of those on the 661 Committee voted in favour of an Iraqi proposal, and they frequently did so. They were concerned that the Iraqi government should not be seen to be helping the Iraqi people and improving their conditions. It was clear that they wished to create a rift between the Iraqi people and the government and used the suffering of the former to reach their objective. This made the task of Denis Halliday and Hans von Sponeck, successive UN humanitarian coordinators, difficult, if not impossible. It was stressed by the US and UK representatives at the UN that Hans's role was to administer the oil-for-food Programme and not to be involved in politics. But politics was inseparable from the humanitarian programme and that is why it failed in its application.

As we all waited in vain for the sanctions to be lifted I focussed on the poor understanding of the situation in Iraq among Bula's management and its political owners. The image of Iraq had to be improved and to this end I talked to Irish parliamentarians, explaining the Iraqi case to them, and making them aware of the devastating effect of sanctions on the majority of the Iraqi people.

The Surcharge Crisis

The multifarious problems caused by the sanctions interacted with one another leading to a disastrous situation. The lack of medicines was made more acute because the water treatment plants along the Tigris and Euphrates had been bombed. This necessitated the pumping of untreated human and industrial effluent directly into the rivers which in turn caused an exceptionally high infant mortality rate due to deadly waterborne diseases. Even the fish died, depriving the people of a major source of food. The north of Iraq fared better than the south because there the water sources were mostly uncontaminated mountain springs.

Another economic effect of sanctions was the continuing decline of the Iraqi dinar against foreign currencies, which the programme did nothing to address, and the Iraqi government therefore requested the United Nations to deal with this problem. The UN made a study and recommended that the oil-for-food programme be modified to provide for the injection of $600 million per phase (six months) as cash. This would allow Iraq to purchase cheaper locally produced food and medicine, surely a desirable step. As Iraq could produce its own rice it made more sense to buy that than to purchase it from Egypt, Syria, Australia or Thailand, incurring unwarranted shipping costs and in some cases getting an inferior product. By reinvigorating the local economy, the dinar would hopefully be stabilised and the emigration of skilled professionals from the country halted.

However, it was clear that whatever resolution was passed, actioning it would be dependent on a unanimous vote on the 661 Committee, and with US and UK intransigence, this was never going to happen. The Iraq government therefore came up with a plan for realising the cash component independently.

A little more detail about what went on at that time is provided by a statement to the Serious Fraud Office (SFO), which investigated me between 2008 and 2010. Gerard McGurk, who became the UK representative on the 661 Committee in August 2000, told the SFO that reports of the Iraqi government's intention to impose oil surcharges started coming in shortly after he took up his post. However it proved very difficult to address breaches of the sanctions regime because of political differences on the subject of Iraq at the UN. Consequently the 661 Committee was unable to reach agreement on how to react to the surcharge, and instead an informal meeting was held at the request of the UK and US missions. This is a clear indication of who was in the driving seat and of the reality that political, rather than humanitarian, considerations were paramount.

At the meeting it was agreed that the surcharges were illegal and the so-called Oil Overseers were ordered to notify all lifters of this fact, which apparently they did shortly after UNSCR 1330 was passed on 5th December 2000.[3] No enforcement mechanism was, however, put in place and I have no recollection of receiving any notification, though it is possible that Perenco and Bula failed to pass on such a communication to me. The resolution did on the face of it go some way to implementing the recommendation of a cash component, albeit with the uncertainty of six-monthly renewal, but it came too late.

---

[3] Prosecution substantive submission on abuse of process. The prosecution was arguing against my defence's case that the government had been turning a blind eye to the payment of the surcharge and it was therefore an abuse of process to try me. Their case against this was that though the government may have been slow, because of the difficulties involved, to act against those who paid the surcharge, it had given no indication that it did not intend to do so.

The Iraqi government was kept well-informed about developments at the UN, and was prepared for the worst. On 3rd September 2000 Perenco received a mysterious fax from the DG of SOMO, Saddam Zebin Hassan, marked for my attention, reading: 'You are kindly requested to proceed to Baghdad as soon as possible for discussion regarding crude oil contract.' Involving as it did that awful journey across the desert from Amman, this was no mean demand at short notice. But I guessed it must be important and replied: 'I intend to travel to Iraq on 14th September 2000 and hopefully will be in your office on the 16th.'[4]

Once there I was confronted with the decision of the Iraqi government to impose a surcharge on oil exports under the oil-for-food programme. To compensate for the extra cost to lifters the price of crude would be reduced below the Official Sale Price (OSP) as determined by the 661 Committee. The Iraqi authorities wanted to know (a) how I expected this to be received by the British and Irish governments, and especially by those British MPs who supported FAF, and (b) whether Perenco and Bula would be prepared to accept such an arrangement. I was told the surcharge would be set initially at 10 cents per barrel, but was likely to rise in the next phase, that is the first half of 2001.

On the first question I could reply without difficulty that those who supported FAF would be sympathetic, and those who didn't would be either less tolerant or positively hostile. But question two put me on the spot, for I would be advising Perenco and Bula, and no doubt payment of the surcharge would need to be arranged through me. I therefore requested permission to call both companies by telephone, and obtained their provisional agreement to paying the surcharge this way.

---

[4] Correspondence in my possession which was shared by the prosecution with the defence before my appearance in court. The text is translated from the original Arabic.

I was under no illusion that payment of the surcharge was on paper illegal in Britain under the sanctions regime. But as Rageh Omaar has pointed out, 'by the end of the decade [i.e. 2000], the economic embargo was being ignored more than it was being observed, without any official changes in international legislation having taken place.'[5] There was ample evidence that on the specific and crucial question of oil exports the US and UK were ambivalent, to say the least. Oil was being exported under the noses of US and British forces through the Shatt al-Arab waterway and over the border in the Kurdish enclave and on into Turkey. Furthermore the West was effectively encouraging the Kurdish warlords to raise funds by this means to bolster the Kurdish economy and pay for their own defence. And as I've said, there was a special protocol agreement with Jordan which flatly contradicted the sanctions policy, and also allowed oil to flow in that direction without hindrance.

It was in the interests of the West for the oil to keep flowing, as indeed it had been doing in large quantities through smuggling even before the oil-for-food programme came in. A complete halt to Iraqi crude exports might well have destabilised the world economy. Would the US and UK not, therefore, view the payment of the surcharge leniently, I argued to myself? That is to say, would they not turn a blind eye to this infringement as well?

Other considerations raced through my head. The first was personal. I had developed cordial relations with Saddam's regime, especially with Tariq Aziz and even with the President himself. I knew, however, that this couldn't be relied upon to save me and my family still living in Iraq from reprisals should I refuse. Even my children and their families outside Iraq might be affected.

I had got this far and it didn't feel as if I could now safely turn back. Moreover, concerning my family in Iraq, it felt like Hobson's choice. Like all Iraqis they faced an indefinite period of economic attrition.

---

[5] Omaar, Ibid, p 50.

What was more dangerous, the unpredictable ruthlessness of the regime or the collapse of the Iraqi economy? Was it not my duty, and also my fate, to resist the temptation to run away?

The judge at my trial maintained that my primary motive had been personal financial gain. But in reality this played no part in my calculations at that critical moment. Let me be quite clear on this matter. I had been in business for most of my life, and I certainly hadn't lost the habit of recognising a profitable deal when I saw one. However, I was now driven by a passion to overthrow the sanctions and, furthermore, to play a part in preventing another disastrous military intervention. At the time I believed, naively I now realise, that being a conduit for communication between the Iraqi and British governments provided unique leverage which might enable me to avert an invasion. That opportunity would be lost if I refused to play ball over the surcharge.

There was one other issue. Could I be sure that the money the regime gained through the surcharge would be used to relieve the suffering of the people, or would it be siphoned off, as has been alleged since, for military expenditure and vanity projects? Here I simply had to go with my gut instinct. I knew Saddam was a hard man, but I also believed that he cared about his country and its people. That is why so many Iraqis supported him. But even if I were wrong in this judgement, it was surely a matter of self-interest for him to ensure, as far as he could, the well-being of the people. The sanctions were in large measure based on the notion that if the people suffered enough, they would overthrow the regime. If the perception had developed among a majority of Iraqis that Saddam was uninterested in their suffering, he wouldn't have lasted for long.

On balance, then, the risks of not paying the surcharge seemed to me to outweigh those of paying it. And so I told Saddam Hassan (not, of course, to be confused with the President) that in principle I was not opposed to the surcharge and would, if it were introduced, argue on the boards of Perenco and Bula for its payment. The die was cast, and over a decade later I would pay the price.

It is worth reflecting at this point on what I did not consider, and to ask whether, if I had done, I might have made a different decision. Firstly I couldn't possibly know that in ten years' time the SFO would be in desperate need of a successful prosecution. Secondly, I didn't sufficiently consider the arrangement whereby, though I was acting on behalf of Perenco and Bula, it would be my name registered in SOMO's records, and that as an individual I was much more vulnerable to prosecution. And finally, and perhaps most importantly, I didn't consider that the very fact I was acting for humanitarian reasons rather than financial gain would, paradoxically, count against me. Of course the opposite was asserted by the prosecution, but I believe, and so did Tam, that behind the scenes, in the murky world of political vengeance, it was my humanitarian campaigning which made me a target. It was that which threatened the plan to topple Saddam by squeezing his people.

I was just one of a large number of lifters questioned by SOMO about their attitude to a surcharge, with the proviso that the price would be set in such a way that they would not be financially disadvantaged by it. 80 agreed, 14 refused and 16 remained hesitant.[6] Based on this, the surcharge was introduced in the autumn of 2000 at 10 cents a barrel, and was increased, on the President's orders, to 50 cents at the beginning of 2001. Following adverse reaction by lifters, it was soon reduced to 30 cents for oil destined for the US and 25 cents for other destinations.

In order to trade in oil, lifters were obliged by the Iraqi government to visit Iraq and sign a document obtained from SOMO. The signatory agreed that when the purchaser transferred funds for the oil lift he would

---

[6] Translation in my possession of a meeting held on 21st November 2000 which was attended by various top Iraqi government officials. This document formed part of a jury bundle prepared by the SFO which in the event was not used.

pay the surcharge into a nominated numbered account either in Beirut or in Jordan. The account holder was not named and it was not known if it was an official Iraqi bank account or a personal one. We were simply told that we had to pay this amount when the lift was concluded. If a foreign company refused to pay it would be blacklisted.

Both Bula and Perenco managements were agreeable to the payment of the surcharge because they rightly understood that the way the sanctions were administered, even after oil-for-food was introduced, was not aimed at achieving objectives beneficial to the Iraqi people. They simply wanted sanctions lifted so that they could get on with their lives in peace. At any rate, that was the position of the Iraqis I knew.

The surcharge was not selective, it was universal, a point repeatedly made by the Iraqi authorities. No contract for an oil lift was awarded without the imposition of the surcharge. This fact was known to governments worldwide. At the end of 2001 the 661 Committee introduced a system of fixing the price of crude on a monthly basis, and did so in such a way that there was no wiggle room for offsetting the cost of the surcharge. However, it was not primarily this which convinced the regime to drop the surcharge.

There were around 10,000 participants involved in trading oil with Iraq between 2000 and 2002, and all of them were obliged to pay the surcharge. The income to the Iraqi government from this source came to about $200 million, while the income coming in from the illicit sales through Jordan, Turkey, Syria and the Gulf amounted to $2.2 billion. The press and trade publications regularly brought this fact to public knowledge. The Ministry of Oil openly established a pumping station in the north to load tankers bound for Turkey via the Kurdish enclave knowing that the UN-US-UK coalition would disregard this violation of the sanctions. It was the disparity between earnings from the surcharge on the one hand and illicit sales on the other, together with the evident turning of a blind eye to the latter by the coalition, which prompted the Saddam regime to put an end to the surcharge.

Despite my direct access to Saddam's Deputy Prime Minister, Tariq Aziz, as well as to most senior ministers, I never told them about my oil interest. Tariq Aziz eventually found out, and said he could have helped me if he'd known, but I didn't want to put him in a compromising position. I wished to keep my dealings with him entirely humanitarian, though as I have said, it was mixed with the pleasure of his company. It could well have complicated my relationship with him if he had also been my benefactor.

CHAPTER TEN

IN THE JUGGERNAUT'S PATH

9/11 and Iraq

On the morning of 11th September 2001 three civilian aircraft were deliberately crashed into the twin towers of the World Trade Centre in New York and the Pentagon building in Washington DC. A fourth hi-jacked aircraft crashed in a field in Pennsylvania. There were no survivors from any of the aircraft. The attacks killed 2,996 people, injured over 6,000 others, and caused at least $10 billion worth of damage to infrastructure and property. The US government maintained from the outset that Al-Qaeda, a Muslim fundamentalist organisation headed by Osama bin Laden, and based in Afghanistan, was primarily responsible, but, it was argued, others must have helped.

There are many aspects of 9/11 which lead one to doubt the official line, but let's leave that issue aside. However it happened, it was a terrible crime, though it should be remarked a relatively minor one compared with other examples of mass murder in recent history, some committed by the United States. Its significance was twofold. Firstly, like Pearl Harbour, it shattered the sense that America was immune to attack. But secondly, 9/11 was a very convenient green light to those who wished to change the political and economic geography of the Middle East. And what could be more desirable in that context than neutralising Iraq.

On 26th September 2001 Tony Benn recorded in his diary:

I had a message from an organisation called Friendship Across Frontiers saying they were expecting an American bombing attack on Baghdad this weekend. / Tam Dalyell rang with the same message, so I rang him back. He had rung Number 10 and said, 'I want to convey my anxiety about this to the Prime Minister. Will you give him the message?' 'Well, I may' a woman replied. Tam said he absolutely lost his temper, and he pulled his rank. He said, 'I'm the Father of the House.[1] If I tell you that I want something to go to the Prime Minister, I don't want that sort of reply. I want an absolute guarantee that it will.' So apparently she got frightened and capitulated. / It's now about twenty-five to twelve and I must go to bed.[2]

In the event either our informants were wrong, or there was a last-minute change of plan. But my visit in December was overshadowed by the US hype for an ominously named 'crusade' to eliminate terrorism. If Iraq could be implicated in the attacks on the US of 11th September 2001 this would provide the sought-for vindication for invasion. Such a line of thinking indicated how ignorant, or worse dishonest, the West was about Iraq, for its secular government was the least likely to give support to Al-Qaeda. Not surprisingly, therefore, Donald Rumsfeld, US Secretary of Defence, and his circle failed miserably in their attempt to link Iraq with Bin Laden or his organisation, and this despite the frenzied arguments of Ahmad Chalabi's umbrella opposition party, the Iraqi National Congress.

---

[1] Tam took over from Ted Heath as Father of the House following the general election in June 2001.
[2] Benn, A., *More Time for Politics: Diaries 2001-1007*, ed. Ruth Winstone, London, Arrow Books, 2008, p 10.

Weapons of Mass Destruction

The US consequently changed tactics and made the issue of Weapons of Mass Destruction (WMDs) a pretext for overthrowing the Saddam regime. Before the UNSCOM inspectors left Iraq in the autumn of 1998, Rolf Ekeus, who had stood down as Director the previous year, stated that they had destroyed most of Iraq's capabilities in this area, but the American government now maintained that since then the Iraqis had restocked.

The argument of the Bush administration that Iraq posed a threat to world peace was weak for the following reasons. Firstly, the Ba'athist regime had failed to use WMDs in 1991 when its capability was intact, primarily due to the stark awareness that Iraq's capabilities were dwarfed by the stockpiles of their adversaries, the US, the UK and the Zionist entity. It would therefore have been suicidal for Iraq to use WMDs. Secondly, Iraq's interest in acquiring WMDs was prompted by its wish to deter aggression by the Zionist entity, which had such weapons. It was these weapons which threatened the peace of the region. And thirdly Iraq was willing to collaborate with UN inspectors so long as the objective was to rid the whole region, not just Iraq, of WMDs. The regime was, however, opposed to a re-run of the UNSCOM experience, because its mandate had been unclear and was not given a definite time frame.[3]

But such reasonable considerations were far from the thinking of the US and UK hawks and their Iraqi opposition cheerleaders. What was needed, according to them, was a concerted effort to persuade all concerned that intervention in Iraq was necessary.

Douglas Feith had already proved an asset in this respect. Son of a member of Ze'ev Jabotinsky's Betar movement, which was closely associated with the Zionist terrorist organisation, Irgun, he had inherited some of his father's mindset, and saw Iraq as a dangerous

---

[3] These arguments were presented in a FAF briefing dated 6th January 2002.

threat to the Zionist entity. With Ahmad Chalabi, he was a major player in the efforts to bring about the 1998 Iraq Liberation Act, which made regime change in Iraq official US policy,

Feith, who was by 2001 Under Secretary of Defence for Policy in the Bush administration, set up the secretive Office of Strategic Influence, as part of the War on Terror. Its mission was the planting of biased news stories in the foreign media which were supposed to influence crucial policymakers, particularly in the Middle East, towards a more compliant attitude on US foreign policy. In this strategy, Ahmad Chalabi, with his US funding, was again particularly helpful. Aram Roston comments:

> Chalabi's contribution was to give the allegations [about Iraq's continuing possession of WMDs] flesh and muscle and specificity. The tidbits he provided were often quickly discredited by the intelligence officers, but they had tremendous impact on public opinion. His use of the press helped prepare the political background for war. The *New York Times*, CBS News's *60 Minutes*, PBS's *Frontline*, and *Vanity Fair* became his chosen outlets. The splash from his stories was immense. Saddam, the intelligence services knew, had no ties to the attacks of 9/11, but as Chalabi's friend Fouad Ajami wrote once to explain the war, 'These distinctions did not matter; the connection had been made in American opinion.'[4]

Much was made of Saddam's lack of cooperation with the UNSCOM weapons inspectors, and it was widely believed that the bombing operation, code-named Desert Fox, was a response to Saddam's expulsion of the inspectors. Little was done to dispel this justification. For example on 5th February 2003 Colin Powell,

---

[4] Roston, A., ibid, p xii.

Secretary of State urged the Security Council to act against Iraq giving in part the argument that 'Saddam Hussein forced out the last inspectors in 1998.'[5] However, in 2000 ex-UNSCOM Chair, Richard Butler, a man accused of undiplomatic language in his criticism of Saddam, told a different story about the withdrawal of the inspectors: 'I received a telephone call from US Ambassador [to the UN] Peter Burleigh inviting me for a private conversation at the US mission [...] Burleigh informed me that on instructions from Washington it would be "prudent to take measures to ensure the safety and security of UNSCOM staff presently in Iraq." ... I told him that I would act on this advice and remove my staff from Iraq.'[6]

Moreover, early in 1999 the UN admitted that 'UNSCOM had directly facilitated the creation of an intelligence collection system for the United States in violation of its mandate.' We were told that CIA, and perhaps MI6, agents had been planted in the UNSCOM teams, and a 'black box' was installed at UNSCOM's headquarters in Baghdad to eavesdrop on Saddam's presidential communications network.[7] Rolf Ekeus, Director of UNSCOM from 1991 to 1997, also confirmed in a Swedish newspaper in 2002 that he had tried to resist attempts by the US to use the commission to spy on the Iraqi regime. So it appears that Saddam was well-vindicated in his suspicion of the inspectors.

A similar disregard for truth and a willingness to pull the wool over people's eyes permeated both UNSCOM and the British government. In 1997-98 Scott Ritter, who at that time took an uncompromising view of Iraqi evasion, obtained the approval of his UNSCOM superiors to supply British intelligence with suitable information for their

---

[5] CNN.Com./U.S, 5th February 2003. See http://edition.cnn.com/2003/US/02/05/sprj.irq.powell.transcript.05/.
[6] Butler, R, *Saddam Defiant: The Threat of Weapons of Mass Destruction, and the Crisis of Global Security*, London, Weidenfeld & Nicholson, 2000, p 224.
[7] Fisk, R., *The Great War for Civilisation: The Conquest of the Middle East*. New York: Alfred A. Knopf, 2006. p. 724.

'Operation Mass Appeal.' Commenting later to reporters in the House of Commons, he revealed:

> I was approached by the British intelligence service ... to see if there was any information in the archives of UNSCOM that could be handed to the British, so that they could in turn work it over, determine its veracity, and then seek to plant it in media outlets around the world, in an effort to try to shape the public opinion of those countries, and then indirectly, through, for instance, a report showing up in the Polish press, shape public opinion in Great Britain and the United States.[8]

On 14th February 2003 Dr Hans Blix, Head of the United Nations Munitions, Verification and Inspection Commission (UNMOVIC),[9] presented his first report to the Security Council following the resumption of inspections in November 2002. This stated, among much else, that 'no evidence or plausible indication of the revival of a weapons of mass destruction programme in Iraq had been found.' Blix stated that the Iraqi authorities had become more cooperative and that access to sites, including some that had not previously been inspected, had been problem-free. He therefore urged the Security Council to allow the inspectors to continue their work.

So what did the hawks do? Early in 2002, anticipating that the resumption of weapons inspections by Hans Blix, which occurred in November of that year, would weaken the case for war, Deputy Defence Secretary Paul Wolfowitz charged the CIA with investigating Blix himself. According to one report, Wolfowitz 'hit the ceiling' because

---

[8] Scott Ritter, W., 'How the British Spy Agency MI6 Secretly Misled A Nation Into War With Iraq,' a half-hour video interview with transcript which can be viewed on the Democracy Now site at
http://www.democracynow.org/2003/12/30/scott_ritter_how_the_british_spy.
[9] In 1999 this body had replaced the United Nations Special Commission (UNSCOM) which was set up in 1991, just after the First Gulf War.

the outcome failed to provide sufficient ammunition to undermine Blix and, by association, the new UN weapons inspection program.[10] Blix's report of 14th February 2003 mentioned above was just the kind of thing he and other hawks feared.

The Iranian connection

For those not well-versed in Middle Eastern politics and Western meddling, one of the strangest elements in the build-up up to the Second Gulf War was the working alliance which now developed between Iran and the US. After all, Bush had described Iran as part of the 'axis of evil;' how could his government possibly have collaborated with Iran. But they did.

In the summer of 2002 Ahmad Chalabi managed to do just this through the hard-line Iranian-led Shia Iraqis of the Supreme Council for Islamic Revolution in Iraq (SCIRI). One of the main obstacles to an invasion of Iraq was thereby removed, that is possible resistance by Iraqi Shias, backed by Iran. Aram Roston describes how this was achieved:

> In the summer of 2002 Chalabi flew to Tehran saying he had a sincere message from the U.S. government. First Chalabi met with Iranian government officials to get their blessing for the merger of interests, and then Chalabi talked to SCIRI. The message was simple: the Americans were very serious about their war. They were going to topple Saddam. This time is was for real. Bush the son, the president, would not do what his father had and abandon the Shiites.

---

[10] Pincus, W., and Lynch, C, 'Wolfowitz Had CIA', *Washington Post*, 15th April 2002. See https://www.globalpolicy.org/component/content/article/168-general/34684.html.

Shortly after a meeting took place in Washington DC at which a deal was sealed.

> Out of the public eye, the bond between the Americans and the hard-right Shiites was strengthened in an expansive conference room in the Old Executive Office Building in August 2002. On the one side sat the Iraqis: Kurdish leaders and Ayad Allawi. With them was Ahmad Chalabi. And there as well was the odd man out, a bearded cleric dressed in a robe and turban. It was Ayatollah Abdul-Aziz al-Hakim, brother of SCIRI's leader. Across from the polite and ceremonious Iraqis sat Defence Secretary Donald Rumsfeld and the chairman of the Joint Chiefs of Staff, Air Force Gen. Richard Myers. / But the most dominant presence was a man who was not even in the room. On a giant wall monitor was the face of Vice-President Dick Cheney, joining the meeting via video conference from his home in Wyoming. […] The man Cheney greeted from SCIRI was completely loyal to the government of Iran and was there with Tehran's full approval.[11]

Shifting justifications

In the last months leading up to the invasion of Iraq, Bush and Blair kept on shifting their justifications for military intervention, as if trying to avoid presenting too easy a target to their critics. These ranged from human rights issues and regime change through to democratisation, stabilisation of the region and, of course, removing Saddam's supposed weapons of mass destruction. I believe the undisclosed reasons, were the West's determination to regain control of Iraq's oil and to protect the Zionist entity.

---

[11] Roston, A., op cit pp 222-24.

In the eyes of the US, Iraq's use of petrodollars, both to develop the infrastructure of the country, including health services and education, and to build up agriculture and heavy industry using indigenous technology, constituted a threat to their aim of full spectrum dominance. If such progress were allowed to continue, Western control of the economy would be further loosened, with serious implications for the West in the areas of finance, employment and geopolitics. China and Russia could be expected to benefit from a fully independent Iraq, to the disadvantage of the West, and therefore nothing short of intellectual cleansing and the imposition of a dysfunctional government, on the model of Saudi Arabia, would serve Western interests.

Some Arab leaders wanted Saddam to stand down but their motives were far from humanitarian. They realised that Saddam's Ba'athist regime had set an example of resistance and resilience which might well be infectious and expose them to domestic pressure. Witnessing the remarkable achievements of the Iraqi people, in both peace and adversity, their own people might well conclude that Saddam's Iraq was a beacon for them to follow. There was widespread admiration for a man who dared to cock a snoop at the Americans, but if Arab puppet regimes responded to this pressure, US protection might be put at risk. It would be much easier if Saddam simply stood aside, which he might be inclined to do in order to save his skin. But they underestimated the man.

The 'Dodgy Dossier'

On 3rd February 2003 a British intelligence dossier was released to the press which, in combination with another dossier published the previous September, became infamous as the 'dodgy dossier.' This made a number of unsourced claims about Iraq's military capability which in retrospect proved to be false. Furthermore, a Channel 4 programme broadcast on 6th February 2003 proved conclusively that much of the dossier had been lifted from an article, 'Iraq: Its Infrastructure of Concealment, Deception and Intimidation,' by a graduate student in California, Ibrahim al-Marashi.[12]

On 10th February the Speaker of the House of Commons, Michael Martin, was requested to allow an emergency debate on the dossier, and refused. Tam stood up and repeatedly accused Blair of deception, while the Speaker called upon him ten times to sit down. Eventually he withdrew from the chamber, commenting outside to reporters: 'I'm not blaming the Speaker. [...] It is the prime minister's fault for not either coming himself or sending a minister to explain what is an absolute lie to parliament and the people.'[13]

Heading the list of errors in the dossier was the assertion that Iraq possessed biological weapons of mass destruction, and that these could be deployed within 45 minutes of an order to do so. The impression was given, and wasn't denied, that British forces, if not Britain itself, would be in the firing line. In an article in *The Guardian* after the war Robin Cook revealed that in February 2003 John Scarlett, Chair of the Cabinet Office Joint Intelligence Committee, had briefed him that the weapons in question could only be used on the battlefield and had, in any case, been dismantled and dispersed to avoid detection by inspectors. Re-assembling and deploying them would be a difficult procedure under attack. Cook described the whole affair as 'the most extraordinary failure in the history of British intelligence.'[14] Was it not rather the most extraordinary success in political manipulation?

---

[12] Dr Ibrahim al-Marashi is now an assistant professor at California State University, San Marcos. His ethnic origin is not indicated in the online sources consulted, but since his main area of interest appears to be Iraq, it seems likely he is of Iraqi, or possibly Iranian, descent.
[13] Tempest, M., 'Father of the house given marching orders,' *The Guardian*, 10th February 2003. See
https://www.theguardian.com/politics/2003/feb/10/houseofcommons.uk.
[14] Cook, R., 'Blair and Scarlett told me Iraq had no usable weapons,' *The Guardian*, 12th July 2004. See https://www.theguardian.com/politics/2004/jul/12/iraq.iraq.

Also included in the dossier was the claim that Saddam had attempted to buy 'significant quantities of uranium from Africa,' and President Bush repeated this in his State of the Union address in January 2003, quoting British intelligence. The country concerned was Niger, to which the CIA had sent a former ambassador, Joseph Wilson, in February 2002 to investigate such a possibility. He concluded shortly after, and long before the September dossier was published, that it would be very difficult for Niger to export uranium to Iraq because of the international ownership of the two mining companies involved, and also because of international and local inspection regimes.

After the war Wilson wrote a letter to the *New York Times* posing the question: 'Did the Bush administration manipulate intelligence about Saddam Hussein's weapons programs to justify an invasion of Iraq?' He concluded that it had indeed done so, citing the Niger uranium story as evidence.[15] The sequel was quite shocking. A week later the mercurial Robert Novak, otherwise known as 'the Prince of Darkness,' wrote a reply in the *Washington Post* based on information supplied him by 'two senior administration officials,' one of whom turned out to be no less a figure than Richard Armitage, the Deputy Secretary of State. In it Novak named Wilson's wife, Valerie Plame, as a CIA operative specialising in weapons of mass destruction, and said it was she who had suggested sending her husband to Niger.[16] This blew her cover, illegal under US law, and had very serious consequences for the couple and indeed the country. The ensuing investigation resulted in no charges relating to the leak itself, but Lewis 'Scooter' Libby, Chief of Staff to Vice-President Dick Cheney, was convicted of lying to the investigators in matters relating to Plame. Before he saw the inside of a

---

[15] Wilson, J., 'What I didn't find in Africa,' *New York Times*, 6th July 2003, online at http://www.nytimes.com/2003/07/06/opinion/what-i-didn-t-find-in-africa.html.

[16] Novak, R., 'Mission to Niger,' *Washington Post*, 14th July 2003, online at http://www.washingtonpost.com/wp-dyn/content/article/2005/10/20/AR2005102000874.html.

prison, however, that part of his sentence was commuted by President Bush.[17]

The following July it emerged that Dr David Kelly, a biological weapons expert employed by the Ministry of Defence, was the source of a quote made by BBC reporter Andrew Gilligan which indicated that the dossier 'sexed up' the intelligence evidence. In 2002 Kelly had been working for the Defence Intelligence Staff at the time the Joint Intelligence Committee was compiling the September dossier on the supposed weapons of mass destruction possessed by Iraq. Because he had previously worked as a weapons inspector with UNSCOM he was asked to proof-read sections of the draft about the history of inspections and became increasingly concerned about the way the inspectors' reports were being manipulated to make the case for war. Following his exposure as Gilligan's source, Kelly was aggressively interrogated for breach of confidentiality, and was found dead two days later. I have little doubt that Norman Baker, who examined the case in depth, is right in his suspicion that Kelly was murdered, and that there was at least collusion at the highest level in facilitating his demise.[18]

Lord Goldsmith's evolving advice

A major problem which faced the warmongers, Bush and Blair, was the unwillingness of other members of the Security Council to acquiesce in a resolution authorising war against Iraq. On 30th January 2003 the Attorney General, Lord Goldsmith, wrote a memo to Tony Blair indicating that existing UN resolutions were insufficient for this purpose. On 7th March he wrote another memo which left wiggle-room for considering that existing resolutions were, on the contrary, adequate, so long as there was 'hard evidence of non-compliance and non-cooperation' by the Iraqi regime. By 17th March, when he wrote

---

[17] Baker, N., *The Strange Death of David Kelly*, Methuen, York, 2007, pp 112-14.
[18] Ibid p 349.

a final memo on the subject, Goldsmith stated baldly that the use of force in Iraq was lawful.

This was not the opinion of Elizabeth Wilmshurst, Deputy Legal Advisor at the Foreign and Commonwealth Office, who just three days after Goldsmith's last memo resigned her post, saying in her resignation letter that 'the process that was followed in this case was lamentable.'[19] And in November 2008 Lord Bingham of Cornhill, one-time Lord Chief Justice and Senior Law Lord, gave his opinion that Goldsmith had produced 'no hard evidence' which justified the use of force. In his view the invasion was 'a serious violation of international law and of the rule of law.'[20]

There has been much speculation about why the Attorney General changed his mind so dramatically and over such a short period of time, but clearly he came under pressure to do so. No doubt he wished to please his patron, the Prime Minister, but it seems probable to me that Zionist sympathies also played a role. There is no doubt that the Zionists were in favour of regime change in Baghdad, and that Lord Levy took this view. Much later, in June 2015 Goldsmith attended an 'Iran Freedom Rally' in Paris at which he warned those present about the dangers of extremism and Islamic fundamentalism, and advocated regime change in that country as well, if necessary by military means. For years Zionists had been playing the same tune.[21]

In a particularly hard-hitting submission to the Chilcot Inquiry, Philippe Sands QC said of the final legal advice given by the Attorney General: 'I have been unable to find support in any academic article in an established United Kingdom legal journal for the view on which the previous British government relied.' Sands went on to point out that a

---

[19] BBC News (24th March 2005). 'Wilmshurst resignation letter' (http://news.bbc.co.uk/1/hi/uk_politics/4377605.stm).
[20] BBC News (18 November 2008). 'Iraq war "violated rule of law"' (http://news.bbc.co.uk/1/hi/uk_politics/7734712.stm).
[21] You can listen to his five-minute speech at https://www.youtube.com/watch?v=RkM_usGKBMs.

Dutch Inquiry had recently concluded 'unanimously and without ambiguity – that the war was not justified under international law.'[22]

The Atlantic Summit

On 16th March 2003 the US, UK, Spain and Portugal held a one-day 'Atlantic Summit' in the Azores, mirroring to a degree the Atlantic Conference in Placenta Bay, Newfoundland, between Franklin D Roosevelt and Winston Churchill on 14th August 1941. Although the US was not at the time of the latter at war with Germany, the two leaders defined the goals they would pursue after the hostilities had been concluded. While the stated objective of the Atlantic Summit was to explore the possibility of a UN resolution on Iraq, in reality it was more about what they wished the world to believe about their intentions. On its conclusion, the participants, US President George Bush, British Prime Minister Tony Blair, Spanish Prime Minister Jose Maria Aznar and Portugal's Prime Minister Jose Durao Barroso, issued a statement entitled: 'A Vision for Iraq and the Iraqi People.' It was full of fine sounding aspirations, many of which now ring distinctly hollow. Envisaging that military action against Iraq was a certainty, it undertook 'a solemn obligation to help the Iraqi people build a new Iraq at peace with itself and its neighbours.'

The statement referred to Iraq's 'rich mix of Sunni and Shiite Arabs, Kurds, Turkomen, Assyrians, Chaldeans, and all others – who should enjoy freedom, prosperity, and equality in a united country.' In reality it was about to set some of those groups at each other's throats and thereby to tear the country apart. It spoke of the damage inflicted by Saddam's regime to the natural resources of Iraq. What damage there

---

[22] Sands, P., letter to Sir John Chilcot dated 10th September 2010. See https://www.scribd.com/document/38686920/Philippe-Sands-Chilcot-inquiry-submissions. The whole document is a stunning indictment of the government's policy and procedure at that time.

was came from US and UK bombing and the sanctions regime which prevented spare parts from being delivered. It said 'all Iraqis should share the wealth generated by their national economy.' Wasn't this precisely what they disliked about Saddam's regime, that he had used petrodollars to fund a welfare state? How was privatisation going to improve matters?

The fine-sounding phrases rolled on: 'We will fight terrorism in all its forms. Iraq must never again be a haven for terrorists of any kind.' If they are referring to the firing of scud missiles at the Zionist entity, then that illegal entity should also be described as terrorist for its much deadlier attacks. The reality is that terrorism, as normally defined, came to Iraq as a result of the coalition intervention. There was none to speak of before it. And lastly, the statement reassuringly talked of a 'temporary' military presence. Is a period of eight years, or more correctly fifteen years, since there are still US forces in Iraq, temporary? And this despite the fact that there were no WMDs.[23]

The words of the Brazilian lyricist and novelist, Paulo Coelho, come to mind:

> Thank you, great leader George W. Bush. [...]
>
> Thank you for revealing to the world the gulf that exists between the decisions made by those in power and the wishes of the people. Thank you for making it clear that neither José María Aznar nor Tony Blair give the slightest weight to or show the slightest respect for the votes they received. Aznar is perfectly capable of ignoring the fact that 90% of Spaniards are against the war, and Blair is unmoved by the largest public demonstration to take place in England in the last thirty years.
>
> Thank you for making it necessary for Tony Blair to go to the British parliament with a fabricated dossier written by a

---

[23] Archive of the US Department of State. See https://2001-2009.state.gov/p/eur/rls/rm/2003/18761.htm.

student ten years ago, and present this as 'damning evidence collected by the British Secret Service'.

Thank you for allowing Colin Powell to make a complete fool of himself by showing the UN Security Council photos which, one week later, were publicly challenged by Hans Blix, the chief weapons inspector in Iraq. [...]

Thank you for not listening to us and not taking us seriously, but know that we are listening to you and that we will not forget your words.

Thank you, great leader George W. Bush.

Thank you very much.[24]

---

[24] Coelo, P., 'Thank You, President Bush,' posted on 11th March 2003 at https://www.opendemocracy.net/conflict-iraqwarquestions/article_1033.jsp.

CHAPTER ELEVEN

THE EXTRA MILE FOR PEACE

It was clear to me that while the American and British governments, together with the exile Iraqi opposition, were rubbing their hands in glee at the prospect of war, the Iraqi government was prepared to do almost anything short of complete capitulation to their enemies' demands, to prevent it. For those of us who believed that war would be a disaster, there seemed, therefore, to be only one option, and that was to support the efforts of the Ba'athist regime. This didn't mean we were uncritical of Saddam, only that we were focussed on a single issue, supporting his willingness to go the extra mile for peace.

Stop the War Coalition

The Stop the War Coalition was established on 21st September 2001 in the wake of the 9/11 attacks ten days earlier. Its objective was to oppose the so-called 'War on Terror.' I attended the inaugural meeting held in the Friends House in Euston, together with around 2000 others, among them such high-profile figures as Tony Benn, Tam Dalyell, George Galloway, Jeremy Corbyn, Tariq Ali and Harold Pinter. Lindsey German, at that time a member of the Socialist Workers Party, chaired the meeting, and became thereafter the Convenor of the Coalition. A Steering Committee was elected with a cross-section of activists on the left, including representatives of Labour Left Briefing and the Communist Party of Britain. Tony Benn was elected

President, a position he held until his death in 2014, and Tam, whom I had nominated for President, became a (or the) Vice-President.[1]

I was a founding member and served on its Steering Committee for a number of years. Friendship Across Frontiers became one of the coalition's many affiliated peace groups, among which were CND and the Muslim Association of Britain. Stop the War's aims, as described in its founding statement, were 'to encourage and mobilise the largest possible movement against the war, [...] to draw together everyone who wants to stop this madness, and to present the anti-war arguments which are squeezed out of the media.'

Acting as a go-between

My visits to Iraq became more frequent after 9/11 and I acted as an unofficial go-between conveying useful information to the governments on each side. My ambitious aim was to increase understanding and reduce tension. In my discussions with diplomats, my many political contacts in Britain, and, as I will relate, my conversations with Julian Coulter, the First Secretary at the British Embassy in Amman, I expressed my view that Iraq did not have any weapons of mass destruction in the vain hope that this would stop a military intervention. Of course I couldn't prove what I said, but my regular contact with senior Iraqi officials and politicians, many of whom I trusted, counted for something, and I was eventually vindicated in my opinion.

There were others who played a role as unofficial go-betweens. David Samuels comments that 'Iraq certainly tried to use other back channels to try to reach US officials, including the Lebanese-American

---

[1] I've not been able to verify whether Tam was sole VP or shared this position with others, nor how long he served in this position. Others who served as VPs were Tariq Ali, Louise Christian, George Galloway, Caroline Lucas, Alice Mahon, Kamal Majid, Keith Sonnet and Walter Wolfgang.

businessman, Imad Hage, who conveyed messages to Richard Perle in the run-up to the war.'[2] I'll come to Susan Lindauer, who is the focus of Samuels's article, later, and I've already mentioned that Jany le Pen, may have had a similar role. It wasn't, however, only the Iraqis who sought such channels. Both sides stood to benefit from unofficial contacts.

Curious manoeuvres were employed to extract information from me surreptiously. It was on my way back to Britain from one of my visits to Iraq around 2002 that I met Julian Coulter in Amman. This was at the request of Dr Thamir Ogali, ex-Director General of the Ministry of Oil, and ostensibly concerned his application for a UK visa. In reality the First Secretary was interested in interrogating me and had indicated to Ogali that I should be asked to call in at the British embassy in Amman in connection with his visa application. The implication was that without my help, Dr Ogali might not be issued the visa, and I wasn't keen to antagonise someone with the kind of connections Ogali undoubtedly had.

This ruse became transparent once I realised that the First Secretary was only interested in whether I had met Saddam, which of course I denied. For my part, I took the opportunity to inform him of the dire situation which had arisen in Iraq by that time and also to emphasise that I did not believe Iraq had weapons of mass destruction. This was, however, of no interest to him, and he continued to pursue a line of inquiry aimed at gathering intelligence about the President. As in other situations where I was cross-questioned in this way, I had no option but to stonewall.

---

[2] Samuels, D., 'Susan Lindauer's Mission to Baghdad,' *New York Times Magazine*, 29th August 2004. See http://www.nytimes.com/2004/08/29/magazine/susan-lindauer-s-mission-to-baghdad.html.

My last trip to Iraq

My very last visit to my homeland, which I'll probably never see again, was in mid-January 2003, and was in response to the request of five Labour MPs who were opposed to the war. These were Tony Benn, Alan Simpson, Jeremy Corbyn, Alice Mahon and Tam Dalyell. My task was twofold. Firstly I was to sound out my contacts and give my opinion about whether or not the regime possessed WMDs. And secondly I was to make a similar assessment about whether, or for how long, Iraq would be able to withstand an invasion. I met the Deputy Prime Minister, Tariq Aziz, and Director of Iraqi Intelligence, General Aboush, both of whom told me that there were no WMDs, and that any capability they had had was destroyed in the early nineties. Other senior Iraqi officials gave me the same account.

My gut instinct told me this was the truth. But by then Iraq was preparing for the worst. In fact they had been expecting an attack ever since 9/11 and had assumed that the build-up to attack Afghanistan was in reality directed at Iraq. Even though they were, in a sense, wrong, because Afghanistan *was* attacked, Alan Simpson and Alice Mahon assured me that in the longer term the real target of the build-up was indeed Iraq and I relayed this information to the Iraqi government.

Tariq Aziz added that if there were an attack, those responsible would regret it; Baghdad would become the United States' Stalingrad. I was taken to see many weapons caches in the rural areas surrounding Baghdad, and it seemed that the army aimed to make a stand in the capital and its immediate vicinity. In the event such confidence in their military capability proved naïve, or was simply bluster, but in the longer term the West has paid a high price for its interventions across the region. The main beneficiary, at least in the short term, has been the Zionist entity.

The Iraqi government was, however, at that stage prepared to go the extra mile for peace. I was asked to convey a message to my contacts in the British government that the Iraqis would be willing to send high-level representatives to a meeting with Lord Levy, Tony Blair's Middle East advisor, in any capital in Europe. Considering Levy's strong support for Zionism, an ideology considered a mortal danger to both the Palestinians and Iraq, this was a remarkable offer.

But then, just before my departure for Britain via Amman I was hastily told by a senior Iraqi contact that this offer had now been withdrawn, and I was not to mention it to any of my political contacts. My reading of what had happened was that a new channel of communication had opened up with the US government via Susan Lindauer, an American woman working for the UN where she had close links with the Iraqi mission in New York. Her second cousin, Andrew Card, was White House Chief of Staff under George W Bush, and she unsuccessfully attempted to use this connection to lobby the President in the hope of preventing an attack on Iraq.

In the immediate run-up to the war it must have seemed to the Iraqi leadership that Lindauer, with her CIA connections, offered greater possibilities than a rather desperate attempt to win over Lord Levy. Once the war was over, however, she was a dangerously well-informed critic of US policy. In 2004 she was arrested by the FBI and indicted for 'acting as an unregistered agent of a foreign government,' and, which she denied, receiving $10,000 from Saddam's government.[3] The following year she was imprisoned for 'psychological evaluation,' and was eventually released on the grounds of a 'lengthy delusional history.' I ask myself who was really deluded!

Human shields

FAF collaborated with an organisation called Truth, Justice and Peace, established by Ken O'Keefe, an ex-US marine, ex-US citizen

---

[3] Samuels, D., op cit.

and 'lawfully declared world citizen'[4] in sending 'human shields' to Iraq. Ken described the rationale of this strategy thus:

> In 2002 I initiated the TJP Human Shield Action to Iraq because I knew that the invasion of Iraq had been planned well in advance, that it was part of a 'Full Spectrum Dominance' agenda as laid out by the Project For A New American Century.[5]
>
> I knew that protests had no chance of stopping the invasion, and […] I argued that the only viable way to stop the invasion was to conduct a mass migration to Iraq. A migration in which people from around the world, especially western citizens, would position themselves at sites in Iraq that are supposed to be protected by international law, but which are routinely bombed when it is only Iraqi, Palestinian, generally non-white, western lives who will be killed. I felt 10,000 such people could stop the invasion, or at the very least, expose the invasion for what it was from the start, an act of international aggression, a war crime and a crime against humanity.
>
> When our two double-decker buses travelled from London to Baghdad through Turkey, it was ever clear that the people of Turkey also could sense the power of this act, and they were the biggest participants in it.[6]

FAF's contribution was moral and financial. My dealings were largely with Sue Darling, an ex-diplomat who had resigned from the service in protest at Margaret Thatcher's foreign policy. Those volunteering for these missions often lacked the funds required and so where necessary FAF provided the wherewithal. I was at City Hall, near

---

[4] See Ken's website: https://kenokeefe.wordpress.com/about/.
[5] The correct wording is 'Project for the New American Century.'
[6] See https://kenokeefe.wordpress.com/?s=human+shield.

Tower Bridge, on 25th January to see the buses of the first wave depart on the two-week overland journey to Iraq. Other volunteers departed by air, and on 21st February I was at Heathrow to see off the third wave. There was extensive press coverage of all the 'waves,' and this helped to raise their profile. Unfortunately, however, we didn't get the ten thousand volunteers we'd hoped for, but rather around a hundred, and this was insufficient to make the US/UK alliance think again. As Ken said, it was a missed opportunity.

Tony Benn's trip to Baghdad

Immediately after attending the send-off of the first wave, I went to see Tony Benn at his request to discuss his planned trip to Iraq where he was to meet with Saddam with the objective of averting war. We spent an hour discussing the type of questions he might put to the President, and I explained to him the logistics of the journey. He was concerned about the visit because between the invasion of Kuwait and the beginning of Operation Desert Storm he had flown to Baghdad where he had had a meeting with Saddam with the aim of procuring the release of 500 human shield hostages who had been captured by Iraqi forces. He had assured the President that Iraq would not be attacked so long as he released the UK and US civilians. As it turned out he *did* release the hostages, but the US and its allies nevertheless launched a major attack on Iraq.

Tony therefore insisted that he should be accompanied on his visit to Baghdad. Reluctantly I agreed to join him in order to ensure the success of his visit, and he welcomed this idea. Immediately after our meeting I called Tariq Aziz's office and requested that he approach Saddam to obtain his agreement. I said that he should emphasise the importance of Benn's proposed visit, as I knew that the President had not given interviews throughout the years of sanctions, and might well refuse. But despite what had happened in the past, he trusted Tony and agreed to this last-ditch attempt to avert war. The next day Tony called me to say that Tariq Aziz had undertaken to take care of his arrangements in the country, and eventually someone from George Galloway's office volunteered to accompany him.[7] I confess I was relieved, as I wasn't in the mood for yet another trip across the desert. I did, however, write to my friend, Sabah, in Baghdad asking him to offer whatever assistance might be needed.

Tony, who was a vegetarian, records another aspect of our discussion in his diary:

> *Saturday 25 January*: In the afternoon, Riad al-Tahir came to see me to talk about the trip. He said that you've got to be careful, you've got to take your own water, you can't eat vegetables because they're never washed, and if they are, it's in impure water; it's difficult to be a vegetarian because everybody in Iraq eats meat, got to be careful with the cheese, and so in effect. I decided to take my own food for a week. Bananas I can buy there, I presume, but I'll take bread and butter, cheese, figs, and powdered milk and teabags and my little boilette water heater. It'll be a camping trip really, but I don't want to get ill.[8]

Tony's interview of Saddam was broadcast by Channel 4 News on 4th February 2003, the day after the publication of the 'dodgy dossier,' and transcripts appeared in the press. Incidentally, the Saudi-financed newspaper, *Al-Sharq Al-Awsat*, later alleged that I benefitted financially from the President's TV interview, though I didn't receive a single penny for my part in arranging it. When confronted with the facts, the newspaper editors agreed that they had been mistaken. Undoubtedly

---

[7] George originally volunteered himself.
[8] Benn, A., *The Benn Diaries: The Definitive Collection*, ed. Ruth Winstone, London, Hutchinson, 2017, p 563. The complete text of Tony's interview of Saddam Hussein appears at Appendix Three.

someone else *did* benefit financially, and I have an idea who it was, but it certainly wasn't me.

Protest marches across the globe

On February 15th 2003 Stop the War, with its affiliated organisations, CND and the Muslim Association of Britain, organised the largest demonstration in British history with the aim of preventing the outbreak of hostilities. Among the marchers, estimated at upwards of a million, were the Algerian revolutionary and ex-President, Ahmad Bin Bella, US politician, the Rev Jesse Jackson, Nicaraguan actress and human rights advocate, Bianca Jagger, British MPs Charles Kennedy (leader of Lib Dems), Michael Foot (ex-leader of the Labour Party), Tony Benn (ex-Chairman of the Labour Party, ex-Secretary of State for Industry, and ex-Secretary of State for Energy), Mo Mowlam (ex-Minister for Northern Ireland), Alice Mahon, Diane Abbott, George Galloway and Jeremy Corbyn,. Trade Unions leaders were also well represented.

The march started from the Embankment at midday and those at the front began to arrive at Hyde Park an hour-and-a-half later. Speakers at the rally included the Mayor of London, Ken Livingstone, the playwright, Harold Pinter, George Galloway, Tony Benn, Bianca Jagger, Charles Kennedy and myself. At 4.30 Ms Dynamite sang a song and then the huge crowds began to disperse. A few Iraqi families had attended, but there was no official representative. Meanwhile Tam attended a 50,000-strong rally in Glasgow, and across the globe an estimated 36 million people took part in protests in up to sixty countries over that weekend.[9] A rally of three million people in Rome is listed in the Guinness Book of Records as the largest ever anti-war rally.

---

[9] Callinicos, A., 'Anti-war protests do make a difference,' *Socialist Worker*, 19th March 2005. See https://socialistworker.co.uk/art/5932/Anti-war%20protests%20do%20make%20a%20difference.

The invasion of Iraq was strongly opposed by some long-standing US allies, including the governments of France, Germany and New Zealand, all of these arguing that there was no evidence of WMDs in Iraq and that an invasion could not be justified in terms of the UNMOVIC report. Even in the US a CBS[10] poll found that 63% of Americans wanted Bush to find a diplomatic solution, and 62% believed the threat of terrorism directed against the US would increase if Iraq were invaded.

Reaching out to the opposition

It was clear to me that I needed to engage with those who didn't share my views, and an opportunity arose shortly before the outbreak of hostilities when I was interviewed by the BBC, together with Hamid al-Bayati of SCIRI and later Iraqi ambassador at the UN, and the future (2006-10) Oil Minister, Hussain Shahristani. However, these two opponents of Saddam refused to engage with me in any way over the future of our country. Both failed to see that just because I didn't agree with them we weren't obliged to be enemies. Whether or not the sanctions had served the interests of the Iraqi people was now of no consequence, and so it should have been possible to put that on one side. But unfortunately it seems to be a common human characteristic to become fixed in a tribal attitude of 'them and us'.

What if?

The report on my discussions with Iraqi officials during my January trip had been circulated in the House of Commons through Tam Dalyell. I believe he presented it personally to the late Robin Cook, then Foreign Secretary, and that this may have played a small part, at

---

[10] Originally an acronym for Columbia Broadcasting System, but now used as the title of this American broadcasting organisation.

least as an excuse, in his decision to resign. 'I can't accept collective responsibility for the decision to commit Britain now to military action in Iraq without international agreement or domestic support,' he said. 'The reality is that Britain is being asked to embark on a war without agreement in any of the international bodies of which we are a leading partner—not NATO, not the European Union and, now, not the Security Council.'[11] Andrew Marr, regarded Cook's performance as 'without doubt one of the most effective, brilliant resignation speeches in modern British politics.'[12]

The UK government was marching to war on a lie as Iraq did not have weapons of mass destruction, and there was no UN Security Council resolution authorising military action. Clare Short, Secretary of State for Overseas Development, was aware of the report but she wavered and unfortunately did not resign like Robin Cook. However, even Cook's decision came too late, as Tam comments.

> Robin Cook's resignation speech in March 2003 earned him cheers and plaudits – it will be a remembered parliamentary event. But if he and Clare Short, who was also later to leave the government, [had] joined those of us who, on a technical motion, *de facto* had voted against war a month earlier (as we begged them to do), I have no doubt that 50 more Labour MPs would have voted against war and Blair would not have been able to forge ahead. I am afraid, *de mortuis nil nisi bonum*,[13] that Cook, had he not become Blair's creature on sufferance due to events in his private life,[14] would have by

---

[11] Hansard, 17th March 2003. See https://publications.parliament.uk/pa/cm200203/cmhansrd/vo030317/debtext/30317-33.htm#30317-33_spnew0.

[12] BBC News, 18th March 2003. See http://news.bbc.co.uk/1/hi/uk_politics/2859431.stm.

[13] Speak nothing but good of the dead.

[14] Cook had had an affair with one of his staff some years earlier and when this was revealed he divorced his first wife.

2002 become leader of the Labour Party. He resigned when he did because he foresaw that he was about to be sacked and decided to leave the government in spectacular fashion on a high moral tone. I could not quite forget that, when I asked to see him in Livingston, once part of my constituency, about Iraq after my return from Baghdad in 1998, he curtly responded that I could make an appointment with a junior minister in London, as he did not have time to give me that 10 minutes for which I asked during the long summer recess.[15]

What if Robin Cook had not dithered? What if those fifty other Labour MPs had voted against war? And what if Tony Blair had been forced to back down on his support of the US policy? Tam may well have found the answer to these questions:

The real tragedy of the British government's co-operation in attacking Iraq was brought home to me when, in 2004, on a visit to the Truman Library at Independence, Missouri, I was told, 'When we heard that the British Labour Prime Minister – a Labour Prime Minister – was enthusiastic for military action, we thought that the Bush administration must have a good case.' They doubted – and so did many others – whether even Bush would actually have embarked on the Second Gulf War if America had been alone.[16]

FAF vindicated

After the war, which I'll come to in the next chapter, the Pentagon and the CIA established the Iraq Survey Group, which was tasked with searching for the alleged WMDs. The Duelfer Report, released on 30th

---
[15] Ibid, p. 261-63.
[16] Ibid, p. 263.

September 2004, concluded that Saddam had ended Iraq's nuclear programme and destroyed its chemical weapons stockpile in 1991, and had terminated its biological weapons programme in 1995. So what FAF had maintained, based on what I had picked up in Iraq, proved to be correct. There were effectively no WMDs in Iraq after 1995. The US and UK invaded my homeland in 2003 on the basis of a lie.

1. Friends House, Euston, where the Stop the War Coalition was founded shortly after 9/11

2. Tony Benn

3. Douglas Feith

4. Tony Blair

5. Blair meets Bush at the White House in 2004

6. Dick Cheney

7. Protest march against the Iraq war, 15th February 2003

8. A bomber's-eye-view of Baghdad

9. Paul Bremer with members of the Iraqi Governing Council in December 2003: (left to right) Mowaffak al-Rubaie, Paul Bremer, Ahmad Chalabi, Adnan Pachachi and Adil Abdul-Mahdi

CHAPTER TWELVE

BACK UNDER THE YOKE

The Second Gulf War

On 18th March Tam invited me to observe the crucial House of Commons debate and the subsequent vote from the Distinguished Strangers' Gallery. I anticipated that the government would be defeated as the opposition was strong, particularly among the Liberal Democrats. Many MPs were determined to prevent Tony Blair pursuing his own criminal agenda of attacking a sovereign state. But alas he won and from then on war became inevitable. It was a very sad day for me, my family and my friends. We were anxious about what would become of Iraq, especially as the people had already suffered so much and struggled for so long just to achieve a degree of normality and to live in peace with the rest of the world.

I don't want to dwell too much on the war. Many of our supporters assumed during the first days of conflict that Iraq would resist, but militarily it was no match for the numerically and logistically superior US and British forces. It appears that in acknowledgement of this reality, orders were given by many commanders in the field not to fire on the invading forces. Like everyone else I watched the unfolding tragedy compulsively on television, but unlike most others, I remember it all as if it were yesterday. It was my country which was being systematically destroyed, and it was shameful to witness Iraq's powerlessness in the face of such an onslaught.

One of the most useful weapons of politicians when they face censure for their actions is people's short memory; and memory is especially short where national pride is at stake. Most of us have more of that than we think, and seek to divert attention away from our own national misdeeds. It helps the British, for example, not to remember their illegal actions in Iraq, both recent and historical, by huffing and puffing about Putin's actions in Ukraine. But to counteract this tendency to forget, let's just recall the salient points of the 2003 war.

'Operation Iraqi Freedom,' was to have begun by 'decapitating,' that is assassinating by bombing, the top 55 officials in the regime. However, when intelligence indicated that Saddam was at the Dora Farms area on the outskirts of Baghdad visiting his sons Uday and Qusay, this plan was abandoned in favour of a massive attack on the farms launched on 19th March 2003. This killed one civilian and injured fourteen others, including a child, but Saddam and his sons were not there.

The invasion was led by the US, supported by troops from the UK, Poland and a number of other states and groups, including rebel Kurdish Peshmerga fighters, and began in earnest on 20th with an air strike on the Presidential Palace and other government buildings in Baghdad. The land invasion across the Kuwaiti border began the day after that, and while special forces occupied my home town of Basrah and the neighbouring oilfields, the main invasion moved north. Devastating air strikes soon knocked out the Iraqi command and control systems, undermining the possibility of coordinated resistance. Nasiriyah fell on 24th March. A second front was opened on 26th March when airborne troops joined up with Kurdish rebels near Kirkuk. On 9th April Baghdad, on 10th April Kirkuk and on 15th April Tikrit all fell, after which Saddam and other members of the regime went into hiding.

On 11th April we learnt that a pack of cards had been issued to troops with the names and pictures of 52 officials who were wanted by the invaders, with Saddam as the ace of spades and Tariq Aziz as the eight of spades. Whatever faults the regime may have had, this way of hunting down its adherents, many of whom I knew personally, as if it were just a game, was particularly shocking to me. To rub salt into the wound, Hoshyar Zebari, a Kurd who became the Minister of Foreign Affairs shortly thereafter, and whose London home was Crockford's Casino, rang me suggesting I go and celebrate with him. He was getting in the champagne.

It is estimated that 30,000 Iraqi combatants and over 7000 civilians died, while the coalition forces lost 196. The coalition figure is probably accurate, that for Iraq should be treated with great scepticism, for the coalition wasn't interested in counting, and in the devastation of war the Iraqi authorities were in no position to do so. On 1st May President George W Bush posed for photographs on board the aircraft carrier USS Abraham Lincoln as it lay safely out of harm's way off the coast at San Diego. This ship had just returned from the Gulf and Bush chose the occasion to announce the end of major combat operations in the Iraq War. Behind him was a large sign reading 'Mission Accomplished.'

Establishing the occupation

In April, 2003, immediately following the completion of the ground offensive, a military occupation was established. On 22nd May the Security Council passed Resolution 1483 which lifted trade sanctions and set a six-month timetable for the winding up of the oil-for-food programme. The resolution assumed that there still were WMDs to discover and destroy, while proclaiming the right of Iraqi self-determination and control of its own natural resources. A Coalition Provisional Authority (CPA) was established, funded by the US Department of Defence and reporting directly to Donald Rumsfeld, Secretary of Defence. This body, with sweeping executive, legislative and judicial powers, was initially led by Jay Garner, but he was replaced a few weeks later by Paul Bremer for reasons I'll describe.

The CPA was given the responsibility under Security Council Resolution 1483 to authorise and oversee expenditures from Iraq's oil revenue, subject to certain conditions. These were that disbursements should be transparent, that they should be subject to scrutiny by a new International Advisory and Monitoring Board (IAMB), and that Iraqis should have a 'meaningful input' into decisions. IAMB was made up of UN financial experts, the IMF, the World Bank and the Arab Fund for Social and Economic Development. For the purpose of implementing the CPA's responsibilities, Garner arranged the opening of an account called the Central Bank of Iraq – Development Fund for Iraq (usually referred to as the DFI) at the US Federal Reserve Bank of New York. Into this the funds of the old oil-for-food escrow account and further oil revenues were to be transferred.

The CPA appointed the Iraqi Governing Council, consisting of a cross-section of favoured political and tribal leaders, as the provisional government from 13th July. Under its mandate the CPA was also to encourage the formation of a fully independent representative government which would ensure equal rights and justice in due course.

In June 2004 an Iraqi Interim Government was appointed by the US and its allies, and replaced the CPA. Its priority was initiating the trial of Saddam, who had been arrested the previous December. Following elections (of a kind) in January 2005 the Iraqi Transitional Government was set up with the primary task of writing a new constitution. Once this was adopted, fresh elections were held in December of that year for a new Iraqi National Assembly. This resulted in a coalition government, with Nouri al-Maliki as Prime Minister and warlord Jalal Talabani as President and therefore titular head of state. They were both to remain in post for more than eight years.

Devilish details

This all sounds like a great achievement, and indeed that is how it was presented by Bush and Blair. Three years after a bloody war, Iraq had its own government, and Jalal Talabani and Nouri al-Maliki were set for a remarkable eight-year stint as President and Prime Minister respectively. But this is to ignore the chaotic conditions in the country which resulted from cynical clandestine arrangements, devils buried in the detail of coalition statements, and the emerging government's legislation. There is not enough space in this book to examine this labyrinth in all its twists and turns.[1] But it conformed to ideas which had been around for a long time.

In *The Prince*, Nicolo Machiavelli recommended a ruthless policy combining settlement building, pampering, division and crushing,[2] which the Zionist entity has pretty much followed. However, this doesn't gain it many brownie points around the world, and so the US and UK, not wishing their humanitarian credentials to be questioned, imposed their will on my homeland by getting others to do their dirty work. One obvious solution was to employ private security firms on a massive scale, and not to put their methods under too much scrutiny. Another was to invite the Zionists and the Badr Brigades to pursue their own agendas in Iraq, or at least not to hinder them in doing so.

The Zionists, in the form of Mossad, remained firmly undercover, and news therefore only occasionally leaked out. A 2003 article in the newspaper *Maariv* was the source of a story about Zionist commandoes who were in Iraq to assassinate 500 scientists.[3] As for the Badr Brigades, uninformed Westerners simply regarded them as further evidence of how benighted Iraq had become. The fact that they were the military wing of the Iran-based SCIRI, that they were officered by Iranians, that they served Iran's geopolitical ambitions in the region,

---

[1] Aram Roston's very readable book, *The Man who Pushed America to War: The Extraordinary Life, Adventures, and Obsessions of Ahmad Chalabi*, New York, Nation Books, 2008, is a pretty good source. Another is the BRussells Tribunal website at http://brussellstribunal.org/.
[2] Machiavelli, N., *The Prince*, Florence, 1532, English translation, Harmonsworth, Penguin Books 1961, p 37 (*inter alia*).
[3] See 'Israeli Commandos in Iraq to Assassinate 500 Scientists,' dated 18th April 2003 and appearing on the Information Clearing House site at http://www.informationclearinghouse.info/article3006.htm.

and, most importantly, that the occupiers gave them a green light to do what they liked, went largely unnoticed.

Firmly on the agenda of the occupiers was the transformation of the Iraqi economy so that it served their interests. Under the Ba'athists the Iraqi economy from one which was centrally planned and where foreign ownership of businesses was prohibited, to an arrangement that served their interests. The state ran most large enterprises, and protected the economy with tariffs on foreign goods. The CPA now lost no time in issuing a number of orders which entitled foreign companies to invest in Iraq on so-called equal terms with Iraqi investors, allowed them to transfer their revenue out of the country, granted them immunity from actions in the courts, and granted them tax concessions for operating in Iraq. Those companies working with the CPA were exempted from any tax, and all tariffs were suspended, thus removing the protection of Iraqi producers.

These measures were clearly in the interests of the US and acted against the interests of Iraq. Moreover it is arguable that they were illegal under international law, which prohibits an occupying power from changing the laws of the occupied country except under certain conditions. Interestingly, as I will relate later, when a puppet Iraqi government was established, it steadfastly refused to endorse these arrangements by passing a hydrocarbon law which would have legitimised them. No doubt they feared a backlash from the Iraqi people. However, by then control of the oil industry was in any case firmly back under foreign control.

The IAMB found the CPA Administrator, Paul Bremer, un-cooperative, and reported that there was a lack of transparency in, and financial control of, the CPA's dealings. Approximately $20 billion was paid into the DFI in its first year, in addition to which the CPA was responsible for administering $18.4 billion allocated by Congress for Iraqi reconstruction. However, Bremer relied almost exclusively on funds drawn from the DFI, allegedly because the money from Congress was subject to much greater scrutiny. Iraq was thereby denied a considerable pot of money which could have been used to accelerate the country's recovery and would have gone some way to compensating its people for the damage caused to its infrastructure.

From the very outset, the occupiers focussed on Iraq's ethnic and religious diversity, rather than on the continuing sense of unity and national identity. When it came to appointing the Iraqi Governing Council, for example, the CPA chose thirteen Shias, five Sunnis, five Kurds (who are mainly Sunni), one Turkoman and an Assyrian. Three of its members were women. On the face of it, this may seem wise, but by focussing on difference, rather than national unity, the effect was to resurrect the old imperial tactic of divide and rule.

There was also a wish on the part of the US, and no doubt also of the Zionist entity, to detach Iraq from its Arab identity. The colours of the Arab nation are red, white, black and green, and these appear in the flags of Egypt, Syria, Jordan, Kuwait, Libya, Sudan, Yemen, the UAE and Palestine. Since 1921 the Iraqi flag had also been made up of these colours but the members of the Governing Council now proposed a completely different flag, designed by the London based brother of one of the members of the Council. It contained none of the Arab colours and emphasised the ethnic divisions. However, that was a step too far for ordinary Iraqis and caused such outrage that it had to be abandoned.

There was widespread insensitivity in the way the occupation was applied. The assumption was that everything which had gone before had been bad, and needed replacing. The achievement of Ba'athist rule in the emancipation of women, for example, was dismissed out of hand, with particular reference being made in UN resolution 1483, in the context of human rights, to resolution 1325 on the rights of women. Though the resolution welcomed 'the first steps of the Iraqi people in this regard' the reference was to the post-war situation, and took no account of what had been achieved before.[4] This was insulting to the

---

[4] See https://www.treasury.gov/resource-center/sanctions/Documents/1483.pdf.

many Iraqi women who had achieved so much, and gave no credit to the Ba'athist regime for encouraging this development.

But the worst effect of the occupation was the destabilisation of the country and the bloodbath which ensued as a result. The occupiers claimed that they were surprised by the degree of resistance they encountered, but it was widely predicted. Tariq Aziz had, indeed told Tam, Albert Reynolds and myself as much as we left his house in 1998.

De-Ba'athification

When a country or group of countries with one political ideology conquers another with a different view of the world, the instinct of the victor or victors is usually to eliminate the alien system. The first stage in such a process is to demonise the leader and regime of the country to be attacked, and in doing this a comparison with Hitler and the Nazis is always useful. Accordingly, following the recommendation of Ahmad Chalabi, De-Ba'athification was consciously modelled on the de-Nazification of Germany.[5] This ruled out any consideration of the merits of the Ba'athist regime; the Ba'athists were Arab nationalist and socialist in their orientation, and that didn't suit the West or the Zionist entity.

The occupation might have been somewhat less arduous if Jay Garner had not been thrown out as Administrator of the CPA within a few weeks of his appointment.[6] Garner had some experience of Iraq, and in preparing himself for the job had worked closely with military

---

[5] Ahmad al-Chalabi, American's favourite for post-war leadership of the country, expressed the opinion that 'Iraq needs a comprehensive programme of de-Ba'athification even more extensive than Germany after World War II. You cannot cut off the viper's head and leave the body festering.' Sunday Business Post (Ireland) 2nd March 2003. Chalabi died in Baghdad on 3rd November 2015 aged 71.

[6] In what follows I have referred to an excellent article by Pfiffner, J., 'US blunders in Iraq: De-Baathification and Disbanding the Army,' *Intelligence and National Security*, Vol 25, No 1, p 76-85, February 2010. See http://pfiffner.gmu.edu/files/pdfs/Articles/CPA%20Orders,%20Iraq%20PDF.pdf.

planners who at least took a pragmatic view of the way forward. At that stage US policy had been to remove only high-ranking Ba'athists from their positions in the military and civil administrations, the reasonable assumption being that the skills of many ex-Ba'athists, together with the existing economic and social infrastructure, would be essential to the security and reconstruction of the country. He also planned to institute some form of self-government within ninety days.

In an interview with Greg Palast on the BBC Newsnight programme a year after his removal, this sequence indicates pretty clearly why he was so quickly removed:

> *Garner*: I just think that we're better by establishing a government and re-establishing basic services and getting things picked up, and letting that government through their own electoral process decide what's good for their country.
> *Palast*: Let them decide whether to privatise the oilfields?
> *Garner*: Yes.[7]

Paul Bremer, Garner's replacement, had a radically different approach. This was a policy of 'deep de-Ba'athification,' which effectively amounted to Sunni cleansing for it was based on sectarian thinking, and resulted in the removal from the economy of much of the well qualified personnel. Even more disastrously, he disbanded the Iraqi Army, throwing hundreds of thousands out of work and creating a disaffected, humiliated and armed section of the population. This became a major source of destabilisation, and to some extent anyway, I believe this is what was intended. But the genie had been let out of the bottle, and would reveal itself a few years later.

So how was this engineered? The appointment of Bremer in place of Garner, and the application of a policy of 'deep de-Ba'athification,'

---

[7] See http://news.bbc.co.uk/1/hi/programmes/newsnight/3552737.stm. This reads rather peculiarly because the text is made up of subtitles that are generated live for the BBC Newsnight programme.

appear to have been in part the work of Douglas Feith and Ahmad Chalabi. Feith and Chalabi were to occupied Iraq what Henry Morgenthau had been to occupied Germany. Regardless of whether or not you consider there to be parallels between Ba'athism and Nazism, the fact is the defeat of these political systems was followed in both cases by calls for the wholescale dismantling of the countries where they had held sway. Feith and Morgenthau were, respectively, leaders, if not originators, of such calls.[8]

Feith's appointment in the Bush administration was helped by his relationship with two other neocons, Richard Perle and Paul Wolfowitz, and he in turn repaid Perle by influencing the decision to appoint him Chairman of the Defence Policy Board Advisory Committee. It was Feith's Office of Special Plans which worked out the details of de-Ba'athification in collaboration with the Americans' favourite Iraqi, Ahmad Chalabi;[9] and it was Feith who presented the plan to Bush in March 2003. It seems, however, that the wool was successfully pulled over Bush's eyes. Other members of the administration, who would certainly have opposed it, were simply kept in the dark. Bush himself, when asked why the policy changed, replied 'Well, the policy was to keep the army intact. Didn't happen.'[10] This is how James P Pfiffner concluded his essay on the question of who gave the authority for a change of plan:

> [... N]either President Bush nor the White House staff followed any regular policy process before the momentous

---

[8] Henry Morgenthau Jr. was US Secretary of the Treasury under Franklin D. Roosevelt. His so-called 'Morgenthau plan,' devised in 1944, was designed to make it impossible for Germany to wage war again. It was adopted in modified form at the Second Quebec Conference attended by Roosevelt and Churchill, and in the memorandum written by the latter it was envisaged that Germany should become 'primarily agricultural and pastoral in its character.' Morgenthau was, like Feith, a convinced Zionist.

[9] See Roston, A., Ibid.

[10] Draper, R., *Dead Certain: The Presidency of George W. Bush*, New York, Free Press, 2007, p 211, quoted by Pfiffner, Ibid.

decisions to disband the Iraq Army and de-Ba'athify the government were made. But what is known is that the decision was made *against* the judgement of Jay Garner, the senior CIA officer in Iraq, and military planners. In addition it was made *without* consultation with Secretary of State Colin Powell, National Security Advisor Rice, Chair of the Joint Chiefs of Staff General Myers, Vice Chair General Peter Pace, General McKiernan, CIA Director George Tenet, or Intelligence Community lead for the Middle East Paul Pillar.[11]

The CIA station chief of Baghdad warned Bremer that he 'was about to fire the key technicians who operated the electric, water and transportation infrastructure of the country. "By nightfall, you'll have driven 30,000 to 50,000 Ba'athists underground. And in six months, you'll really regret this."'[12] The Director of the CIA, George Tenet commented after the event: 'In fact, we knew nothing about it until de-Ba'athification was a *fait accompli*.'

Pfiffner points the finger of suspicion towards Vice-President Dick Cheney's office, with the remark that this was 'known for its opacity and lack of leaks.'[13] It seems probable to me that Feith, Perle, Cheney and Wolfowitz, cooked up the policy together in the secure surroundings of Cheney's office and decided Bremer was the right man for the job. Whether or not he was present, Ahmad Chalabi was an important figure in the background, manipulating his American backers to do his bidding.

---

[11] Pfifner, ibid, p 85.
[12] Pfiffner, Ibid, p 79.
[13] Ibid, p 85.

The aftermath

Following the defeat of Iraq, there was widespread looting and disorder. The National museum was ransacked and some of the most important monuments were destroyed. The same happened to government buildings, and much of the documentation they contained was removed. In this general chaos there was just one ministry which was protected by the occupying forces, and you can probably guess which it was. The Ministry of Oil remained undisturbed!

The US strategy of alignment with the Shia population, and therefore necessarily with the Iranian government, was a recipe for disaster. Under the Ba'athists it is true that the Sunnis were in the dominant position, and the Tikritis even more so, but this didn't mean that the Shia majority had no power in Iraqi society. In any case, you were never asked what sect you belonged to, and even if this was obvious, it was not the determining factor in appointments as it became under the occupation. The Ba'athist government was formed from a wide cross-section of the population, and there was widespread support for it even in Shia areas, as indeed we had witnessed among the Marsh Arabs on our 1993 trip. Reversing the power balance on the basis of political expediency, and doing so by drastic measures like the disbanding of the army, showed at best an arrogant lack of understanding of how Iraqi society had functioned under the Ba'athists and was a major cause of destabilisation.

A majority of the army and top government officials and academics were Sunni and many of them were Ba'athist members. They now found themselves unemployed and in danger of execution, if not by the Americans, then by marauding Shia militias. They therefore had little to lose by aligning themselves with the Arab nationalist and religiously conservative Jeish Mohammed, or Mohammed's Army of Ansar, based in Falluja. Following the murder of four private security contractors nearby, the US launched an assault on the town, in which around 200 resistance fighters and forty Americans were killed. Under pressure from the Iraqi Governing Council and international public opinion, a truce was then negotiated which at least took the pragmatic step of giving a former Ba'athist general the task of keeping the peace.

Meanwhile, Muqtada al-Sadr, the Shia cleric, took control of the streets of Baghdad, with the help of his 1000-man strong Iranian backed Mahdi Army. Realising they'd lost control of the situation, the CPA closed down Muqtada's newspaper and following mass anti-American demonstrations, attempted to arrest the cleric himself. He took refuge in the Imam Ali mosque in the holy city of Najaf, which the US army then besieged. In August, following an intervention by Aytollah al-Sistani, Muqtada declared a national cease fire and negotiated an arrangement whereby the Mahdi army became part of the national armed forces.

Countless Iraqi lives, and a significant number of coalition lives as well, were lost as a result of this chaos. Indeed it was responsible for vastly more casualties than the war itself. In January 2003 I had been told by reliable sources that this was exactly what would happen, for guerrilla warfare would be the only viable option open to those who wished to resist and disrupt the infinitely better equipped invading forces.

The statistics vary enormously, but in addition to the estimate of 30,000 Iraqis killed in the actual invasion, when account is taken of the aftermath, and the effects of damage to essential infrastructure such as water treatment plants and hospitals, the estimates of total casualties range upwards from 158,000 in the period 2003 to 2011, the great majority being civilians.[14] As early as 2006 the British medical journal, *The Lancet*, published an article estimating 'excess deaths' (that is

---

[14] Iraq Body Count report, 2nd January 2012. See
https://www.iraqbodycount.org/analysis/numbers/2011/.

deaths above the death rate before the conflict) at 654,965 up to that time.[15] By comparison, coalition losses numbered less than 5000.

George Bush and Tony Blair were largely responsible for this slaughter which was initiated by a disproportionate bombing campaign resulting in the destruction not only of military targets but also of vital infrastructure. The aim was clearly to undermine the stability of the country. Were we to understand that this was the action of civilised nations, which preached human rights to the world? These leaders were egged on by the so-called Iraqi opposition, the Zionists, the oil barons, multinational corporations, bankers and the media, and they drew their inspiration from the Project for the New American Century.[16] All of these had their own reasons for supporting the US agenda, hardly a propitious situation in which to achieve peace and harmony. Indeed, did making war on faraway countries ever achieve peace and harmony? Alas, the world has not learned from its bloody history. The glossy concepts of civilisation and democracy are over-used to deceive the silent majority. The truth is that in 2003 the old colonialists' philosophy of spreading corruption and division was reinvented in the Middle East and set to work restoring itself with a vengeance.

None of the Iraqis I met had been in favour of the US invasion; on the contrary they had wished to avoid it, and therefore up to the last minute had sought opportunities for dialogue. Nevertheless the Western, and especially the American, media, reflecting political agendas, contended that the people welcomed the invading forces. American televiewers were persuaded in its aftermath that the war had

---

[15] Burnham, G., Doocy, S. & Roberts, L, 'Mortality after the 2003 invasion of Iraq: a cross-sectional cluster sample survey,' The Lancet, Vol 368, No 9545, pp 1421–1428, 21 October 2006. See
http://www.thelancet.com/journals/lancet/article/PIIS0140-6736%2806%2969491-9/abstract.

[16] The Project for the New American Century was established in 1997 as a neoconservative think tank based in Washington DC. It aimed 'to promote American global leadership' in the belief that this was 'good both for America and for the world.'

been for the benefit of the Iraqi people. But the British were from the start more sceptical, and once it was revealed that the justification, namely Saddam's supposed possession of WMDs, was false, Tony Blair was increasingly regarded as a war criminal.

On 31st May 2003 I wrote a memo to Tam expressing my deep concern. Among the points I made were the following

- The three months' rations distributed before the war are coming to an end and there are no plans to replace them. Furthermore the occupying forces have stood by while the Ministry of Trade's storage and distributions facilities are looted. As a result famine looms.
- Water and electricity supply are non-existent or at best unreliable. As a result sanitation is dire, and this threatens in particular the lives of children. Following the war in 1991 these services were restored in record time, so why are the occupiers taking so long. Instead of taking up the offers of Iraqi engineers, they contracted the multi-national Bechtel to restore these services, which it has singularly failed to do adequately.
- Security is at an all-time low. People fear for their lives, children are abducted, rape is common. The only public buildings which are secure are the Ministry of Oil, the British and US embassies and the army bases.
- Health care was already bad before the war, but it has been further degraded by pillaging and the lack of clean water and electricity.
- Sectarian and ethnic conflict is on the verge of breaking out, and once started is unlikely to end soon.
- The 'deep de-Ba'athification' policy is having a disastrous effect on unemployment, family well-being, morale, and security.
- The exiles are back in Iraq but continue to work against each

other, causing the majority to distrust them.
- John Sawers, the British Special Representative in Baghdad, lacks a basic knowledge of the country. He stated on BBC Radio 4 that Iraq's water and power facilities suffered from 25 years of neglect. This is a travesty. Extraordinary efforts were made to put these services back in order after the 1991 war, and despite the sanctions, they were maintained in working order until the 2003 war. Why doesn't the Foreign Office take the advice of those who know the country well.

In April 2004 Oliver Miles, a foreign office Arabist and experienced Middle East diplomat with impeccable credentials, developed in conversation with his family the idea of an open letter from retired ambassadors. Once drafted, he sent it to about five colleagues who amended and improved upon it, and encouraged him to look for more signatories. Having found many others who were willing to sign, he arranged with Reuters to release the letter to them at the same time as sending it to No. 10, while alerting No. 10 through the FCO that this was what he planned. Here is some of the letter:

> We the undersigned former British ambassadors, high commissioners, governors and senior international officials, including some who have long experience of the Middle East and others whose experience is elsewhere, have watched with deepening concern the policies which you have followed on the Arab-Israel problem and Iraq, in close co-operation with the United States. Following the press conference in Washington at which you and President Bush restated these policies, we feel the time has come to make our anxieties public, in the hope that they will be addressed in Parliament and will lead to a fundamental reassessment. […]

The conduct of the war in Iraq has made it clear that there was no effective plan for the post-Saddam settlement. All those with experience of the area predicted that the occupation of Iraq by the Coalition forces would meet serious and stubborn resistance, as has proved to be the case. To describe the resistance as led by terrorists, fanatics and foreigners is neither convincing nor helpful. Policy must take account of the nature and history of Iraq, the most complex country in the region.

Referring to the several hundred killed in Falluja in the previous month, Miles writes: 'Phrases such as "We mourn each loss of life. We salute them, and their families for their bravery and their sacrifice," apparently referring only to those who have died on the Coalition side, are not well judged to moderate the passions those killings arouse.'[17] Among the fifty ex-ambassadors and ex-senior officials joining Miles as signatories were Sir James Craig, former ambassador to Syria and Saudi Arabia, and Sir Crispin Tickell, former permanent representative of the UK to the UN. So far as Iraq is concerned, they and all the others who signed might as well have been talking to a blank wall.[18] At least, however, they left a mark to indicate that decency and fairness was not dead in all quarters.

---

[17] Oliver Miles, in kindly agreeing to this quote of part of the letter, provided my editor with the original script and the details given about its production and distribution. Miles served as UK ambassador in Libya, Luxembourg and Greece. The letter can be viewed online, in a slightly different format, at: http://news.bbc.co.uk/1/hi/uk_politics/3660837.stm.

[18] Oliver Miles points out that the letter had one significant success. 'Standing with George W. Bush in the White House Rose Garden Tony Blair had given the impression that he was going along with Bush in abandoning the long-held position that the Israeli settlements in the occupied territories were illegal and an obstacle to peace. [...] The day after we sent the letter Mike O'Brien, Minister of State at the FCO, told the press that it was quite wrong to suggest that any principle had been abandoned. The British position remained unchanged.'

Those Iraqis who were brought in from abroad to govern Iraq had no interest in the country's future. The British and Americans knew that they were a bunch of thieves. Moreover, democracy does not mean bringing in more mobile phones and enabling people to watch satellite TV. The economy was in tatters and no attention was paid to social needs or security. Most of those who had served Iraq for years, especially those in the armed forces, were thrown out of their jobs. This was a terrible blow to families whose breadwinners had held secure positions in the army or the police. The US and UK governments deliberately set out to dismantle the entire professional sector in Iraq and to render the Iraqi military dormant, thus providing the trusted Zionist entity with full spectrum dominance in the region.

After a trip to Amman in September 2004 (going to Baghdad was out of the question) I was interviewed by Felicity Arbuthnot[19] of Global Research and told her that I'd 'met a wide spectrum of people, including Kurds, who in spite of their differing backgrounds and politics were united in condemnation of the occupation, mistrust of the US appointed government and the horror of continuous loss of Iraqi lives.' US soldiers were adopting the motto 'No better friend, no worse enemy,'[20] thus earning the hatred of ordinary Iraqis. Brutal search methods were used. I was told of one UK educated Christian friend whose house was raided at 5 a.m. 'The situation was largely defused due to his fluent English – and his offering them beer.' He thus avoided his home being trashed and his belongings and valuables stolen.

I told Felicity about another UK graduate's experience at a check point. His hands were visibly on the wheel, when his mobile phone rang; he instinctively tried to reach it and was almost shot; only his

---

[19] Felicity had earlier collaborated with Pilger in the production of 'Paying the Price.'
[20] 'No better friend, no worse enemy,' was a phrase coined by General James 'Mad Dog' Mattis to describe the US marines. Addressing a group of Iraqi tribal elders he said: 'I come in peace. I didn't bring artillery. But I'm pleading with you, with tears in my eyes: if you "mess" with me, I'll kill you all.' See https://www.warhistoryonline.com/history/general-jamesmattis-x.html.

shouted explanation in English saved him. The soldier coolly responded that he could have killed my friend and he could have justified in it five minutes. Iraqis, I said, have become unpeople, whose lives count for nothing. I concluded my interview by saying that Iraq was 'a country now run by foreigners, including Israelis,' and indeed the methods used against Palestinians, like house demolitions and random killings, were being repeated in Iraq.[21]

Things went from bad to worse, and it became more apparent day by day that the minority sectors of the Iraqi community, the Christians, the Sabians and the Turkomans, were being targeted. The only Iraqis who benefitted were the warlords of the Kurdish sector, Talabani and Barzani, who were in the process of establishing their independence from the central government. Meanwhile the central government was actively encouraging the sectarian divide by selecting officials on the basis of whether they were Sunnis or Shias, rather than on their abilities and experience. One government had been dismantled in order to create another which was allied to Iran and served a section of Iraqi society.

It could be argued that the previous regime also favoured one section of Iraqi society, namely the people of Tikrit, Saddam's tribal home. However, while it is true that the Tikriti clan had more pull than others in Iraq at that time, its members did not govern exclusively. Saddam's ministers came from all sections of Iraqi society, not only from the Tikriti clan. The governments which followed the downfall of Saddam were all selected on a sectarian basis. In order to become part of the governing elite you had to be affiliated with a certain sect, regardless of how popular you were or what kind of majority you could muster. The guiding principle was that Iraqis should be divided on the basis of sect and ethnicity.

---

[21] Arbuthnot, F., 'A country now run by foreigners, including Israelis ...', online article for Global Research, 29th October 2004 at http://www.globalresearch.ca/a-country-now-run-by-foreigners-including-israelis/550.

In my view the 325-member Iraqi Council of Representatives elected in December 2005 at the National Assembly was nothing more than a fig-leaf to deceive international public opinion that the occupiers had established democracy in Iraq. There were numerous irregularities and disruptions to these apparently democratic processes, which were in reality, just the reverse of what they seemed. The infrastructure of the country was in tatters, the electricity supply was unreliable, water was contaminated, hospitals were struggling to cope, there were no social services to speak of, education was neglected, transport was not functioning properly, the manufacturing sector was dismantled and above all there was no security. As Aram Roston remarks in his book on Chalabi, 'Fewer and fewer Iraqis called the hell they were living in "liberation."'[22]

I believe this situation was deliberately engineered by the occupying forces to strip Iraq of all its professional class. It amounted to an intellectual cleansing of the country in order to bring in a new governing class of illiterates dependent on American and British rule. With little remaining indigenous ability to manufacture, produce or invent, the US/UK alliance was in a position to control the country behind the public front of a powerless puppet regime.

As if this were not enough, Iraq, the very cradle of civilisation, was also culturally destroyed. The invading forces stood by while historical documents and other artefacts dating back to before the birth of Islam were destroyed. The occupiers showed no concern to preserve historical remains and even allowed their forces to establish bases at archaeological sites while excavations were still in progress. As historians and archaeologists sought to reveal the secrets of one of mankind's most ancient civilisations, American soldiers simply regarded the sites as convenient places to set up camp.

When I look at Iraq today I feel very sad. It has been damaged to such an extent that a whole generation of artists, engineers and doctors

---

[22] Roston, Ibid p 330.

has been forced to leave. Moreover, the situation is not getting any better as exemplified by the continuation up to the present of the 'International Zone' in Baghdad, popularly known as the 'Green Zone,' or what I started to call the 'Green Zone Texan Bubble.' Set up immediately after the war in 2003, it consists of a highly fortified 10-square-kilometre area in the Karkh district containing the Republican Palace, the National Assembly building and the Al-Rasheed Hotel. It is still heavily fortified and provides a base for the government, foreign embassies and private military contractors. It is, however, far from secure, as numerous attacks on it over the years have proved.

If the elections which took place under occupation had been legitimate one would have expected government officials to be able to move around the country freely, yet for over a decade the ministers and their officials have been confined to this fortified area. On the few occasions that they venture out, they are guarded by highly paid mercenaries, of which there were at one point around 20,000 in the country. Moreover, visitors and most journalists coming to the country never stray outside the zone, and therefore gain a very distorted view of Iraq.

The main change since the occupation began is the extent of bribery and corruption. I wonder if Iraq has ever experienced such corruption in its entire history. Nothing can now be done in the country unless a bribe is paid. Particularly guilty are those who constitute the new police force. All contractual arrangements are subject to abuse. If there has been any marginal improvement, I have not heard about it and neither have my friends who are now in Syria, Jordan or the UAE. Most of the honest people who were capable of running the oil industry and who were still in situ after the war, have now been forced to leave or have been imprisoned.

CHAPTER THIRTEEN

WHAT TO DO NOW?

FAF revises its strategy

FAF had been founded to campaign against the sanctions. Now that they were about to be lifted, we needed to review what role FAF might continue to play. In a mailing I sent out on 16th April 2003 I listed the issues which seemed most urgent:
- The invading armies should be withdrawn immediately.
- All Iraqis should be allowed to participate in the political process.
- The interim administration should be run by Iraqis.
- Law, security and essential services should be the priority of the Iraqi interim administration.
- The Iraqi interim administration should have exclusive responsibility for the awarding of contracts.
- The Blair Government and Bush Administration should be brought to account for the current humanitarian disaster in Iraq.
- The invading armies should pay reparation to the families of civilians killed and for damage to infrastructure.
- The invading armies should be held responsible for the cost of clearing mines, depleted uranium munitions and cluster bombs.
- The World Bank and IMF should in view of their ideological position be barred from any involvement in Iraq.
- Muslim communities worldwide should be encouraged to unite against (a) destructive fundamentalism and (b) the

occupation and illegal settlement of Iraq and Palestine.
- The world community should challenge America's intention of leaving their 'footprint' in the region.
- Independent monitoring visits by MPs and NGO representatives must be maintained in both Iraq and Afghanistan.
- An Iraqi judicial organisation should investigate human rights violations and promote reconciliation.

But clearly, as a small unstructured organisation, and only one part-time secretary, we were not in a position to undertake such am ambitious programme of campaigning. We therefore came to focus our efforts on five main issues:
1. An end to the occupation, and drawing a parallel with the occupation of Palestine.
2. The maintenance of a unified Iraq.
3. Control by Iraq of its natural resources.
4. A transparent investigation into the justification, conduct and aftermath of the war.
5. The correct treatment of political prisoners.

I will deal with the first four of these in this chapter. Chapter Fourteen will be devoted to political prisoners and assassinations.

During the period from January 2003, as war loomed, up to January 2009, when I became increasingly preoccupied with preparing my defence, I worked frenetically to realise this agenda. I supplied my supporters in parliament and elsewhere with briefings containing all the information I could get from Iraq, I wrote directly to senior politicians in the UK, US, France and elsewhere, and I commented, both positively and critically, on radio, television and newspaper reports, and on documentaries and interviews. I gave numerous interviews myself to a wide range of broadcasting stations, I collaborated with the Stop the

War Coalition and I reached out even to those who took a very different view from me. The spirit of that time came back to me recently when my ex-secretary sent me a USB stick containing more than 700 documents relating to our campaign, almost all of which I wrote or drafted.

Tam, who had from the outset in 1993 been FAF's patron, became Father of the House in 2001, which raised our profile still further. But in 2005 he decided to retire from politics, and therefore didn't put himself forward as a candidate in the May General Election of that year. He was happy to remain our patron, but encouraged me to find another member of parliament to represent our campaign in the House. This was less easy now that there wasn't a clear body of opinion in the Labour Party opposing government policy on Iraq. MPs were wary of committing themselves sufficiently to take on the patronage, fearing that it could affect their political careers.

I was therefore very grateful to Harry Cohen, who agreed in April 2007 to join Tam as our second patron. His credentials were impressive. Together with just eleven other Labour MPs he had the previous October supported Plaid Cymru and the Scottish National Party in their call for an inquiry into the Iraq War. He was, moreover, a signatory to the Jews for Justice for Palestinians (JFJFP) statement 'Two Peoples. One Future'.[1] In writing to thank him for his acceptance I acknowledged his 'exemplary' and 'continuous support since 1990 of the Iraqi people during their plight under the draconian sanctions.' I regretted, however, that matters had 'hardly improved since Blair's occupation of 2003.'

---

[1] JFJFP was founded in 2002. The 'about us' page of its website is headed by this quote from Rabbi Elizabeth Tikvah Sarah: 'The Torah teaches: "Justice, justice, you shall pursue" (Deuteronomy 16:20). To secure a lasting settlement to the conflict between Palestinians and Israelis so they can live in peace and security, thrive side by side, and co-operate together, Jews today are obligated to pursue justice on behalf of both peoples.' See https://jfjfp.com/what-we-believe/.

'End the occupation!'

I felt it essential to maintain a hard line on ending the occupation, and therefore on regarding resistance as legitimate. It was not for us to judge the methods used; our job was to exert pressure on the British government for a change of policy. Four decades earlier Bertrand Russell had eloquently expressed this position when answering a letter about the anti-Apartheid campaign:

> It is presumptuous for those of us not faced with conditions such as those which obtain in South Africa to determine the form of struggle. I believe that our efforts in Britain should be concentrated on making known the nature of the regime and on mobilising public opinion ...[2]

This philosophical underpinning of our uncompromising position didn't, however, protect us from the accusation that we were supporting terrorists, for in the eyes of the US and UK governments the resistance was illegitimate. In my view, though, there was no difference in principle between our stance, and allied support of resistance movements across Europe during the Second World War. The Germans likewise regarded the Maquis, which inevitably had civilian blood on its hands, as terrorists.

Moreover, we came under suspicion of being loyal to the fallen regime, which was not at all the case. Our frustration was with the occupation, the injustices this enabled and the lack of tangible progress on the road towards a real, rather than an imitation democracy. I have little doubt, however, that from then on, and possibly from much earlier, I was under covert surveillance by the security services, and had it not

---

[2] Russell, B., letter to Mr Hougham dated 27th November 1964, and included in Russell, B,, ed. Feinberg, B., and Kasrils, R., *Dear Bertrand Russell: A Selection of his correspondence with the general public 1950-1968*, London, George Allen and Unwin, 1969, p 88.

been for the support I enjoyed at a high level in Parliament and elsewhere I suspect I would have found myself in trouble with the law much sooner than I did.

It became increasingly clear to me that the plight of Palestinians and Iraqis was intimately linked, and it therefore made sense for FAF to collaborate with pro-Palestinian organisations. On 15th April 2003, as the war was still raging, I wrote to Betty Hunter and Carol Regan of Palestine Solidarity Campaign suggesting that I speak at their rally on 17th May, advancing the argument, which I also used in my speech at the rally, that 'Iraq and Palestine are interlinked and the invasion of Iraq is part of the so-called "Road Map"[3] to a solution on Israel's terms. Both the Iraqi and Palestinian peoples are victims of occupation by America and its Zionist ally.'

And in July 2003 I distributed an opinion piece developing this argument:

> Unless the Iraqi people reject the legitimacy of the council appointed by the CPA, encourage resistance to occupation and support non-cooperation with occupying authorities, then there is a bleak future for Iraq, the Arab nations and the Palestinian people. The struggle in Iraq and Palestine against occupation represents the last flicker of hope before the otherwise inevitable total Zionist control, by proxy, of the Arab Nation.

During President Bush's visit to London in November 2003 we collaborated with the Stop the War Coalition in arranging a series of protests and a march against the occupation and the illegal war. From

---

[3] The Road Map was a plan for peace in occupied Palestine drawn up by the so-called Quartet, consisting of the US, the EU, Russia and the UN. It was published by the G.W. Bush administration in April 2003 and was a variation on the two-state solution. Among other things it required the Palestinians to recognise the legitimacy of the Zionist entity as a Jewish state. By the end of Bush's term of office, the Road Map was effectively a dead letter.

December we added the slogan 'end the occupation!' at the foot of all appropriate FAF communications.

We had no wish to make sectarian distinctions in our support for those in Iraq opposing the occupation. But the truth was that on the Shia side all parties, whether they declared themselves against the occupation or not, ended up collaborating with the occupiers and their stooges. For example, Muqtada al-Sadr, leader of the Mahdi Army, owed a great deal of his support to his anti-occupation rhetoric among the population of Sadr City, a poor district of Baghdad. But when it came to the crunch, he allied himself with SCIRI, the Islamic Da'wa (Call) Party and Ahmad Chalabi's gang to form the United Iraqi Alliance which under Ibrahim al-Jaafari of Da'wa won the December 2005 elections by a small margin.

The Iranian-born Ayatollah Ali Sistani, of Najaf, never took a clear anti-occupation line, and indeed he encouraged his followers to engage in the elections under occupation in 2005. We made a number of attempts to engage Sistani in a debate about his position, but he declined to respond. Equally fruitless was our call on Mahmoud Ahmadinejad, shortly after his election as President of Iran in 2005, 'to support the Iraqi resistance to occupation and to denounce the US appointed government in Iraq.'[4] The geo-political advantages to Iran of US intervention no doubt underlay this silence. He was happy enough to support the Palestinians resisting occupation, but not the Iraqi resistance.

The SCIRI-linked Badr Brigades were opportunists, for while they despised the US as 'the Great Satan,' they nevertheless took advantage of the green light given to them by the Americans, and wreaked havoc by terrorising Sunnis until many left the country, taking their invaluable skills and knowledge with them. In doing this dirty work the Badr Brigades were an important, though undeclared, ally of the Americans

---

[4] Letter dated 28th June 2005

and its personnel were rewarded by being given positions in the new Iraqi police force, which they now dominate.

The Islamic Da'wa Party even took a firm stance against the 2003 war and Ibrahim al-Jaafari, who was living in London at that time, ensured that the party took part in the UK anti-war demonstration. Nevetheless Da'wa returned from exile in Iran at the beginning of the occupation, establishing itself in Nasiriyah and was also willing to collaborate with the 'Great Satan' to further its interests.

With his US passport and neocon support, Ahmad Chalabi had naively believed that his adopted country would hand over the government of Iraq to him immediately after they had removed Saddam and subdued the country. His anti-occupation rhetoric was, however, belied by his insistence that US troops should remain in sufficient numbers to protect his regime for as long as it proved necessary. I had asserted for years that Ahmad Chalabi lacked any credible support in the country and here was the proof.

After all sorts of skulduggery, Chalabi fell out with the Americans, and in the absence of their support he was done for. He served as President of the Interim Governing Council for one month, was Deputy Prime Minister under Ibrahim al-Jaafari for 20 days in 2005, and was Minister of Oil for eight months. In a survey in 2004 only 0.2% of Iraqis thought he was 'the most trustworthy leader in Iraq,' and the *Daily Telegraph* reported that secret UK government documents seen by the paper described Chalabi as 'a convicted fraudster popular on Capitol Hill.'[5] All of this did not prevent him, however, from making an eye-watering amount of money out of the opportunities offered him by the invasion and occupation.

---

[5] Smith, M., 'Ministers were told premier was seen as stooge,' *Daily Telegraph*, 24th September 2004. The premier referred to was Ayad Allawi, of whom the documents said he 'was seen [in Iraq] as "a western stooge" and "lacked domestic credibility."' The article indicated that the same description applied to Ahmad Chalabi. See https://www.telegraph.co.uk/news/worldnews/northamerica/usa/1472540/Ministers-were-told-premier-was-seen-as-stooge.html.

The only credible resistance to occupation came from the Sunni Jeish Mohammad, or Mohammed's Army of Ansar, based in Falluja. I considered its struggle legitimate, but this was naturally not how the occupiers saw it. The democracy which had apparently been achieved was unreal, and I decided it would only weaken our position if we compromised. No less a figure than US Secretary of State, Condoleezza Rice, had implied in February 2005 that free and fair elections could not take place in Lebanon until the 'contaminating influence' of Syrian occupation was removed.[6] And yet she praised the elections under occupation in Iraq.[7] Moreover, the oil industry, contrary to all the fine-sounding sentiments expressed at the Atlantic summit, was no longer under the control of the Iraqi government.

In November 2006 'The Way Out' statement was published by two organisations called The BRussells Tribunal [sic] and the International Anti-Occupation Network respectively. The first signatories were Denis Halliday and Hans von Sponek, and sixteen professors soon joined them, as did I and many others. Their two principal demands were that 'US forces must negotiate an immediate withdrawal with the Iraqi resistance,' and that 'the American people must hold their leaders responsible for the crimes of aggressive war.' The opening statement read:

> In the November 2006 congressional elections,[8] the American people expressed their clear rejection of the Bush administration's war in Iraq. However, a broad movement of opinion is needed to force U.S. leaders to heed the will of their own people and, still more, the people of Iraq.

---

[6] News 24 Archives, 1st March 2005. See https://www.news24.com/World/News/Rice-wants-free-Lebanon-polls-20050301.
[7] US Department of State Archive, document dated 31st January 2005; see https://2001-2009.state.gov/secretary/rm/2005/41414.htm.
[8] These were mid-term elections, in which the Democratic Party made sweeping gains, securing control of the House of Representatives and the Senate.

U.S. military leaders admit that their invasion and occupation of Iraq have produced 'chaos'. The logical conclusion is that the U.S. presence itself, based on criminal aggression and multiple crimes against humanity, is responsible for such chaos, and that to bring about stability, the United States should withdraw immediately.[9]

Perhaps this initiative did something to change public opinion, for by 2007 even 55% of Americans believed the war had been a mistake. Now in retrospect people around the world can see how hollow and dishonest the coalition's assurances about the necessity of war were. Officially the military occupation ended in 2004, but the reality was that the country remained under American occupation. Indeed in 2007 the US involvement in Iraq was strengthened with 'the Surge' of an additional 20,000 troops.

Don't divide Iraq!

The relatively recent creation of Iraq following the defeat of the Ottomans during the First World War led many in the West to conclude that it wasn't a viable state. According to this view, described as the 'primordial' approach,[10] the three Ottoman provinces of Baghdad, Basrah and Mosul, which were themselves not homogeneous, had been unsuccessfully glued together by the British, and now that the US was in control, they could just as easily be unglued. Such a way of seeing things was particularly attractive to the Zionists, who feared a large modernised state near enough to threaten their presence in Palestine. Not surprisingly, therefore, the Zionist model of divide and rule was followed in Iraq.

---

[9] See http://www.brussellstribunal.org/WayOut.htm.
[10] See Dr Toby Dodge's submission to the Iraq Inquiry at page 2 of http://webarchive.nationalarchives.gov.uk/20131205144012/http://www.iraqinquiry.org.uk/media/37045/dodge-submission.pdf.

It is thought that Philip II of Macedon coined the phrase 'divide and rule.' In his *Art of War* Machiavelli also wrote about this strategy: 'a Captain ought [... to] endeavour with every art to divide the forces of the enemy [...].'[11] And more recently the Zionists have applied it in their treatment of the Palestinians, a people whose very existence as a society they refuse to acknowledge. It is difficult to rule a land populated by a people who have a firm sense of their common identity, and a determination to preserve it. Accordingly, the Zionists discriminate between the indigenous people of Palestine based on whether they are Muslims or Christians or 'Israeli Arabs,' or Druze or Bedouin, in the hope that this will destroy their sense of corporate identity and consequently their will to resist.

Though committed in public statements to maintaining the unity of Iraq, the occupiers' policy of divide and rule underlay its whole strategy. The deal brokered between the US government and SCIRI by Ahmad Chalabi in 2002 was intended to place the Americans on the side of the 60% of Iraq's population who were Shia at the expense of the Sunnis, who had almost continuously supplied Iraq with its heads of state since its emergence as an integrated country.[12] This policy was presented as being only fair in view of the population makeup, but it ignored two realities.

Firstly, Saddam had also recognised the need for national unity and integration. A majority of his ministers came from Shia or other non-Sunni backgrounds. Certainly his regime was far from perfect, and certainly the Tikriti clan had too much power, but all other sections of Iraqi society were represented in the makeup of the government and civil society, and I personally never witnessed any discrimination

---

[11] Machiavelli, N., *The Art of War*, 1520, online at https://www.marxists.org/reference/archive/machiavelli/works/art-war/ch06.htm.

[12] If you remove the autonomous Kurdish Region's population, perhaps 80% of whom are Sunnis, from the figures, the Sunni minority in the remainder of Iraq shrinks even further, to perhaps around 30%. The one exception to Sunni rule was Abdul-Karim Qasim, leader of 1958 coup and PM until 1963, who was Shia.

against officials, or indeed against myself, on the basis of sect or ethnicity. Secondly, as mentioned earlier, the deployment of the military wing of SCIRI, the Iranian-trained and officered Badr Brigades shattered the unity of Iraq and laid waste to its intellectual resources. Now the Sunnis were, at best, to be thrown out of employment and effectively disenfranchised. Many of them felt their only choice was between emigration and joining such militant Sunni resistance groups as Jeish Mohammed.

Meanwhile the Kurdistan Region, with around one fifth of Iraq's population was granted federal autonomy under the new constitution and was to be protected by coalition and even Mossad forces. The Kurdistan Regional Government established itself in the capital Erbil and governed, and still governs, almost entirely independently of the national government. The warlord, Masoud Barzani, was elected president in 2005, a position which he held until 2015.

In the more than eighty years of Iraq's existence up to 2003, turbulent though these may have been, Iraqis had strengthened their sense of Arab national identity. This patriotic feeling was intensified by the struggle to survive during the sanctions years, and could have stood Iraq in very good stead, had the aim not been to undermine this beneficial force. Even some Iraqi collaborators with the occupiers, who had believed all Bush's talk of peace and democracy, began to realise that not everything was as they had imagined.

For example, Falah al-Jibouri,[13] an Iraqi-born US resident who helped with the pre-invasion brokering, told Greg Palast that all those whom he and his colleagues had named as political leaders and who had stopped Iraq's army from firing on US troops, were arrested. Such people, and particularly Sunni officers in the army, who were a primary target of de-Ba'athification, now realised that they faced a stark choice between joining the Islamic resistance or imprisonment, and possible execution, by the Americans. By choosing the first option, they brought

---

[13] He writes his second name Aljibury in America.

their military know-how to the Wahabi rebels, led by Musab al-Zarqawi.[14]

Black gold

Dividing Iraq's oil out among foreign companies separated Iraq from control of its principle resource, indeed of its future. Aljibury (alias al-Jibouri) told Greg Palast that when word got out about the plans to sell off the oilfields the pipelines began to blow.

> Although he had been at the centre of planning for invasion, Aljibury now saw the greed-crazed grab for the oil fields as the fuel for a civil war that would rip his country to pieces:
> 'Insurgents,' he said, 'and those who wanted to destabilize a new Iraq have used this as means of saying, "Look, you're losing your country. You're losing your leadership. You're losing all of your resources to a bunch of wealthy people. A bunch of billionaires in the world want to take you over and make your life miserable." And we saw an increase in the bombing of oil facilities, pipelines, of course, built on – built on the premise that privatization [of oil] is coming.'[15]

A matter of particular concern to me was the safety of my colleagues in the Ministry of Oil who had remained at their posts during the war. As it happens, and no doubt with good reason, the Ministry of Oil building was not damaged, while the seats of all the other ministries, along with educational institutions and medical centres, were trashed by the Americans and their expatriate Iraqi lackeys.

---

[14] Palast, G., Unreported: The Zarqawi Invitation, 2006. See https://web.archive.org/web/20060618005914/http://www.zmag.org/content/showarticle.cfm?SectionID=15&ItemID=10399.
[15] Ibid.

I got some insight into the situation in the oil industry on 20th and 21st of October 2003 when I was invited to attend the first post-war oil conference[16] in Geneva by the British company which had organised it. This had been scheduled to take place before the invasion, and I had been listed to chair one of the sittings. However, on the first day I was asked to relinquish my role on the grounds that Thamir Al-Ghadban, who was soon to become the Interim Minister of Oil in the first post-2003 US/UK selected government, considered me inappropriate. I then learnt that my friend Dr Falih al-Khayat, the Deputy Minister of Oil before the occupation, who had been scheduled to chair the aborted pre-war conference, had been barred from the post-war conference by the Americans. A graduate of Manchester University where he had studied electrical engineering, he had worked with BPC and was, on the face of it, ideally suited to the task. But this very capable and genuine person was a true patriot, and that wasn't what the Americans wanted. Instead he was forced to seek asylum in Amman.

Expatriate Iraqis from all over the world flocked to Geneva to promote themselves and to gain the approval of the American and British intelligence officers who were visibly present. Throughout the proceedings empty promises were made to major oil companies, and as a result the conference, unlike the pre-2003 conferences held in Baghdad, Paris and Geneva, was a failure. At these earlier conferences, international contractors had been invited to develop major and minor fields or Western Desert exploration blocks, which is how Perenco and Bula had become involved in the Rafidain oil field development project and the Block 4 exploration respectively. The failure of the conference gave a green light to the Americans to ravage the country. Behind political posturing, Dick Cheney's global engineering, construction and services company, Kellogg Brown Root (KBR), out-manoeuvred the

---

[16] Officially called The Iraq Conference (IC).

French company, Total, to gain control of the Majnoon field near Basrah, as well as the other oil fields in Iraq.

Iraq's interest and future seemed of little consequence, and though it was quite reasonable to promote the country's potential in terms of profitability, the official with whom delegates were supposed to negotiate had no clear mandate to act in this capacity. Instead we were treated to the sad spectacle of resurfaced Iraqi professionals sucking up to the US/UK Intelligence Services and the exile-dominated CPA. I recorded my notes about some of those attending the conference in a letter to Falih to which I've added further comments.

Thamir Ghadban, the new CEO of the Ministry of Oil, was not the man I knew. Both Hans von Sponeck and Enrica, of Finast, agreed with me that he'd remodelled himself in a way which made him unrecognisable. He was later involved in drafting the new constitution, and the still unapproved hydrocarbon law. [*Editor's note*: In October 2018 he became Deputy Prime Minister and Minister of Oil.]

Falah Khawaja revelled in the power of organising a meeting of the Iraqi team. He was the only delegate who publicly condemned the outgoing government and remained a senior employee in the Ministry of Oil despite the change in leadership. *Ghazi Haider* was more open than in the past but stayed on the fence. With others he formed Feipco Amatco Petroleum for Oil Services Ltd in 2008. *Natiq al-Bayati* was unchanged and friendly. He was the least affected by the euphoria of the gathering, and his contributions were practical and forthright. He went on to become a top Iraqi Oil Ministry official, dealing with contracts and licensing.

Many of those present wouldn't have dreamt of attending previous conferences. *Issam al-Chalabi*[17] made it clear he was interested in being reinstated as Oil Minister, a position he had held from 1987 to 1990. He publicly condemned the sabotage of pipelines and the resistance attacks on the oil installations, and was willing to accommodate the demands

---

[17] No relation of Ahmad al-Chalabi as far as I know.

of the new order. Quite by accident while dining at a restaurant on Lake Geneva, I encountered him with the Iraqi Team, who were meeting with *Dominic Simpson*, MD of Kyoll. I'm fairly sure the latter was unofficially representing the Foreign Office and Intelligence Service.

Falah al-Jubbari,[18] nicknamed 'the King Maker,' was a close associate of the US Republican administration. He selected Fadhal Othan, Dr Hashim al-Khursan and Thamir Ghadban to be Ministry executives. Though he was at the conference, he didn't to my knowledge attend any of the proceedings.

In 1964 *Tariq Shafiq* had been among the founders of the Iraq National Oil Company, and served as its Vice Chairman and Executive Director. He made an effort to rekindle his role in shaping Iraq's oil policy, having been side-lined by the CPA. He warned against privatisation by an un-elected Government, but his main interest was in doing business.

Dr Salah al-Shaikhly, who had earlier accused me of being Saddam's man in Europe, was a key member of the expatriate opposition and Iraq's ambassador to London after the war. He was keen to play some role but found himself brushed aside. He maintained that the US invasion was not motivated by oil, though I can't believe he really thought that oil played no part in US calculations.

Talib Naji Talib, Director of Comantec and working with Fluor, seems to have played some role, together with *Riadh Habboush*, in preparing the ground for the conference. He'd been employed in the South Oil Company before he left for the States.

I hadn't seen *Farouk al-Kasim*, a Basrawi, since 1968 when he resigned from IPC and emigrated with his Norwegian wife. He had met her in London in the fifties while training as a geologist at Imperial College. He played a crucial role in the development of Norway's oil policy, for which he was paid rather more than the Prime Minister. He was just as I remembered him; ambitious, mild-

---

[18] See note in the index entry for this delegate.

mannered, but good at promoting himself. He earned himself the thankless task of drafting the new Iraqi hydrocarbon law, but when this was altered by political horse-trading until it was unrecognisable, he disowned it.

Sabah Juma, like many, sailed with the wind. In 2007 he signed a statement opposing a unilateral decision by the Iraqi Kurdistan region to negotiate its own oil contracts, without the endorsement of the central government in Baghdad. My old friend, *Dr Hashim al Khursan*, expressed himself in favour of privatisation, and was pro-US in his stance, but was content to remain in Tunisia.[19]

Dr Ashti Abdullah, a Kurd from Sulaymaniyah, was Chair of the exploration company, ECL. He was working in Basrah on reservoir engineering and at that time he had no connection with political organisations. But in 2006 he became the Kurdish Regional Government's Minster of Natural Resources. And lastly there was *Saadalla al-Fathi*. From 1980 to 1986 he had served as President of the Refineries and Gas Industry Administration, and from 1986 to 1994 was head of the Energy Studies Department at the OPEC Secretariat. I felt his heart was in the right place, but he also sat on the fence.

I had expected Dr Thamir al-Ogali, who I believe became Bechtel's rep in Baghdad shortly after, and Fadhil Ali Othan, who turned down the offer of CEO at the Ministry, to be there, but they stayed away.

In 2004 the American government employed the consulting firm BearingPoint to help in drafting an oil law for Iraq (also known as the hydrocarbon law) which was finally approved by the Iraqi cabinet in 2007. Among other provisions, it permitted production share agreements (PSAs) guaranteeing a profit to foreign oil companies and authorised the governorates to conclude independent deals with oil

---

[19] I wasn't in favour of the privatisation of Iraq's oil industry, but I respected those who were, so long as there wasn't a political agenda behind their view. It was my meeting with my old school colleague, Hashim, and the Oil Minster, Abdul-Karim Tayih, while they were on a visit to the UK in 1975, which prompted me to set up Petcon.

companies. But this proved so unpopular both with the Iraqi parliament and the people that the law was never, to my knowledge, endorsed. An opinion poll found that 63% of Iraqis opposed the law on the grounds that Iraq should control its own oil. It was encouraging to discover that the patriotic spirit of my countrymen had not been entirely extinguished.

When I heard about the hydrocarbon law I sent out a FAF mailing, dated 13th April 2007, making the following points:

> Iraq is not a third world country starved of indigenous technical capability, nor is it short of funding to develop the existing oilfields. Such contracts [with foreign companies] are not therefore suitable for Iraq.
>
> Iraq's current priority is stability and an end to the occupation. There should be a referendum if the government wishes to change its constitution or its economy from a managed to a market economy. Iraq's oil industry could recover effectively by using revenue from oil sales and, where necessary, bringing in international companies on limited term contracts. It is unacceptable to lock Iraq into long-term contracts without fully consulting the Iraqi population. […] Such a system would also open the door for foreign contractors to utilise 'third country national' cheap labour rather than Iraqi manpower, and would thereby deny future generations of Iraqis training in the skills necessary to an independent country.

But in reality, though the lack of a firmly established legal framework for the oil industry might have deterred some, the very same companies which had run the IPC back in my early days with the company, that is Exxon Mobil, Shell, Total and BP, were soon, with the addition of Chevron and some small firms, back in the saddle. The CPA orders allowing foreign companies to invest on equal (i.e.

advantageous) terms with Iraqi firms and to transfer money out of the country, had not been repealed, and therefore provided sufficient protection and encouragement to foreign investors. Of greater concern to them was the instability and violence which the occupation had unleashed.

David Whyte, writing in the British Journal of Criminology, strongly condemned US/UK policy on the issue of Iraq's oil in the following terms:

> The scale and intensity of the appropriation of Iraqi oil revenue makes the 2003 invasion one of the most audacious and spectacular crimes of theft in modern history. The institutionalisation of corporate corruption that followed the invasion can only be understood within the context of the coalition forces' contempt for universal principles of international law enshrined in the Hague and Geneva treaties.[20]

Demanding an inquiry

I took every opportunity to join the chorus of voices demanding a transparent investigation into the justification, conduct and aftermath of the war, the eventual outcome of which I'll examine in Chapter Fifteen.

On 23rd May 2007, for example, I tagged this demand onto the end of a rant I wrote to the Prime Minister, who had just visited Iraq, and who only had another month to run in office. I reproduce some of the letter, which was copied to Gordon Brown, Harry Cohen, Ian Taylor and Paddy Ashdown, because it expresses well my mood at the time.

---

[20] Whyte, D., 'The Crimes of Neo-Liberal Rule in Occupied Iraq,' British Journal of Criminology, Vol 47, Issue 2, 1st March 2007, Pages 177–195. See https://doi.org/10.1093/bjc/azl065.

The instability, the sectarian/ethnic divide and the imminent slide into the abyss are manifestations of the Iraqi diaspora in government. None of its members have the capability or inclination to serve (except when it comes to themselves). They are incapable of governing, not because of a lack of security (there is, after all, a 150,000-strong multi-national force presence, not to mention numerous armed militias), but because of their conduct in promoting nepotism, corruption, and lust for hoarding personal wealth. The Iraqi people outside the Green Zone have rejected them for these reasons. [...]

It is regrettable that you have made so many visits to Iraq since the invasion, yet you made none during the period of sanctions. You would have seen capable, experienced and highly motivated Iraqi professionals driven by their patriotic wish to serve. What a contrast to those now ruling in the Green Zone. Alas many of these dedicated Iraqis are currently either in detention or have been forced to leave Iraq, a situation which represents a tremendous loss of intellectual and skilled capacity to the nation.

We urge you, and the PM elect, to pursue an independent inquiry into the conduct leading to the war.

I don't for a moment suppose that Blair read this, but it relieved my feelings. It's just possible, though, that Gordon Brown, who was shortly to become the Prime Minister, did so, and maybe it added a little more weight to the argument of others for the inquiry which he long opposed, but then announced two years later.

CHAPTER FOURTEEN

POLITICAL PRISONERS AND ASSASSINATIONS

The term 'political prisoner' is not neutral. It implies criticism of a government detaining anyone for political rather than legal reasons. This doesn't mean that such prisoners are free of any fault, but rather that the motivation for detaining them is not primarily legal. Consequently, this description is normally used of detainees in so-called pariah regimes. Saddam's Ba'athist government carried this label once it moved out of favour with the West, and consequently those it detained were generally regarded as political prisoners, whether or not this description fitted the case. The post-2003 regime in Iraq is regarded as 'legitimate,' at least officially, and therefore those it detains are generally not referred to as political prisoners. These prisoners, we are expected to believe, have been legally detained and are undergoing due process to determine whether they are guilty of the crimes with which they are charged.

The problem with this lop-sided view of political detention is that it tends to ignore the legal aspects of detainees in pariah regimes, and the political dimension of cases in so-called democratic regimes. I believe that the primary reason I was investigated and imprisoned was political, which is not to deny that I broke the law by paying the surcharge. But because the British government is not considered to 'do' political detention, it was impossible for me to defend myself as a political prisoner. The nearest I could get to doing so was to maintain that the case against me was an abuse of process, and that argument failed.

There is no doubt that Saddam, and at least by collusion Tariq Aziz also, used what most people in the West would regard as unacceptably violent means to control the country. But natural justice would have demanded that they be given the chance to explain, and have heard, why they acted as they did. They were, however, seen as guilty in advance and were treated accordingly. Their trials, and those of many others, were therefore a sham. Moreover, their detention lacked the basic elements of fairness and humanity which anyone accused of a crime should expect. In the case of Saddam his execution was a political showpiece, rather than the decent and discrete ending of a life which we would demand even for an animal.

In the labyrinthine world of international politics anything can happen. Let's suppose someone had managed to convince the US government following 9/11 that the best bulwark against Islamic terrorism would be strong leadership in the Arab world, and that as a result Saddam and his regime had been rehabilitated as responsible guardians of stability in the region. In these circumstances he, Tariq Aziz and many others wouldn't have been detained, and if their human rights record had been challenged, their argument, that they acted in the interests of the state and its people, would have been accepted by the great, if not the good, as reasonable.

In such a scenario I also believe that my co-defendant and I would not have been prosecuted by the Serious Fraud Office. Nor would Oscar Wyatt, who like me was on friendly terms with Saddam, have done time in a Texan jail. Oscar, a Texas oilman, was as far as I know, the only other person in the world, apart from myself and my co-defendant, to have been charged with paying the surcharge. He met Saddam in 1990 and secured the release of two dozen oil workers who had been held hostage following the Iraqi occupation of Kuwait, for which he was hailed as a hero. However, a decade and a half later he was charged in New York with taking advantage of his relationship with the President to gain the first contract for an oil lift under the oil-for-food programme. In 2007, at the age of 83, he pleaded guilty to paying millions of dollars to the Iraqi government in surcharges, and under a plea-bargaining arrangement was sentenced to one year and a day in prison.[1]

I find it significant that Wyatt, whom I met a couple of times and whose son I knew quite well, shared with me the experience of being personally acquainted with the Iraqi President. Was that the primary reason why we were both prosecuted, and that after us no one else was charged? To have continued to prosecute, especially if large companies with almost unlimited funds to spend on their defence had been involved, might well have brought quite unsavoury facts to light.

Saddam Hussein

Campaigning against the atrocious mistreatment of Ba'athists who had loyally served their country, often for many years, and who were now incarcerated for long periods without trial, and without proper arrangements for them to be legally represented, became a major part of our work.

As I have mentioned, Saddam was arrested in December 2003. This followed a massive US intelligence operation called 'Red Dawn,' the name of a 1980s film. He was found in a 'spider hole' in the town of Ad-Dawr, near Tikrit, and gave himself up without resistance. Later

---

[1] Leonard, T., 'Oscar Wyatt admits Iraq oil-for-food bribes,' *The Telegraph*, 1st October 2007; see http://www.telegraph.co.uk/news/worldnews/1564798/Oscar-Wyatt-admits-Iraq-oil-for-food-bribes.html; and Kearney, C., 'Texas oilman Wyatt sentenced to year in prison,' Reuters, 27 November 2007; see http://www.reuters.com/article/us-un-iraq-trial-idUSN2751695120071127. Incidentally, Wyatt had two high-profile British connections. His son was implicated in the divorce of the Duchess of York, and his wife was a friend of Lord Lloyd Webber and Sir Elton John. But these latter friends in British high places were of little use to him in the US. The Volcker Report had this to say about Wyatt (page 171): 'American oil trader Oscar Wyatt, a long-time and loyal oil customer of Iraq, was a rare exception to the Government of Iraq's ban on allocating oil to companies and individuals from the United States after the initial phases.'

television pictures showed him undergoing a medical examination, and being 'treated like a cow,' in the words of a senior Vatican clergyman.

The Americans handed Saddam over to the Iraqi Interim Government to be tried, but there were grave doubts internationally that the trial would be fair, and that the Americans would not influence the outcome. Accordingly, in June 2005 an International Emergency Committee for Iraq was formed which had as its main aim ensuring that Saddam and other top Ba'athists were tried fairly. Four prominent figures shared the chairmanship, namely ex-Malaysian Prime Minister Mahathir Mohamed, ex-US Attorney General Ramsay Clark, ex-Minister of Foreign Affairs of France Roland Dumas, and ex-President of Algeria Ahmed Ben Bella. Ramsay Clark joined Saddam's panel of defence lawyers at the Iraqi Special Tribunal set up for the purpose. From the time of Saddam's arrest, FAF joined in the demands that Saddam be tried fairly, and supported the efforts of the International Emergency Committee.

The Trial began in October, four days after the referendum on the new constitution, but the new Iraqi rulers badly botched the arrangements, most particularly in respect of security. Saddam was brought to trial alongside seven other top Ba'athists, including his half-brother and former chief of intelligence, Barzan Ibrahim al-Tikriti, and Taha Yassin Ramadan, former Vice-President. Saddam rejected the legality of the proceedings, maintaining that he was still the President. Four defence lawyers, including Khamis al-Obeidi, who was representing Saddam, were killed as the trial proceeded, another was wounded, and the chief judge at the beginning of the trial resigned due to government interference in the proceedings.

In June 2006 Ramsay Clark and the Human Rights lawyer Curtis Doebbler, who was also on the defence panel, called for adequate security for defence lawyers, and described the trial as unfair. In their view Saddam and his co-defendants were effectively being tried by the US, with only the appearance of Iraqi involvement. Saddam's eldest daughter Raghad, living in Amman, dismissed the proceedings as a farce, and said her father had deported himself like a lion.

Two days before his execution, the Ba'ath Party website carried a letter from Saddam urging Iraqis to unite, and not to hate the people of countries that invaded Iraq, but only their leaders. He declared himself ready for a martyr's death. A member of his defence team confirmed the authenticity of the letter, which he said had been written after he was condemned to death on November 5th. An unscientific sampling of opinion about the letter in a Baghdad street drew the following comments: 'When Saddam says in his letter that he offered himself for sacrifice for Iraq and called for unity, whether you agree with him or not, all Iraqis want unity and want foreign forces to leave the country.' Another, from Mosul, said that many Iraqis would hear Saddam's message and do what he said out of love for him. A third thought hanging Saddam would damage Iraq's image and cause an upsurge in terrorism. And finally a Kurd didn't want Saddam executed before everyone knew what he had done to his people.[2]

The night before his execution Saddam ate some chicken and rice with a cup of hot water and honey, and the next morning, at 5 a.m., he was escorted by American troops from Camp Cropper, near Baghdad airport, to Camp Justice, in the city centre, where he was handed over to the Iraqi police. At dawn, he was led to the gallows with a government camera recording the procedure up to the point where his head was put in the hangman's noose.[3] He told Mowaffak Al-Rubaie, who witnessed the execution, that he had no remorse or fear: 'I am a

---

[2] See
https://web.archive.org/web/20071007234244/http://www.redbolivia.com/noticias/News%20in%20English/36246.html.

[3] This can be viewed, if you don't consider it too ghoulish, at:
https://www.youtube.com/watch?v=1yAWVddk2mU, accompanied by entirely inappropriate Arabic music. An unofficial filming, recorded on a mobile phone, is also available at: https://www.youtube.com/watch?v=eqwTvHIU43c. Though of poorer quality, this has the advantage that you can hear the taunting shouts of those surrounding Saddam, and also his recitation of the Shahada on the scaffold.

militant and I have no fear for myself. I have spent my life in jihad and fighting aggression. Anyone who takes this route should not be afraid.' He was led before a judge, who read out the verdict finding him guilty of crimes against humanity. As the verdict was read out he cried: 'Long live the nation! Long live the people! Long live the Palestinians!'

After that he became calm as he was led to the gallows carrying a copy of the Quran. He asked for this to be given to another co-defendant who was about to be executed. It was cold and cramped in the execution room, and there was a bad smell. A large number of witnesses jostled each other for position, and threw insults at the condemned man. After the noose was tied round his neck Saddam recited the Shahada[4] and waited for the trap door to open. At last it was over and subsequently his body was taken to Al-Awja, his birthplace near Tikrit, where he was buried near other family members.[5]

There was widespread condemnation of the way Saddam was tried and executed. Human Rights Watch said that the 'execution follows a flawed trial and marks a significant step away from the rule of law in Iraq.'[6] Amnesty International, which opposes the death sentence, also commented on the unfairness of the trial.[7] Two day before his execution, the International Federation for Human Rights had called in vain for a moratorium on the death sentence and for Saddam to be treated as a prisoner of war under the Geneva Conventions.[8]

---

[4] The Shahada is the Muslim declaration of faith: *Ashadu an la illaha, illa Allah, wa Mohammad al-rasul Allah*, I declare that there is no God but God, and Muhammed is the messenger of God.

[5] This account of Saddam's death is based on Santora, M., 'On the Gallows, Curses for U.S. and "Traitors"', *New York Times*, 31st December 2006. See http://www.nytimes.com/2006/12/31/world/middleeast/31gallows.html?ex=13252 21200&en=472d36ebe903eabd&ei=5088&partner=rssnyt&emc=rss.

[6] See http://pantheon.hrw.org/legacy/english/docs/2006/12/30/iraq14950.htm.

[7] See https://web.archive.org/web/20070103205025/http://web.amnesty.org/pages/irq-281206-statement-eng.

[8] See https://www.fidh.org/spip.php?page=article&id_article=3925.

For me Saddam's execution was a personal matter. Though I was not a close friend of the President, and though I was well aware that he could be extremely ruthless, as several of my decisions recorded in this book testify, I knew him, nevertheless, as a human being, and one to whom I could relate. We ate together, we exchanged gifts and we visited each other's farms. Much though he may have deserved the full force of the law, I was disgusted at his treatment. Moreover, I couldn't overlook the fact that, like him or loathe him, Saddam represented the ideal of national unity within a socialist state, an outlook dear to me but like a red rag to the West. Had he remained the imperialists' friend, he would most probably have lived out his days without the indignity, and no doubt trauma, which he suffered in his last years. For we live in a hypocritical world in which extreme violence is condemned with great moral self-righteousness by the very people who initiate yet greater violence and destruction, and all in the name of democracy and human rights.

You may well say that I have underplayed the horror of Saddam's regime, and that is a reasonable criticism. But in a situation where a distorted history has been written by the victors, you might perhaps consider forgiving me for not adding further to the condemnation of a man who cannot now defend himself, and who during his trial had little chance to do so either.

Tariq Aziz

I was much closer to Tariq Aziz than I was to Saddam. Campaigning on his behalf was easier than for Saddam, as the latter had been so demonised that it was difficult to persuade people that he deserved any sympathy. The ex-Deputy Prime Minister, on the other hand, was well-known abroad and was regarded with some respect by many. Moreover, he was a Chaldean Christian, which shouldn't have made any difference, but it did. It also helped that Tam had come to know and like him.

Number 43, the eight of spades, on the American list of the 55 most wanted Iraqis,[9] gave himself up voluntarily to the Americans in April 2003 in the hope of ensuring the safety of his family. Rather over a month later, on 4th June, Tam secured an adjournment debate about Tariq Aziz's case in the House of Commons, which he opened in enigmatic form:

> Over 41 years as a Member of this House, I have initiated just over 100 Adjournment debates. On no occasion have I known less about the subject than I do about today's issue of the detention of Tariq Aziz. I do not know where he is. I do not know in what conditions he is held. Is he in Baghdad? Is he in the continental United States? What are the circumstances in which he went into the hands of the coalition?[10]

After a long diversion on the subject of protecting ancient epigraphic clay tablets in Iraq, for which the Speaker politely reprimanded him, and which was probably designed to give the government minister, Bill Rammell, time to arrive and take his place, Tam handed over to Robert Marshall-Andrews. The latter expressed the wish that Tariq Aziz would 'be tried in all the circumstances we would regard as humane, humanitarian and in the best tradition of our own form of justice.' After saying he was glad to see that the Minister was now in his place to hear him, he went on:

---

[9] He was later upgraded to number 25.
[10] See Hansard, 4th June 2003, Vol 406 cc280-8, for a full record of the debate. View online at http://hansard.millbanksystems.com/commons/2003/jun/04/tariq-aziz#S6CV0406P0_20030604_HOC_521.

The wider question pertains to the legality of actions taken by the coalition in the invasion of Iraq. ... [T]he more powerful a man, woman or nation is, the more important it is that legality is observed by that man, woman or nation state. ... What concerns us – it concerns me as a friend of America, which I have always been – is the effect that that form of apparently arbitrary justice will have on America's reputation and that of its allies.[11]

Bill Rammell opened his reply in the kind of emollient language expected of the Parliamentary Under-Secretary of State for Foreign and Commonwealth Affairs. 'I am genuinely grateful for the opportunity that has been accorded us by the Father of the House in raising a matter that is important to all of us.' On specifics, he confirmed that the ex-Deputy Prime Minister and Foreign Minister was in US custody in Baghdad, and that

the International Red Cross has been notified and given access to the detention centre where Tariq Aziz and other detainees are being held. We are trying to establish what medical treatment the detainees are receiving, but I can assure Members that all prisoners of war are being treated in accordance with international law and the Geneva conventions. [...] This is certainly not the victor's justice that the Father of the House is concerned about.[12]

The Minister may have been sincere, but in this case, as we will see, he was at least badly informed. Here is part of what I wrote to *The Independent* on 29th April 2008 under the title 'Trial of Vengeance':

---

[11] Ibid.
[12] Ibid.

> His Excellency Tariq Aziz, former Deputy PM of Iraq, has been imprisoned for over 5 years, together with other senior officials, by the US-supported sectarian Government.
>
> According to his family his lawyers have been denied free and safe access, since [he gave himself up in] 2003. He has also been denied regular family visits and phone calls. He is currently accommodated in a cell with two other detainees and lacks proper facilities. [...] This conduct by the multinational and the sectarian government is in blatant violation of his human rights as stipulated by the Geneva Conventions and International Law. It is also in total contradiction of the explicit declared reason for regime change.
>
> I found Tariq Aziz to be an extremely pragmatic and intelligent man, well versed in international affairs, who consistently reached out to find a peaceful resolution of the sanctions issue for the nation he faithfully served. He certainly is not a man of vengeance.

In April 2005 Tariq Aziz managed to address a letter to world public opinion in which he appealed for his case, and many others like it, to be handled fairly. He wrote: 'We have been in prison for a long time and we have been cut [off] from our families. No contacts, no phones, no letters. Even the parcels sent to us by our families are not given to us. We need a fair treatment, a fair investigation and finally a fair trial. Please help us.'[13] There was after that some improvement in the conditions of his detention. In August of that year he was finally allowed to see his family again, though they were not permitted to know where he was, and were therefore taken to the prison in a bus with blacked out windows.

---

[13] Barnett, A., 'The extraordinary pleas of Saddam's right-hand man,' *The Guardian*, 29th May 2005. See
https://www.theguardian.com/world/2005/may/29/iraq.antonybarnett.

Five years rolled by and then on 17th January of 2010, we learnt that Tariq Aziz had suffered a massive stroke. Four days later I received an email from his son, Ziad Aziz, from which I quote:

> [My father's] medical situation is still not made clear to us. We, his family, and his lawyer have been denied any access to him. We do not have any further information about his situation or if there were any further complications or, for that matter, any improvements.
>
> Furthermore, his lawyer was denied access to the court proceedings which took place this week, and as I mentioned above, he was denied any access to his client until his return to Camp Cropper [from which he had been taken to the US forces hospital at their base in Balad].
>
> These actions by the Iraqi courts and the added loss of speech will severely diminish my father's ability to defend himself against the charges brought against him. These actions are in strict violation of his human and civil rights granted to him by international and Iraqi law.
>
> I have constantly demanded that my father be released on humanitarian grounds. I have said over and over that my father is a very old and very sick man, and today my fears have come true. The poor medical attention he is receiving at Camp Cropper, the physical strain he is suffering being moved from and to the court, the less-than-human conditions in the court's detention cell where the detainees can't even wash their clothes, let alone sleep or eat, and of course the psychological stress have all led to his deteriorating medical condition. I demand that he be released immediately so he can receive the proper medical care that he desperately needs,

especially now. There can be no delays as his life in hanging by a thread.[14]

Between 2008 and 2010 Tariq Aziz was at last tried on a number of different charges, for the last of which, concerning the persecution of Islamic parties in 1991, he was in October 2010 sentenced to death. When one considers the West's attitude to Islamic parties today, there is a certain grim irony about the charge on which he was found guilty. There was widespread international condemnation of the trial as it was rightly considered to be politically motivated, and this probably saved him from execution.

I had come to enjoy a close relationship with Tariq Aziz. I had eaten at his house, had held long conversations with him, and had met his charming family. I believed him to be a sincere patriot and a good man, and realised that what I was going through (I had by then been charged with breaking the sanctions) bore no comparison with his suffering. I copied Ziad's email to all my contacts, including Clare Short, Secretary of State for International Development under the Blair administration, Denis Halliday and Hans von Sponeck, ex-UN Humanitarian Coordinators, and Nicholas Allen, Middle East and North Africa Director of the Middle East Group at the Foreign and Commonwealth Office. I received numerous expressions of support and offers to do what they could, but in truth neither I nor they could do much more than protest. Perhaps this had the effect of marginally improving the conditions of Tariq Aziz's detention; one would like to think so. But for another five years he languished in gaol, before death from cancer finally released him from his suffering in June 2015.

In an obituary Hans von Sponek and Denis Halliday wrote this:

> It does not matter to us that our words of sadness and respect for Tariq Aziz – a leader during many dark days of his

---

[14] Transcript of the email as sent out in a FAF mailing.

country – will be used by some to discredit us for alleged support of a dictatorial regime.

Tariq Aziz impressed us again and again by his commitment with which he cooperated with the United Nations when we served at different times as UN humanitarian coordinators in Baghdad. His relentless efforts to prevent the 2003 war will not be forgotten. He was a hard but highly principled task master without whom the inadequate UN Security Council response to human suffering in Iraq would have had an even worse impact.

We had a good idea how the scales of justice would react were it possible to quantify the weight of wrong-doing against the people of Iraq contributed from within Iraq and [that which originated] from the outside.[15]

They were outspoken in their criticism of former US Secretary of State, James Baker, the Vatican, and leaders in Europe and elsewhere for their lack of humanity and statesmanship. 'Not even our own organisation, the United Nations, could muster the courage to demand fair treatment for a man whom the organisation had known over decades as a convincing and credible defender of Iraq's rights.'[16]

Intellectual cleansing

The destruction of Iraq required the removal of its skills and knowledge. Again Palestine, though different in certain respects, served as a model. During the twenties and thirties, as the Zionists set up their proto-state, they introduced procedures which excluded non-Jews from the workforce. In the lead-up to the declaration of the

---

[15] Von Sponeck, H., Halliday, D., 'Obituary: Tariq Aziz,' *Common Dreams*, 12th June 2015. See https://www.commondreams.org/views/2015/06/12/obituary-tariq-aziz.
[16] Ibid.

Zionist entity in 1948 life was made so insecure by Zionist gangs that many of those with money and connections left the country. The Palestinians who remained made strenuous efforts to replace that loss, but it took time, and the Zionists made sure they benefitted from the vacuum. Then as the Zionists set up their system of control, three further methods of intellectual cleansing were adopted, assassinations of prominent figures, a ban on the return of refugees and large-scale detentions.

Iraq was not settled by a foreign people in the way that Palestine was, but the similarity in the methods used by the occupiers is striking. The exclusion from the workforce was achieved by de-Ba'athification. The Badr Brigades and other militias were the equivalent of the Zionist gangs who frightened the intelligentsia out of the country. The vacuum created by the purging of Sunnis in high positions was filled by Shias loyal to Iran. Those who had fled the country had to be particularly foolhardy to return, for hired assassins were likely to gun them down. And those that dared to remain, if they were Sunni, were liable to find themselves enduring long periods of detention, without trial or proper legal representation, and in inadequate and degrading conditions of the kind endured by Saddam Hussein and Tariq Aziz.

As far as these methods of intellectual cleansing were concerned, FAF could do little more than draw them to the attention of appropriate ministers in the British government and urge them to bring pressure to bear on the Americans and their Iraqi quislings. But as Tam pointed out, even among intelligent MPs there was often a lacuna of understanding, or perhaps it was an unwillingness to understand. That is why we focussed on the specific issue of political prisoners, the ex-President and ex-Deputy Prime Minister being top of our list. There were many others, and the unstated reason for their incarceration was often the skill and knowledge which they possessed and which the country so desperately needed.

As the word got around that FAF was lobbying MPs and humanitarian organisations on behalf of political prisoners, we received numerous cries for help from the families of detained Ba'athists. We therefore found it necessary to develop a short questionnaire to collect the necessary information; this consisted of variations on the following questions:

- What form of communication do you have with your relative?
- In what condition is s/he held, and is s/he in need of, and receiving medical treatment?
- Are you or any of your family allowed to visit?
- Does s/he have legal representation?

I asked myself how democracy could thrive in Iraq if those competent patriots who previously governed were in jail, often without access to a lawyer or any prospect of a fair trial. These men[17] were imprisoned despite their previous commitment and service to their country over many years, and in the meantime the British and Americans imposed an administration which presented a façade of democracy to the world.

On 12th March 2007 I raised with Ann Clwyd, the Prime Minister's Envoy on Human Rights, my concern about some detained scientists:

> I would like to call for your intervention arising out of a disturbing report from Iraq that 22 Iraqi scientists are in detention. To date their families have not been informed of their whereabouts, nor have any charges been brought. It appears they are victims of their past scientific achievements and of the fact that they are all Sunnis.

---

[17] I know of no women politicians who were imprisoned, but some female government scientists were.

Your co-operation will be of immense value to maintaining and upholding human rights for all:

01. Dr Rafid Mohammed Al Omar – Physician
02. Dr Tariq al Mashhadami – Prof of Organic Chemistry
03. Dr Nasir al-Tikrity – Physician
04. Dr Saad al-Hayani
05. Dr Fahed Abdul-Karim al-Dulaimi – Physicist.
06. Dr Jasim al-Khaldi – Archaeologist
07. Dr Salah Khalid Khadom – Economist
08. Dr Waleed al-Jubori – Plastic Surgeon
09. Dr Ali al-Nasiri – Sociologist
10. Dr Anwar Alani – Physicist.
11. Dr Nabeel Mohammed al-Obaidi – Bacteriologist
12. Dr Basil Raziq – Chemist
13. Dr Tawfiq Saddi – Rocket Engineer
14. Dr Suleiman Adil al-Dulaimi – Mig21 Engineer
15. Dr Salam Mukhus al-Hayali
16. Dr Jaber Amin al-Bawi – Rocket Engineer
17. Dr Sabri al-Qaysi
18. Dr Asim al-Mohawdi – Nuclear Scientist
19. Dr Yousif al-Kubaisi
20. Dr Iman Omar Abdul-Aziz – Female physicist specialising in Rocket Fuel
21. Dr Hosan al-Musali
22. Dr Shoja al-Hashawi[18]

I got the usual pro-forma reply, but I never heard anything more about these scientists, and a superficial search on the internet came up blank in all cases. I am, therefore, led to fear the worst.

---

[18] Letter dated 12th March 2007, FAF reference 30.03.07. See http://www.uruknet.info/colonna-centrale-pagina.php?p=m31514&l=&size=&hd.

Denis Halliday and Hans von Sponeck were very supportive of my efforts on behalf of prisoners as they shared my view that their detention and treatment was not only unjust, but also unwise. Almost all of those who had been incarcerated were loyal and hardworking patriots. In addition to those already mentioned, there were the former Minister of Culture, Hamid Yussef Hamadi, the former Minister of Trade, Dr Mohammed Saleh Mahdi, and the former Minister of Oil, Dr Amir Rasheed. We contacted a number of MPs to intervene on their behalf but all our efforts failed to bring them to a fair trial or to secure their release. No one was sufficiently interested and their situation deteriorated.

CHAPTER FIFTEEN

A TALE OF TWO TRIALS: PART ONE, TONY BLAIR

Two people went on trial in the summer of 2009.

The first, Tony Blair, was to be tried in the court of public opinion. The presiding judge of the most important part of the trial was Sir John Chilcot, Chair of the Iraq Inquiry set up in 2009. No official charges were to be brought, but everyone understood roughly what they would have been. That Anthony Charles Lynton Blair did knowingly mislead parliament into agreeing to an illegal war on the basis of false evidence drafted for the purpose. That he did thereby cause the death and wounding of an incalculable number of Iraqis and the death of 179 and wounding of 222 Britons. That he destabilised the region still further. And that he soiled the reputation of the UK for fair and transparent dealing and adherence to international standards.

Two months later I was charged in court with 'Making funds available to Iraq except under the authority of a licence granted by the Treasury.' The evidence was that on four oil transactions with SOMO in 2001 I paid a surcharge imposed by the Iraqi regime. I did pay those surcharges and I did know that they were illegal. Since, however, around eighty companies and individuals in the UK committed the same offence, in most cases paying far more than I did, and yet none of them, other than my co-defendant, were ever prosecuted for it, I have reason to think that in reality I was, in this respect like Blair, facing undeclared charges. These were that Riad el-Taher did consort with the Queen's enemies, and that he did disturb through his campaigning the smooth functioning of the foreign policy of Her Majesty's government. You will note that I was *not* charged with endangering anyone's life, and indeed I may well have saved some.

The Chilcot inquiry is announced

On 15th June 2009 the then Prime Minister, Gordon Brown, announced an inquiry, to be conducted by Sir John Chilcot, together with four other privy counsellors. Its aim would be to identify the lessons that could be learned from the Iraq conflict. He stated, however, that 'the committee will not set out to apportion blame or consider issues of civil or criminal liability.'[1] He also pointed out that

> we have had four separate inquiries already into some of the events surrounding Iraq: we have had the Foreign Affairs Committee inquiry, the Intelligence and Security Committee inquiry, the Butler inquiry and the Hutton inquiry. It is not as if many of the issues have not been addressed; they have been addressed, but it is important to look at the matter in the round. What we want to do—I think that sometimes we forget this—is learn the lessons, so that they can be applied for the future.[2]

Let's recall the most significant of these previous inquiries. The Hutton report investigated the circumstances surrounding David Kelly's death, and was published at the beginning of 2004. It's enough to say that I agreed with Paul Routledge who wrote in *The Daily Mirror*, that it was an 'establishment whitewash' that stank 'to high heavens.'[3] The BBC had taken the brunt of the flak for having substantially told

---

[1] Hansard 15th June 2009, column 24. See
https://publications.parliament.uk/pa/cm200809/cmhansrd/cm090615/debtext/90615-0004.htm
[2] Ibid, column 30. See
https://publications.parliament.uk/pa/cm200809/cmhansrd/cm090615/debtext/90615-0005.htm
[3] CNN.com, 29th January 2004. See
https://web.archive.org/web/20040221151253/http://edition.cnn.com/2004/WORLD/europe/01/29/hutton.press/.

the truth about the 'sexing up' of intelligence to make the case for war. Tony Blair and his government had got off that one virtually scot-free. The Butler Review (of Intelligence on Weapons of Mass Destruction), published in July of the same year, had been more critical. It had found that the intelligence the government used to justify its involvement in the Second Gulf War was unreliable because the Secret Intelligence Service hadn't checked its sources adequately, had relied on third-hand reports, and had given too much weight to the accounts of Iraqi dissidents. I had repeatedly warned my contacts in parliament on this last point.

There was much disquiet among MPs that this new inquiry would take a year to deliver its report, and it was pointed out that it would, conveniently for the government, appear after the next general election. What would they have thought had they known that the Chilcot report would not appear for another seven years, by which time not only one, but two general elections would have passed. Whatever redeeming features the report may have had, and I admit that my scepticism was only partly vindicated, the anger felt by many British people about the way they had been misled, had by 2016, that is 13 years after the war, to some extent subsided. Moreover, the Labour Party had not been in power since 2010, and was therefore less vulnerable. Chilcot may not have intended to kick the issue into the long grass until it was no longer so explosive, but that's effectively what happened. And Tony Blair lived on to fight another day.

Sir John described the Inquiry's task as follows:

> Our terms of reference are very broad, but the essential points, as set out by the Prime Minister and agreed by the House of Commons, are that this is an Inquiry by a committee of Privy Counsellors. It will consider the period from the summer of 2001 to the end of July 2009, embracing the run-up to the conflict in Iraq, the military action and its

aftermath. We will therefore be considering the UK's involvement in Iraq, including the way decisions were made and actions taken, to establish, as accurately as possible, what happened and to identify the lessons that can be learned. Those lessons will help ensure that, if we face similar situations in future, the government of the day is best equipped to respond to those situations in the most effective manner in the best interests of the country.

The committee members of the Inquiry, in addition to Sir John, were Sir Lawrence Freedman, Sir Martin Gilbert,[4] Sir Roderic Lyne and Baroness Usha Prashar.

Scepticism about the inquiry

In the view of Oliver Miles, author of that letter to Tony Blair in 2004, the question the Chilcot Inquiry should have addressed was as follows: 'Was this a war of aggression and therefore a war crime?' He added sardonically: 'There were two views about its legality, and the then Attorney General seems to have held both of them.' Expanding on this he continued:

> What about the alleged links between Saddam Hussein and al-Qa'ida? – it seems there were no such links. What happened to the civil planning for after the fighting? – according to Clare Short, who was a member of the Cabinet, there 'were preparations that were then all junked, because of the hubris and deceit that went into preparing for war'. Were the arguments for and against war ever assessed by the FCO, and was formal advice submitted to the then Secretary of State, the Cabinet and the Prime Minister? Here is Clare

---

[4] Sir Martin Gilbert became seriously ill in April 2012, after which he was no longer able to contribute to the inquiry. He died on 3rd February 2015.

> Short again: 'All the Cabinet meetings were little chats: they were never a proper consideration of all the options.' Is it true that the Iraq experts invited to No 10 in November 2002 (two of whom also took part in the seminar organised by the Inquiry on 5th November) decided not to tell Tony Blair whether they thought an invasion was wise or not because they thought he wouldn't listen? We have heard a lot recently about the freedom of experts to give advice which is unpalatable to the Government, so why the self-censorship?
>
> We need to know more about the exchanges between George Bush and Tony Blair. According to Colin Powell, the then US Secretary of State, he and Jack Straw[5] sometimes tried to get Blair to hold Bush back. 'Jack and I would get him all pumped up about an issue. And he'd be ready to say, "Look here, George". But as soon as he saw the President he would lose all his steam.' Can this be true?[6]

Miles summarises the criticisms of the composition of the Inquiry committee, and goes on to voice his own:

> None is a military man, Sir John Chilcot was a member of the Hutton Inquiry and has been closely involved with the security services, Baroness Prashar has no relevant experience, Sir Roderic Lyne was a serving ambassador at the time of the war, and so on.
>
> Rather less attention has been paid to the curious appointment of two historians (which seems a lot, out of a total of five), both strong supporters of Tony Blair and/or the

---

[5] Secretary of State for Foreign and Commonwealth Affairs in Blair's government, 2001 to 2006.
[6] Miles, O., 'The key question – is Blair a war criminal?' in *The Independent on Sunday*, 22nd November 2009. See
http://www.independent.co.uk/voices/commentators/oliver-miles-the-key-question-ndash-is-blair-a-war-criminal-1825374.html.

Iraq war. In December 2004 Sir Martin Gilbert, while pointing out that the 'war on terror' was not a third world war, wrote that Bush and Blair 'may well, with the passage of time and the opening of the archives, join the ranks of Roosevelt and Churchill' – an eccentric opinion that would seem to rule him out as a member of the committee. Sir Lawrence Freedman is the reputed architect of the 'Blair doctrine' of humanitarian intervention, which was invoked in Kosovo and Afghanistan as well as Iraq.

Both Gilbert and Freedman are Jewish, and Gilbert at least has a record of active support for Zionism. Such facts are not usually mentioned in the mainstream British and American media, but the Jewish Chronicle and the Israeli media have no such inhibitions, and the Arabic media both in London and in the region are usually not far behind.

All five members have outstanding reputations and records, but it is a pity that if and when the enquiry is accused of a whitewash, such handy ammunition will be available. Membership should not only be balanced; it should be seen to be balanced.[7]

As could be expected, Oliver Miles's carefully considered assessment of potential Jewish-Zionist bias in the committee soon drew condemnation from certain quarters, and this was reflected in the establishment press. An editorial in *The Times* on 25th November commented:

> Oliver Miles's contribution to the debate is extraordinary and disgraceful [...]. Sir John and the members of the enquiry panel are eminent in scholarship and public service [...]. They

---

[7] Ibid.

should be left to get on with their deliberations without a volley of snide attack and irrelevant innuendo.[8]

Three days later Richard Ingrams wrote in his weekly column in *The Independent*:

> The ambassador's comments and the attention paid to them by *The Times* may be helpful in the long run, if only by drawing attention to the Israeli dimension in the Anglo-US invasion of Iraq in 2003, a dimension that hitherto has scarcely been mentioned. Yet it is a fact that the campaign to overthrow Saddam Hussein was initiated well before 9.11, by a group of influential American neocons, notably Perle, Feith and Wolfowitz (once described as 'the godfather of the Iraq war')[9] nearly all of whom were ardent Zionists, in many cases more concerned with preserving the security of Israel than that of the US.

---

[8] The correct text was supplied by Oliver Miles to my editor. On 17th February 2010 *The Times* published a letter from Oliver Miles repudiating this attack, following his complaint to the Press Complaints Commission. Here is what he wrote:
'Sir, In a leading article commenting on the Chilcot inquiry into the Iraq war ("A search for truth", November 25) you described my views on the inquiry as "extraordinary and disgraceful", but you did not quote those views or inform readers where they could be found. Your reference was to an opinion piece I wrote in the *Independent on Sunday* (November 22), and I believe you have misrepresented my views.
I do not "already know [my] view of Chilcot's work". I do not believe the inquiry to be "a defensive response to public anger". I am not a "zealot" and do not "hold all such inquiries to be tainted until and unless they arrive at the right answer". Indeed, my article was generally supportive of the inquiry.
I am concerned that my observation that two of the five members of the panel are Jewish was interpreted as a statement that the panel "has too many Jews on it", suggesting prejudice against Jews. I do not believe that I have written anything to support such a charge. Oliver Miles, Former British Ambassador to Libya.'
[9] Richard Perle, Assistant Secretary of Defence for Global Strategic Affairs; Feith, Douglas, Under Secretary of Defence for Policy; Paul Wolfowitz, US Deputy Secretary of Defence.

> Given that undeniable fact, the pro-Israel bias of Sir Martin Gilbert and Sir Lawrence Freedman, both of them supporters of the 2003 invasion, is a perfectly respectable point to raise. It is equally legitimate to ask if at any point the panel will investigate or even refer to the US neocons and their links to Israel. Call me snide if you like, but I very much doubt they will.[10]

In a FAF briefing acknowledging the contributions of Miles and Ingrams, I voiced my own doubts about what could be expected from the Inquiry:

> It is no secret that the campaign for regime change in Iraq was driven by ardently Zionist neo-cons in America. It is regrettable that the Conservative opposition leadership were so influenced by the pro-Zionist Conservative Friends of Israel lobby that they blindly supported Blair's quest for a pre-emptive war. In doing so they plunged the national interest into the abyss. For all these reasons our expectation of the Chilcot report will be marginal [...]

That was, in retrospect, a rather overstated judgement. My scepticism at the time did not, however, deter me from submitting evidence to the inquiry. The inquiry's public hearings were concluded in February 2011, but there were repeated delays in issuing the report after that, largely as a result of a decision to grant those criticised in the report a right of reply. And so it wasn't until 6th July 2016 that it finally appeared.

---

[10] Ingrams, Richard, 'Will Zionists' links to Iraq invasion be brushed aside?', *The Independent*, 27th November 2009.

The Iraq Inquiry report

At 11 o'clock on 6th July 2016 Sir John Chilcot launched *The Report of the Iraq Inquiry*[11] at the Queen Elizabeth II Centre in Westminster. The repeated delays had created among many the suspicion that the report would be a whitewash, but it issued, on the contrary, a devastating judgement on the two fundamental questions which the inquiry, in Sir John's own words, was charged with investigating:

- whether it was right and necessary to invade Iraq in March 2003; and
- whether the UK could – and should – have been better prepared for what followed.

At the beginning of his statement Sir John put it this way:

> We have concluded that the UK chose to join the invasion of Iraq before the peaceful options for disarmament had been exhausted. Military action at that time was not a last resort. We have also concluded that:
>
> - The judgements about the severity of the threat posed by Iraq's weapons of mass destruction – WMD – were presented with a certainty that was not justified.
> - Despite explicit warnings, the consequences of the invasion were underestimated. The planning and preparations for Iraq after Saddam Hussein were wholly inadequate.
> - The Government failed to achieve its stated objectives.

---

[11] The full report, executive summary and Sir John Chilcot's statement can all be viewed by clicking on the appropriate links at http://webarchive.nationalarchives.gov.uk/20171123122743/http://www.iraqinquiry.org.uk/the-report/. At the time of writing if you just type in http://www.iraqinquiry.org.uk/, which was the address of the original inquiry site before archiving, you are redirected to the relevant National Archive pages.

And at the end of his statement he summarised:

> Military action in Iraq might have been necessary at some point. But in March 2003:
>
> - There was no imminent threat from Saddam Hussein.
> - The strategy of containment could have been adapted and continued for some time.
> - The majority of the Security Council supported continuing UN inspections and monitoring.

What about Oil and Palestine?

It will be noticed that the emphasis in Chilcot's summing up is on risk assessment, the assumption being that the stated motives of the UK, that is national security and the application of international law, were the only ones which needed to be considered. The reality is that states are rarely motivated only by such narrow considerations. Two obvious ones arise in the case of the invasion of Iraq, that is oil supplies and the security of a nearby Western ally, the Zionist entity.

Oil is hardly mentioned at all, and never as being a major Western motive for regime change. There are five references to oil in the Executive Summary; two refer to smuggling under the sanctions regime, one to the oil-for-food programme, one about the control of oil revenue, and the last about oil policy under the post-war provisional authority. As I said in Chapter Four I am convinced that from the moment Iraq nationalised its oil industry, the Western powers were looking for a way to regain control of the country's oil resources. In 2003 they achieved it.

Secondly, nowhere in its twelve volumes and 2.6 million words is there any indication of the part the Zionist entity undoubtedly played in the whole affair. 'Israel' is mentioned only twice in the 150-page executive summary, and that superficially in relation to a hoped-for resolution of the Israel-Palestine conflict. Moreover, a key figure in the relationship between Tony Blair and the Zionist entity, Lord Levy, does not appear in the list of those mentioned in the report which appears as 'Annex 3: Names and posts.' He was either not called to give evidence, declined to appear, or requested that his participation not be revealed.

Lord Levy was for nine years Tony Blair's special envoy to the Middle East, as well as a personal friend of the Prime Minister. Levy organised the funding of Blair's 1997 election campaign, persuading prominent figures such as Alex Bernstein and Robert Gavron to contribute substantially. They, as well as Levy, were all ennobled by Blair after he came to power. Levy continued to be the Labour Party's main fundraiser right up to Blair's departure in 2007, which makes it difficult to believe that the latter didn't feel in some way beholden to him. Levy's close ties to Zionist leaders were strengthened through his son, Daniel Levy, who served as assistant to both Ehud Barak and Yossi Beilin. An indication of how important the Zionists regarded him came on December 4th 2003, a few months after Iraq was invaded, when he was honoured with the 'Israel Policy Forum (USA) Special Recognition Award.'

That this important aspect of the story was not even mentioned may well be due to the inclusion on the inquiry committee of the two prominent Jewish historians which drew the criticism of both Oliver Miles and Richard Ingrams. Those who more openly doubted the impartiality of the Chilcot committee appear, therefore, to have been at least partly vindicated.[12] Having said all this, Chilcot's damning

---

[12] Gilad Atzmon, an ex-Israeli political commentator and saxophonist, made the same point the day after the Iraq Report was published, quoting the same passage from the article by Oliver Miles reproduced earlier in this book. Atzmon's article appears on his own website at: http://www.gilad.co.uk/writings/2016/7/7/chilcot-israel-and-the-lobby.

assessment of Tony Blair's action gave me some hope that we were at last on the way to uncovering his crimes.

But how did Blair and his closest associates react to the report? Well, exactly as one would expect. No regret, no remorse! Tony Blair and Ann Clwyd both said they would do it again.

For whose benefit, one is bound to ask? Certainly not those who opposed the regime and experienced thirteen years of draconian sanctions; nor did they help ordinary unengaged Iraqis whose only error was to be living in their native country at the time. Members of my extended family, for example, lost their homes, their roots, their heritage and their culture, and are now scattered across the globe. Practically all my school friends and work colleagues have suffered a similar fate. Hardly any of them now live in Iraq. Our Christian friends have also lost everything since 2003.

Yes, Iraq's rulers made many political mistakes which had adverse effects on the lives of its people. But these pale into insignificance compared with the chaos which Blair and Clwyd, through their partnership with George Bush, unleashed upon an entire nation. The forced exodus since 2003 which this has caused has spilled over to the entire region, most particularly affecting Libya, Yemen and Syria. It has caused shock waves within the EU and fuelled extremism in the Middle East.

There were many voices of reason immediately before the war, but equally there were those of vested interest, especially the so-called Iraqi opposition in the US and UK, which was motived by self-gain and hatred of Saddam. These political schemers were encouraged when Whitehall and the White House granted them the status of a government in exile, despite the lack of indigenous support in their homeland. On the other hand Ann Clwyd's friends, the Kurdish warlords Talabani and Barzani, were able to turn the sanctions regime to their advantage because it created the conditions for a lucrative and illicit oil trade with Turkey which the West intentionally ignored.

Did the opposition represent the whole of Iraq? Did they have any experience of governance? The answer to both these questions is a definitive 'no.' It is quite evident that the puppet regimes which have ruled Iraq since 2003 can only operate with a degree of safety within the green zone and with the aid of mercenaries beyond it.

I'm not a Saddam apologist, as Clwyd once accused me of being. I judged Saddam's policies on their merits; some I agreed with, others I didn't. How I wish that Blair and Clwyd could have witnessed the deprivation experienced by Iraqis during those years of sanctions. If they had paid attention to that, rather than listening to the treacherous sanctions-supporting Iraqis living in the UK they might not have destroyed an entire nation.

Blair can't be charged

I have said that the charges against Blair were in people's minds rather than being represented in specific judicial actions. But there was, and continues to be, much discussion about bringing Blair to justice, and a serious attempt was made to do just this by former Iraqi general, Abdulwaheed al-Rabbat. Supported by his solicitor, Imran Khan (not to be confused with the Pakistani cricketer and politician),[13] and represented in the High Court by Michael Mansfield QC, he brought a private prosecution for war crimes against the ex-Prime Minister.[14] Mansfield argued that the offence of waging an aggressive war had effectively been assimilated into English law since the time of the

---

[13] Imran Khan had acted for the family in the Stephen Lawrence inquiry, the report of which was published in 1999. Michael Mansfield also represented the family in their earlier unsuccessful attempt to prosecute the police officers involved in Stephen Lawrence's murder.

[14] As I will relate in the next chapter, Mansfield expressed an interest in taking on my case, but by then I was committed to Sir Desmond de Silva.

Nuremberg trials.[15] Moreover, 'the Chilcot inquiry's conclusion that the invasion of Iraq was unnecessary and undermined the United Nations required the prosecution of Tony Blair. [...] The aim of the case was to force Blair – as well as the former foreign secretary Jack Straw and the former attorney general Lord Goldsmith – to answer for their actions in court.'[16]

However, in their ruling on 31st July 2017 the Lord Chief Justice, Lord Thomas of Cwmgiedd and Mr Justice Ouseley, though sympathetic to Mansfield's arguments, maintained that there was no crime of aggression in English law, and that Blair could not therefore be prosecuted on this basis. Here are some of the comments made by Imran Khan on the outcome:

> [Rabbat] is extremely disappointed with the judgment of the high court in London which brings to an end the hope of prosecuting Tony Blair, Jack Straw and Peter Goldsmith for the crime of aggression in invading Iraq in 2003.
>
> The invasion and subsequent occupation resulted in the deaths of hundreds of thousands of individuals as well as the displacement of over 4 million others including General al-Rabbat who has had to seek sanctuary and refuge in another country.
>
> Iraq has been left decimated and in a state of chronic instability. Despite all of this, and the clear findings of the Chilcot inquiry which laid bare the conduct of those that should be held to account, the high court has confirmed that

---

[15] The trials of prominent Nazis organised by the victorious allies after World War II.
[16] Bowcott, O., 'Tony Blair prosecution over Iraq war blocked by judges,' *The Guardian*, 31st July 2017. See
https://www.theguardian.com/politics/2017/jul/31/tony-blair-prosecution-over-iraq-war-blocked-by-judges.

there is to be no accountability. Those responsible are to remain unpunished. This is not justice. […]

It is now the responsibility of the UK parliament to end this deplorable state of affairs and introduce legislation which ensures that the crime of aggression can be prosecuted in the criminal courts here.[17]

---

[17] Ibid.

1. Walking in the English countryside became a favourite pastime

2. On the Devon coastline

3. Paul Volcker

4. Lord Goldsmith

5. Where the hearings in my case took place, and where I was sentenced

6. The long-awaited Iraq Inquiry report, which vindicated much that I'd said, was launched by its Chair, Sir John Chilcot, in 2016

CHAPTER SIXTEEN

THE TALE BEHIND MY TALE

Levantine politics, British style

And so we come to my own trial. I use this word more in its colloquial sense than to describe a specific judicial process. In reality my appearances in court never reached the stage of a full jury trial. It consisted, rather, of a series of preliminary hearings which aimed at establishing whether the case brought against me should be dropped on the grounds of abuse of process.

This book is in great measure about the suffering of my fellow Iraqis and the denial of their right to self-determination. Though I was profoundly affected by what happened to me between 2008, when I was first detained, and 2011, when I was convicted and sentenced, in the greater scheme of things, my distress was a side-show. It belongs in my memoir, but I could have kept it very short. I took a risk when I decided to pay the surcharge, it was illegal under British law to do so, and I paid the price.

However, it's not quite as simple as that. The fact that only two other people were ever prosecuted for this offence, and one of those was in the United States, whereas the Volcker report identified 139 companies worldwide who paid the surcharge,[1] raises the question about what process was at work. Why were only I and two others convicted for this offence? I pose this question not in the 'why me?' spirit of a victim, but rather as a believer in the idea that justice should not only be done, but be seen to be done. British people are proud of their apparently

---

[1] I believe eighty companies and individuals paid the surcharge in Britain alone.

incorruptible legal system, but my case indicates that it is far from what it seems. That is why I'm going to explore in some detail the background to my case.

The expression 'Levantine politics' is used to describe impenetrable, even inexplicable dealings behind the scenes by invisible operators, and involving improbable alliances, unjust decisions, and often cruel administration. Certainly Arab politics often displays these characteristics. But if I had ever been tempted to think that politics in Europe and America was more straightforward and honest, and that in Britain, at least, a sense of fair-play would ensure the equitable enforcement of the law, the scales were about to fall from my eyes.

Starting in 2005, but especially after 2009, I was drawn into a maelstrom where natural justice played no part. I do not dispute that I broke British law, deriving from UN resolution 661, in paying the surcharge imposed by Saddam Hussein's regime. I assumed, however, that the British and American governments were not in earnest in their public adherence to this policy, since their actions indicated to me and many others quite the opposite. For the vast majority of those who took the risk of paying the surcharge, this view of the matter paid off. My disadvantage was that I could be regarded as a sole oil trader (even though I was acting as a director for Perenco and Bula), and that the Serious Fraud Office urgently needed an easy scalp after years of poor results. Moreover, as Tam intimates in his introduction to this book, my long campaign against the sanctions, and thereafter against the occupation, made me enemies in high places, and probably sealed my fate.

The Volcker Committee

This sorry story begins with my interrogation by the Volcker Committee. In April 2004 UN Secretary General Kofi Annan had appointed a committee to investigate alleged corruption and fraud in the United Nations oil-for-food Programme in Iraq. It was to be chaired by former Federal Reserve Chairman, Paul Volcker,[2] the other members of the inquiry being South African Justice, Richard Goldstone and Swiss Professor of Criminal Law, Mark Pieth. In 2005 I was interviewed for four and a half hours by staff employed by the committee and admitted paying the surcharge, while pointing out that these remittances were not bribery in the ordinary sense, since the charge was mandatory for all lifters in the oil-for-food programme. Many were therefore paying it, as the UN, US and British authorities were fully aware, yet in the period 2000-2001, during which the surcharge was in force, they chose to disregard this breach to protect their own economic and strategic interests.

The interview focused almost exclusively on my connection with Galloway, and I believe it was him that they intended to nail. Their interest in me was in what I could tell them about 'Gorgeous George.' But the fact was that after taking George on his first visit to Iraq, I had had little further contact with him. We were both on the Stop the War Coalition Steering Committee and both of us objected to the war and the occupation. We shared various platforms but our approaches were different. He moved on and FAF and I were not directly involved with him after that.

I was shown numerous documents related to Galloway's involvement with the Ministry of Oil and the oil lift. Their greatest interest was in his UK associates, but most of those mentioned had no trading links with Iraq. They were politicians, members of the press or those engaged in political or religious activities. Did I know these people, and what information had I about them? I couldn't, of course,

---

[2] Volcker was at the time director of the United Nations Association of the United States of America. The full title of the inquiry was 'The Independent Committee into the United Nations Oil-for-Food Programme. Manipulation of the Oil-for-Food Programme by the Iraqi Regime,' hereafter referred to simply as the Volcker Committee, while the report it issued is referred to as the Volcker report.

help them much in this direction. Very little time was spent discussing my oil involvement which, according to the report when it came out, amounted to one quarter of his payment of surcharges[3]. I believe the situation changed later to my disadvantage when the SFO concluded, in its wisdom, that Galloway was too difficult a fish to catch.

The Volcker report

The Committee's final report, which was published in October 2005, found that 'oil surcharges were paid in connection with the contracts of 139 companies.' This compared with 2,253 companies which paid so-called 'humanitarian kickbacks', that is bribes to obtain contracts for the delivery of humanitarian goods.[4] Astrazenica and Glaxosmithkline were prominent among the latter, yet neither was prosecuted.

One should, it seems to me, distinguish between ad hoc deals of this kind and the payment of a charge, albeit one outlawed internationally, which was imposed across the board by a still recognised government. The distinction is blurred, deliberately it seems to me, in most of the discussion of the surcharge by also referring to the latter payments as kickbacks. It is certainly curious, if nothing more, that as far as Britain was concerned, the SFO file on the whole issue of the 'oil-for-food scandal' appears to have been closed quite soon after my conviction.

The prosecution in my case five years later claimed that I was named as someone who had paid the surcharge. However, the only reference to me in the main report occurs in a footnote on page 168. The text to which the footnote refers comes under the subheading, 'Vitol's Financing of Surcharge Payments by Hamida Na'ana.' There we read:

---

[3] I paid $501,934 spread over four contracts. Galloway paid $2,103,034, also spread over four, but larger, contracts.
[4] Volcker Report, Summary of Report, page 1. See
https://www.ethz.ch/content/dam/ethz/special-interest/gess/cis/center-for-securities-studies/resources/docs/un_iic_final_report_27Oct2005.pdf.

In at least one instance, Vitol[5] funded the payment of surcharges by an individual beneficiary by paying a sufficiently high commission to cover the surcharge. During phases X and XI,[6] Vitol purchased oil allocated to Hamida Na'ana. Ms. Na'ana is a Syrian journalist who received oil allocations from Tariq Aziz to compensate for her efforts in writing a book and articles about Iraq and its leaders. The contracts with SOMO to purchase Ms. Na'ana's oil allocations in Phases X and XI were not signed by Vitol but by a Panama-registered company, Devon Petroleum. However, Ms Na'ana dealt directly with Vitol. She communicated regularly with Gilles Chautard, a French-speaking trader at Vitol, and forwarded her invoices and received her payments from Vitol.

The footnote marker at the end of that paragraph details the evidence for it, including:

Riad El-Taher interview (Aug 31, 2005) (describing Devon Petroleum as an agent of Vitol with respect to Iraqi oil purchases). Mr. El-Taher is an Iraqi engineer based in the United Kingdom, who ran Friends Across Frontiers [sic], an organization that campaigned against Iraqi Sanctions. Vitol purchased some of his allocations through Devon Petroleum.[7]

However, in the 'Summary of Report' on page 1, we are told:

---

[5] A global energy and commodity trading company, founded in Rotterdam.
[6] The phases were six month periods which were introduced by the oil-for-food programme, commencing with its introduction in December 1996. Phases X and XI refer to late 2001 and early 2002.
[7] Independent Inquiry etc., p. 168, footnote 340.

> Beyond the narrative set forth in this volume, the Committee releases today a set of eight comprehensive tables identifying contractors under the Programme and other actors of significance to Programme transactions (such as non-contractual beneficiaries of Iraqi oil allocations and parties that financed oil transactions). These tables can be accessed at the Committee's website: http://www.iic-offp.org.

Except that they can't now be accessed there, because you are redirected to a Chinese site with a similar address but no connection to the Volcker report. A search of the web proved equally fruitless, as did an online request for information on the UN website. Even the main volume is not included on the UN site, but must be searched for elsewhere.[8] Presumably it was in these comprehensive tables that my payment of the surcharge was mentioned. I never knew about the tables, and have only recently discovered that they existed.

The main report singled out two countries (Russia and France), four individuals (George Galloway heading the list) and five companies for particular attention in connection with payment of the surcharge. If the US and UK had really been serious about catching the big fish, the Volcker report indicated who they were. Neither Perenco nor Bula were mentioned. The Committee's interest in me appeared largely exhausted once they realised I had no useful information about George Galloway's contacts and had confirmed that Vitol, that is the end-purchaser in the Hamida Na'ana case, effectively paid the surcharge, as was often the case in such deals.

I was called by a member of the Volcker Committee shortly before the publication of the report to reassure me that I only appeared in a footnote of the report; he didn't mention the tables in which there was evidently detailed information about Bula, Perenco and me. He assured

---

[8] See https://www.ethz.ch/content/dam/ethz/special-interest/gess/cis/center-for-securities-studies/resources/docs/un_iic_final_report_27Oct2005.pdf.

me that if the British government's lawyers didn't take any further action within the following three months I should regard the matter as closed. More worryingly, this official also confirmed that there had been a transcript of my evidence to the Volcker Committee, but said that it couldn't now be found. If this had survived it would, I believe, have revealed that I admitted paying the surcharge, and this could later have been regarded as a mitigating circumstance in my defence. As it was, I was accused of *not* having admitted it, but had no evidence to back my denial of this assertion.

The Attorney General, Lord Goldsmith

I have already described how Lord Goldsmith vacillated in March 2003 in his advice to the Prime Minister on the legality of military action against Iraq without an *ad hoc* UN resolution. In the war which followed the cooperation of Saudi Arabia was an essential element in the military strategy. No doubt, leaving aside commercial considerations, this was one of the reasons Goldsmith was lent upon, and in turn himself lent on the SFO in 2006, to discontinue an investigation into bribes paid by BAE Systems to Saudi Arabia.

The revelations of the Volcker report in 2005 had left the government, and therefore its chief legal advisor, in a quandary. One can imagine that they were in no particular hurry to open an investigation into breaches of the sanctions imposed on Iraq. This could have opened a can of worms, for large multinational companies were involved and they could be expected to defend themselves vigorously. In cases related to the oil-for-food programme it would not be difficult for them to demonstrate that the government had applied a double standard on sanctions, insisting on their enforcement at home, turning a blind eye in the field. Moreover, much might have been made of large-scale smuggling of Iraqi crude under the noses of British forces without them lifting a finger to prevent it. In these circumstances it would be particularly difficult to bring successful prosecutions and the government could end up with egg on its face.

However, I guess the furore following the cancellation of the BAE case made a diversionary action attractive. It might not get far, but a few million pounds of public money may well have seemed an acceptable price, and they might at least catch a couple of companies and unsuspecting sole traders. There was, for example, that thorn in their side, Riad el-Taher, who refused to collaborate and had done so much to whip up opposition to the sanctions and the ensuing war. He should at least get his just desserts.

And so a year and a half on from the publication of the Volcker report, Goldsmith announced in February 2007, that the SFO was to begin an investigation into breaches of the sanctions on Iraq, and that they would get all the resources they needed for the job.

The degree to which Goldsmith was dependent on his patron, the Prime Minister, who had launched what many regard as an illegal war on his advice, became very clear following Blair's announcement on 10th May 2007 of his intention to stand down. On 22nd June, two days before Blair handed over the leadership of the Labour Party to Gordon Brown, Goldsmith also resigned his post as Attorney General to take effect the same day that Blair accepted the stewardship of the Chiltern Hundreds (that is resigned his seat in the House of Commons).

Investigating the Investigators

Following a number of financial scandals in the City during the 1970s and 80s a committee was set up under Lord Roskill to consider how serious fraud could more successfully be combatted. The outcome was the Criminal Justice Act 1987 which established the Serious Fraud Office. The SFO is accountable to the Attorney General, and its jurisdiction extends across England, Wales and Northern Ireland, but not Scotland. Ironically, however, following the dawn of the new century, the SFO often found *itself* under unwelcome scrutiny.

In 2003 Robert Wardle took over from Rosalind Wright[9] as Director and the following year he initiated an ill-fated investigation into

> suspected accounting irregularities related to BAE and the Al-Yamamah deal,[10] focusing on the relationship between BAE and two small travel firms which made arrangements for Saudi officials on behalf of BAE. ... [But] in December [2006], the SFO drops the Saudi probe after 'representations' from the British government about the need to safeguard national security. The move sparks outrage from transparency campaigners. The decision followed a *Daily Telegraph* article, citing unnamed authoritative sources, saying Saudi Arabia had given Britain 10 days to halt the SFO inquiry or lose a contract for 72 Eurofighter Typhoon combat jets being built by BAE systems and consortium partners.[11]

This branched out into a number of related investigations on £2 billion worth of secret payments to Saudi Arabia, but pressure mounted from BAE, Lord Goldsmith and eventually the British ambassador to Saudi Arabia, to pull the plug on the whole operation.

---

[9] Rosalind Wright served as director from 1997 to 2003 and was credited with having restored its 'tarnished reputation.' See https://www.theguardian.com/business/2002/jun/09/corporatefraud.observerbusiness.

[10] A massive and ongoing 'weapons for oil' deal between Britain and Saudi Arabia, initiated by Margaret Thatcher in the mid-eighties.

[11] 'BAE Systems: timeline of bribery allegations,' *Daily Telegraph*, 21st December 2010; see http://www.telegraph.co.uk/finance/newsbysector/industry/defence/8216172/BAE-Systems-timeline-of-bribery-allegations.html.

Wardle, it seems, did his best to resist the pressure, to the extent that his friends believed 'Goldsmith would have sacked him if he could have got away with it,' but eventually he was forced to give way. For public consumption Tony Blair cited 'alleged threats by Saudi's Prince Bandar[12] to make it easier for terrorists to attack Britons' if the investigation were not stopped. Two months later, in February 2007, just as Wardle landed the 'fantastically thankless task' of investigating breaches of the Iraqi sanctions regime, Goldsmith reduced his expected five-year contract extension to just one year. He had become the fall guy for the BAE disaster.[13]

But that wasn't the end of investigations into BAE. In January 2007 another investigation was started into payments by BAE to South Africa, and the next month the SFO revealed it had six investigations against BAE under way. In June the US Department of Justice began its own probe.

Nothing deterred, Wardle set about forming a fifty-strong and £22 million funded team, under the leadership of the senior investigating lawyer, Roddy Gillanders, to investigate breaches of the Iraq sanctions. It was envisaged that the project should be reviewed after three years, but I've not found any evidence that it was.

In April 2008, Wardle's shortened term of office came to an end, and he was succeeded by Richard Alderman, but under this new leadership controversy still didn't let up. In April 2008 the BAE crisis came to a head when Campaign Against the Arms Trade and anti-corruption campaigners Corner House[14] won their case against the decision by Wardle to pull the investigation. The appeal judge, Lord

---

[12] Prince Bandar bin Sultan al-Saud was then head of Saudi Arabia's National Security Council and son of the crown prince.
[13] Leigh, D., 'The fall guy,' *The Guardian*, 18th April 2008, online at https://www.theguardian.com/world/2008/apr/18/bae.armstrade.
[14] The Corner House supports 'democratic and community movements for environmental and social justice.'

Justice Moses and Justice Sullivan rejected the SFO's argument that it was powerless to resist the Saudi threats.

> So bleak a picture of the impotence of the law invites at least dismay, if not outrage. Had such a threat been made by one who was subject to the criminal law of this country, he would risk being charged with an attempt to pervert the course of justice.[15]

The abandonment of the Saudi case, and the success of the appeal placed Wardle and the SFO in an unenviable position. As the OECD and other critics had pointed out, he had failed to bring a single prosecution over bribery allegations since taking on this project in 2007. David Leigh wrote in *The Guardian*:

> He has been defeated because the politicians have stopped him, or the laws have proved unworkable, or the sheer difficulties of digging out information from offshore banks and dodgy foreign governments have been too great. Taxpayers' money gets spent by the suitcase-full, company offices are raided, investigators travel all over the world, 13 inquiries are currently in train, and Wardle has bid to the treasury for around £2.5m for a dedicated overseas corruption team. But nothing so far has got results.[16]

In September 2009 talks broke down between the SFO and BAE over a plea-bargain in a bribery case relating to the supply of equipment to Tanzania, the Czech Republic and South Africa. A figure of between £500 million and £1 billion being mentioned as the price. In February 2010 BAE agreed to pay the US Department of Justice a $400 million

---

[15] Walker, P., 'SFO wrong to drop BAE inquiry, court rules,' *The Guardian*, 10th April 2008, online at
https://www.theguardian.com/world/2008/apr/10/bae.armstrade.
[16] Leigh, D., op cit.

fine, and £30 million to the UK Treasury, after which the SFO said it would not seek to prosecute BAE for allegations it had been investigating for six years.

Then between November 2011 and February 2013 the SFO accidentally sent 2000 evidence bags which contained information about third parties back to a witness in a BAE bribery case, and was accordingly fined.[17] And between May and October of 2012 the SFO lost 32,000 pages of data and 81 audio tapes linked to the al-Yamamah deal.[18]

During Alderman's term of office it was revealed that documents were obtained by means of an improperly conducted raid and as a result an investigation into the property developers, the Tchenguiz brothers,[19] had to be dropped. The SFO also dropped its probe into Bernie Madoff's London dealings[20] and turned down the proposal that it should investigate LIBOR-rigging by UK banks.[21] Alderman allowed his chief executive, Phillipa Williamson, to work two days a week from her Lake District home, while charging expenses of £27,600 for travel and hotel bills for her three days in London. She and others, among

---

[17] Information Commissioner's Office. See https://ico.org.uk/about-the-ico/news-and-blogs/2015/03/serious-fraud-office-fined/
[18] See http://www.bbc.co.uk/news/business-23622364.
[19] The Tchenguiz brothers, Vincent, the elder, and Robert, were born to Iraqi Jewish parents, Victor and Violet Khadouri. The family emigrated to Iran, where they changed their name to Tshenguiz, but after the Iranian revolution in 1979 they moved to England. Following the collapse of the Icelandic Kaupthing Bank in 2008, Robert Tchenguiz was investigated by the SFO, but the case was dropped in 2012 due to 'insufficient evidence'. He then sued the SFO for false imprisonment and damage to his businesses, the case being eventually settled by the SFO paying £4.5 million to the two brothers in compensation as well as 80% of Robert's legal expenses.
[20] 'Bernie' Madoff was an American fraudster and a former stockbroker, investment advisor, and financier.
[21] LIBOR (the London Interbank Offered Rate) is the average of interest rates estimated by leading banks in London. The LIBOR-rigging scandal related to the manipulation by bankers of this rate in order to profit from trading or to give a false impression of creditworthiness.

them Roddy Gillanders who was leading the Iraq investigation, were eventually paid large unauthorised severance packages at the end of Alderman's tenure.

When this scandal was investigated by the Public Accounts Committee in 2013, a year after Alderman was succeeded by David Green, Margaret Hodge, the chair, put Alderman on the spot: 'Your chief executive is in the Lake District. A quarter of your time is abroad talking to people about legislation. Is that really the way to lead an organisation?' Green complained that he now faced a dilemma in being legally obliged to make an ex-gratia payment to an ex-employee, which had been blocked by the Treasury. 'I think I would get the money out of Mr Alderman,' shot back Hodge.[22]

This, then, was the chaotic and success-hungry organisation to which my fate was now entrusted.

---

[22] Osborne, A., 'Ex-SFO chief Richard Alderman attacked over 'shocking' stewardship,' *Daily Telegraph*, 7th March 2013; see
http://www.telegraph.co.uk/finance/financial-crime/9916461/Ex-SFO-chief-Richard-Alderman-attacked-over-shocking-stewardship.html.

CHAPTER SEVENTEEN

A TALE OF TWO TRIALS: PART 2, MYSELF

Arrested and bailed

On 7th August 2008 Charmaine and I were abruptly woken when the police, acting together with officers from the SFO, raided my home in force at seven o'clock in the morning. More than twenty officers were involved, most of them fanning out in the back garden and in front of the house, the others banging on the door and ringing the bell. It was a very frightening and intimidating experience both for Charmaine and me. Whereas companies had been given forewarning of investigation, it came for us like a bolt out of the blue.

At that time I had a bad knee and was walking on crutches. I told the police that it would take me some time to come downstairs, but they were very impatient. When I opened the front door and asked what the problem was, they pushed me aside and marched into the house.

One of the officers read me my rights and said that I was under arrest for violating United Nations sanctions. I replied that I had already admitted paying the surcharge, an admission which was later to be used against me. I was extremely shocked believing, as I did, that this whole business was water under the bridge. The government had known perfectly well that such payments had been made by every lifter in the oil-for-food programme. How else could it have continued to operate, if indeed there was any intention that it should continue?

The search went on for almost three hours. My office in the garage at the back of the house was the main focus of their attention. Most of the documents they took related to Petcon, which had ceased trading in

2003, together with much of my FAF correspondence. They were incredulous that I didn't have a mobile phone or computer. A phone cable ran from the house to the office but was no longer connected and they suspected therefore that I was hiding a computer. They kept insisting that I must have a computer and asked me how I received emails. I told them my secretary, who was, unlike me, computer-literate, downloaded them, and printed them out for me. After I gave them her address they marched off to her house and threatened to get a warrant for her arrest if she didn't cooperate. She said, 'Go ahead, there is nothing to hide.' I felt bad that this happened to her without my being able to warn her, because she was in no way involved in my political and humanitarian work.

An officer at last allowed us to get dressed, leaving the door open while he and his colleagues stood there with their backs turned. Before Charmaine left they also searched her car and personal bags. About midday I was taken to Hayes police station where I was formally detained for questioning.

In the police station my tie was taken off and I had to undo my belt and take off my shoes. Even my crutches were taken away from me and I was left in a solitary cell for six hours reading the two charge files detailing the accusations against me. I attempted to meditate to calm myself down, but this was difficult because of distressing cries coming from a mentally disturbed detainee in the next cell. It's hard for me to convey my terrified state of mind during those long hours. I felt I had been forgotten, an impression which was reinforced by my being given nothing to eat or drink. Admittedly there was a bell which I could ring in case of emergency, but I hesitated to use it for fear of making my situation worse. When at last I was visited by a guard, I was simply told that the duty solicitor assigned to my case had not yet arrived.

Eventually I was allowed to call Tam who suggested his son might be able to represent me, but I foolishly told him I didn't need a solicitor. The officer who had agreed to my call overheard what I was saying and took the phone from me. He urged Tam to impress upon me the need for a solicitor during the interview which would follow. I later realised the value of this intervention in the midst of all this chaos. Here was a flicker of human compassion in a very dark time. The same officer told me that the search of my house had been relatively benign compared with what others experienced, and this was because they had found so little of relevance.

Finally the unimpressive and badly-dressed solicitor turned up and advised me to reply 'no comment' to every question, even when asked my name. But I couldn't bring myself to accept this legalised absurdity. The interview lasted over an hour as we had to go through the file page by page, all my comments being carefully noted down. At one point I produced a portable magnifying glass which I always carried with me in case I forgot my reading glasses. The SFO lawyer jumped on me and accused me of hiding a mobile, which indeed it did resemble. Showing him it, I said: 'No, it's not a mobile telephone,' at which he looked rather foolish.

I suppose their main interest in finding a mobile phone was that they wished to check my contacts and see whether any of them had terrorist links, or whether they would reveal the identity of Saddam's friends around the world. I believe it was the hope of discovering such information which was the primary reason for my arrest. Perhaps through their search they might find more useful political ammunition than the violation of UN sanctions. But instead of dropping proceedings against me when they found nothing of importance, they decided to make a case out of my payment of the surcharge alone.

When we had finished I was released on unconditional bail. As I couldn't walk the SFO officer who had attended the interview gave me a lift home and on the way told me that Charmaine had been calling them and was very concerned. While my bail was unconditional, my lawyer was advised that I should remain living at my Hinchley Wood home, that I should surrender my current and old passports and that I should undertake not to apply for travel documents which would enable me to leave the country. I duly complied with these requirements.

I was in a daze. I didn't understand what was happening nor where I should go for help. I had no knowledge about lawyers nor how to find a good and avoid a bad one. Someone I knew suggested I contact a Pakistani who seemed very enthusiastic about handling my case and correctly advised me that I would qualify for legal aid. I had a briefing with him in the office of another Pakistani, a barrister, in Holborn. To my surprise he arranged the meeting at 7 a.m. on a Sunday, but I took this to be a positive sign that he wanted to get on with the case. Both the barrister, who was also present, and the solicitor were well versed in the language used by lawyers with their clients: 'Everything is in hand, we have a winnable case, the prosecution doesn't have a leg to stand on.'

The subsequent meeting was scheduled to take place on another Sunday morning at the same early hour. Nobody was there, and so I rang the barrister whose details were indicated on the name plate. I was told that there had been a mistake. 'We tried to reach you, but got your answer-phone.' At this point I began to realise that I was dealing with an unprofessional organisation. Later I discovered to my amazement that the offices of the solicitor were in a very busy area above a shop in Camden Town, not in Holborn. It turned out that these were immigration lawyers with no knowledge of criminal law or cases brought by the SFO. They were just using the offices of the barrister as a front and the only time they could have access was in the early morning. It was back to square one. Who should I trust and where was I to go from here?

By chance I was invited one evening to a soirée held by the colourful and controversial Australian-born advertising model-turned-political-activist Lady Michèle Renouf, and among her guests was Sir Desmond de Silva, a criminal lawyer of Sri Lankan and Scottish descent, and very much an establishment figure. Lady Renouf suggested I talk to him as he specialised in serious crime. He was enthusiastic about my case as he had had past dealings with the United Nations and told me he would ask a solicitor to call me the next morning.

In view of my previous experience, I was somewhat surprised to receive the promised telephone call from a Palestinian solicitor, Zena Haddad, who said that her specialism was fraud and that my case therefore particularly interested her. We met the next day and I was encouraged by her background, guessing that this would help her to understand the political implications of my case. Had things not moved so quickly two barristers at Tooks Chambers, Michael Mansfield, who called himself a 'radical lawyer,' and the Palestinian QC, Michel Massih, might have taken my case, because both expressed an interest when I met them at a celebration of Libya's Revolution Day at the Dorchester on 1st September. I can't help wondering how they would have handled my case, though whether the outcome would have been any different is impossible to tell.

Anyway I felt the die was cast, and a few weeks later Sir Desmond arranged for us to meet in a Lebanese restaurant in Shepherd Market, Mayfair. The three of us, Sir Desmond, Zena and myself, would be joined there by Lady Renouf, together with a barrister named Paul Mylvaganam, (also of Sri Lankan descent) and a retired Lebanese-Palestinian judge.

My confidence was markedly restored and I now believed my case would be won. Sir Desmond and Zena said they would do their utmost to kill the case before it even reached court, which were just the encouraging words I wanted to hear. I stopped dealing with the Pakistani lawyer and appointed Sir Desmond, shortly after which he, Zena and I met in his chambers. They assigned a firm of solicitors, Attridge and Charles, as Zena, being a freelance lawyer, needed a practice to assign her to the case. I was told this firm could provide backup with their own solicitors.

The tedious process of reading and assessing documents, which was quite alien to me as an engineer, went on for months in preparation for a series of briefings. It was not yet clear whether I would have to defend myself in court or whether the case against me would be dropped. The result was that I had hardly any time for my FAF work and in any case, the unofficial conditions of my unconditional bail meant that I couldn't safety travel abroad, which was an essential part of my campaigning. The first long briefing, with the SFO, was spent going through the documentation, and having my reply to every question carefully recorded.

Charged

On 12th August, almost exactly a year after my initial arrest, and just two months after the announcement of the Chilcot Inquiry, I was charged, as recounted earlier, with contravening the UN sanctions on the basis of four transactions in 2001, and was advised to get my own solicitor. The gravity of my situation gradually sank in. I had not remotely anticipated this kind of treatment for something which, however mistakenly, I couldn't see as a criminal act. I was frankly terrified and of course it was a shocking experience for Charmaine as well. I had never had any dealings with the law, whether with solicitors or the police. It was the first time in my life that I had been inside a police station other than for registration purposes, and I had never been put in a cell.

In this crisis I replayed in my mind all the events in my life which might have led to the situation in which I now found myself. Where had I gone wrong? Was it a question of who I had crossed? Or was I the victim of some process set in motion by the intelligence services of those countries whose policies I had opposed? Hadn't the main part of the Volcker Report identified the big boys who had paid the surcharge, while only mentioning me in passing? Had I not, indeed, been assured by a member of the Volcker Committee that no further action was expected against me?

If I found answers to some of these questions, perhaps I could find a clue as to how I might extract myself from this trauma. An unexpected and rather strange visit to me in 2004 by an ex-colleague now appeared in a new light. He didn't make friends easily as he was rather sensitive and argumentative by nature, and so I wouldn't have called him a friend. His request, out of the blue, to come and stay with me therefore appeared strange to me.

While he was with me he spent much of his time on the phone talking to Iraqis in Baghdad and the USA. One of those in America was Falah al-Jibouri who had assisted the 'opposition' and was, as I wrote earlier, interviewed by Greg Palast in 2006. At one point, after talking to Falah, he asked me directly: 'Why do you continue upsetting the Iraqi government when you are no longer dealing in oil?' This veiled warning and his calls, which were clearly to Iraqis working with the US administration both in Iraq and America, were rather disconcerting, not to say alarming.

My guest evidently couldn't comprehend that I saw oil-lifts as a way of helping the Iraqi people. He thought that my campaigning was intended to sweeten the Iraqi authorities into granting me oil allocations from which I would benefit personally. I spoke out because I saw the dire effect of the sanctions on millions of people. He had lived in Iraq, had seen and experienced what I had seen and experienced, and had then left the country. With the change in regime, he now saw the possibility of high office in Iraq, and accordingly joined a Shia sect and the largely Shia Al-Fadilah (Virtue) party. It did him little good.

It is Iraqis such as these who, by collaborating with the US and UK, caused the destruction of my country. Bush and Blair, with their manipulation of the UN system, played the major part but without the assistance of these Iraqis who facilitated the entry of foreign troops there would have been no occupation. They bear a heavy responsibility for what has happened.

Perhaps if I had at that stage, post–2003, ceased to be politically active I might have avoided the upheaval of imprisonment and substantial financial loss. I have no doubt that singling me out and charging me was politically motivated, though to this day I do not know for certain who was behind it. Someone, somewhere, evidently instigated this abusive process.

Preliminary hearings

At last, on August 12th 2009, I was ordered to appear in court to answer the charges arising out of the United Nations Act of 1946 and the Iraq (United Nations Sanctions) Order 2000. The relevant text in section 1 of the first reads:

> If ... the Security Council of the United Nations call upon His Majesty's Government in the United Kingdom to apply any measures to give effect to any decision of that Council, His Majesty may by Order in Council make such provision as appears to Him necessary or expedient for enabling those measures to be effectively applied, including (without prejudice to the generality of the preceding words) provision for the apprehension, trial and punishment of persons offending against the Order.'

Article 3 of the Iraq (United Nations Sanctions) Order 2000 reads:

> Any person who, except under the authority of a licence granted by the Treasury under article 5— (a) makes any funds available to the government of the Republic of Iraq or any person who is resident in the Republic of Iraq, or (b) otherwise remits or removes any funds from the United

Kingdom to a destination in the Republic of Iraq, is guilty of an offence.'

From then on my case was in earnest. My lawyers inundated me with files and papers which I was asked to read carefully, after which we would meet and go laboriously through them making comments. I studied these documents in my house in Hinchley Wood, or if the weather was fine, I would go to the nearby Hampton Court Palace gardens, where I would work on a bench.

I felt very isolated, a state of mind which was not helped by the decline, for a number of reasons, in my relationship with Charmaine. The gap this had left in my life was all of a sudden filled by Karen Audin, whom I met at a yoga class. Karen now gave me the strength to carry on through all the trouble which awaited me, and soon I came to believe that she would be my final life-companion. She touched my soul, and made my world beautiful, but though I cared deeply for her, I found it impossible to show my emotions adequately. This would eventually lead to difficulties between us.

Between March 2010 and the end of that year there were a number of hearings at Southwark Crown Court, a designated serious fraud centre. I never denied paying the surcharge, but pointed out that doing so was normal practice by all those lifting oil in Iraq at that time. If what I did was considered worthy of prosecution, then the charge should have been applied to all those who lifted oil under the oil-for-food Programme during the period between 2000 and 2002, not to me and my co-defendant alone. After all, the SFO only had to look at the Volcker Report to know who the main culprits were.

The details of my case were widely reported in all the national and international newspapers, and it was predicted that many further cases would follow. Indeed, after my conviction the SFO promised this would be so. In the event, the very opposite happened.

The lawyers intended to rely on two arguments in my defence. These were, firstly that the UN 661 Committee officials had clearly turned a blind eye to surcharge payments, and as the British government was represented on the Committee, it was well aware of this policy. Indeed it could be argued that the British and American representatives on the Committee were the driving force behind the lack of action by the 661 Committee. To prosecute me in these circumstances would therefore constitute an abuse of process. The occupiers knew that the surcharge was being paid by all lifters in the oil-for-food programme, but were afraid of the consequences of enforcing the surcharge ban. If oil exports had been stopped completely the implications would have been serious, for the majority of oil exported from Iraq was destined for American refineries. A spike in the price of oil per barrel could have had a direct impact on the economic situation worldwide, and so it was better to accept the murky *status quo*.

The second line of defence was that I had acted under duress, since I had family in Iraq and could not be confident that they would remain safe if I refused to pay the surcharge. In the event, this argument was never put, since I was persuaded to plead guilty after the abuse of process argument was discounted and my co-defendant changed his plea.

Although the Volcker Committee were told that 'the United Nations warned traders and companies by letter that surcharge payments were illegal'[1] I never saw such a letter, and I never met anyone else who did. All those engaged in the oil-for-food programme had to be approved by the Department of Trade and Industry as well as the Foreign Office before applications for oil allocation were submitted via the UK mission to the UN 661 Committee. It should therefore have been a relatively easy matter to have informed lifters in an adequate way about the consequences of paying the surcharge.

---

[1] Volcker Report, p. 18.

As I have said, I believe the SFO knew that the case against me rested on shaky ground. If you read between the lines of four paragraphs in the 'Prosecution Substantive Submission on Abuse of Process' you may well reach the same conclusion. After stating that the prosecution's case in this matter 'relies principally on the statement of Gerard McGurk ... UK representative on the Iraq Sanctions Committee,' we read:

> 13.2. The reports of oil surcharges started to come through shortly after he [McGurk] started in post (in August 2000) [...] There could be no assumption prior to this time that any oil traders might be paying surcharges to the Iraqi regime.
>
> 13.18. Even if there were such a policy [of turning a blind eye] ... there is nothing to suggest that it was known to either defendant, or that either of them acted in any different way as a result.
>
> 13.19. From the wider point of view of public confidence in the administration of justice, the effect of any such policy would depend on the reason for adopting it. There was clearly a very difficult and sensitive diplomatic situation at the UN over Iraq. A decision to soft-pedal over surcharges for a while in the interest of wider political harmony, for example, could not give rise to an abuse of process where that was unknown to the defendants at the time.
>
> 13.20. It is emphasised that this is merely a hypothetical example to illustrate the submission that proof of such a policy is only the first stage in what the defendants have to prove. The prosecution is unaware of anything to support such a hypothesis.[2]

---

[2] Prosecution Substantive Submission on Abuse of Process dated 5th November 2010 in my possession.

It seems clear to me from the above that the prosecution lawyers were preparing themselves for the possibility that my defence might convincingly argue that though I could not know when I made the first surcharge payment that the UK government, following the US lead, would turn a blind eye, it was a reasonable assumption that they would do so in view of their lack of action to stop oil smuggling across the borders of Turkey and Jordan and down the Shatt al-Arab waterway; moreover, the prosecution was well aware that the 661 Committee was divided on the subject of the surcharge, and that this made action against those who paid it difficult. I learnt at the time of my visit to Baghdad in mid-September 2000 that many high-profile companies had agreed to pay the surcharge, and it seemed improbable, as indeed it has turned out, that such companies with offices in England would eventually be prosecuted.

In order to outflank this defence the prosecution adopted two strategies. The first was to limit my 'blind eye' defence to the surcharge alone, and not to the wider issue of smuggling of oil across Iraq's borders, which was also a breach of the sanctions. The other strategy had been to link my case to the more straightforward one of the Pakistani oil-trader, Aftab Hasan, and thereby to reduce the possibility of wider issues being brought in.

Meanwhile, I received substantial high level support. Hans von Sponeck made a robust statement supporting me as did Tam, Denis Halliday and Tony Benn. In addition, my accountant of 35 years standing, Alan Howell, and many others supported me with character references.[3]

The hearings which followed were sterile, unreal even. My name was mentioned but I might as well not have been there. Fifty-five years after I came to England I felt for the first time truly alien. All the arguments were between the judge and the defence and prosecution barristers, while I wasn't allowed to say anything. I just sat there like a

---

[3] The editor of this book was among these.

lemon. My future was at stake but I felt I was not really part of the judicial process. It was particularly frustrating when the prosecution barrister indicated that I was Saddam's man in the UK and I was given no opportunity to reply.

In October 2010 there was agreement in court that 'an arguable abuse of process might arise if the UK Government had a policy of deliberately turning a blind eye on UK companies, nationals or residents paying illegal surcharges on the purchase of oil from Iraq, or facilitating such payments.' The following month the prosecution rebutted this argument on the grounds set out in the Prosecution Substantive Submission already quoted. Unfortunately the judge took the prosecution's side and the case continued. At that point I would love to have stood up and defended myself along the lines I've already indicated, but I wasn't allowed to do so.[4]

At one point the SFO claimed, as indeed I had been told back in 2005, that there was no record of the Volcker Committee's interview of me, which suggests that all the records leading up to and including that interview were destroyed. And yet the prosecution used the Volcker Committee's proceedings as evidence against me, stating that I had at first denied the payment of the surcharge, but when confronted had admitted to it. I clearly remember that interview, and the truth is I admitted to paying the surcharge right at the outset. As I have said, only half an hour was spent talking about the surcharge, the other four hours being devoted to George Galloway's involvement with the oil-for-food programme and the question of whether I was involved with him politically.

Just once during these endless hearings did the learned judge, Nicholas Loraine-Smith, take any notice of me. I was listening to a statement which he was making and I closed my eyes to concentrate. Loraine-Smith turned to the barrister and said: 'I presume that the man sitting behind you, Sir Desmond, is your client. I suppose when it comes

---

[4] Prosecution Substantive Submission.

to a jury trial you have to be much more attentive to the court or things could go against you.' I just managed to hold myself back from answering that if I had been asleep my head would not have remained upright.

A crucial point was reached when the Deputy First Secretary at the British Mission in New York, Carne Ross, was called by my team to give evidence and be cross-examined. This was particularly effective as he indicated that the government had indeed turned a blind eye to the payment of the surcharge and took no action against those who complied with the Iraqi demand. So we assumed that the case would be thrown out of court. The judge stated that he was 'uncomfortable' with the cross-examination of Ross and would be interested to know more about the position of the British government. At this point he ordered the court to rise for lunch.

We were all hopeful that if the prosecution failed to produce an argument which would support their stance the case would be dismissed. Nevertheless, the recess made me very uneasy, and with good reason. After lunch a lady from the ex-DTI was brought in and put forward a very weak argument against Ross's testimony, but to my dismay my legal team failed to cross-question her. It would have been useful to my case to know what precisely her position in the DTI was, and what limitations there were on what she could say. I guess phone calls had been made during the recess which resulted in the judge's astonishing change of position. Whatever the cause, the judge decided to proceed with the case. From then on I lost hope and anticipated that things would get worse as the court hearings proceeded wearily on from one sitting to another.

The decision of my legal team, against my objection, to agree to the SFO's suggested linking[5] of my trial with that of a Pakistani oil-trader, Aftab Hasan, was most unfortunate. Where cases are joined in this way, there is an assumption that the position of the two defendants is

---

[5] The legal term is 'consolidating'.

essentially similar. In reality, his case was completely different from mine. He had an office in Baghdad but had no family connection with Iraq and no interest in the Iraqi people. He was buying any available oil allocations simply for financial gain. I didn't seek oil allocations or pressurise the Iraqi government into granting me them. They were given to me both because of my campaigning work on behalf of the beleaguered Iraqi people, and because I was reliable. My background in the oil industry, albeit as an engineer, was known and I was able to ensure the lifts, shipments and payments into the UN escrow account. Unlike his position, mine was one of principle and patriotism. I objected to the imposition of draconian sanctions on humanitarian grounds. I was appalled at reports that over 500,000 Iraqi children had died as a result of shortages of food and medical supplies.

My case was political and I could not have had better witnesses to support the fact that I was acting not as an oil trader but as someone who was motivated to help the Iraqi people. That is why I was so angry about the decision of the 661 Committee, caused by the refusal of the US and UK members to support it, not to grant the Iraqi government a cash component under the oil-for-food programme. I believed that war was avoidable and when it came, that it caused irrevocable damage to the country of my birth, and in particular to my family and friends. I was also, like many others, opposed to the occupation.

There were no doubt reasons why my legal team accepted the coupling of my trial with that of Al-Hassan, but it was this which ultimately worked to my disadvantage. My co-defendant had no serious grounds for defence and pleaded guilty once the abuse of process defence was rejected. He had lifted oil and there were documents to show that he had benefited to the tune of $10 million. The mitigating circumstances which applied in my case, and which Zena had worked tirelessly to corroborate, were inapplicable to his.

Once the Pakistani had pleaded guilty my room for manoeuvre was restricted. In fact it was Hobson's choice; either I pleaded guilty or, as

I was told by my defence team, I would face the possibility of a seven year prison sentence. The judge gave my team half an hour to make up its mind whether to advise me to plead guilty or not, giving the impression that if I chose the first option I would receive a suspended sentence.

My defence team knew I dreaded the prospect of incarceration. Sir Desmond told me that he had no remaining defence and that in my position he would plead guilty. I considered the alternative of not doing so, for it occurred to me that the defence of duress hadn't been tested.[6] But without the support of my lawyers, and with the uncertainly of how a jury would see my case, it seemed at that moment better to do as I was advised. I assumed that the chances of going to prison would thereby be reduced, but it wasn't sufficiently explained to me that my guilty plea stripped me of all rights to defend myself further and that there was a possibility, which became a reality, that I would have to pay the whole legal costs of my defence.

Sentencing

The days leading to the sentencing were very upsetting and unnerving. I was stepping into the unknown. The terror of those six hours' detention in Hayes Police Station came back to me and when it came to the day of sentencing I was expecting the worst. On 25th February I was driven to Southwark Crown Court by friends and was grateful for their company. I sat in the dock in a daze hearing the judge making much of Aftab Hasan's illness and then handing down a suspended sentence to him.

Now at last the Judge Loraine-Smith turned to me and summed up my case. He conceded: 'It must seem to you to be unfair to be in the dock while many others are not.' But he maintained that I had benefited financially from my illegal dealings with SOMO, and in addition to this

---

[6] I have since learnt that such a defence is rarely successful on its own.

said that I had lied to the UN Volcker Committee. I felt that my legal team should have challenged the evidence for the prosecution's allegation on this issue earlier in the proceedings, because it was now too late to do so. The judge proceeded to sentence me to ten months in prison and ordered me to arrange for £500,000 of my assets to be seized after my release.

I was furious and dismayed at the judge's complete misunderstanding of where I was coming from. He had assumed that I was a regular oil trader, while in reality I had only traded in oil during the oil-for-food Programme, and for humanitarian reasons. Until then my professional life had been in engineering and particularly engineering design. I was incredulous when I later read the SFO's crowing press release on my sentencing in which the SFO Director, Richard Alderman, commented: 'I am pleased with this result. The offences committed here denied humanitarian aid to the people of Iraq.' What a travesty! It was, after all, the sanctions, and the veto by the US and UK of the cash component, which had denied Iraq humanitarian aid.

Shocked and disillusioned I was led down to a cell and felt the full humiliation and powerlessness of my situation. All my possessions, including a mobile phone which Karen Audin had by now bought me, an electric shaver, a toothbrush and a tube of toothpaste, were recorded, put in a bag and removed. My legal team came to see me, and they were also shocked. They encouraged me to sustain my strength for a maximum of two weeks during which time they would do all they could to get me D-categorisation which would allow me to be transferred from Wandsworth (where I was to be detained initially) to an open prison.[7] There was some basis for their optimism as I was clearly qualified to be treated in this way, but their telling me this gave me false

---

[7] D category prisoners are 'Those who can be reasonably trusted not to try to escape, and are given the privilege of an open prison.'

hope that my stay in Wandsworth would be brief. You could say it was, but it certainly didn't feel like it.

CHAPTER EIGHTEEN

AT HER MAJESTY'S PLEASURE

Wandsworth prison

Once my personal possessions had been confiscated, I was handcuffed and taken in a prison van to Wandsworth. Through a tiny darkened window I saw familiar parts of London flashing by as music blared out. It was a horrendous journey, the cell in the van being so small that while sitting my knees were just two inches from the front. It was difficult to move and I felt claustrophobic. At last we reached Wandsworth where my fellow-prisoners and I remained locked in the van feeling neglected for another forty minutes. Some of them became very agitated, shouting and banging on the door to attract attention.

Finally we were led into the prison. All my clothes were replaced with prison garb, and we were then taken into an induction suite. This was where the dehumanising process really began, for from that moment I simply became prisoner number 7728. Curiously that figure had several associations for me because it contained within it the birthdates of my son and daughter, of Karen Audin, and my own official birthdate. I wondered, and still wonder, whether this was just a coincidence or some message from another realm. At any rate, I clutched at this straw as a good omen; I hadn't much else to hold onto.

The duty doctor called me out as my solicitor had delivered my food supplement to the prison authorities and his approval was required for this to be given to me. He was inquisitive about my case as he had been opposed to the Blair war. The nurse noted down the intervals at which the supplement was to be given to me, and told me that I would be given my dose each time, rather than being left to self-administer. At the time

I was surprised to hear what harm food supplements can do, but realised afterwards that this was a generous ruse to help me when I was locked up and feeling abandoned. Being required to leave the cell and go the dispensary for half an hour every morning was a godsend.

A kind person from a voluntary organisation asked me whether there was anyone I would like to inform and I said that my family were not aware of what had happened and I would like to make a phone call. He took the details and made a phone call on my behalf to inform my daughter of my situation.

I was asked to pair up with a boisterous Nigerian man called Eddy and I agreed once he had assured me that he didn't smoke. He was upset because he'd lost the friend who'd come with him from another prison. He knew the system very well, which was in some respects a bit of luck for me for he taught me how to conduct myself in a way which was appropriate to prison life. The first thing he told me was not to look at the cell door because if you did so, anticipating that it would open, you would go mad. I was to imagine the door did not exist and that's what I tried to do, though not always successfully. The problem with Eddy was his addiction to 24/7 television. He said he couldn't sleep unless it was on, regardless of what was showing.

Karen Dabrowska came to visit me on my first night which was a very pleasant surprise. How she managed it is a mystery, because one was not supposed to be allowed a visitor for the first two weeks. It was a great relief to leave the cell and spend an hour with a familiar face, drink some tea and eat a Mars bar. It was she who then planted in me the idea of writing my story as a way of lifting my morale and using my time constructively. And here seven years later is the result!

I was in the induction wing for a few days and while there the other prisoners were very kind to me. Many realised I was in prison for the first time and kept on asking me how I was. Some of the more privileged prisoners used to supply me with the only luxury they could put their hands on, which was milk cartons. There were no separate toilet facilities in the cell, the latrine simply being separated off by a small curtain. The so-called exercise amounted to walking round and round a small spit-splattered concrete area. I met a number of Algerian prisoners who had committed various crimes and we established an understanding, helped by our common language.

On the last day in the induction wing the senior officer told me that, owing to Tam Dalyell's letter to the governor, the latter was asking about my welfare. I explained why I had been imprisoned and he was very understanding and concerned about what had happened to me. But the order then came for us to be moved to C Wing and I could no longer take advantage of this officer's support. We packed our bedding and clothing and were taken to the new wing where we sat down in a locked room.

Eddy, with whom I was hoping to stay, knew the officer responsible for transfers and managed to get a cell on the ground floor. But the officer told me that as Eddy had already been allocated a cell I would have to be placed somewhere else. At last everyone had been assigned a cell apart from a young Albanian Muslim in his twenties, called Ahmet, and me. And so I had to pair up with him. My only real concern was that he shouldn't smoke, and luckily he didn't. The cell assigned to us on the fifth floor was cramped and had only a small window. But one important compensation was that the toilet was separate from the living area, a great luxury compared with the previous wing's facilities.

What my new cellmate noticed immediately, however, was that there was no television. He went berserk. He protested he couldn't stay in a cell without a TV, but once the door was locked there was nothing he could do. I was very concerned and tried to calm him down. I asked him if he read or if he had any other pastimes, but these didn't seem profitable lines of enquiry. I spoke to him primarily for my own peace of mind because I knew that if he were anxious it would undoubtedly affect me. I then asked him if he played chess and when he said he would like to learn I offered to teach him. His mood lightened immediately and he became excited at the prospect. We had no chessboard so he suggested I make something from cardboard. Motivated by his insistence and enthusiasm I managed to draw a chessboard on the table which, apart from the bunk bed and two chairs, was the only furniture in the cell. We spent the whole evening creating that board with hardly any tools or measures, and in no time it was ten o'clock and we were both ready for bed.

The next morning he was still very eager to finish our task. We designed the various pieces by cutting them out of cardboard and he spent some time learning the moves of the various pieces. Then we started to play. By concentrating hard he soon became a good player and the time it took for the game to reach a conclusion increased from ten to thirty minutes or longer.

After a couple of days of no television I was told we would be transferred to a lower floor because I had complained that my knees were not up to climbing five flights of stairs every time I came back from collecting a meal or from the daily three-quarters-of-an-hour exercise period. Prisoners over fifty were not normally placed on the higher floors, and so I kept on reminding them of their promise. One day, quite by chance, I met a senior officer on the landing and when I explained my problem he expedited the move to a lower level. Ahmet was very apprehensive that he would be moved away from me and begged the senior officer to let us stay together, which he did. Our chess games became for both of us our salvation, preserving our sanity and giving us something to talk about.

Our new cell, C2-15 on the second floor, was in quite a different environment and became a more permanent home. Playing chess and learning the moves had diverted Ahmet's attention away from his television addiction, and he had become an interesting character to spend time with. But now we had a television again, he reverted to his former ways and was as undiscerning in his viewing as Eddy had been. But at least he was very clean, though not in his language which was that of an experienced villain; he'd already been in and out of prison several times. Otherwise he was respectful and protective of me and I managed to restore some element of self-regard in him.

On 5th March an article about my case appeared in *The Times*. Under the headline 'Outcry grows over jailing of engineer who broke Iraq oil sanctions "to help the West,"' Sean O'Neill, the Crime and Security Editor, said that my case was causing concern. *The Times*, he said, had seen evidence of my contacts at the British embassy in Amman, and of how I had informed diplomats there that Iraq had no WMDs. He quoted Hans von Sponek as saying that I was 'a concerned and committed person who spoke out on the injustices of international policy. If he broke the rules then he is accountable for his own actions. But he is a small fish.' And Denis Halliday had said that my prison sentence indicated double standards on Iraq; the 'big guys' had got off scot free. Tam had pointed out the absurdity of sending a harmless old man like me to jail at a time when there was a policy of trying to reduce the prison population.[1]

My photo at the bottom of O'Neill's article caught the attention of officers and fellow prisoners, and this encouraged them to read the article. Realising that I had effectively been convicted for a political offence, I became quite a celebrity. The prisoners in my wing started banging on the door, offering their assistance and asking me to help them better themselves through education. They thought that I might be able to assist them in their future careers, improve their command of English or advise them about what to study. We shared newspapers, and the prisoners serving meals gave me more than I needed. My cellmate happily benefitted from the excess.

I wanted to get out of the cell as much as possible and so I put my name down for Friday prayers. My cellmate, although a Muslim, never prayed and was hesitant to come. I told him I didn't know how to pray

---

[1] O'Neill, S., 'Outcry grows over jailing of engineer who broke Iraq oil sanctions "to help the West,"' *The Times*, 5th March 2011, p 18. See image 3 after p 291.

either but we could copy the others, and he agreed to accompany me. This way we got to know the other Muslim prisoners and eventually I was nominated to be the race relations coordinator, the best-paid job in the prison with the additional exceptional privilege of giving access to all wings. This, however, never happened because of my transfer to Ford open prison in West Sussex. I do wonder whether it was to avoid granting me this responsibility with its accompanying freedom which speeded up my transfer.

But I'm getting ahead of myself and want to say a bit more about my time at Wandsworth. My fellow prisoners represented a cross-section of hardened criminals, thieves, fraudsters, immigration offenders awaiting deportation and so on, all of whom I tried to respect in a non-judgemental way. In prison you don't ask too many questions.

I befriended one VIP prisoner from Russia who explained to me that China wouldn't go to war in a conventional sense with the West, but would use investment in the Euro as a means to undermine its weakest aspect, that is the monetary system. One day I watched him playing chess with a black prisoner in the yard, and after one of his moves, I made a harmless remark. When his opponent reacted abusively, I thought it best not to defend myself in front of the other spectators. A few days later, standing outside my cell I saw the black man doing his cleaning duty in the common area. He approached me and asked if he should clean my cell as compensation for his bad behaviour and my non-reaction to it. I said it wasn't necessary, but he insisted. It's interesting that even a villain can show a different side of themselves if treated well.

My daily routine was writing letters, reading the papers and, when we were allowed out, exercising as much as I could. Mornings were the most difficult time, for then anxiety crept up on me. I therefore very much appreciated the nurse who had arranged for me to leave my cell as soon as it was opened to take my medication. Every morning, notwithstanding Eddy's advice, I looked forward to the door being unlocked at 8 or 8.30, and when there was a delay I would become apprehensive. Some mornings we used to calm our nerves at such times by playing chess. Getting out of that enclosed environment with its small window on the world was such a relief.

I made a number of further friends, all specialists in various aspects of prison life. Some organised my visiting rights, others advised me on how to apply for the right categorisation. Eddy continued to be my 'minder' and introduced me to a number of useful old lags. They helped me to find a way to get things moving. I became a well-known person within the wing where I mixed with lawyers and bankers. And so gradually the days became more bearable and less stressful.

Telephone facilities were inadequate and were tightly controlled. So long as I had built up enough credit by working or attending classes, I could make calls of up to ten minutes at a time, but had to wait five minutes between them. The washing facilities were atrocious. Most meals were excellent, far superior to hospital food, but there were no eggs, free range or other. On Sundays we were given forms to complete for the meals we wanted during the following week.

After long delays I was, with the assistance of my fellow prisoners, registered for classes. I started to study journalism, painting and IT, for which I was paid £1 per attendance. This money was credited to me in the form of points which could be used to buy foods unavailable as part of standard prison fare, such as bananas, oranges, ketchup, sardines, tea bags, honey and chocolate. As I have mentioned, they could also be used for telephone calls, and could be traded to obtain stamps from other prisoners. Stamps couldn't be bought in the prison shop and therefore had either to be requested from friends and relations outside, or obtained from other prisoners who had some to spare in return for something they required. The majority of my classmates were hardened criminals who joined up simply to get credit to buy a few 'luxuries' from the Thursday shop. We were given a list of these in advance so that we could plan our shopping.

After the first fortnight I was allowed visits every two weeks. I was required to give the name, telephone number, address and relationship of those I wanted to visit me. Once that was approved an invitation would be issued, the visitor on arrival would be taken to the visitor hall, and after being searched I would be taken to see him or (more usually) her. A small canteen served tea, coffee and chocolate, all of which had to be consumed there and then, and I was searched again on return to my cell. Visits normally lasted an hour.

After I'd been visited by a few friends I received a request from Karen Audin to be issued with an invitation. After that I reserved all my visit slots for her because she had such a profound effect in raising my morale. Looking forward to the visits, and between them the phone calls, of someone for whom I cared deeply made prison life much more tolerable.

Some of my supporters didn't even know me but they still made the effort to voice their concern and write to their MPs. Their action was a demonstration that we are here on earth to help one another. Life without a friend is not a fulfilled life. We must extend our support to one another through life's journey if it's to become truly meaningful. It was obvious to my supporters that putting me, a 72-year-old, in prison, and thereafter tagging me, served no useful purpose while costing the taxpayer a mint. What was it supposed to achieve? The idea that prison is a corrective institution is contradicted by the fact that some hardened criminals enjoy being there, preferring to be locked up rather than working eight hours a day in an open prison. It is difficult only for those people who are new to the system.

Before the end of my time at Wandsworth I was attending two classes in the morning and another two after lunch and as a result I was free to leave the wing from the morning until 4 p.m. and was out of the cell four days a week. By the time I came back I would be tired, and so would watch television for a while, then do some yoga and meditation despite the limited space, and go to bed.

At six one morning at the end of March Ahmet was moved out to attend a hearing, and that was the last I saw of him. For a few days my life then became a nightmare. A Nigerian boy, whom I couldn't stand, moved in just three hours later, though fortunately he was moved the next day. After that I was left on my own for a whole day before a third cellmate, a Kuwaiti, came in for just half a day. These constant changes preyed on my mind and made me feel dangerously exposed. I had to remind myself that one should never give in to despair, as there is always light at the end of the tunnel.

The morning after that, the officer responsible for PE knocked on the cell door at 7 a.m. and asked: 'Do you want to go to the gym?' This was a special privilege, and for me it was another godsend. While I was exercising, Bert de Boer, a Dutch-Canadian prisoner whose cell was on the ground floor, was ordered to a different prison. He had shared a cell with Daniel McCann, a fellow banker from Jersey who was around my age. The banker was apprehensive about losing his cellmate and so some of my friends asked if I would like to move in with him. The movement officer, a firm but fair lady with a pleasant nature, had heard about the constant changes in my cell and took it upon herself to move me in with the banker the same morning.

My new cellmate might have been an agreeable companion, had he not had a routine quite different from mine. Alas, like Eddy and Ahmet, he was addicted to watching TV; at 6 a.m. on it went, regardless of the fact that I was still sleeping. I told him I didn't want to complain but could he at least wait until 8 am: 'You are not going anywhere so why do you want to watch the news at 6 am? You can just as easily watch it at 8.' He took my complaint badly, and sulked.

While this habit of many prisoners to switch on the TV at the earliest possible hour was very annoying, its purpose was obvious. It masked the vulnerability which most of us felt at that time of the day. I simply dealt with it differently, either by doing yoga or playing chess.

Appeal upheld and re-categorisation

Early one morning I was told that I would be taken to the appeal court. You might have thought I would have been pleased, but I hated the idea of another hellish journey in a prison van, and so I asked my solicitor, Zena, to argue the case that there was no necessity for me to attend. Fortunately, after a stressful few hours I heard that they had sorted it out and I was excused attendance. I must admit that on this occasion Daniel was supportive in my hour of need.

A week before my move from Wandsworth the appeal against my sentence was heard in court and the length of imprisonment was reduced from ten months to eight, as a result of which my release date would be brought forward. This news was received with euphoria in the wing and all my prisoner comrades assumed that I would be released immediately. They came in droves to congratulate me, almost as if they had won their own appeals. A successful appeal for one prisoner was a joy for all.

Then, however, I found out by phoning my family and my solicitor that my release date had been put back again. My worry about this was further stoked by a sadistic officer, of Pakistani or Bangladeshi origin, who remarked as I walked past him to post a letter, that my imminent move from Wandsworth following D-categorisation would have the effect of delaying my home detention curfew. This was because open prisons didn't have facilities for attaching tags, and it would therefore be better for me to stay in Wandsworth. I was very unsettled by this remark.

Why did this officer tell me such a thing? When I asked him to explain what he meant he said that he didn't have time to discuss it. Then luckily on my way back from class I saw the same kind black female officer who had organised my cell move and told her of my distress. She suggested I go straight to a meeting room on the ground floor instead of making frustrating phone calls as she had seen me doing before in such circumstances. When I arrived there I found the governor of the wing holding a consultation meeting with inmates and told her about my fears. She assured me that regardless of where I was imprisoned, the process of home detention would remain the same. She then asked who had told me that a move to Ford would adversely affect me, and I replied, honestly, that I did not know his name. I could, of course, have identified him, but realised that as he had taken advantage of my vulnerability once, he could do so again if he had a grudge against me. So I kept quiet.

My application for re-categorisation was at this point about to be approved, after which I would be moved to Ford open prison, though as so often there was a delay. From the start I had clearly qualified for Category D status which is given to those who are considered low risk and can reasonably be trusted in open conditions. I should, therefore, have been sent to an open prison within a couple of weeks of conviction as my legal team had predicted. The whole time I was at Wandsworth the Church of England and Roman Catholic chaplains, as well as the Muslim Imam, had argued my case for D-categorisation. And yet I was only given this status after nearly two months, at the very point when I was about to gain exceptional freedom of movement within Wandsworth, indeed only shortly before I was released on home detention. It was the African Catholic chaplain who told me I was on the list to be moved. My sense of joy was only slightly dampened by not knowing what the conditions in an open prison would be like. But I felt sure it could not be worse than Wandsworth.

On the night before I was due to move a small slip of paper was pushed under the cell door stating I had to pack up and be ready at six the next morning. I was moving but still didn't know for sure where I was going. As arranged, early the next day, together with other prisoners who were being transferred, among them the Jersey banker, Daniel, I was taken to an area where we waited for a couple of hours. We were then put into a small prison van in the charge of a sympathetic driver. He played comforting music *en route*, and gave us food and drink to sustain us on the journey to Ford Open Prison near Arundel.

Ford Open Prison

The journey took three hours. Once there, I could feel the air and see the sun all day, and was free to interact with people in a way I hadn't done since the beginning of my sentence. We were efficiently inducted by an inmate who was supervised by a prison officer, but as we had arrived on an Easter bank holiday weekend nothing else happened after that until the end of the shutdown. I was grateful that I had arrived at Ford in time to benefit from this opportunity to relax.

My stay in Ford was very short but every day I was there was absolutely beautiful. The sun shone, I was wearing more comfortable prison clothing and I was allowed to eat in a canteen rather than in my cell. I could move around as I liked, even crossing the surrounding green fields. I again shared a cell with the Jersey banker who in these new surroundings was much more bearable. When I awoke in the morning I could see the sun shining and hear the birds singing. I had the key to my cell and could unlock it when I wanted and have a shower in a clean washroom. And I could use a clean toilet. It was heaven!

I called Karen Audin and told her it was fantastic to be in Ford. Her visits to Wandsworth, together with our telephone conversations, had sustained me and brought light to my darkened soul, and I was immensely grateful to her. But now she reminded me, quite correctly, that I was still in prison. After a few days it did finally dawn on me that she was right, and that there was still a fence around this apparent paradise. If I had stayed in Ford for a longer period the euphoria would no doubt have worn off. You may not be locked up in an open prison, your cell key is in your hand, you can open it and come and go when you feel like it, you have contact with people in eight other cells, you are not confined as in a normal prison, and do not have to put up with your cellmate's mood and behaviour. But as Karen said, it was still a prison.

My ecstatic state arose from the comparison with Wandsworth. The efficiency at Ford was unparalleled. Quite unlike Wandsworth, where one often got no response to requests, here I received a reply within twenty-four hours. For example, at Wandsworth I was once left for about three weeks without any access to the phone. I complained persistently until one humane officer took up the issue and resolved it within five minutes. The majority of the other officers were bullies with psychopathic tendencies. Some of the prisoners were difficult, but not the majority, and I do not see why the officers had to exceed their mandate and punish their wards more than they were already being punished through their incarceration.

Moreover, the facilities at Wandsworth were very poor. They had a gym but it was rat-infested and dirty. With a few exceptions, the officers were unconcerned about the prisoners' welfare and did not respond to complaints about the unhealthy environment. That made me all the more grateful to those unusual officers who got to know me and were kind. One offered to let me use a quiet room to do yoga away from the noise and smell of other prisoners. However, there was little ventilation and no fresh air to breathe there. The only benefit of the gym was that it was possible to have a shower in cleaner facilities than those in the wing. Even the food at Ford was better than at Wandsworth, and that was about the only aspects of that prison about which I couldn't complain, and we didn't have to wash our plates!

In Ford I continued to do yoga, which took place in the church hall, and thereby met the chaplain who invited me to come to the Easter service. The same evening they were organising the Easter service and invited me to join in, which I did. To my surprise I had my feet washed by the chaplain and all the congregation said a prayer to bless me. I also attended prayers with the Muslims and in these few days I was involved in various sporting activities as a referee. My days at Ford passed very quickly and joyfully.

After the bank holiday Monday I met an officer who told me she believed I would not be at Ford for long. She suggested I ought to check with the Home Detention Unit to find out exactly when I was going to be released. Accordingly I made an appointment and to my joy, and everyone else's, I learnt that my release had been scheduled for 27th April. I phoned my family and Karen Audin and told them the good news. The next day I packed and was ready to go, but when I came to the last gate the officer responsible for the release was not there. I was ordered by the gatekeeper, an unresponsive woman, to wait. There was no indication as to what was happening until at last, two hours later, the release officer arrived apologising that he had been detained in a meeting. He was surprised I had not been told he would be delayed.

Release on a tag

And so at last I put on my suit again and left Ford with a plastic bag marked 'HM Prison Service' in bold print. Although I had been told by my daughter that her husband would be there to meet me at the gate, I hadn't been able to call him to tell him when to pick me up. This was because I had used up all my prison credit. So I found myself in a very embarrassing position. If I were to travel home by public transport, everyone would know from my bag that I had just been released from prison. But then I discovered to my great surprise and delight that my mobile, which was with my belongings, was still charged after all this time and I managed to call Karen to tell her I'd been released. She contacted some friends to ask them to collect me, and when at last they arrived it was a euphoric reunion.

We went first to my daughter's house in Brighton where, after a while, Karen joined us. After that I drove with Karen to my own house in Hinchley Wood in time for the 3 p.m. appointment to fit the home detention monitor. As it turned out, the pleasant lady who fitted the tag didn't actually arrive until the evening. She attached it to my left ankle and explained what the rules were without making me feel anxious. The home detention curfew meant I had to stay at home between seven in the evening and seven in the morning. It was bearable because at least I had the freedom to step outside the house, go to yoga classes, and visit friends so long as I was home before 7 p.m.

A week later I rang Charmaine, told her the good news about my release, and thanked her for all her support while I was in prison. During the conversation I mentioned that Karen had arranged for me to be picked up at the prison gate. I was aware that she was in a new relationship and so I didn't anticipate her reaction. She took the news badly that Karen was still on the scene, and so our conversation came to an abrupt end. It was a shock to realise that she had continued to blame Karen for the break-up which, as I've indicated, had come about for quite different reasons. Fortunately, she was later able to view the matter more philosophically, and described our relationship as part of life's colourful tapestry.

This final restriction of my liberty lasted for about two and a half months, after which the tag was removed. I had completed half of my reduced eight-month sentence and was now a free man again, albeit with a debt of half a million pounds to the authorities.

Outcry grows over jailing of engineer who broke Iraq oil sanctions 'to help the West'

Sean O'Neill Crime and Security Editor

The imprisonment of a campaigner who carried messages from Baghdad to London in the build-up to war saying that Iraq had no weapons of mass destruction is causing rising concern.

Riad el-Taher, 72, has been held in Wandsworth jail, South London, for the past week after being sentenced to ten months for breaches of United Nations sanctions against Saddam Hussein's regime. Friends of el-Taher say that he paid kickbacks on allocations given to him under the Oil-for-Food programme to "keep his seat at the table" and glean information which might prevent the war or lead to a relaxation of sanctions. El-Taher had direct access to Tariq Aziz, Saddam's deputy prime minister, who has since been executed.

The Times has seen evidence that el-Taher briefed diplomats, including the MI6 attaché, at the British Embassy in Amman, Jordan, and repeatedly passed on the message that Iraq did not have any nuclear, chemical or biological weapons. Security sources declined to comment on the contact.

Two former directors of the UN's humanitarian programme in Iraq have told The Times that they believed el-Taher was a courageous campaigner whose primary motive was to lessen the suffering of ordinary people in Iraq.

El-Taher, an oil engineer, fled to Britain in the 1970s to escape Baathist rule but returned to his native country to help to rebuild it after the Gulf War. Distressed by the hardship suffered by Iraqis because of sanctions, he set up Friendship Across Frontiers to campaign for their removal. He lobbied MPs, organised trips to Iraq for Western politicians and lobbied the Foreign and Commonwealth Office.

His political contacts included the late Robin Cook, the former Foreign Secretary, and Clare Short, who was the International Development Secretary. He also briefed senior MPs, including Tam Dalyell and Tony Benn. El-Taher attended the Iraq Inquiry, also known as the Chilcot Inquiry, with Ms Short last year and has also given written evidence to Sir John Chilcot, the Inquiry's chairman.

El-Taher is one of only a handful of people to be prosecuted out of 169 companies and individuals that paid kickbacks under the Oil-for-Food programme.

Hans von Sponeck, head of the programme from 1998 to 2000, said: "Riad el-Taher was a concerned and committed person who spoke out on the injustices of international policy. If he broke the rules then he is accountable for his own actions. But he is a small fish."

Denis Halliday, a former head of the humanitarian programme in Iraq, said that the jailing of el-Taher showed continuing "double standards" over Iraq. "What is appalling is that the real culprits, those who cheated most on sanctions, are the big guys — governments, politicians and major companies in Australia, the US, India, France and Russia who paid millions of dollars in kickbacks to Saddam," he added.

Judge Nicholas Loraine-Smith, who sentenced el-Taher at Southwark Crown Court last week, seemed to acknowledge that many guilty people would never stand trial, saying: "It must seem to you to be unfair to be in the dock while many others are not."

El-Taher pleaded guilty to sanctions breaches in the hope that he might receive a suspended sentence. But the judge concluded that his primary motive was financial gain and that he had made $140,000 (£86,000) from selling his oil allocations. His lawyers are to appeal against the sentence and apply for bail.

Mr Dalyell, the former Father of the Commons, called for el-Taher's immediate release, adding: "At a time when the Justice Secretary wants to reduce the prison population it seems preposterous to be sending a 72-year-old man, who poses no threat to the public, to jail in such controversial circumstances."

Jack Straw, page 21

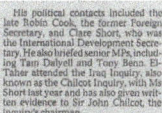

Riad el-Taher: carried messages from Baghdad to London before Iraq War

1. Wandsworth Prison

2. Interior of Wandsworth Prison

3. Article about my case by Sean O'Neill in *The Times* on 5th March 2011

4. Ford Open Prison: paradise by comparison, but still a prison

5. Outside Peter Kyle's constituency office in Hove following my expulsion from the Labour Party in 2017

6. The Victory Arch in Baghdad which survived the attempt post-2003 to demolish it

CHAPTER NINETEEN

AFTERSHOCKS AND AFTERTHOUGHTS

A £70,000 bill

My sentence included the requirement to pay £500,000 to the Crown. The money I owed was based not on the modest (in oil trading terms) profit of £97,000 which Bula and Perenco made on the four transactions for which I was prosecuted, but on the amount I had paid in surcharges. My legal team advised me that this was as good a deal as I was likely to get, and I didn't therefore appeal against it. Accordingly I sold my Hinchley Wood house, paid the amount demanded, and reconciled myself to this loss with the thought that I didn't really need a three-bedroom house anyway. The modest flat I acquired in Hove in 2013 was quite adequate for my needs.

Then, like a bolt from the blue, I was once again summoned to appear in court and ordered to pay a further £70,000 towards the costs of the defence. I should have realised that this was coming, but I didn't. It was one of the penalties of being found guilty that the legal aid I had received was now forfeited. If I could have proved that I would be reduced to poverty, I might have argued my way out of such a large repayment, but Judge Loraine-Smith, who was again presiding, described me as 'a man of means', and so that was that.

The Garda on my case

A year or two after my release, my lawyer was unexpectedly approached by the Irish Garda. They said that they would like to interview me, either in Ireland, or a Garda officer would come to see me at my home in England. Having been a director of Bula and having worked with the Irish government in my campaign against sanctions, and in particular with the ex-Taoiseach, Albert Reynolds, the US authorities were now apparently leaning on their Irish counterparts to take similar action against me as the British authorities had done. However, in the course of the conversation, the Garda admitted to my lawyer, off the record as they said, that the Irish government had no interest in pursuing the case, but were simply going through the motions to satisfy the Americans. All I had to do was to ignore the request, which is, of course, what I did. I never heard any more about it.

Expulsion from the Labour Party

The last aftershock also came like a bolt out of the blue. On 9th March 2017 I received an email with an attached letter from the Labour Party head office. It contained the following message:

> It has been brought to our attention with supporting evidence that you were convicted of four counts of 'Making funds available to Iraq except under the authority of a licence granted by the Treasury' in February 2011. This is incompatible with membership of the Labour Party.

The letter went on incongruously:

> Chapter 2.1.4.D of the Labour Party's rules states:
> 'iii – where the NEC [National Executive Committee] determines it is appropriate and based on a conviction for a serious offence or subject of a serious ruling form [sic] HM Court and Tribunals Service, resolve that a member is

> ineligible to be or remain a Party member subject to the provisions of Chapter 6.1.2 below of the disciplinary rules.'

That sub-clause only makes sense in the context of what preceded it:

> Where a member has been convicted of a serious criminal offence or subject of a serious ruling from HM Courts and Tribunals Service, the NEC shall have the right to impose the appropriate disciplinary action from the following options:
>
> i. Suspension from membership or from holding office and representation of the Party for the duration of any prison sentence imposed, included a suspended sentence.
> ii. Referral of disciplinary case to the NCC [National Constitutional Committee]'

The following paragraph of the letter reads:

> You are therefore ineligible to remain a member of the Labour Party and have been removed from the national membership system. You are no longer entitled to attend local Labour Party meetings.

Clause 6.1.2 of the rule book concerning applications for re-admission was quoted, stipulating that such an application would only be considered after five years had elapsed; at my age that meant never.

I was absolutely dismayed by this totally unexpected decision. The offences for which I had been convicted had occurred in 2001, and I was convicted, and I had served my sentence in 2011, that is sixteen and six years respectively before my expulsion. After such a time lapse should the slate not have been wiped clean? I believe that my conviction was legally 'spent' by late 2015. Option (i) above suggests that the rule makers had in mind a recent conviction, not one years earlier. It seems probable in the nature of things that there are other Labour Party members who have been convicted of serious offences in the past, but who continue to enjoy their membership undisturbed. Moreover, the officials at Labour Party HQ could have availed themselves of option (ii), that is of referring my case to the NCC for disciplinary consideration. But of course that would have given me the chance to defend myself, which presumably is what they didn't want.

Why, then, was I targeted in this way? The phrase used by Tam in his introduction to this book comes again to mind: 'a process of nasty, political vengeance.' In this case, however, the motive may have had as much to do with internal divisions within the Labour Party.

I had been a member of the Labour Party back in the nineties, but resigned over Tony Blair's support for the sanctions policy. Following the election of Jeremy Corbyn as Labour leader in September 2015 and the formation of the grassroots pro-Corbyn Momentum organisation which evolved out of it, I was inspired to re-join. I should emphasise that the application form contained no declaration that I had never been convicted, nor did the rules of the party make a historic conviction a disqualification for membership. Meanwhile on 2nd July 2016 Brighton and Hove Labour Party, the largest branch in the country, was suspended by the national Labour Party amidst allegations of intimidation and vote-rigging, and subsequently it was split into three constituency branches. Whatever the truth of the allegations, there is little doubt that the real motivation of the Labour Party National Executive was to disrupt the strongly pro-Momentum faction in Brighton and Hove.

In early 2017, as the AGM of the Hove Constituency Labour Party approached, I had agreed to stand for election to its executive committee. In my personal statement I wrote that after graduation as a design engineer 'I worked in the oil industry … I managed the first Arab engineering company financed [by] OAPEC and also worked for OPEC.' I said that I had travelled extensively in the region. This, and the fact that I was known to be an Iraqi, might have been the cue to further investigation, yet at no point was I asked about my past. On 5th February I was duly elected with nine others, eight of whom were, like me, Momentum members. This was something of a disaster from the point of view of the new Labour Progress MP for Hove and the only Labour MP at that time in both Kent and Sussex, Peter Kyle. He had hoped his supporters would take over. Thereupon Ivor Caplin, who had been the Labour MP for Hove between 2001 and 2005 and who was a committed Zionist, appears to have told Kyle, a close friend, about my history. The latter then presumably laid the matter before the NEC in the expectation that I would be expelled. Meanwhile Caplin called on me to 'do the right thing' and stand down prior to my expulsion. But I wasn't about to do their dirty work for them.

Salt was rubbed into my wound when the day after my expulsion *Private Eye* published a piece about this debacle in its 'HP Sauce' column. They must have been tipped off about my expulsion before it happened, because otherwise they wouldn't have had time to include this comment. I'm indirectly described as an 'ex-con' with an alliance to a criminal dictatorship, which is a distortion on two counts. Firstly my relationship with Saddam was in no way on the level of an alliance. And secondly it painted a grossly distorted picture to present me as someone who had cosied up to a dictator while failing to mention that Western leaders, some of them socialists, regularly did the same. The Americans had done it with Saddam, and Tony Blair did it with Gaddafi.

The anonymous author was kind enough to quote me saying: 'I have been an active campaigner on issues to do with the Middle East and strongly believe that human rights should be central to an ethical foreign policy.' I had acted as I did to 'alleviate the suffering of the Iraqi people.' But sarcasm follows with '… he persuaded Tony Benn and Tam Dalyell to support his plea that he was nothing more than a misunderstood altruist.' The last paragraph puts the boot in by quoting the judge's verdict that my primary motive was financial.

There seemed some chance that *Private Eye*, which prides itself on being non-partisan, would publish my side of the story, and so I wrote a letter to the editor, Ian Hislop, putting my case. I insisted that Tony Benn's and Tam Dalyell's support for me had not been naïve, but rather based on sound evidence. I pointed out that 'the profit made from oil-for-food transactions was paid to two companies, Bula and Perenco, on whose boards of directors I served. I had no individual access to this money, most of which was used, as I wished, to campaign against the sanctions.' I went on: 'The payment of £501,934 relates to the surcharge on oil-for-food transactions imposed by the Iraqi regime. It was not an individual backhander to Saddam; all oil lifters who wished to continue in the programme at that time had to pay it.' I concluded that this matter was much more complex than the *Private Eye* columnist had presented it, and deserved more careful analysis, something which my forthcoming book would aim to provide.

The response came in the following issue in a piece by 'Ratbiter' entitled 'Riad Politik.' The author claimed that *Private Eye* could take credit for my expulsion, though in reality I was expelled a day before the piece in 'HP Sauce' appeared. 'El Taher,' it goes on, 'had been aiding an Iraqi regime soaked in blood, so Labour must have felt it had no choice.' Did anyone at *Private* Eye, or indeed in the NEC, consider that at the same time as I committed my offence, our Labour government under Tony Blair was supporting a sanctions regime which was killing far more people, especially woman and children, than the supposedly wicked Saddam?

You might think that I live in an opulent detached mansion from the description of where I was interviewed for the local BBC news: '… his attractive home on Hove's aptly named Grand Avenue.' It is true that the street in which I live is rather impressive, but I live in a small second-floor flat of a quite ordinary building. That is all I could afford after the half million charge imposed by the court and the other expenses to which I've referred. Not that I want anyone's sympathy. I long ago stopped being concerned about material possessions above the basic minimum.

The writer summarises my interview with *Brighton and Hove News*, in which I mentioned that I had known Jeremy Corbyn since 1990 and had shared a platform with him many times as fellow members of the Stop the War Coalition. Referring to my letter to the *Eye* he points out, correctly, that Greg Hadfield, Secretary of the Hove branch, had taken up my case, suggesting that my expulsion might have been affected by two additional factors, my being the only BAME (Black Asian Minority Ethnic) member in the local party, and my support for the Palestinians. Hadfield also, interestingly, maintained that publishing the fact of my conviction could be regarded as a breach of the 'Rehabilitation of Offenders Act.' Reported in a neutral way, some of this could be seen as positive, but the slant was very clear; I'm referred to as a 'convicted crook,' for example.

I would like to take this opportunity to thank all those in Momentum and the Brighton Labour Party, and especially Greg, who supported me through this ordeal and attempted to get the expulsion reversed. In the end I felt it was more important for me to publish this book than to expend my energy on other, probably fruitless, attempts to persuade people to see matters differently.

The failure of our campaign

I pass on now to ask myself where I, where we, went wrong in our campaign against the sanctions, the war, and the occupation. What was the missing ingredient which might have made a difference? For alas, in the end all was lost. The US and British governments were following an agenda which took no account of suffering on the ground. All of their rhetoric was directed to supporting their long-term aims. Their championing of the Iraqi opposition had to do with the fact that it said the things they wanted to hear, and because it was at hand. Tam comments:

> Such information as was available to London and Washington came overwhelmingly from Iraqi exiles who had fled Saddam, loathed his regime and were happy to goad Britain and the Untied States into hostility and armed conflict, with a view to restoring their own positions within Iraq.
>
> Repeatedly I asked the Prime Minister and others whether they were sure their information came from untainted sources. Equally repeatedly and perhaps understandably, they declined to reveal their sources – least of all to me. My criticism of Blair is that he did not ask probing questions as to how exactly crucial information on which possible military action would be based had been obtained and from whom. And this criticism applies equally to members of his Cabinet who were also in a position to ask questions – had Cabinet members delved deeper, I doubt if Britain would have been complicit in the bombing of Baghdad. This begs the question of *why* they didn't delve deeper. I thought there was a simple answer – that to meddle in any subject outside a minister's own portfolio was, to put it mildly, frowned upon by Downing Street, while to question the Prime Minister's judgement on Iraq was to invite dismissal from the Cabinet, however senior one was.[1]

The truth of what Tam said about the unreliable sources on which the West enthusiastically built its case for war was revealed in a *Daily Mail* article just a week before I was sentenced to jail. Rafid Ahmad

---
[1] Dalyell, T., *The Importance* ... , p 261.

Alwan al-Janabi, alias 'Curveball,' one of Ahmad Chalabi's dissident 'informers,' admitted that he had deliberately fabricated stories to persuade the world that toppling Saddam was justified. For example, he said that he had worked in a team which assembled germ-production units on trucks at a seed purification plant near Baghdad, that these could be moved from site to site to avoid detection by the UN inspectors, and that there were plans to build mobile bio-chemical factories. In a speech at the UN making the case for the US-led invasion, Colin Powell referred to this 'eye-witness' who had testified to these military preparations. In reality the whole story was a fabrication. Commenting on what he had done, Curveball told *The Mail*: 'Maybe I was right, maybe I was not right. They gave me this chance. I had the chance to fabricate something to topple the regime.'[2]

The great advantage Tam had over almost all his parliamentary colleagues was that he had been to Iraq and 'had talked deeply and at length to Iraqis and those who knew about the issue.' He realised that the information gained from Western intelligence agents in Iraq was, in the circumstances, as unreliable as that from the supposed 'opposition,' and that there was no substitute for direct contact with the country and its people.[3] A smokescreen was erected by the West which obscured the fact that, unlike Saddam's regime, the leaders of the opposition had no local popular power base. Saddam's success was doubtless partly due to the ruthlessness of the Ba'athist government, but it was also a tribute to what Saddam had done for his country.

We learned later that all our efforts before the war had been fruitless as Tony Blair had made up his mind, regardless of what we communicated about the situation on the ground. According to the secretary of the Roman Catholic Archbishop at that time, Cardinal

---

[2] 'Defector who told the West about Saddam's weapons of mass destruction admits he lied,' *Daily Mail*, 16th February 2011; online at
http://www.dailymail.co.uk/news/article-1357295/Iraqi-defector-told-Blair-Bush-Saddams-WMDs-admits-lied.html.
[3] Dalyell, T., *The Importance ...*, p 261.

Hume presented Iraq's case to Tony Blair's wife, Cherie, when she attended mass. He believed, like many other religious leaders, that the British policy towards Iraq was wrong and harmful. But even that had no effect.

As we have seen the attitude already existed in high places as early as 1998 that a war must be waged against Iraq and that world public opinion must accordingly be prepared to accept it. Even more shockingly, a United Nations agency had been involved at the highest level in helping to promote this war rather than seeking a peaceful resolution. This was the UN in which we Arabs had placed such naïve trust, the international body which we believed would eventually, for example, deliver justice to the Palestinians. Saddam's suspicion of the weapons inspectors was, it turned out, justified, and his consequent restriction of their freedom of action understandable. The four-day punitive Operation Desert Fox in December 1998, designed to teach Saddam who was boss, was a taste of what further misery the world community had in store for my country.

That same year Denis Halliday resigned as UN Humanitarian Coordinator overseeing the oil-for-food programme, bringing to an end a 34-year career in the UN. In 2003 he received the Gandhi International Peace Award, and in his acceptance speech said the following about his resignation.

> I was driven to resignation because I refused to continue to take Security Council orders, the same Security Council that had imposed and sustained genocidal sanctions on the innocent of Iraq. I did not want to be complicit. I wanted to be free to speak out publicly about this crime.
>
> And above all, my innate sense of justice was and still is outraged by the violence that UN sanctions have brought upon, and continues to bring upon, the lives of children, families – the extended families, the loved ones of Iraq.

There is no justification for killing the young people of Iraq, not the aged, not the sick, not the rich, not the poor.

Some will tell you that the leadership is punishing the Iraqi people. That is not my perception, or experience from living in Baghdad. And were that to be the case – how can that possibly justify further punishment, in fact collective punishment, by the United Nations? I don't think so. And international law has no provision for the disproportionate and murderous consequences of the ongoing UN embargo – for well over 12 long years.[4]

As I've already mentioned, Halliday's successor, the German diplomat, Hans von Sponeck, together with his colleague, Jutta Burghardt, head of the UN World Food Programme in Iraq also resigned, and for similar reasons, in 2000. A resounding condemnation of UK and US policy on Iraq appeared in a 2001 article in *The Guardian* co-authored with Denis Halliday:

The UK and the US, as permanent members of the council, are fully aware that the UN embargo operates in breach of the UN covenants on human rights, the Geneva and Hague conventions and other international laws. It is neither anti-UK nor anti-US to point out that Washington and London, more than anywhere else, have in the past decade helped to write the Iraq chapter in the history of avoidable tragedies.[5]

Both sides in the conflict saw me as a potential asset, and this appeared to give me the opportunity to avert war by alerting the Iraqi

---

[4] Halliday, D., words of acceptance – Gandhi International Peace Award – 30 January 2003. See http://gandhifoundation.org/2003/01/30/2003-peace-award-denis-halliday-2/.
[5] v Sponeck, H. & Halliday, D., 'The hostage nation,' *The Guardian*, 29th November 2001, online at
http://www.theguardian.com/world/2001/nov/29/iraq.comment.

government to Western thinking, while answering the concerns of British government officials about Iraq. I have to confess now that this was a great illusion.

Tam was convinced that if George Bush Jr and Tony Blair had witnessed what he had seen they would have adopted a different attitude. He may have been right but personally I now doubt this as well. It is my belief that policies are set by economic and strategic interests rather than leaders' perceptions. If it is inconvenient for politicians to see the reality staring them in the face, they will find ways of obscuring or distorting it.

For example, back in December 1996 US Ambassador to the UN and later Secretary of State, Madeleine Albright, was interviewed by Lesley Stahl on a TV programme called 60 Minutes. Stahl, commenting on the sanctions, posed the following question: 'We have heard that a half million children have died. I mean, that's more children than died in Hiroshima. And, you know, is the price worth it?' Albright replied: 'I think this is a very hard choice, but the price – we think the price is worth it.'[6] Worldwide public opinion was outraged, and this increased the pressure to make the oil-for-food programme work.

My naivety

Our campaign failed not because its case was weak but because the US and UK were entrenched in their blinkered view of Iraq, and also because we had insufficient time for the truth to emerge in the way that it eventually did. But I must confess that I revealed my naivety in my campaigning. I had not understood, for example, that politics is in reality about playing the media. George Galloway knew exactly how this was done, but he was too much of a maverick to make a lasting impression. Others like Tam Dalyell, Tony Benn, Alan Simpson and Harry Cohen were not comfortable at this game, and when confronted

---

[6] '60 Minutes', 5th December 1996.

with tragic events like those in Iraq wanted to tell the media in unembellished form what they had seen. But their views tended not to make the headlines in a world where the primary motive was to sell papers. And they were no match for the well-oiled government propaganda machine.

With hindsight, I was also naïve in my perception of democracy and the role MPs could realistically play. The Gulf War and the imposition of the sanctions prompted me to write handwritten letters to all 628 MPs. My assumption was, wrongly as it turned out, that they needed to be informed and that they were voting in support of the war and sanctions because they were misled by the media. This was as futile an exercise as my letter to George Bush senior back in 1992. MPs are only likely to be influenced by letters written by their own constituents, and even that isn't at all certain.

It was naïve of me to think that the 200,000 Iraqi families living in the UK, many of them bogus refugees, would flock to support their country. To my disappointment I found the majority weren't interested. They talked about the situation and what was happening to their families and friends, but shied away from engaging in any positive activity to support their own people. Fear is embedded in the character of Muslims generally and Arabs in particular. The tribal system demands total respect for the leader, an attitude which may partly reflect the fear of God demanded by Islam. Consequently they have a culture of avoiding open challenges to authority, even when living abroad. Privately they're often critical, and rarely idolise their leaders, but they're unwilling to be vocal or support opposition figures publicly.

Many British people were aware of the real motivation behind British and American policies. The so-called Iraqi opposition which their leaders supported had no coherent argument other than hatred of Saddam, naked self-interest, the wish to gain political standing or a combination of these. Some were paid informants working for US and UK intelligence. But it must also be said that the Saddam regime often foolishly shot itself in the foot. For example, the persecution of Iraqis of Iranian origin like Mowaffak al-Rubaie was ultimately counter-productive, driving many of them straight into the arms of the West.

Ann Clwyd, Labour, and Emma Nicholson, Lib Dem, used the suffering of the Marsh Arabs and the Kurds to justify their support for the Iraqi opposition. One can understand the grievances of these peoples, but they cannot be regarded as a credible and unified opposition. I might not have objected to supporting them if it had been otherwise. In fact there was no credible Iraqi opposition inside or outside the country. Emigré opponents of the regime were fragmented and self-serving and had no power base in Iraq. Consequently when they came riding in on the tops of American and British tanks they failed miserably to establish a secure and lasting government in Iraq.

Another example of my naivety was my assumption that the best way to publicise the situation in Iraq was to invite journalists to the country. Most of them had pre-conceived ideas which shaped and filtered what they saw and heard. Even those excellent journalists like Tim Llewellyn, whom I took to Iraq another two times after that first official trip there, had their wings clipped by editors back home. The BBC, for example, had screened his programmes at unsocial hours or at the same time as popular programmes and the impact of his reporting was consequently diminished. It's not surprising that he resigned.

No doubt there will be readers of this book who think that my greatest naivety was my belief that developing a relationship with Saddam, regarded by many as a tyrant of the worst order, could have a beneficial outcome for the Iraqi people. But I had no illusions about the President; he was a man who ruled with an iron hand. So, however, was Stalin, but Churchill didn't shy away from a friendly relationship with him. Circumstances sometimes dictate the way you act when trying to resolve a problem. The subsequent negative outcome should not in hindsight be taken as an indication of naivety.

I thought that FAF could contribute to changing the world for the better by informing people of the facts. But I was forced to conclude that the world of politics is driven by sinister motives such as self-aggrandisement and economic gain. I am not a prophet and have never professed to be one. Nor was I born to change the world single-handedly, but I believed that together with others an improvement in the international order was possible. That was the root of my naivety.

Disillusion with democracy

I'm not bitter, but I *am*, disillusioned, in the true sense of that word. Democracy was throughout my life a burning ideal, but I have lost faith in the democratic system, both in the West and in Arab world. I now know that politics has become corrupt and has little ethical basis. I also learned that Parliament is not sovereign, but provides a mandate for abuse of privilege. There are fair-minded and just individuals, but the system itself is not even-handed.

As I said earlier, attempts have been made to bring Tony Blair to account for his action in bringing suffering to an entire nation, not to mention the families of UK combatants. To date he has refused to acknowledge the devastating failure of his policies to establish democracy and provide a secure and prosperous future for Iraqis. Iraq has become a failed state built on corruption and ethnic and sectarian division. His insistence that he acted correctly has a ripple effect resulting both in a lack of respect for politics and in the media's ditching of decent moral standards. Punishment of Blair would be clearly understood as a deterrent to others, instead of which we see a Prime Minister who was very economical with the truth getting off scot free and, to cap it all, who was later rewarded by being appointed Peace Envoy to the Middle East. As Imran Khan put it bluntly in his comments on the failed private prosecution of Blair: 'This is not justice.'

We are all living in the delusion of democracy. Admittedly it is better in the UK than in some other countries, but even here people are not free to challenge the system. If I had chosen to pursue my own interest and ignored what I witnessed on my visits to Iraq under sanctions I would neither have been prosecuted, nor imprisoned, nor would my life savings have been wiped out.

What is democracy? I believe the basic minimum is a parliamentary system with free elections and secret ballots, a free press, free markets, and the unshackling of citizens from limitations to their development such as lack of education and health care. Iraq before 2003, like Libya before 2011, offered free education and medical care, using their oil wealth to pay for it. Certainly neither of these countries under their autocratic rulers were models of democracy, but they had started down the long road which leads to fully just societies. Even when I lived in Iraq in the 1950s we had a parliament and elections which were probably more democratic than what passes for democracy post-2003. And yet the Western powers, in their wisdom, decided to destroy my country and Libya, and unleashed chaos instead. The rise of ISIS in both countries is a direct result of these misguided Western policies.

The citizens' collective right to change governments in a democratic state is of little value if they suffer from poor living standards and gross inequalities in education and health care. When I first came to the UK I saw democracy as the system of government in a utopia where all citizens were equal in every way, including their right of access to their elected rulers. Blair stated that one of the objectives of the Second Gulf War was to establish democracy and free elections in Iraq. Elections have taken place, but have Iraqi citizens since 2003 enjoyed security, free medical treatment or education, or freedom to choose where to live or seek employment in accordance with their talents? The answer is a definitive 'no.'

Yet Blair continues to deceive the public that he has established democracy where before there was none. Democracy in the UK has evolved over many centuries, with universal adult suffrage only being achieved within the last hundred years. Even now education and health care are under constant threat; elections are, by comparison with these, a luxury and are only worth having if those who are elected fulfil their responsibilities conscientiously.

If other Arab rulers had followed Iraq's and Libya's example in using their oil resources to provide health care and education for all, and to eradicate poverty, illiteracy and corruption we could more realistically talk about an Arab Spring. Instead we see the mirage of democracy in the superficial glass and concrete development of the Gulf region. This serves the foreign contractors rather than the Gulf and the wider Arab world.

Meanwhile, in the aftermath of Blair's 2003 war, the region is on fire. There is mass emigration of professionals and ethnic and religious minorities, while extremism, emergencies, and dysfunctional governments fill the chaotic vacuum. Advantage has been taken of the sectarian nature of Iraq to divide and rule, while the wealth of the country has been sequestered, undermining education and medical care. The oil flow which used to pay for it is now controlled by multinationals and social justice has been replaced by a global economy controlled by the very rich. Freedom of movement is severely restricted by the requirement to obtain permits to travel around the country, and like Palestine, Iraq is now littered with road blocks at which permits to travel have to be produced.

The so-called Arab Spring

People could be forgiven for believing that the revolution in Tunisia, following the self-immolation of Mohammed Bouazizi in 2011, and the copycat uprisings which followed across the Arab world, were evidence of a new democratic spirit which would transform the Middle East. There is no doubt that the Tunisian uprising was spontaneous and sprang from the grass-roots. What followed across much of the Arab world was, however, orchestrated by the West, and was therefore selective and compromised. For example, the one other spontaneous uprising, that in Bahrain, received little encouragement from the West, while the present chaos in Syria resulted from Western support for the ill-defined opposition in that country.

The Arab Spring, named after the so-called Prague Spring in 1968, an unsuccessful uprising against Soviet occupation, might more appropriately be called the Arab disaster. Many European socialists lent their support to these disturbances without understanding the cultural and political environment in which they took place. True, President Mubarak was overthrown in Egypt, but why? It was, I believe, because the US and the Zionist entity had come to view the old guard leadership in that country and, by the way, in Saudi Arabia, as spent forces.

The American claim to be promoting democracy and fighting terrorism by supporting grass root uprisings across the Arab world is disingenuous when you consider US support for the Zionist entity, the Badr Brigades, Saudi Arabia and Qatar. The last of these is not only useful as a strategically-placed location for its regional military forces. As an oil-rich state Qatar has used its considerable wealth to conduct labyrinthine diplomacy with such diverse players as the Muslim Brotherhood, Hamas, Hezbollah, the Zionist entity and Iran. By making the Qatari leadership dependent on them, the Americans are able to use this power to finance, and withhold finance, to fine tune their covert policy in the region. Moreover, from their military base in the Emirate they can conveniently launch military operations to achieve whatever objective seems the flavour of the month. What better way could there be of weakening the whole region, except, of course the Zionist entity, than by setting the natives at each others' throats.

Syria, Yemen and Libya have been devastated as a result, with the same kind of cultural and intellectual cleansing occurring there as has happened in Iraq. From a Western perspective, all this chaos provides a good opportunity to export expensive weapons to the region, so that the people there can more efficiently kill one another. And, of course, there is the reward of oil, now firmly back in the control of multinationals, often the same ones which were kicked out by independent countries decades earlier. Medical care and education has been undermined across the board, for backwardness and poor health serve the long term security of the Zionist entity.

I realise this is a particularly jaundiced view of Western involvement and liberal fervour in the Middle East, but there is evidence to support the view that the US and UK only support those uprisings which they think are in their interests. The reforms in Tunisia have stagnated, Egypt is facing meltdown, Saudi Arabia. with Western backing, supports the ex-Yemeni government, while Iran is supporting the Houthi rebels. Ironically, at the same time the US allows Iran to undermine stability and progress in Iraq.

And where did all this start? The 2003 war on Iraq with its promise of democracy, was certainly not the first step, but it was a defining moment. From then on the clock was well and truly set back to a former imperial age which we believed to be behind us. Meanwhile the Zionist entity can pretty much do what it likes. What fools we have been!

CHAPTER TWENTY

TOWARDS JOURNEY'S END

Winding up FAF

In July 2011, just after being released from my tag, I decided it was time to wind up Friendship Across Frontiers. Disillusionment played its part, but the fact that many of my contacts in parliament had moved on or died, was also a consideration. Accordingly I sent out this letter to FAF supporters:

> FAF was formed in 1993 in the aftermath of the Gulf War and the imposition of the draconian sanctions. After his first historic visit to Iraq, British Parliamentarian Tam Dalyell suggested the formation of an organisation to encapsulate the aspirations of those Iraqis who opposed the sanctions. I was then disappointed to discover that Iraqi exiles were either committed to the so-called opposition groups who supported the sanctions, or if they opposed the sanctions, would go no further than expressing their outrage in private.
>
> I believe that since its formation FAF has achieved a tremendous amount in raising public awareness, and more particularly awareness among MPs of all parties, and generally in stimulating debate of the relevant issues. FAF's affiliation to various organisations opposed to the war and occupation of Iraq, as well as Palestine, gained it a higher profile and wider public support.
>
> Times have changed since the occupation of Iraq in 2003 and the world has moved on. Meanwhile in the country itself

there has been a marked deterioration in upholding human rights, in fighting corruption and in promoting fairness. But I no longer have access to those who govern Iraq, and most of the MPs who were associated with FAF have now left parliament. I have concluded, therefore, that it is time for me to hand over the struggle for the liberation of the Iraqi, as well as the Palestinian, peoples to others.

I have no regrets about the years I devoted to assisting the Iraqi people in their quest to break the sanctions regime. The prolonged legal proceedings from 2008 leading to my eventual incarceration have, of course, some bearing on my decision to step aside. Equally I believe I have done my share. The price I paid is minor in comparison to the colossal losses incurred by the majority of the Iraqi people. I feel deep sorrow for the needless loss of Iraqi lives as well as for the young British and US combatants who placed themselves in harm's way. This war and occupation is not a British or American war but a misadventure by the coalition of the neo-cons and Bush-Blair in their quest for oil and self-advancement.

For my part it is time for closure in active politics. But those who care about their fellow beings cannot remain blind to injustice or oppression and therefore the struggle will go on. In this context I would like to extend my profound thanks and appreciation to Tam Dalyell, our founder and patron, and a very dear friend, for his relentless efforts on our behalf, and also to his fellow patron, Harry Cohen, for his persistent support and encouragement. Our struggle against oppression could not have been achieved without their unstinting involvement. Special thanks are also due to the Rt. Hon. Tony Benn, President of the Stop the War Coalition (to which we affiliated just before 2003), which has become an umbrella organisation for promoting justice and truth.[1] May it continue to present the voices of the masses fairly.

Finally my thanks go out to all those who voiced their opinions and provided a platform whether in Iraq, the UK or Ireland. I wish you all persistent light and bliss.[2]

The balance sheet of US-British intervention

On 24 August, as a final mailing, I sent out some statistics about Iraq to supporters, highlighting the injustice which had been perpetrated against the Iraqi people by the hawks of war and the engineers of deceit. I had the Rt Hon Tony Blair primarily in mind, but also Lord Mandelson, who is reported to have acquired great wealth as a beneficiary of the 2003 invasion. When I spoke of the losses, I meant what I said. You can make up your own mind how valuable you think the gains were.

Mike Wood was kind enough to reply to my balance sheet with these validating words: 'Thank you very much indeed for your latest letter and for the statistics you provided which underline the validity of the position you have consistently taken. Thanks for everything you have stood for during your period of active political involvement and for your contribution to try and make the world a more peaceful and just one.'

Thoughts of a free man

Do I feel guilty? Hardly at all. Would I do it again knowing what I now know? Yes I would. Sanctions were an unwarranted collective punishment. It was right for all Iraqis and indeed anyone else to break the sanctions. The UN, which instituted them, will remain an

---

[1] Tony Benn died on 14th March 2014.
[2] Document in the possession of the author.

The balance-sheet of US-British intervention

Losses
1 million widows.
4 million orphans.
2.5 million civilian casualties.
800,000 missing.
240,000 prisoners (20,000 held by the US occupier).
4.5 million refugees, including professional and educated Iraqis.
2.5 million displaced within Iraq.
76,000 AIDS cases (compared with 114 cases prior to 2003).
70% divorce rate since 2003.
40% of Iraq population below the poverty line.

'Gains'
550 political parties.[3]
126 foreign security companies.
43 locally registered militias.
220 newspapers.
45 TV stations.
67 radio stations.
4 mobile phone networks costing $12 billion, each owned by the supporters of the invasion:
Kork – Warlord Barzani
Asia – Warlord Talabani
Zain – 50% Ahmad Chalabi and 50% Kuwait
Ather – Abdul-Aziz al-Hakim (of the Badr brigades)

---

[3] This is one estimate. The fact that the invaders provided funding to political parties at such a desperate time predictably provided a strong incentive to found spurious groups with the aim of extracting financial benefit. And in so far as these groups were not spurious, this device further divided the country.

undemocratic organisation so long as the veto remains a privilege of the paramount five. My only serious regret is the devastating effect my imprisonment had on my nearest and dearest.

Do I feel bitter? No. I have learnt that bitterness destroys you. I accepted that what I had been through was all part of life's journey, and in any case I benefited greatly by moving away from engineering and oil. I owed this attitude to my practice of yoga which, as the reader will have gathered, came to play an important part in my life.

Viewed in the broader scheme of things, rather than on the basis of legal niceties, the way I was treated when I made the decision to help my compatriots contains a sombre message. But this book is not offered to the public because I want sympathy for what happened to me, for my suffering was much less than that of millions of my fellow-countrymen. Moreover, I wasn't alone in paying a high price for taking a principled position on Iraq. I have described how the humanitarian commissioners, Denis Halliday and Hans von Sponeck, head of the UN World Food Programme in Iraq, Jutta Burghardt, all resigned from highly paid and prestigious positions in the UN because they could no longer stomach the inhumanity of the sanctions regime.

All of us who were prominent in opposing Western policy suffered in one way or another. Scott Ritter appears to have been entrapped into sexual misdemeanours for which he has done time, Susan Lindauer was accused of being an Iraqi agent, also served time and was then released labelled deluded, and David Kelly ended up dead.[4] My own terror and misery are part of the story which I have told. But my primary aim has been to inform and enlighten others about the injustice and double-standards of the so-called mother of democracy. My hope is that it should lead people in Britain in particular, and in the West in general, to reflect on how matters might be improved.

---

[4] As I've said, I don't discount the possibility that David Kelly was murdered, but Carne Ross believes he committed suicide.

I have another purpose, though. In 1991 I faced the loss of my business together with all I had striven to achieve with Petcon. Financial ruin destroyed my faith in the future and brought me to the edge of a nervous breakdown. My visit to Iraq in 1991 confronted me with the amazing resilience of the people who faced much greater losses than I, and this gave me the strength to fight on their behalf. The decision to devote all my energy to this project was a crucial step on my road to recovery. I now entered the world of enlightened politics and recording this personal journey has been a way of tying up loose ends and taking stock of what I have learnt.

What Chilcot didn't say

One loose end remains. I have said that Chilcot left oil and Palestine out of the picture, but this is really only the beginning of the problem. It seems to me he that he didn't mention these vitally important factors in Western calculations, to which Blair was a party, because he and his fellow inquiry members were all deeply imbued with a Western view of the world. This in large measure derives from the age of European imperialism, now co-opted by the US and expressed in the simple phrase 'we know best.' The West knows best about democracy, about human rights, about peace-keeping, about economics, about gender roles (or lack of them), about sexual mores and diversity, about child rearing, about religion (or lack of it), about history and about punishment. I'm not saying that this overarching viewpoint is universally held in the West, but it is dominant, especially among those who make decisions affecting all of us.

From this position it makes sense for the West to try by every means possible to replace the worldviews and customs of other cultures with their own. Such a policy also makes Westerners feel more secure, for a world where there is a diversity of outlooks is unsettling. This cultural imperialism may be attempted through agencies of the United Nations, though national institutions like the British Council, through the internet and the media, through Western teachers in schools and universities, through the teaching of English, through the promotion of Western cultural events and so on. Or it may become more coercive, as in the imposition of sanctions and other forms of penalties on countries which do things differently from the West. And ultimately, it may become one of the arguments for military intervention. When challenged about his support of the US policy in my homeland, Blair often replies that he still thinks it was right to depose Saddam. Right in whose eyes? Many Iraqis might justifiably say, as indeed the Americans once did: 'Yes, he was a son of a bitch, but he was our son of a bitch.'

In a mailing on 'The Zionist connection' in June 2005 I wrote that trying to impose pro-US 'moderation' on Muslim leaders in the Arab world and beyond 'was one of the contributing factors fuelling extremism.' When such leaders colluded with the West, those who wished to preserve their way of life and protect it from what they saw as Western decadence resorted to desperate methods such as martyrdom (suicide bombing). 'It has become acceptable for most Muslims to admire those who heroically stand up to the US-imposed administration.'

How could Chilcot argue that oil and Palestine didn't fall within his remit? He described the Inquiry's task as 'considering the UK's involvement in Iraq, including the way decisions were made and actions taken, to establish, as accurately as possible, what happened and to identify the lessons which can be learned.' Is it really credible to believe that considerations about oil and Palestine did not affect 'the way decisions were made'? Of course not! But equally it was never on the cards that the report would reflect a profound Western willingness to take a long hard look at itself in the mirror. For such a willingness was, and remains, entirely absent.

The Executive Summary of the Chilcot report contains twelve pages (86 numbered paragraphs) of 'lessons' to be learnt from the Iraq fiasco.

But nowhere in it is there a recognition of the imperial nature of Western foreign policy. While the report recognises the necessity for cultural understanding of the enemy in the conduct of war and any occupation which follows it, there is little indication of a true respect for the outlook and beliefs of the people in the targeted country. I believe a much more radical approach is needed in such situations. I'm going now to attempt a list of what I think Chilcot should, though to be fair in his position and within the parameters he was set he probably couldn't, have said. I do this, however, with one reservation. The report contains 2.6 million words, and so you won't be surprised to hear that I haven't read them all. It is therefore possible that some of what I say was included, in one way or another; I feel confident, however, that much of it was not.

1. In his submission to the Iraq Inquiry, Stephen Pattison, Head of the United Nations Department at the FCO from 2000 to 2003 cited Mark Malloch Brown, then head of the United Nations Development Programme, as saying that 'the Iraqis were extremely competent in their own right,' and added that it was a generally held view (presumably in the FCO) 'that Iraq was in many ways an efficiently run state, with a functioning civil service etc.'[5] Chilcot should at least have expanded on this. Iraq under the Ba'athists was probably the most developed welfare state in the Middle East. The government funded its efficient social services, health service, and excellent educational provision with the revenue it earned from its nationalised oil industry.
2. The intellectual cleansing of Iraq, partly due to de-Ba'athification, and partly to the blind eye the occupations forces turned to the activities of Shia militias such as the Badr Brigades, needed to be highlighted. It caused a massive emigration of highly skilled and educated people from Iraq, and they have been difficult to replace.

---

[5] The Iraq Inquiry, Stephen Pattison's submission, paragraph 43.

This has had a serious effect on the country's recovery. Surely there were lessons to be learnt from that disastrous experience. A search for the word 'emigration' comes up with a zero on the Iraq Inquiry website.

3. The way in which both the American and the British governments rode roughshod over public opinion is also missing. There are four occurrences of the phrase 'public opinion' in the Executive Summary, three of which relate to its 'management.' And if you have a sceptical frame of mind, the fourth instance of this phrase has a similar meaning, for it emphasises 'the need for sustained communication of key strategic messages to inform public opinion about the objectives and progress of the military campaign ...'

4. The government shouldn't consider regime change a legitimate foreign policy objective except in cases where there is a clear risk, and not just a hypothetical one, to the UK. This risk should be directly attributable to the regime in question, and it should be properly assessed, if necessary by an independent inquiry which looks carefully at the reasons for the policy adopted by that regime, and the possibility of a negotiated settlement of the dispute between the two countries.

5. The use of Western oil companies as a front for control of oilfields in other parts of the world should be recognised as destabilising, and therefore undesirable. In reality these companies, though apparently independent, are the long arm of the states in which they are based.

6. The principle of non-intervention in the internal affairs of sovereign states should be revived, and the grading of states according to whether the West approves of them or not should be abandoned.

7. When the balance of power in a region is threatened by the manufacture or attempted manufacture of new weapons systems, the first response should be to consider whether there was already

an imbalance, to which the new development is a response. There may then be a possibility of negotiating a balanced disarmament agreement. Iraq constantly drew attention to the Zionist entity's possession of WMDs, and the need for regional disarmament.

8. Prime Ministers should consider carefully before appointing personal envoys to parts of the world about which they want to be well-informed. Is there sufficient reason for by-passing the normal diplomatic channels? If it's considered that there is sufficient reason, persons considered for this position should be chosen to ensure that the information and advice provided by them is impartial. A well-known Zionist, with close family connections to the Zionist entity should, for example, have been considered an unsuitable candidate as Personal Middle East Envoy.

9. Equally, Prime Ministers should consider whether anyone they appoint to the position of Attorney General might have a conflict of interest. For example, if the person appointed is known to have Zionist sympathies, this is a reasonable ground for treating any advice they give concerning the Middle East with scepticism. It should, at least, be counterbalanced with advice from a more neutral position.

10. In considering its foreign policy in the Middle East, the government should be constantly aware, as the people of the Middle East are, of how the Zionist entity presents its interests as identical with those of the West. Moreover, the composition of any inquiry into events in the Middle East should be such that it does not give a disproportionate voice to those known to be sympathetic to, or defensive of, the Zionist entity. Not acting with great sensitivity in this way to the fears of those living in the region is likely to result in continuing unrest with attendant risks to UK citizens.

11. The government's foreign policy should be based on enlightened self-interest, which is to say that it should consider ALL the effects

of its policies, both short and long-term. Where necessary it should distance itself from the UN's tendency over recent years to support intervention in order to impose reforms on countries which may not want them. In particular, it should consider the dangerous effect of pressurising Muslims to adopt Western liberalism. This is likely to fuel violent resistance and a retreat into fundamentalism.

12. The government should reconsider its support for the Zionist entity in terms of the UK's own interests. In order to do this effectively, it will need to brave the well-oiled Zionist propaganda machine which portrays all opposition to their plans as anti-Semitic. It may also wish to consider that the continuation of the Zionist entity, as an exclusive Jewish state, is a threat not only to the whole of the West, but also to Jews themselves.

Resolution through yoga

As I go down a road by which no one returns, I look back across the landscape I've passed and see youthful exuberance, culture shock, excitement, pleasure seeking, joy, love, ambition, regret, anger, disappointment, despair, idealism, sadness, political engagement, terror, pain and disillusion.

Women have played a significant part in my life. I love them for their beauty, just as I love and am fascinated by the beauty of nature in all its manifestations – water, air, matter and life, enormous galaxies and infinitely small sub-particles. To appreciate beauty is to appreciate life and without it there would be no meaning or reality.

We all face happy and sad times in life, but I have learnt that if we deal with the down-times by denial rather than acceptance we gain nothing. I was already approaching this saner attitude when I was introduced to yoga. In 2000 I developed arthritis in my left knee, the legacy of years of playing competitive squash combined with the inevitable effects of ageing. The consultant was not of the opinion that an early intervention was necessary, and advised physiotherapy. And so I started attending weekly sessions at the British School of Osteopathy in the Borough area of London.

After a few months I was advised to take up yoga, and though reluctant I joined a class at a new health club housed in a disused Victorian water pumping station beside the River Thames in Surbiton. Among the facilities available there were an Olympic size pool, a sauna, steam rooms, a gym and, of course, classrooms, in one of which a hatha yoga class was led by our mentor, Maia (known as Khaton), a committed and experienced teacher. She soon overcame my reservations and gradually my enthusiasm grew. The fact that I was the only male in a group which otherwise comprised beautiful women may have played its part in my conversion. But it was Maia who was the essential catalyst in carrying us through this wonderful practice of mind, body and soul. I found it of immense benefit, and it came to take priority over most other engagements in my life.

I used to carry instructions with me on my visits to Iraq, and before the 2003 invasion many of my friends there attended the informal classes I arranged. Even the Minister of Culture, Hamid Yussef Hamadi, recognised the benefit of yoga in dealing with stress and enabling well-being. For me the key to yoga is steady development, at your own pace, and not in competition with others. Your achievement at any particular time is governed by your perseverance, thought, diet, outlook and state of health. It is an on-going practice with no limits, and your physical condition is no obstacle as there are always alternatives available.

I wish I had started yoga much earlier, and I encourage my grandchildren to take it up. Yoga and the ego are incompatible which means that when you practise it you are at one with the world and living 'in the now.' Your thoughts and worries are placed outside the practice so that your mind is refreshed. Instead of fighting situations which you can't change, and thereby ruining your health, you learn to accept what life brings. When much later I mentioned to Maia that I might be sent to prison she replied: 'Try to accept it.' At the time I found this cold and uncaring, but it was acceptance without bitterness which enabled me to survive my initial twenty-four hours of incarceration. I fought outwardly as far as I could; inwardly I refused to allow bitterness to enter my soul and destroy it.

And so when visitors came to see me in Wandsworth, at least after the initial shock had worn off, they were surprised to witness my calm state of mind, which arose from the positively uplifting effect of my yoga practice. Some even thought I was enjoying my incarceration! Far from it. But adversity is a good teacher, and I capitalised on the opportunity it gave me. Karen Audin could not be with me all the time, and so I had to find a way of living in the now and enjoying the situation as it was. I am happy with the person I have become as a result.

Each morning, while waiting anxiously for the rattling of the warden's keys, I calmed myself with the following text:

> The joy I have found in my yoga practice is something more permanent, something that stays with me, deep down. Ultimately, it's the joy of finding that connection with yourself. You don't need anybody when you're in that space. You feel content with your surroundings, and with everything around you. Finally you come to a point where nothing matters. You're not striving, you're not pushing, it's just OK. Inner joy is all about letting go and being content with who you are, and with everything around you.
>
> We each have our own story, our own dreams, aspirations, flaws and failures, and we will each have our own personal experience of this quest for joy. But let's start by becoming conscious and respectful of our body as the vessel that carries us through life. […]

Let us free ourselves of any stigma concerning our social standing or what possessions we own. To have been given the gift of life alone is extraordinary enough, and we should be grateful and humble. We should not be embarrassed to give thanks, regardless of our religious beliefs. The moment you remove yourself from the centre of the Universe (and it's hard, I know!) and acknowledge with thanks that you are blessed to be alive, is the moment you free yourself.

Let us learn to love our children, friends and family unconditionally, never judging, controlling or manipulating but with fair compassion and reason. Everyone we know is a bird in flight like ourselves, sometimes lost, often in need of protection but ultimately seeking their own truth.

Let us take responsibility for the world around us. We are all in this together, and the more we give service to others the richer we will feel for it. Being environmentally conscious in even the smallest way will make a difference. Be informed, not indifferent. And let us return favours whenever we can. From the simplest offer of taking on the school run for an overworked neighbour, to organizing a charity jumble sale/sky dive or volunteering to help out at the local old people's home.

Finally, let's try to relinquish control ourselves. Let's quieten our busy minds, through meditation, mantra, or simply a country walk, finding time to reflect and bask in the beauty of nature. Let life take its course. Let the sunshine in, let the soul come alive, let go - let God! This is joy.[6]

---

[6] I was sent this text while I was in prison, but I don't know who wrote it. I've traced it on the web where it appears anonymously in two parts here:
http://aibolita.com/fitness/34974-and-a-whole-new-chapter.html and
http://aibolita.com/fitness/34817-let-life-take-its-course-let-the-sunshine-in-let-the-soul-come-alive-let-go-let-god-this-is-joy.html.

What about the time left to me? I want to continue to love and be loved and to care for those who need me. When this journey will end is not for me to say, but I want to continue to see, feel and experience and to change darkness to light. In this, the practice of yoga has been of immense benefit to me.

I would like to end with a poem by Karen Audin which gave me comfort and inspiration when I was in prison and most needed it. We weren't, alas, destined to become life-companions, but I'm eternally grateful to her for the spiritual inspiration and support she gave me.

That Special Place

They may have taken away my liberty
But there is a peaceful place
That I can see
So when at times it seems too much
I know I can just get in touch
With that stillness that resides in me
The place where I am always free.

APPENDIX ONE

TIMELINE

Some dates are approximate

1939-1941	Born in Basrah (exact date not recorded)
1956	Move to UK, to study engineering in Southend
1959	Move to Brighton to study at College of Technology
1961	Complete engineering course & graduate in Brighton; return to Southend
1962	Marry Doreen Saunders, honeymoon in Zermatt.
July 1963	Drive to Iraq with Doreen. First appointment with BPC
1966	Birth of son
	Four months' military service
1968	Ba'athists take power in Iraq
1968	Birth of daughter
1970	Move back to Britain. Work for Shell on Teesside.
1971	Move to Kuwait to take up post with Kuwait Oil Company
1972	Short contracts in Libya, then with British company, Coppas
1973	Join McDermott Engineering and Construction - work with them until 1980
1975	Divorce Doreen

1976	Establish Petcon, engineering supply, procurement and consulting company
1980	Join AREC in Abu Dhabi/UK. Petcon meanwhile run by fellow directors. Naturalised as a British citizen Marry Pauline
1984	Leave AREC and start free-range poultry farm in Hampshire
1985	Re-engage with Petcon supplying engineering equipment to Iraq via Jordan
July 1990	Last trip to Iraq before war
August 1990	Iraq invades Kuwait, UN sanctions imposed; begin political involvement
Autumn 1990	Divorce Pauline
1991	US led action to remove Iraq from Kuwait (Gulf War I)
Spring 1992	Visit Iraq to see my family
1993	Visit Iraq with Tam, George Galloway & Tim Llewellyn; establish FAF
1995	Buy farm at Shejeera on Tigris River
1996	Negotiations on behalf of Perenco & Bula with Iraqi Oil Ministry
1998	Visit Iraq with Tam Dalyell and Albert Reynolds Visit to Iraq with Canon Andrew White
Dec 1998	Operation Desert Fox: US/UK air attacks on Iraq continue up to May 1999
May 1999	Church Delegation to Baghdad

2001	9/11 attacks on the US
March 2003	US-led invasion of Iraq (Gulf War II)
April 2003	Fall of Baghdad
August 2005	Interviewed by Volcker Committee
October 2005	Volcker Report published
7th Aug. 2008	Police raid my house; detained and interrogated
12th Aug. 2009	Charged with violation of UN Sanctions
25th Feb. 2011	Convicted & sentenced to 10 months' custody; to Wandsworth prison
April 2011	Transferred to Ford open prison and shortly after released on tag
July 2011	Tag removed & wound up FAF
2012	Ordered to pay £70,000 court costs
2013	Informed by my lawyer that the Irish Garda wanted to interview me
6th July 2016	Chilcot Report published
9th March 2017	Expelled from the Labour Party
March 2018	Diagnosed with terminal prostate cancer
9th Nov 2018	Died in Hove at the age of c79

APPENDIX TWO

IN THE FOOTSTEPS OF SIR PERCY

Tim Llewellyn on some provocative re-drawing of borders in post-war Iraq

Umm Qasr, Iraq [May 1993]

TAM DALYELL, MP, descendant of Scots warriors, dark-suited under the Iraqi sun, articulate, emphatic, is the model of the upright Briton. It is a type that still, despite everything, impresses Arabs, even the hard-eyed officials in Ba'ath Party uniforms, one of whom reminds him, he says, of a Labour political agent in the Scottish border country. Mr Dalyell has the bearing, the aura, of a colonialist, born to rule, but he condemns colonialism's negative consequences at every opportunity. Thus he confesses regularly and publicly to our hosts during our voyage through Iraq that his parents worked in Mesopotamia 70 years ago on the staff of Sir Percy Cox, the British High Commissioner in Baghdad. He apologises. The Iraqis forgive him. They are like that.

Sir Percy was one of the colonial officials who, after the collapse of the Ottoman Empire, intrigued on Britain's behalf against Arab independence. He sketched defining lines in the sand between our mandated territories of Kuwait, Transjordan and Iraq, and Saudi-ruled Arabia. Mr Dalyell excuses himself for not having inherited his parents' Arabic, a failing for which he was once mildly reprimanded by President Nasser. He is forgiven again.

This indulgent attitude may soon be constrained. On this journey a cloud of anglophilia envelops us, but it is hard to understand why. It is embarrassing. The ghost of Sir Percy is present, and his spiritual descendants are at work, in Whitehall and elsewhere, at their post-Gulf war drawing-boards.

Their most recent skilled handiwork is evident at Umm Qasr, Iraq's only remaining working port, on the Khor Az Zubbayr, a deep-water inlet which is the country's one existing navigable outlet to the waters of the Gulf. Here, the seeds of a forest of future disputes and battles are being planted by the Gulf war allies, with 'Oh Simon– you and your come-to-bed eyes' Britain as prime mover and expert cartographer in the Cox tradition.

Umm Qasr was developed in the 1970s as an alternative port to Basra, about 40 miles to the north, on the Shatt al-Arab. Basra was overloaded, and the shallow waters of the Shatt aggravated the problem. Umm Qasr became even more important during the Iran-Iraq war, when Iran closed the Shatt and eventually laid long siege to Basra. Iraq built its only naval base at Umm Qasr, from which it launched sorties against the Iranians, and, later and suicidally, the allied armada.

Basra continued to diminish in importance. It had only just been rebuilt when it was clobbered comprehensively by the allies in January and February 1991. That March it was torn apart yet again from the inside by rebels, rioters, assorted Iranians and the just plain vengeful in the brief but murderous uprising that followed Saddam Hussein's defeat and short-lived loss of control.

Basra remains shut off from the Gulf by silt and sunken shipping. Umm Qasr is therefore essential to Iraq's waterborne trade — exports of fertiliser, petrochemicals and other petroleum products — or will be so, when Iraq can trade again.

During the Iran-Iraq war of the 1980s, with Kuwait's approval, the town, port and base of Umm Qasr expanded a half-mile or so south of Sir Percy's 1923 boundary (reaffirmed by Britain after a border shindig in 1961). The border, without Kuwaiti demur, shifted south, just beyond the naval base. After all, so it was said, Iraq was defending its Arab brothers, especially Kuwait, which was, we were led to believe, firmly in the Ayatollah's sights.

Now the frontier is back where it was in 1923, redrawn by a special United Nations Boundary Commission, approved by the Security Council, slap through the middle of Umm Qasr. This leaves the naval base and about a dozen civilian houses in what is now, *de jure*, Kuwait, though there is not a Kuwaiti in sight and nor has there been in any strength or settlement throughout history. The nearest properly Kuwaiti-populated area is an oilfield some 40 miles south of Umm Qasr.

Further west, six oil-wells used by Iraq until 1991 have now been handed to Kuwait, as have tracts of Iraqi farmland. Farmers have already been firing at UN and other observers. This is no Coxian line in the sand, but one through bricks, mortar and homesteads. The pre-war border disputes that partly caused the crisis in 1990 have not only not been settled even-handedly but have been compounded. If the Iraqis are angered by this piece of post-war diplomacy now, they will be barking mad when 1990 is as vague a memory to outsiders as Iraq's 1980 occupation of Khorramshar, in Iran, is now, and the caravan has moved on.

Saddam Hussein, it might well be said, invited such punitive, peremptory treatment when he invaded Kuwait and caused everyone so much trouble. But all Iraqis — Saddam supporters, neutrals, opposition and quiet critics alike, and even many far-sighted Kuwaitis — are horrified by this rubbing of Iraq's nose in the sand. 'A recipe for future disaster,' said Mr Dalyell, looking aghast at the sand-swept bollard in the middle of one of Umm Qasr's main roads, marker of the new frontier. We walked round it, without hindrance, into the new, expanded Kuwait, to talk to 'Kuwait's' new Iraqi residents. 'I'm not leaving unless I'm shoved out. I'm an Iraqi,' said Amina, a 21-year-old mother of five more Iraqis. Next door, in a stone house he owns with a large front garden, is Ahmed, an Iraqi army officer. I suppose he is the last Iraqi soldier in Kuwait. The allies should know about it. United Nations soldiers drive up and down occasionally, observing the idiocy, but do nothing to interfere with us or the 'displaced' Iraqis.

It is hard to envisage Kuwait ever pressing its claims on Umm Qasr; but come the day when Iraq needs the port and the base, and is an approved member of the international community again, there either will have to be some western diplomatic U-turn or this half-usable town will threaten anew the relationship between Iraq and the rest of the world, particularly Kuwait. The new border, and its extension seawards, also raises the possibility that Iraq's territorial waters will be changed to its disadvantage. It has little enough already.

Iraqis see all this as a western plot to keep the Gulf states at each others' throats, easily divisible, ruleable and targetable for our weapons — either to sell to them or to bombard them with, depending on the political season. It is, in fact, part of a policy of trying to squeeze the Iraqi people until Saddam Hussein's pips squeak, a futile campaign. He is firmly in control of all Iraq except Kurdistan, and cares nothing for the suffering of his people, whether induced by such indignities as the new Kuwaiti border or the disease, malnutrition, inflation and massive unemployment brought about by sanctions.

'Why are you trying to make enemies of us?' asked an Iraqi businessman, a Christian, from Zhako in the north, a graduate of Manchester University. 'I love England, I speak and read English, and I follow Manchester United. We want to do business there, have holidays there ... I want my children to go to college there. I don't want to learn French or Japanese. Nor do they. They may have to.'

He stared glumly out of the car window at the gigantic picture of Saddam in his Somerset Maugham rig — Panama hat and linen suit — beaming down on his people. Tam Dalyell had no answer for him. Perhaps Sir Percy Cox would have been able to find a few words.

Tim Llewellyn was Middle East correspondent of the BBC.[1]

---

[1] *The Spectator* Archive, 4 June 1993, Page 14. Reproduced with kind permission of the author, who also provided some corrections to the text as it appears at http://archive.spectator.co.uk/article/5th-june-1993/16/in-the-footsteps-of-sir-percy/. This piece was written shortly after our 1993 fact-finding mission to Iraq and the year after Llewellyn stood down as BBC Middle East correspondent.

APPENDIX THREE

TONY BENN'S INTERVIEW WITH SADDAM HUSSEIN
4th February 2003

Benn: I come for one reason only - to see whether in a talk we can explore, or you can help me to see, what the paths to peace may be. My only reason, I remember the war because I lost a brother. I never want to see another war.

There are millions of people all over the world who don't want a war, and by agreeing to this interview, which is very historic for all of us, I hope you will be able to help me be able to say something to the world that is significant and positive.

Saddam: Welcome to Baghdad. You are conscious of the role that Iraqis have set out for themselves, inspired by their own culture, their civilisation and their role in human history. This role requires peace in order to prosper and progress. Having said that, the Iraqis are committed to their rights as much as they are committed to the rights of others. Without peace they will be faced with many obstacles that would stop them from fulfilling their human role.

Benn: Mr President, may I ask you some questions. The first is, does Iraq have any weapons of mass destruction?

Saddam: Most Iraqi officials have been in power for over 34 years and have experience of dealing with the outside world. Every fair-minded person knows that when Iraqi officials say something, they are trustworthy. A few minutes ago when you asked me if I wanted to look at the questions beforehand I told you I didn't feel the need so that we don't waste time, and I gave you the freedom to ask me any question directly so that my reply would be direct.

This is an opportunity to reach the British people and the forces of peace in the world. There is only one truth and therefore I tell you as I have said on many occasions before that Iraq has no weapons of mass destruction whatsoever. We challenge anyone who claims that we have to bring forward any evidence and present it to public opinion.

Benn: I have another [question] which has been raised: Do you have links with al-Qaeda?

Saddam: If we had a relationship with al-Qaeda and we believed in that relationship we wouldn't be ashamed to admit it. Therefore I would like to tell you directly and also through you to anyone who is interested to know that we have no relationship with al-Qaeda.

Benn: In relation to the inspectors, there appears to be difficulties with inspectors, and I wonder whether there's anything you can tell me about these difficulties and whether you believe they will be cleared up before Mr Hans Blix and Mr ElBaradei come back to Baghdad?

Saddam: You are aware that every major event must encounter some difficulty. On the subject of the inspectors and the resolutions that deal with Iraq you must have been following it and you must have a view and a vision as to whether these resolutions have any basis in international law. Nevertheless the Security Council produced them. These resolutions - implemented or not - or the motivation behind these resolutions could lead the current situation to the path of peace or war. Therefore it's a critical situation.

Let us also remember the unjust suffering of the Iraqi people. For the last 13 years since the blockade was imposed, you must be aware of the amount of harm that it has caused the Iraqi people, particularly the children and the elderly, as a result of the shortage of food and medicine and other aspects of their life. Therefore we are facing a critical situation. On that basis, it is not surprising that there might be complaints relating to the small details of the inspection which may be essential issues as far as we are concerned and the way we see the whole thing. It is possible that those Iraqis who are involved with the inspection might complain about the conduct of the inspectors and they complain indeed.

It is also possible that some inspectors either for reasons of practical and detailed procedure, or for some other motives, may complain about the Iraqi conduct.

Every fair-minded person knows that as far as resolution 1441 is concerned, the Iraqis have been fulfilling their obligations under the resolution. When Iraq objects to the conduct of those implementing the Security Council resolutions, that doesn't mean that Iraq wishes to push things to confrontation. Iraq has no interest in war. No Iraqi official or ordinary citizen has expressed a wish to go to war.

The question should be directed at the other side. Are they looking for a pretext so they could justify war against Iraq? If the purpose was to make sure that Iraq is free of nuclear, chemical and biological weapons then they can do that. These weapons do not come in small pills that you can hide in your pocket. These are weapons of mass destruction and it is easy to work out if Iraq has them or not. We have said many times before and we say it again today that Iraq is free of such weapons.

So when Iraq objects to the conduct of the inspection teams or others, that doesn't mean that Iraq is interested in putting obstacles before them which could hinder the efforts to get to the truth. It is in our interest to facilitate their mission to find the truth. The question is does the other side want to get to the same conclusion or are they looking for a pretext for aggression? If those concerned prefer aggression then it's within their reach. The superpowers can create a pretext any day to claim that Iraq is not implementing resolution 1441.

They have claimed before that Iraq did not implement the previous resolutions. However, after many years it became clear that Iraq had complied with these resolutions. Otherwise, why are they focusing now on the latest resolution and not the previous ones?

Benn: May I broaden the question out, Mr President, to the relations between Iraq and the UN, and the prospects for peace more broadly, and I wonder whether with all its weaknesses and all the difficulties, whether you see a way in which the UN can reach that objective for the benefit of humanity?

Saddam: The point you raised can be found in the United Nations charter. As you know Iraq is one of the founders and first signatories of the charter. If we look at the representatives of two superpowers - America and Britain - and look at their conduct and their language, we would notice that they are more motivated by war than their responsibility for peace. And when they talk about peace all they do is accuse others they wish to destroy in the name of peace. They claim they are looking after the interests of their people. You know as well as I do that this is not the truth.

Yes the world would respect this principle if it was genuinely applied. It's not about power but it is about right and wrong, about when we base our human relations on good, and respect this principle. So it becomes simple to adhere to this principle because anyone who violates it will be exposed to public opinion.

Benn: There are people who believe this present conflict is about oil, and I wonder if you would say something about how you see the enormous oil reserves of Iraq being developed, first for the benefit of the people of Iraq and secondly for the needs of mankind.

Saddam: When we speak about oil in this part of the world - we are an integral part of the world - we have to deal with others in all aspects of life, economic as well as social, technical, scientific and other areas. It seems that the authorities in the US are motivated by aggression that has been evident for more than a decade against the region.

The first factor is the role of those influential people in the decision taken by the president of the US based on sympathy with the Zionist entity that was created at the expense of Palestine and its people and their humanity. These people force the hand of the American administration by claiming that the Arabs pose a danger to Israel, without remembering their obligation to God and how the Palestinian people were driven out of their homeland.

The consecutive American administrations were led down a path of hostility against the people of this region, including our own nation and we are part of it. Those people and others have been telling the various US administrations, especially the current one, that if you want to control the world you need to control the oil. Therefore the destruction of Iraq is a pre-requisite to controlling oil. That means the destruction of the Iraqi national identity, since the Iraqis are committed to their principles and rights according to international law and the UN charter.

It seems that this argument has appealed to some US administrations especially the current one that if they control the oil in the Middle East, they would be able to control the world. They could dictate to China the size of its economic growth and interfere in its education system and could do the same to Germany and France and perhaps to Russia and Japan. They might even tell the same to Britain if its oil doesn't satisfy its domestic consumption.

It seems to me that this hostility is a trademark of the current US administration and is based on its wish to control the world and spread its hegemony. People have the right to say that if this aggression by the American administration continues, it would lead to widespread enmity and resistance. We won't be able to develop the oil fields or the oil industry and therefore create worldwide co-operation as members of the human family when there is war, destruction and death.

Isn't it reasonable to question this approach and conclude that this road will not benefit anyone including America or its people? It may serve some short-term interests or the interests of some influential powers in the US but we can't claim that it serves the interest of the American people in the long run or other nations.

Benn: There are tens of millions, maybe hundreds of millions of people in Britain and America, in Europe and worldwide, who want to see a peaceful outcome to this problem, and they are the real Americans in my opinion, the real British, the real French, the real Germans, because they think of the world in terms of their children.

I have 10 grandchildren and in my family there is English, Scottish, American, French, Irish, Jewish, Indian, Muslim blood, and for me politics is about their future, their survival. And I wonder whether you could say something yourself directly through this interview to the peace movement of the world that might help to advance the cause they have in mind?

Saddam: First of all we admire the development of the peace movement around the world in the last few years. We pray to God to empower all those working against war and for the cause of peace and security based on just peace for all. And through you we say to the British people that Iraqis do not hate the British people.

Before 1991 Iraq and Britain had a normal relationship as well as normal relations with America. At that time the British governments had no reason to criticise Iraq as we hear some voices doing these days. We hope the British people would tell those who hate the Iraqis and wish them harm that there is no reason to justify this war and please tell them that I say to you because the British people are brave - tell them that the Iraqis are brave too. Tell the British people if the Iraqis are subjected to aggression or humiliation they would fight bravely. Just as the British people did in the Second World War and we will defend our country as they defended their country each in its own way.

The Iraqis don't wish war but if war is imposed upon them - if they are attacked and insulted - they will defend themselves. They will defend their country, their sovereignty and their security. We will not disappoint those who believe in the principles of justice. And we will uphold the principles of justice and right that we strongly believe in.[1]

---

[1] Reproduced with the kind permission of Channel 4 News, by whom it was broadcast to a record audience of around 1.5 million. The transcript which appears here comes from the BBC News website, and is dated 4th February 2003. It bears the title 'Full text of Benn interview with Saddam,' and can be viewed at: http://news.bbc.co.uk/1/hi/uk_politics/2726831.stm. It has been slightly edited and reformatted for easier reading.

APPENDIX FOUR

TAM DALYELL'S OBITUARY OF TARIQ AZIZ

The Independent, 6th June 2015

Deputy Prime Minister of Iraq, Born 1936
Tariq Aziz
Politician who was loyal to Saddam Hussein but was seen by many as the human face of the Iraqi regime

Tariq Aziz was the civilised face of the Iraqi regime. He was Deputy Prime Minister from 1997, having served Saddam Hussein in the same position from 1979 to 1983. In between he had been Foreign Minister. The regime could not have had a more skilful spokesman.

In 1998, with the former Irish Prime Minister Albert Reynolds, I went to Baghdad to discuss possible ways of ending sanctions. We were invited to Aziz's far from sumptuous home for supper. Our host – in appearance often compared to Groucho Marx – was charming, well-informed, with a superb command of English and a dry wit.

Whatever murky past deeds may – and almost certainly did – have taken place – I believe that he was a man of genuine beliefs. He told us, 'You may think that Saddam and I are extremists; we are as nothing to what will come if these sanctions and this bombing do not stop. I hope you realise that by your actions of sanctions and bombing you are creating a whole generation of young Arabs who will grow up hating you.'

His remarks were all the more powerful since as a Chaldean Christian he came from one of the minorities that were neither Arab or Muslim but played an important part in the diverse society which became the Iraqi state.

He knew about Sir William Willcocks, the British engineer who had dammed the Tigris and the Euphrates and to whom my father had been military secretary. He recounted stories to us of my father's friends, Gertrude Bell and Freya Stark, indomitable travellers in the Arab lands.

He was also proud of the religious tolerance he claimed existed in Iraq; he made a strong point of the existence of a small but ancient Jewish community in Baghdad. He was also vehement that he and his colleagues in the regime had no prejudices against the Kurds. The subject on which he would not be drawn, understandably so, was the position of the Tikriti clan, the Praetorian Guard of Saddam Hussein.

Tariq Aziz was born in the small village of Tell Kaif, near Mosul, in 1936; his father was a waiter. He changed his name when he was 20 from Michael Yuhanna to Tariq Aziz, which means 'Glorious Past', to tone down hostile sentiments towards his religious upbringing and his community.

After studying English at the Baghdad College of Fine Arts he became a teacher and journalist, chief editor of the monthly *[Saut] Al-Jamaheer*, published by the Iraq-backed Arab Liberation Front, and *Al-Thawra*, the Ba'ath Party's newspaper. He had joined the Ba'ath movement in 1957 while working with Saddam to overthrow the British imposed monarchy.

His background made him a target of Muslims from time to time, but he was protected by Saddam, who believed in a secular society. He was the target of a serious assassination attempt in 1980 by Iranian militants, and reminded me of this in a telephone call in 2002 when I asked about relations between Iraq and Al-Qaeda. He told me that Osama bin Laden had twice tried to have Saddam assassinated on the grounds that he was a bad Muslim.

Aziz worked for the Ba'ath press in Syria until 1966 and got into some difficulty by urging reconciliation between Saddam and his Syrian counterpart Hafez el-Assad. Stories abound of how Aziz watched colleagues, with whom he was chatting moments before, being taken to a room to be executed. It was said that he defended putting the victims of hangings on public display. This is strenuously denied.

As Foreign Minister, Aziz enlisted US support for Baghdad during the eight-year Iran-Iraq war, and also worked closely with [Yevgeni][1] Primakov, architect of Iraq's economic ties with the Soviet Union.

Extreme anger with the Kuwaitis was one of the bees in his bonnet. He thought Iraq had been their protective shield against Ayatollah Khomeini, but when Iraq had asked Kuwait for financial help in 1990, the Kuwaitis increased oil production to dampen oil prices on a world scale, to the detriment of the Iraqi economy, and also refused Iraq a loan.

It was Aziz who negotiated on the eve of the outbreak of hostilities in 1991 with the US Secretary of State, James Baker, in a last-ditch attempt to stop the conflict. Aziz told me of the letter passed across the table written by President Bush for delivery to Saddam. He told me how he had taken the letter, opened it and then, slowly reading it, underlined passages. Some of the other diplomats were bewildered. After 25 minutes he looked up, pushed the letter back and said he could not deliver the letter to Saddam as President Bush's language was inappropriate for addressing a head of state.

The point of telling me and Reynolds this story was clearly to give the message that, if Prime Minister Tony Blair or William Hague, the Opposition leader, wanted to address the Iraqi government, that they should do so with politeness and dignity. My parliamentary colleagues thought I was naïve but I really do believe, as I told him on my return from Iraq, that if Blair had been willing to so approach the Iraqi government he might have elicited a more co-operative and helpful response.

In the light of the revelations from the 1981 National Archive at Kew about Margaret Thatcher's directives that the British defence industry should sell arms to Iraq, little wonder that Aziz expressed such

---

[1] Tam gave Primakov's first name as Yuri.

astonishment to me that the British military reaction at the time of the Gulf War should have been so hostile from friends and military suppliers.

The interesting question is the relationship between Aziz and Saddam. I suspect there was more than an element of sycophancy. But in one respect Aziz was safer than many of the Sunni group because he was a Christian and would never have a power base to rival Saddam's. As editor-in-chief of the party paper he had been useful to Saddam in his rise to power. He was also useful in that Saddam, apart from an enforced sojourn in Egyptian prisons, had little international experience.

Aziz had another advantage. Unlike many Iraqis he was not educated at a British university. Huge numbers of those of an ability to cope internationally had been educated either in Britain or the US and were therefore suspect.

As Minister of Information he was again useful to Saddam, able to tell the Russian government that there was no need for a Communist Party in Iraq – making the comment which I believe to be true rather than apocryphal: 'If the Communists want to become martyrs then we shall oblige them.' Even James Baker was able to say of Aziz: 'He was a very professional negotiator and did a very good job with an extraordinary bad brief.'

It is far from clear exactly what happened to Aziz after the coalition forces rode into Baghdad in 2003 and he was taken into captivity. His French lawyers, the human rights experts Mathieu Faupin and Emile Ludot, were denied direct contact with their client, but told me that through Iraqi sources they had learnt that Aziz was held in sheer squalor without proper medical attention. Some of us in Parliament before the last election made efforts to get him a trial. It was up to the US, we were told, and we got nowhere. Aziz deserved a fair trial, in front of an international court. My instinct is that at the bar of history his reputation will be partially restored.

In 2009 he was given a 15-year jail sentence for his alleged role in the killing of dozens of merchants in 1992, and another seven years for his part in the forced displacement of Kurds. He suffered a severe stroke the following year. The Iraqi authorities denied access to his lawyer, who was prevented from attending the court proceedings which took place the same week. These actions, and the loss of speech he had suffered, severely diminished Aziz's ability to defend himself. Many significant Iraqis think these actions were a violation of Aziz's human and civil rights granted to him by international and Iraqi law.

He was sentenced to death on 26 October 2010 for the persecution of members of rival Shi'ite parties. The truth is that even many of those who disliked Aziz because of his association with Saddam were offended that a man who had many qualities, who had worked hard for Iraq, should be treated in such a disgraceful way. In my opinion, Aziz, who died in prison, will join in history a long list of Iraqi martyrs.

Michael Yuhanna (Tariq Aziz), journalist and politician: born Tell Kaif, Iraq 28 April 1936; Deputy Prime Minister of Iraq 1979-83, 1997-2003; Minister of Foreign Affairs 1983-97; married (two sons, two daughters); died 5 June 2015. [2]

---

[2] Dalyell, T., 'Politician who was loyal to Saddam Hussein but was seen by many as the human face of the Iraqi regime,' The Independent, 6th June 2015, p 42. This obituary is reproduced in its entirety with the kind permission *The Independent* newspaper.

ENDPIECE

John Pilger's prescient essay on the root causes of terrorism and what we can do about it

From Pol Pot to ISIS: The blood never dried (16 November 2015)

In transmitting President Richard Nixon's orders for a 'massive' bombing of Cambodia in 1969, Henry Kissinger said, 'Anything that flies on everything that moves'. As Barack Obama wages his seventh war against the Muslim world since he was awarded the Nobel Peace Prize, and François Hollande promises a 'merciless' attack on the rubble of Syria, the orchestrated hysteria and lies make one almost nostalgic for Kissinger's murderous honesty.

As a witness to the human consequences of aerial savagery - including the beheading of victims, their parts festooning trees and fields - I am not surprised by the disregard of memory and history, yet again. A telling example is the rise to power of Pol Pot and his Khmer Rouge, who had much in common with today's Islamic State in Iraq and Syria (ISIS). They, too, were ruthless medievalists who began as a small sect. They, too, were the product of an American-made apocalypse, this time in Asia.

According to Pol Pot, his movement had consisted of 'fewer than 5,000 poorly armed guerrillas uncertain about their strategy, tactics, loyalty and leaders'. Once Nixon's and Kissinger's B-52 bombers had gone to work as part of 'Operation Menu', the west's ultimate demon could not believe his luck. The Americans dropped the equivalent of five Hiroshimas on rural Cambodia during 1969-73. They leveled village after village, returning to bomb the rubble and corpses. The craters left giant necklaces of carnage, still visible from the air. The terror was unimaginable. A former Khmer Rouge official described how the survivors 'froze up and they would wander around mute for three or four days. Terrified and half-crazy, the people were ready to believe what they were told... That was what made it so easy for the Khmer Rouge to win the people over.' A Finnish Government Commission of Inquiry estimated that 600,000 Cambodians died in the ensuing civil war and described the bombing as the 'first stage in a decade of genocide'. What Nixon and Kissinger began, Pol Pot, their beneficiary, completed. Under their bombs, the Khmer Rouge grew to a formidable army of 200,000.

ISIS has a similar past and present. By most scholarly measure, Bush and Blair's invasion of Iraq in 2003 led to the deaths of at least 700,000 people - in a country that had no history of jihadism. The Kurds had done territorial and political deals; Sunni and Shia had class and sectarian differences, but they were at peace; intermarriage was common. Three years before the invasion, I drove the length of Iraq without fear. On the way I met people proud, above all, to be Iraqis, the heirs of a civilization that seemed, for them, a presence.

Bush and Blair blew all this to bits. Iraq is now a nest of jihadism. Al-Qaeda - like Pol Pot's 'jihadists' - seized the opportunity provided by the onslaught of 'Shock and Awe' and the civil war that followed. 'Rebel' Syria offered even greater rewards, with CIA and Gulf state ratlines of weapons, logistics and money running through Turkey. The arrival of foreign recruits was inevitable. A former British ambassador, Oliver Miles, wrote, 'The [Cameron] government seems to be following the example of Tony Blair, who ignored consistent advice from the Foreign Office, MI5 and MI6 that our Middle East policy - and in particular our Middle East wars - had been a principal driver in the recruitment of Muslims in Britain for terrorism here.'

ISIS is the progeny of those in Washington, London and Paris who, in conspiring to destroy Iraq, Syria and Libya, committed an epic crime against humanity. Like Pol Pot and the Khmer Rouge, ISIS are the mutations of a western state terror dispensed by a venal imperial elite undeterred by the consequences of actions taken at great remove in distance and culture. Their culpability is unmentionable in 'our' societies, making accomplices of those who suppress this critical truth.

It is 23 years since a holocaust enveloped Iraq, immediately after the first Gulf War, when the US and Britain hijacked the United Nations Security Council and imposed punitive 'sanctions' on the Iraqi population - ironically, reinforcing the domestic authority of Saddam Hussein. It was like a medieval siege. Almost everything that sustained a modern state was, in the jargon, 'blocked' - from chlorine for making the water supply safe to school pencils, parts for X-ray machines, common painkillers and drugs to combat previously unknown cancers carried in the dust from the southern battlefields contaminated with Depleted Uranium. Just before Christmas 1999, the Department of Trade and Industry in London restricted the export of vaccines meant to protect Iraqi children against diphtheria and yellow fever. Kim Howells, parliamentary Under-Secretary of State in the Blair government, explained why. 'The children's vaccines', he said, 'were capable of being used in weapons of mass destruction'. The British Government could get away with such an outrage because media reporting of Iraq - much of it manipulated by the Foreign Office - blamed Saddam Hussein for everything.

Under a bogus 'humanitarian' Oil for Food Programme, $100 was allotted for each Iraqi to live on for a year. This figure had to pay for the entire society's infrastructure and essential services, such as power and water. 'Imagine,' the UN Assistant Secretary General, Hans Von Sponeck, told me, 'setting that pittance against the lack of clean water, and the fact that the majority of sick people cannot afford treatment, and the sheer trauma of getting from day to day, and you have a glimpse of the nightmare. And make no mistake, this is deliberate. I have not in the past wanted to use the word genocide, but now it is unavoidable.'

Disgusted, Von Sponeck resigned as UN Humanitarian Co-ordinator in Iraq. His predecessor, Denis Halliday, an equally distinguished senior UN official, had also resigned. 'I was instructed,' Halliday said, 'to implement a policy that satisfies the definition of genocide: a deliberate policy that has effectively killed well over a million individuals, children and adults.'

A study by the United Nations Children's Fund, UNICEF, found that between 1991 and 1998, at the height of the blockade, there were 500,000 'excess' deaths of Iraqi infants under the age of five. An American TV reporter put this to Madeleine Albright, US Ambassador to the United Nations, asking her, 'Is the price worth it?' Albright replied, 'We think the price is worth it.'

In 2007, the senior British official responsible for the sanctions, Carne Ross, known as 'Mr. Iraq', told a parliamentary selection committee, '[The US and UK governments] effectively denied the entire population a means to live.' When I interviewed Carne Ross three years later, he was consumed by regret and contrition. 'I feel ashamed,' he said. He is today a rare truth-teller of how governments deceive and how a compliant media plays a critical role in disseminating and maintaining the deception. 'We would feed [journalists] factoids of sanitised intelligence,' he said, 'or we'd freeze them out.' Last year, a not untypical headline in the Guardian read: 'Faced with the horror of Isis we must act.' The 'we must act' is a ghost risen, a warning of the suppression of informed memory, facts, lessons learned and regrets or shame. The author of the article was Peter Hain, the former Foreign Office minister responsible for Iraq under Blair. In 1998, when Denis Halliday revealed the extent of the suffering in Iraq for which the Blair Government shared primary responsibility, Hain abused him on the BBC's Newsnight as an 'apologist for Saddam'. In 2003, Hain backed Blair's invasion of stricken Iraq on the basis of transparent lies. At a subsequent Labour Party conference, he dismissed the invasion as a 'fringe issue'.

Here was Hain demanding 'air strikes, drones, military equipment and other support' for those 'facing genocide' in Iraq and Syria. This will further 'the imperative of a political solution'. The day Hain's article appeared, Denis Halliday and Hans Von Sponeck happened to be in London and came to visit me. They were not shocked by the lethal hypocrisy of a politician, but lamented the enduring, almost inexplicable absence of intelligent diplomacy in negotiating a semblance of truce. Across the world, from Northern Ireland to Nepal, those regarding each other as terrorists and heretics have faced each other across a table. Why not now in Iraq and Syria? Instead, there is a vapid, almost sociopathic verboseness from Cameron, Hollande, Obama and their 'coalition of the willing' as they prescribe more violence delivered from 30,000 feet on places where the blood of previous adventures never dried. They seem to relish their own violence and stupidity so much they want it to overthrow their one potentially valuable ally, the government in Syria.

This is nothing new, as the following leaked UK-US intelligence file illustrates:

> In order to facilitate the action of liberative [sic] forces... a special effort should be made to eliminate certain key individuals [and] to proceed with internal disturbances in Syria. CIA is prepared, and SIS (MI6) will attempt to mount minor sabotage and *coup de main* incidents within Syria, working through contacts with individuals... a necessary degree of fear... frontier and [staged] border clashes [will] provide a pretext for intervention... the CIA and SIS should use... capabilities in both psychological and action fields to augment tension.

That was written in 1957, although it could have been written yesterday. In the imperial world, nothing essentially changes. In 2013, the former French Foreign Minister Roland Dumas revealed that 'two years before the Arab spring', he was told in London that a war on Syria was planned. 'I am going to tell you something,' he said in an interview with the French TV channel LPC, 'I was in England two years before the violence in Syria on other business. I met top British officials, who confessed to me that they were preparing something in Syria... Britain was organising an invasion of rebels into Syria. They even asked me, although I was no longer Minister for Foreign Affairs, if I would like to participate... This operation goes way back. It was prepared, preconceived and planned.'

The only effective opponents of ISIS are accredited demons of the west - Syria, Iran, Hezbollah and now Russia. The obstacle is Turkey, an 'ally' and a member of Nato, which has conspired with the CIA, MI6 and the Gulf medievalists to channel support to the Syrian 'rebels', including those now calling themselves ISIS. Supporting Turkey in its long-held ambition for regional dominance by overthrowing the Assad government beckons a major conventional war and the horrific dismemberment of the most ethnically diverse state in the Middle East.

A truce - however difficult to negotiate and achieve - is the only way out of this maze; otherwise, the atrocities in Paris and Beirut will be repeated. Together with a truce, the leading perpetrators and overseers of violence in the Middle East - the Americans and Europeans - must themselves 'de-radicalise' and demonstrate a good faith to alienated Muslim communities everywhere, including those at home. There should be an immediate cessation of all shipments of war materials to Israel and recognition of the State of Palestine. The issue of Palestine is the region's most festering open wound, and the oft-stated justification for the rise of Islamic extremism. Osama bin Laden made that clear. Palestine also offers hope. Give justice to the Palestinians and you begin to change the world around them.

More than 40 years ago, the Nixon-Kissinger bombing of Cambodia unleashed a torrent of suffering from which that country has never recovered. The same is true of the Blair-Bush crime in Iraq, and the Nato and 'coalition' crimes in Libya and Syria. With impeccable timing, Henry Kissinger's latest self-serving tome has been released with its satirical title, 'World Order'. In one fawning review, Kissinger is described as a 'key shaper of a world order that remained stable for a quarter of a century'. Tell that to the people of Cambodia, Vietnam, Laos, Chile, East Timor and all the other victims of his 'statecraft'. Only when 'we' recognise the war criminals in our midst and stop denying ourselves the truth will the blood begin to dry.[1]

---

[1] Reproduced with kind permission of the author. It appears on his website at
http://johnpilger.com/articles/from-pol-pot-to-isis-the-blood-never-dried.

ANNOTATED INDEX

Some explanations by the editor

This index, which was completed several months after the rest of the book, has a dual function. Firstly it indicates, in the usual way, the pages where the bold printed entries can be found. But secondly it provides selected supplementary information about many of the people, places, organisations, events and concepts mentioned in the book; that is to say, information which will generally not be found by searching the pages indicated.

The decision about what to include in these notes and how to present them has been entirely mine. I had always in mind one of Riad's aims in writing his book, which was to leave a permanent record of his life for his family. I reflected that with the passage of time much that is now common knowledge would not remain so. While editing this book I was surprised to discover how much I myself had forgotten.

But there is a further point. I guess many of us, if my own experience is anything to go by, have a hazier idea of the world around us than we'd like to think. For example, when did this, that or the other thing happen and what was the sequence, how does the United Nations function, and what is the background to so-called Islamic extremism? These notes can't do more than fill in a few gaps, but I felt this was better than nothing for a text which is, at times, quite dense.

Riad generally avoided the words and expressions 'Israel' and 'Israeli,' 'Middle East' and 'Middle Eastern.' This policy, which he shares with many, arises from the well-founded belief that language shapes our perception of the world, and that these particular words and expressions tend to lock their users into a Western-centric view which he rejects. The problem is that most people are unaware of this issue, and since I wanted my notes to be easily understood by the general reader, I decided to revert to common usage. This is a compromise, but in my view a reasonable one.

Abbreviations have been used to keep the detail compact, but only where I thought the risk of misunderstanding was low. In case of difficulty please refer to the list on pages xii to xiv and to a supplementary list at the end of this index. Ministerial positions, such as PM (prime minister), refer to the British or Iraqi governments, unless otherwise stated. Where there is no indication to the contrary, these were the positions occupied at the relevant time in the narrative.

For the purposes of this index 'war' means the 2003 Gulf War unless otherwise indicated. Distances are all given in kilometres, the unit of distance measurement used in Iraq. To convert to miles multiply by 0.62, or roughly estimate the figure by taking 2/3 of the number in kilometres. Where an index entry is a state I have felt free in some cases to include references to the associated nationality. So 'Turkey,' includes 'Turk' and 'Turkish,' 'Pakistan' includes 'Pakistani' and so on.

Arabic names are entered in the order they are used, unlike the practice of indexing Western and other names where the surname comes first. This is to avoid the problem that there is no consistent system of family names in Arabic, and also because Arabs are often referred to by their first name even by those to whom they are not known. In cases where the last name is commonly used internationally, as with Nasser and Gaddafi, or where the first name is Christian, there are double entries.

Another problem with Arab names, including those of places, is that there is no agreed standard system of transliterating Arabic into Roman script. This partly relates to the language of the person doing the transliteration. For example, where we would write 'Shalabi,' the French write 'Chalabi,' for them a reasonable, but for English speakers a misleading, transliteration of the Arabic letter 'shin.' A further complication arises in non-Arabic speaking Muslim countries, where Arab names are often used in modified form. So, for example, Riad's Albanian cell-mate was called Ahmet, the Turkish form of Ahmed, and Mohammed Ali, the Khedive of Egypt in the first half of the nineteenth century, was Mehmet Ali in his native Macedonia.

There are three basic vowel sounds in Arabic, equivalent to 'a', as in 'bat', 'i' as in 'bit' and 'u' as in 'boot,' but where these are short, they are generally not indicated in Arabic script. Moreover, across dialects there is much variation, especially with unstressed vowels. This leads to inconsistent spelling of names like 'Ahmad' which is more commonly written, and pronounced, 'Ahmed,' or 'Muhammad,' which appears more commonly as 'Mohammed.' Long vowels are sometimes indicated in transliteration, sometimes not; for example 'Rashid' is the same name as 'Rasheed,' the latter indicating more accurately the correct pronunciation, while 'Mahmoud' may be written 'Mahmood' or, less helpfully, 'Mahmud.' The very common ending of words, 'ah,' can be written with these two letters, as in 'Basrah,' but 'Basra' (pronounced, incidentally, 'Bassra,' not 'Bazra') is also widely found, and the second spelling appears in some quoted text in this book..

Arab family names are often preceded by the word 'al' or 'el' meaning either 'family/tribe' or 'the'. For example, 'al-Harbi,' a common name in the Arabian peninsular, means 'tribe of warrior(s)', but in the names 'al-Muhandis' and 'al-Masri' the meaning is 'the engineer' and 'the Egyptian.' Sometimes the 'al' is not added, as with 'Saddam Hussein', which is more correctly 'Saddam al-Hussein', that is 'Saddam of the Husseini clan'. Except where the 'al' appears at the beginning, I've generally written such names with a lower-case 'al' and a hyphen between it and the following name, but other practices are common, that is capitalisation of the 'al,' no hyphen, no space and combinations of these. Where I've known the preference of the person concerned in writing their own name, I've not imposed mine.

There is, furthermore, no consistency about how and when to transliterate the shadda or strengthening of a consonant. 'Mohammed' (meaning 'commendable') is correctly written with a double 'm', but 'Mohamed' or 'Muhamed' are often found. Where the doubled Arabic letter is represented by a digraph such as 'kh,' 'dh,' 'sh' or 'th', however, doubling is, for obvious reasons, impractical.

There is a consonant in Arabic which is like a 'k' but is produced by a constriction of the larynx. This is often written with a 'q' giving, for example, the spelling 'Al-Qahira,' for Cairo, and 'Iraq'. However, this letter may also be transliterated as 'k', as in 'Irak.' There is a letter indicating a glottal stop which is often indicated in transliteration with an apostrophe, as in 'Qur'an,' but the holy book is more often simply written 'Quran' or 'Koran'. An apostrophe is also sometimes used to indicate the Arabic consonant ayn, which to us sounds more like a vowel and is also produced by a constriction of the larynx. So, for example, the Baath (resurrection, renaissance) party is more helpfully written Ba'ath, a convention I decided to adopt in this book.

In Muslim tradition there are ninety-nine names of God, each of which has a derivative personal name formed by prefixing the word (really two words) 'Abdul' (slave or servant of), such as 'Abdul-Wahid' (servant of The One), 'Abdul-Aziz' (servant of The Mighty), 'Abdul-Rahman' (servant of The Most Compassionate), 'Abdul-Salam' (servant of The Bestower of Peace). These are often written without a hyphen, and in the last two examples the 'l' of Abdul is often (and more correctly) replaced by a doubling of the following letter, giving 'Abdurrahman' or 'Abdur-Rahman' and 'Abdussalam' or 'Abdus-Salam. Suffice it to say here that this eliding of the 'l' only occurs before certain following letters.

All this, and there are many more complications, is to indicate the need for some lateral thinking in searching for Arabic personal, as well as place, names.

Lastly, I have a couple of acknowledgements. For the detail on how MPs voted in the leadup to the 2003 war and on the question of an investigation after it. I am indebted to the compilers of 'TheyWorkForYou.com.' Where such information is not given this is either because it wasn't available or there wasn't a clear pattern. I repeat my thanks, expressed in my foreword, to the organisers of, and contributors to, Wikipedia for the excellent resource they've provided.

I'm also very grateful to Caroline O'Reilly for her additional painstaking help in completing the final revision of the text or this book, and in particular in compiling this index And thanks to Paul Cheston, for twenty-three years courts correspondent of the London Evening Standard, for clarifying at the last minute some of my remaining confusion about how the legal system works. He wrote the case commentaries included in Desmond de Silva's memoir, *Madam, Where Are Your Mangoes*, and lent me his copy of the book. Paul, whom I know through another connection, lives just round the corner in Brighton. Should I say it's a small world? Perhaps it's bigger than we think.

60 Minutes: *148 303+fn*: US tv programme.
9/11: *145 148 161-62 164 215*: i.e. 11th Sept 2001; date on which civilian aircraft were crashed into the N & S towers of the World Trade Centre in NY & into the Pentagon in Washington DC; one further plane crashed in a field in Pennsylvania; overall fatalities nearly 3000.
Abbasids: *116fn*: 3rd caliphate; based in Baghdad; named after Al-Abbas ibn Abd al-Muttalib.
Abbott, Diane: *xxiv, 64 104 169*: Lab MP, voted v Iraq war.
Abdessalam Jalloud: *25*: 1972-77 PM of Libya.
Abdul-Karim Qasim: *114fn 204fn*: leader of 1958 Iraq coup & PM until 1963.
Abdul-Karim Tayih: *30 57fn 210fn*: Iraqi Oil Minister; 1975 visited BP in UK.
Abdul-Karim: *after 14 image 5*: author's 2nd eldest brother, police officer; d 1999.
Abdulwaheed al-Rabbat: *243-44*: Saddam's Army Chief of Staff; Shia.
Aberdeen University: *68*.
Aboush, General: *164*: Director of Iraqi Intelligence.
Abu Dhabi National Oil Company (ADNOC): *31 33*: founded 1971.
Abu Dhabi: *31-33 35+fn 36*: capital & one of 7 constituent United Arab Emirates qv.
Abu Ghraib prison: *76*: 32 km W of Baghdad.
Abu Musab al-Zarqawi: *206+fn*: Jordanian, possibly from Zarqa qv; in 1990s formed al-Tawhid wal-Jihad (Union & Struggle); opposed US presence in Islamic world & its support of Israel; 2004 joined al-Qaeda & pledged allegiance to Osama bin Laden; 2005 following Iraqi govnt offensive v insurgents in Sunni town of Tal Afar, declared 'all-out war' on Shias in Iraq; 2006 killed when safe house bombed by US.
Abuse of process: *138fn 214 246 268 269+fn 271 273*.
Adil Abdul-Mahdi: *after 173 image 9 2003*-4 member of the provisional Iraqi Governing Council.
Adnan Pachachi: *after 173 image 9*: 2003-4 member of the provisional Iraqi Governing Council.
Afghanistan: *145 164 196 236*: landlocked state E of Iran, N of Pakistan; pop 35 m; languages Dari (Farsi/Persian) & Pashto (also spoken in W & NW Pakistan); 1839–1842, 1878–1880 & 1919 3 Anglo-Afghan wars aimed with varied success at British control & denial of Russian penetration; 1978 coup d'état by socialist regime with modernising agenda; supported by Soviets; resisted by Mujahideen (meaning performers of Jihad qv), supported by Pakistan & US; 1979-89 Soviet protectorate; reinforced resistance & US involvement; 1989 Soviets, on point of collapse back home, withdraw; 1996 fundamentalist Taliban declared Islamic emirate; 2001 following 9/11 for which Taliban held responsible, US invasion; interim admin under Hamid Karzai; 2002 UN estab International Security

Assistance Force (ISAF); UK incl; 2014 war declared over but Taliban not defeated.
Aflaq, Michel. See Michel Aflaq.
Aftab Hasan. See Hasan, Aftab.
Ahmad: *after 14 image 5*: author's nephew.
Ahmad Chalabi: *61 80 106 119 146 148 151-52; after 173 image 9; 178fn 181+fn 183-84 193 200 201+fn 204 209fn 300 314*: Shia, with Iranian & Israeli connections; 1992 set up INC; aim regime change; campaigned for US 1998 Iraq Liberation Act; seen by some as replacement for Saddam; played only minor role after 2003; d Baghdad 2015. See Iraqi National Congress.
Ahmad Hassan al-Bakr: *18*: 1968-79 1st Ba'athist President of Iraq.
Ahmadi: *24*: Kuwait, expatriate settlement & HQ of KOC; 37 km S. of Kuwait City.
Ahmed Ben Bella: *217*: 1963-65 Algerian President.
Ahmet: *279-81 285*: author's Albanian cell-mate.
AIDS: *314*.
Air-conditioning: *115*.
Al-Awja: *219*: Saddam's birthplace nr Tikrit, where he was also buried.
Al-Fadilah (Virtue) party: *265*: Shia.
Al-Hakim, Ayatollah Abdul-Aziz. See Ayatollah Abdul-Aziz al-Hakim.
Al-Hakim, Ayatollah Mohammad Sa'id Al-Hakim. See Ayatollah Mohammed Sai'd Al-Hakim.
Al-Khobar: *26*: Saudi coastal town; Persian Gulf; 425 km ENE of Riyadh & 60 km W of Bahrain via causeway.
Al-Qaeda/Al-Qa'eda: *145-46 335 342 347*: 'the foundation'; network of Muslim fundamentalist jihadists; 1988 founded by Osama bin Laden, Abdullah Azzam et al as resistance v Soviet invasion of Afghanistan.
Al-Rasheed Hotel: *40 41 67 90 194*: Baghdad; 1982 constructed to host Non-Aligned Movement conf, but after kamikaze Iranian attack this relocated to New Delhi; now named Royal Tulip Al Rasheed Hotel.
Al-Sabah: *23 51 101*: ruling dynasty in Kuwait qv; Emir nominated by family council.
Al-Sistani, Ayatollah Ali. See Ayatollah Ali Al-Sistani.
Al-Thawra **(The Revolution)**: *342*: Ba'ath Party's newspaper; ceased publication 2003; Chief Editor Tariq Aziz; 2003 replaced by *Iraqi Solidarity News* (*Al-Thawra*), online magazine of Iraq Solidarity Campaign.
Al-Watan al-Arabi, The Arab Nation: *Ch 4 esp 45-56 180 199 205*: concept underlying Arab nationalism.
Al-Yamamah arms deal: *154*. See Thatcher, Margaret.
Albania: *Albanian 279*: secular Balkan state with coastline on Adriatic; 1912 independence from Ottoman Empire; WWII German protectorate; post-war communist regime; 1991 new Western-style constitution; pop c3m, majority Muslim, but substantial minorities.
Albright, Madeleine: *303 349*: 1993-97 US ambassador to UN, 1997-2001 Sec of State.
Alderman, Richard: *255 257 258+fn,275*: 2008-12 Director of SFO.
Algarve: *27*: region in S of Portugal.
Ali al-Nasiri, Dr: *229*.

Allen, Nicholas: *225*: ME & N Africa Director, ME Group at FCO.
Alps, The: *6*.
Amara: *71+fn*: 180 km N of Basrah, on Tigris nr Iran border; involved in 1991 uprising.
Amir Rasheed, Dr: *230*: Minister of Oil; arrested 2003, released 2012.
Amiriyah air-raid shelter: *68-69; after 78 image 6*: 1991 US bunker-buster bomb killed at least 408 civilians.
Amman: *57-58 66-67 76-77 81 90 132 139 162-63 165 191 207 218 264 281*: Jordanian capital; 70 km E of Jerusalem & 40 km E of R Jordan; remains of Roman temple & C8th Umayyad palace; pop 4m, many Palestinian. See also Jordan.
Anglo-Persian Oil Company: *46*: British; founded 1908; BP its successor.
Amnesty International: *219*: London-based NGO founded 1961 to fight human rights abuse.
Annan, Kofi: *86 247*: 1997-2006 UN Sec General; 2004 set up Volcker Committee; d 2018.
Anti-war protests: *161-62 165-67 169+fn 170; after 173 image 7*. See also CND.
Anwar Alani, Dr: *229*.
Appeal against sentence: *xxv 276 286-87 292*.
Arab emigration: *1 18 137 205 308 318-19*.
Arab Engineering Company (AREC): *32-36 39 55-56 295*.
Arab Fund for Social and Economic Development: *177*.
Arab Liberation Front: *342*: Palestinian political party; 1969 founded by Ahmed Hassan al-Bakr qv; previously controlled by the Iraqi Ba'ath Party; member of PLO; monthly newspaper *Sawt al-Jamaheer* qv; may have ceased publication 2003; HQ in Ramallah, W Bank.
Arab Nation, The. See Al-Watan al-Arabi.
Arab Socialist Ba'ath Party: *18fn*: founded 1947; branches in several Arab countries.
Arab Spring: *308-10 351*: 2010-12 wave of uprisings v *status quo*; continuing in Syria.
Arab/Persian Gulf: *3fn 33 330*: sea between Iran & Arabian peninsular (Jazira). See also Gulf, The.
ARAMCO (Arabian American Oil Coy): *31*: formed 1944; since 1988 Saudi Aramco.
Arbuthnot, Felicity: *111 191-92 192fn*: journalist; radical commentator on ME & beyond.
Archaeological sites: *62 114 193*.
Armitage, Richard: *155*: 2001-05 US Deputy Sec of State.
Arms sales: *54 254-56 343*.
Armstrong, Ashley: *26*. Coppas GM.
Army Reserve Officer College, Iraq: *18*.
Army service: *18*.
Arrest (and release on bail) of author 7th August 2008: *259-61 264*.
Art of War, The: *204+fn*: polemic by Nicolo Machiavelli published 1520.
Arundel: *288*: W Sussex, 36 km W of Brighton, 5 km from Ford Prison.
Ashti Abdullah, Dr: *210*.

Asia, mobile phone network post-2003: *214*.
Asim Al-Mohawdi, Dr: *229*.
AstraZenica: *249*: pharmaceutical coy named in Volcker Report.
Ather, mobile phone network post-2003: *214*.
Atlantic Summit: *158-59 202*.
Attridge and Charles: *263*: solicitors, London
Audin, Karen: *267 275 277 284 288-91 323 325*.
Australia: *128 137*.
Austria: *12*.
Author: *after 14 image 3, after 78 image 8, after 130 images 2,5&6, after 246 images 1&2, after 291 image 5.*
Avebury, Lord, Eric Lubbock: *100*: 1962-70 Lib MP Orpington; then House of Lords.
Ayad Allawi: *152 201*: Member of Iraqi Governing Council; 2004-05 PM of Iraq; 2016- present Vice President.
Ayatollah Abdul-Aziz al-Hakim: *152 314*: founding member of SCIRI; succeeded brother, Ayatollah Muhammed Sa'id al-Hakim qv, as leader after latter's assassination; negotiated with US; served on Governing Council post-2003, d 2009.
Ayatollah Ali al-Sistani: *186 200*: 1992 to present, one of four Grand Ayatollahs of Najaf.
Ayatollah Mohammed Bahr al-Ullum: *61*: 1992 appointed to presidential council in exile by INC; 1992-2003 in London; 2003 & 04 rotating President of Iraqi Governing Council; father of Ibrahim Bahr al-Ullum qv; d 2015.
Ayatollah Muhammed Sa'id al-Hakim: *61*: one of four Grand Ayatollahs of Najaf; leader of SCIRI; assassinated 2003; succeeded by brother, Ayatollah Abdul-Aziz al-Hakim qv.
Ayatollah Ruhollah Khomeini: *46 74 343*: 1979-89 First Supreme Leader of Iran, d in office.
Aziz Qurba: *32-36*: GM AREC, Algerian.
Aznar, Jose Maria: *158-59*: 1996-2004 PM of Spain.
Azores: *158*.

B-52 bomber: *346*: US Boeing long-range strategic bomber; introduced 1952.
Ba'athists: *xvii xix xxiv 18fn 31 41 59 64 71 73 75 91 101 132 147 153 161 179-82 184-86 214 216-17 228 264 300 318*: 1968 assumed power; 2003 ousted by coalition forces.
Baby incubators allegation: *47-48*: Kuwait.
Babylon: *title & back cover iii xix 88fn*: c2300 BC small Akkadian town on Euphrates 85 km S of present Baghdad; C19th BC independent city-state under 1st Babylonian dynasty; C18th BC Amorite king Hammurabi king of Babylonia (S Mesopotamia) & city becomes largest in world; 609-539 BC capital of Neo-Babylonian Empire; 588-586 BC King Nebuchadnezzar sacked Jerusalem; est 25% of Judeans (aka Jews/Hebrews) taken into slavery in Babylon; 539 BC fell to Persian king Cyrus the Great & Hebrews permitted to return to Judaea; remains of city in Hillah, Babil Governorate.
Badr Brigades: *178 200-01 205 227 309 314 318*: military wing of the Iran-based SCIRI.

BAE Systems: *252-57*: 1977 formed as state-owned British Aerospace; 1980 privatised; 1999 became BAE Systems; multinational defence, security, & aerospace coy based in London.

Baghdad: *xv xviii 2 5-6 12 13 19 41 46-47 57-58 63 67 68 70 74 76 79 81-83 88-89 90+fn 91-93 96 98 114-16 123 126 135 139 140 149 157 164: Benn's trip 167-69: 172 175 184 186 189 191 194 200 203 207 210 218 221-22 226 265 270 273 299 300 302 329 334-35 341-44*: capital of Iraq; on R Tigris; pop 9m, second largest city in Arab world.

Bahrain: *122 309*: Constitutional monarchy; islands in Persian Gulf off E coast of mainland Jazira; ruling family al-Khalifa; C19th became British protectorate; until 1930s famous for pearl fisheries; 1971 independence as emirate; 1986 25-km causeway to al-Khobar in Saudi opened; 2002 declared a kingdom; 2011 Arab Spring protests; pop 1 ¼ m, incl 2/3m non-nationals; Khalifas Sunni, majority of Muslim nationals Shia.

Baker, James: *226 343-44*: 1989-92 US Sec of State under George Bush Sr.

Baker, Norman: *156+fn*: Lib Dem MP, author of *The Strange Death of David Kelly*.

Balad: *224*: city 80 km N of Baghdad; pop 80,000, largely Shia.

BAME: *298*: UK acronym standing for Black Asian Minority Ethnic.

Barak, Ehud: *241*: 1999-2001 PM of Israel.

Barjessieha: *16 17*: British built compound outside Basrah for BPC employees; now Halliburton (qv) base camp.

Barroso, Jose Durao: *158*: 2002-04 PM of Portugal; 2004-14 President European Commission.

Barzan Ibrahim al-Tikriti: *217*: half-brother of Saddam & chief of intelligence; 2007 executed.

Basil Raziq, Dr: *229*.

Basrah/Basra: *2: youth in 3-6: 6 7 13 15 16 19 41 63 71-73 112 120 175 203 208 210 330*: largest city in S of Iraq; 530 km SE of Baghdad, 100 km from head of Persian Gulf; pop c2.5 m.

Basrah Petroleum Company (BPC): *13 16 22 30 31 131 207 210 265*.

Basrah Port Authority: *5 13*.

Basrah Power Station: *13 14*: Russian built.

Battery hens: *37 39*.

BBC (British Broadcasting Corporation): : *xv xviii 44+fn 45 61 64 66 77fn 79 156 157fn 170 182+fn 189 190fn 232 297 305 333+fn 340fn 349*: public service broadcaster.

BearingPoint: *210*: multinational management & technology consulting firm; HQ Amsterdam.

Bechtel: *35 40 50 188 210*: largest construction & civil engineering coy in US.

Bedouin: *12 13 204*: in Arabic plural of Bedu; in other languages used in singular; a nomadic Arab typically herding camels & goats in the desert.

Beheading: *346*.

Beilin, Yossi: *241*: 1999-2001 Israeli Minister of Justice under Ehud Barak.

Beirut: *146 351*: capital of Lebanon qv; pop estimated over 1m. See also Lebanon; Sabra and Shatila.

Bell, Gertrude: *46fn 65 84+fn 342*: b 1868 d 1926; English writer, traveller, political officer, administrator & archaeologist; explored, mapped & influenced

British imperial policy; travelled extensively in ME, sometimes on camel-back; with T. E. Lawrence supported Hashemite dynasties in Jordan & Iraq.
Benn, Tony: *xxiv 10 93 101 104 108-09 145 161 164: Baghdad trip 167-69: 169; after 173 image 2; 270 296-97 303 312: interview with Saddam Appendix 3*: Lab MP, left of party; 1964-79 various posts in Wilson & Callaghan govnts; 2001 voted President of Stop the War Coalition qv; leading figure in opposing Iraq war.
Bennetts, The Rt Rev Colin: *89*: 1998-2008 Bishop of Coventry; d 2013.
Bernstein, Alexander, Lord Bernstein of Craigweil: *241*: tv executive, Lab benefactor.
Betar movement: *147*.
Bevan, Aneurin (Nye): *10*: Lab MP; 1945-51 Minister of Health; 1956-59 Shadow Foreign Sec; 1959 until his death in 1960 Deputy Leader of Lab Party.
Bingham, Thomas Henry, Lord Bingham of Cornhill: *157*: Senior Lord of Appeal.
Binns, House of the: *72*: seat of Dalyell family in W Lothian, Scotland; aka The Binns.
Biological weapons: *154 156 173 336*.
Birmingham University: *68*.
Blair, Cherie, QC: *301*: lawyer; aka Cherie Booth, wife of Tony Blair qv; 2002 speaking at Medical Aid for Palestinians mtg, which Queen Rania of Jordan also attended, said: 'As long as young people feel they have got no hope but to blow themselves up you are never going to make progress.' See also Tonge, Dr Jenny.
Blair, Tony: *xxiv 50 100 105-08 121 152 154+fn 156 158-59 165 171-72; after 173 images 4&5; 174 177 187-88 190fn 195 197 213 225 231 233-34 235+fn 236 238 241-42: attempted prosecution of 243-45: 252-53 255 265 277 295-97 299-300*: 1997-2007 PM of Lab govnt; 2007-2015 Special ME Envoy for Quartet.
Blix, Dr Hans: *150-51 160 335* : 2000-03 Chair UNMOVIC qv.
Block 4: *134 207*: oil field allocation in W desert of Iraq.
Blunt, Wilfrid Scawen: *48*: lived 1840-1922; English poet & writer; opposed colonialism esp in Ireland & ME; mar granddaughter of Lord Byron; friend of W Churchill; great uncle of Anthony Blunt, art historian & Soviet spy.
BNP Paribas: *136*.
Board for Social Responsibility: *92*: part of General Synod of CofE.
BP. See British Petroleum.
Bramall, Edwin Noel Westby, Field Marshall the Lord: *104*.
Bremer, Paul: *after 173 image 9; 176 179 182 184*: May 03 – June 04 Administrator of Coalition Provisional Authority qv.
Brighton & Hove, City of: *after 14 image 6; 295*: largest city in Sussex, pop 288,000.
Brighton & Hove Labour Party: *295*: 2016 divided into three branches. See Hove Constituency Labour Party.
Brighton & Hove News: *298*: a free local newspaper.
Brighton Technical College: *10*.
Brik: *26*: Tunisian dish.
Britain. See UK.
British Council: *102-03 317*: founded 1934 to promote British culture & fight fascism worldwide.

British mandate in Iraq. See Iraq.
British mandate in Palestine. See Palestine & Zionist Entity.
British mandated territories: *329*: countries UK governed on behalf of League of Nations/UN.
British Petroleum (BP): *15 30 46 211*: formed in 1954 as successor to Anglo-Persian/Iranian Oil Coy.
British Ports Authority: *10*: nationalised authority formed 1947; privatised 1982.
British Railways: *9*: now British Rail; 1948 system nationalised; 1980s partially privatised.
British School of Osteopathy: *322*.
Brown and Root: *50fn*: US engineering & construction coy founded 1919, now KBR.
Brown, Gordon: *102-06 212-13 232 253*: 1997-2007 Chancellor of the Exchequer; 2007-10 PM; voted for Iraq war & v investigation; but set up Iraq Inquiry qv.
BRussells Tribunal, The (sic): *178fn 202*: 2004 hearings in Brussels as part of World Tribunal on Iraq with focus on intellectual cleansing; also used to refer to those who organised hearings; name derived from Russell Tribunal aka International War Crimes Tribunal, Russell-Sartre Tribunal, or Stockholm Tribunal, organised by Bertrand Russell qv & hosted by Jean-Paul Sartre.
Bryan, Jo: *26*: owner of Coppas.
Bula Resources Holdings: *81 86+fn 101 134-39 142-43 207 247 251 292-93 297*: Irish oil coy; Albert Reynolds qv became Chair in 1999.
Bulgaria: *12*.
Burghardt, Jutta: *109 302 315*.
Burleigh, Peter: *149*: 1998-99 US Ambassador to UN.
Bush, George HW: *80 151 304*: 1989-93 Rep US President; father of George W Bush qv.
Bush, George W: *54 247-48 151-52 155-56 158-59 160+fn 165 170 172; after 173 image 5; 176-77 183+fn 187 189 190fn 195 199+fn 202 205 235-36 242 265 303 312 343 347 352*: 2001-09 Rep US President; son of George HW Bush qv.
Butler Review: *232-33*: 2004; Chair Lord Butler; examined intelligence on WMDs used to justify Iraq war.
Butler, Richard: *149*: Australian public servant; 1997-99 Chair of UNSCOM; 2003-04 Governor of Tasmania.
By the Rivers of Babylon: *88+fn*: 2008 booklet by Hope Jones & Andrew White qv.

Cabinet: *UK 95 103 106 154 234-35 299; Iraq 210*: UK decision-making body comprising top ministers.
Cadzow, Brian: *65*.
California: *4fn 154*.
California State University: *154fn*: St Marcos.
Cambodia: *346-47 351-52*.
Cambridge: *68 96*: uni town 97 km N of London.
Cambridge Against Sanctions on Iraq (CASI): *96*: 1997 founded; 2003 dissolved.

Cambridge University: *68*.
Cameron, David: *347 350*: 2010-16 Con PM; in coalition with Lib Dems until 2015.
Camp Cropper: *218 224*: US detention centre nr Baghdad Airport.
Camp Justice: *218*: Iraqi-American military base, Kadhimiya, where Saddam was executed.
Campaign Against the Arms Trade: *255*: founded 1974 by coalition of peace groups.
Campbell, Sir Menzies (Ming): *xxiv 104*: Lib Dem MP; 2006-07 leader of party.
Canada: *265*.
Cancer: *xxi 11 112 225 348*.
Capitol Hill: *82 106 201*: Washington DC; quarter where US Congress & Supreme Court stand; also used to refer to US govnt.
Caplin, Ivor: *296*: 1997-2005 Lab MP for Hove; voted for Iraq war & v investigation; 2018 became Chair of the Jewish Lab Movement which was founded 1903 & known as Poale Zion until 2004.
Cash component: *138 293 275*.
CBS poll: *170*.
Central Bank of Iraq – Development Fund for Iraq (DFI): *177 179*.
Central Electricity Generating Board (CEGB): *10*: UK nationalised body; 1957 founded; 2001 wound up, following privatisation.
Channel 4: *xxiv 7 153 168 340fn*: UK public-service, commercially funded, tv broadcaster launched 1982.
Charge against author: *215-16 225 231 260 264 266*.
Charmaine: *40 62-63 259-61 264 267 291*.
Chautard, Gilles, French-speaking trader at Vitol qv.
Chaudhury, Rifat: *xxv*.
Chemical weapons: *44 71fn 84 127-28 173*.
Cheney, Dick: *152 155; after 173 image 6; 184 207*: 1989-93 US Rep Sec of Defence; 2001-09 Vice-President; neocon.
Cheysson, Claude: *97*: 1973-77 European Commissioner; 1981-84 French Foreign Minister.
Chilcot, Sir John: *xix 157 158fn 231-35 237fn 238 239+fn 240-41 244; after 246 image 6; 264; What Chilcot Didn't Say 316-21*: Chair of Iraq Inquiry qv.
Chilcot Inquiry/Report. See Iraq Inquiry.
Children: *xv 61 63+fn 68-69 94-95 98 111+fn 112 118 128; after 130 image 3; 135 188 273 297 301 303 332 336 339 348-49*. See also Children & grandchildren of author; UNICEF.
Children & grandchildren of author: *v xxv xxvi; after 14 images 4&5; 18 21 27-29 32 140 322 324*.
Chile: *352*.
China: *36 54 153 282 338*.
Cholera: *69 71fn*: intestinal infection typically causing severe diarrhoea & dehydration.
Christian, Louise: *162*.
Christians & churches: *1 74 87 88-93 191-92 204 220 242 332 341 344*: those following & representing teaching of Jesus of Nazareth; contained in Christian Bible; Christianity largest world religion, with c2bl adherents.

Church and Nation Committee of the Church of Scotland: *100.*
Church of England: *88 91-92 287 341 344*: established church; monarch is head.
Churchill, Sir Winston: *71fn 127 158 183fn 236 305*: 1940-45 & 1951-55 PM; 1919-21 responsible for Iraq policy.
CIA, Central Intelligence Agency: *80 127 149-50 151fn 155 165 172 184 347 350-51*: US; formed post WWII on model of British MI6 & Special Operations Executive.
City, The: *11*: refers to City of London; financial centre of the capital; aka The Square Mile.
Civilian casualties in Iraq: *108 186-87 314.*
Clapham, Michael: *xxiv 104*: Lab MP; opposed Iraq war.
Clark, Ramsay: *217*: 1967-69 US Attorney General; joint-chair of Emergency Cttee qv; on Saddam's defence panel.
Clarke, Kenneth: *xxiv 104*: Con MP; numerous ministerial positions; opposed Iraq war; 2017 became Father of the House.
Clash of Loyalties: *7*: film produced in 80s by Latif Jorephani qv, starring Oliver Reed qv.
Clinton, Bill: *107-08*: 1993-2001 Dem US President.
Clwyd, Ann: *100 228 242-43 305*: Lab MP, 2001-05 Vice-Chair Labour Party; 2003-2010 PM's Envoy on Human Rights; supported Iraq war & told Chilcot she would do so again.
CND, Campaign for Nuclear Disarmament: *162 169*: founded 1957; 1st President Bertrand Russell.
CNN, Cable News Network: *45*: American cable & satellite tv news channel.
Coalition: *xviii 1 59 69 143 150 176 178 186-87 190 203 205 212 221-22 312 344 350 352*: 2002 George W Bush said if Saddam didn't disarm US would lead 'coalition of the willing' against him; 2003 48 countries supported US invasion militarily or politically; only UK, Australia & Poland supplied troops.
Coalition Provisional Authority (CPA): *176-77 179-81 199 208-09 211 240*: US appointed; May 2003-June 2004 governed Iraq.
Cockney: *7-8*: London dialect.
Cohen, Harry: *xxiv 92 104 109 197 212 303 312*: Lab MP, co-patron with Tam Dalyell of FAF. See Jews for Justice for Palestinians.
College of Fine Arts, Baghdad: *342.*
Comantec: *209*: London based, metal structures manufacturer.
Command and control systems: *175.*
Communist Party of Britain: *161*: 1988 formed by disaffected Marxist-Leninist section of Communist Party of Great Britain; incl editorship of *Morning Star*; accused CPGB of abandoning 'class politics'.
Communist Party, Iraq: *5 344*: founded 1934; opposed UN sanctions & 2003 invasion.
Comprehensive tables: *251*: accompanying Volcker Report.
Conduits for intergovernmental communications: *94 141 162-63*: aka go-betweens.
Congress: *84 106 179*: Washington DC, seat of US Senate & House of Representatives.
Congressional elections, US, 2006: *202.*

Conservative Party / Conservative & Unionist Party: *77fn 96 104 238*: UK; right of centre; dates back to 1830s or before.
Consolidated Contractors Company: *21*: Palestinian; largest construction coy in ME; formed 1948.
Consolidation of hearings: *270 272+fn*: legal expression; where pending proceedings in same court share legal or factual aspects hearings may be linked & heard together; prosecution, defence & judge must all agree.
Constitution of Iraq: *177 205 211 217.*
Conway Hall: *64*: London, since 1929 home of South Place Ethical Society, changed to Conway Hall Ethical Society in 2012; originally Unitarian church in S Place, Finsbury; now humanist; popular venue for campaign groups.
Cook, Robin: *102 104 154+fn 170 171+fn 172*: Lab, 1997-2001 Foreign Sec; 2001-2003 Leader of the House; opposed Iraq war & resigned from govt in March 2003; d 2005.
Coppas: *27-27*: British engineering coy based in Mitcham qv, Surrey.
Copper: *116 122.*
Corbyn, Jeremy: *xxiv 104 161 164 169 295 298*: Lab MP; voted v Iraq war & for investigation; 2015 elected leader of party; patron of Palestine Solidarity Campaign; accused of antisemitism.
Corner House, The: *255+fn*: campaigns for environmental & social justice; founded 1997.
Cornwall: *63*: county in SW England.
Corruption: *xvii 2 5 39 46 56 61 124-25 187 194 212-3 247 255-56 306 308 312.*
Coulter, Julian: *162-63*:
Coup d'état, 1958: *15*: King Faisal II assassinated, British bases taken over by new regime.
Court hearings: *246 266-75.*
Coventry: *87 89*: cathedral city 156 km NW of London, 35 km SE of Birmingham; heavily bombed in WWII; cathedral destroyed, now replaced.
Cox, Major-General Sir Percy: *45 46fn 65 84 329-32*: 1920-1923 British High Commissioner, Iraq.
Craig, Sir James: *190*: Arabist; 1979–84 Ambassador to Saudi Arabia; signed Oliver Miles' (qv) 2004 open letter; d 2017.
Crime of aggression: *234 244-45 337-40*: not recognised in English law.
Criminal Justice Act 1987: *253*: outcome of Roskill report; estab SFO.
Crockford's Casino: *176*: Curzon Street, Mayfair, London.
Crude oil: *139*. See also oil.
Crusades: *109 146*: C11th to C13th, actions called for by Latin church v Muslim rule in Anatolia & Holy Land.
Cryer, Ann: *xxiv 104*: Lab MP; voted v Iraq war but usually v investigation as well.
Cuba: *83.*
Cultural heritage: *1 123 193 242 309 316-18 334 348.*
Curveball. See Rafid Ahmad Alwan al-Janabi.
Cyprus; *16 89 110*: divided island state in E Mediterranean; 1878-1914 leased by Ottomans to British; 1914 British annexed; 1960 independence; 1974 coup d'état by Greek military junta with aim to unite island with Greece; followed by

Turkish invasion of N of island, where majority Turkish extraction; pop of whole island 1.2m.

Da'wa Party. See Islamic Da'wa Party.
Dabrowska, Karen: *xxi xxiii 100 278*: writer on ME & Islamic affairs.
Dail: Irish parliament formed 1919 before partition in 1923. See also Ireland.
Daily Express + Sunday Express: *68*: UK, normally right-leaning middle market tabloid newspaper, founded 1900; sister *Sunday Express* launched 1918.
Daily Mail + Mail on Sunday: *xxv 77 82fn 105 299-300+fn*: UK, right-wing daily newspaper, founded 1896; sister paper *Mail on Sunday* launched 1982.
Daily Telegraph, The + Sunday Telegraph: *8 126fn 201+fn 216fn 254+fn 258fn*: Conservative newspaper founded 1855; 1961 sister *Sunday Telegraph* launched.
Dalyell, Sir Thomas (Tam): *Introduction & picture xv-xvi: xix xxi xxiii xxvi 46+fn 48 63-64+fn 65fn 66-70 71+fns 72+fn 73-78; after 78 images 7&8; 81 82+fn 83 84fn 85 95+fn 96fn 97 101-02 104-05 107 109-13 122-23 128 142 146+fn 154 161 162+fn 164 169-72 174 181 188 197 221 227 247 260-61 270 279 281 295-97 299-300 303 311-12 329 331-32: Tariq Aziz obituary Appendix 4*: Lab MP; didn't use his title; author often refers to him as Tam; 2001-09 Father of the House of Commons; Patron of FAF; v Iraq war & for investigation; d 26.1.17 aged 84.
Damage to Baghdad: *58-59 206*.
Damascus/Esh-Sham: *12 48*: capital of Syria; in SW of country; 115 km ESE of Beirut, pop 1.7m.
Darling, Sue: *166*.
Date cultivation: *after 14 image 1; 3-5 13*.
D-categorisation: *275 286-87*: UK; granted to low-risk prisoners who can be trusted in open conditions.
de Boer, Bert: *285*:
de Silva, Desmond, QC: *243fn 262-63 271 274*: Barrister; 1987 mar Princess Katarina of Yugoslavia g-g-g-gdtr of Queen Victoria; 2002 UN Chief War Crimes Prosecutor Sierra Leone; 2010 investigated Israeli military operation v 6 civilian ships of Gaza Freedom Flotilla, & esp on Mavi Marmara for UN Human Rights Council; highly critical of Israel; Oct 2011 created Privy Counsellor qv; in his 'episodic memoir,' *Madam, Where Are Your Mangoes?* refers briefly to author's case in this sentence on p.14: 'Later, among the outstanding juniors in chambers was Paul Mylvaganam, who I was to lead in numerous murder trials and a UN sanctions-busting case to do with the Iraq war.'; d 2018.
De-Ba'athification: *181+fn 182-184 188 205 227 318*: coalition policy of removing Ba'athist culture; modelled on denazification.
Defence Intelligence Staff: *156*: UK.
Defence Policy Board Advisory Committee: *183*: US.
Deir el-Zoor: *12*: city in E Syria; 450 km NE of Damascus; major destination for Armenians in 1915 deportations; pop 212,000.
Delegations to Iraq: *63-93*.
Democracy: *89 187 191 193 198 202 205 220 228 304 306-10 315-16*.
Demonstrations against war: *9-10 63 92 159 169 201*.
Department of Defence: *88 176*: US; at Pentagon qv across Potomac R from Washington DC.

Department of Justice: *255-56*: US.
Department of Trade and Industry (DTI): *131-32 136 268 272 348*: UK govnt: 1970 formed; 2007 replaced by Dept for Business, Enterprise & Regulatory Reform, & Dept for Innovation, Universities & Skills.
Desert Fox, Operation: *108 112 148 301*: 1998 continuing into 1999; US/UK bombing raids on Iraqi targets.
Desert Island Disks: *108*: BBC Radio 4 programme; participants choose music & talk about their lives & opinions.
Desert Road, Amman to Baghdad: *Chapters 5 & 6.*
Design engineering: *28 30 35*: development of fit-for-purpose conceptual & detailed designs.
Devon Petroleum: *28 30 35*: Panama-based oil trading coy.
Devon: *63*.
Dichter, Avi: *129*: 2006-09 Israeli Minister of Internal Security & former head of Shin Bet.
Digital telecommunications: *14 18 55*: microwave & telemetering.
Dinar: *41 47 72 79 137*: unit of Iraqi currency.
Diphtheria: *348*: bacterial infection causing sore throat & fever.
Diploma in Engineering: *9-10*.
Discrimination: *16 204-05*.
Displaced persons in Iraq: *45 62 314 332*.
Distinguished Strangers' Gallery: *109 174*: House of Commons.
Divide and rule: *180 203-04 308*.
Divorce: *of author – 43 326; rate in Iraq – 314.*
Doctoral studies: *10*.
Dodge, Sir Toby: *203*: British political scientist; expert on Iraq; gave evidence to Iraq Inquiry qv.
Dodgy Dossier: *153-56 168*: 2003 briefing re Iraq's supposed WMDs; used to justify 2nd Gulf War.
Doebbler, Curtis: *217*: US & international human rights lawyer; on Saddam's defence panel.
Dora Farms: *175*: on S outskirts of Baghdad.
Dorchester Hotel: *263*: Park Lane, London.
Doreen. See Saunders, Doreen.
Doulton's: *48*: US public relations firm; cooked up story of baby incubators qv.
Dresser Industries: *50fn*: Texas-based; services energy & natural resources industries.
Drone attacks: *350*.
Dublin: *101*: capital of Republic of Ireland (Eire); nr Irish Sea coast; pop ½m .
Duchess of York: *216fn*.
Duelfer Report: *172*: findings of multinational Iraq Survey Group on WMDs; post-2003 war.
Dumas, Roland: *217 351*: 1986-93 French Foreign Minister; 2013 revealed on French tv channel, LPC, Britain was planning rebel attack in Syria 2 years before uprising began in Deraa; joint-chair of Emergency Cttee qv.
Dundee University: *68*.
Dunn, Simon: *75*:
Duress: *268 274*.

Dutch senior engineers at KOC: *22-23*.
Dysentery: *69*: infection of the intestines causing diarrhoea containing blood/mucus.

Eagleburger, Lawrence: *47*: US statesman/diplomat; 1992-93 briefly Sec of State.
Ealing: *26*: borough 19 km W of central London.
East Timor: *110 352*.
ECL: *210*: exploration company.
Ecology: *xviii 73 119 121*.
Eddy: *278-80 283 285*: Nigerian cell-mate of author.
Eden, Sir Anthony: *9-10*: 1955-57 PM, now remembered chiefly for Suez policy which caused his downfall; d 1977. See Suez crisis.
Edinburgh University: *68 105*.
Education: *of author – 5-10; in Iraq – 1 16 52 55 118 123 153 193 206 307-08 310 318*.
Edward Heath: *76+fn 146fn*: 1970-74 Con PM; d 2005.
Egypt: *48-50 54 62-63 137 180 309-10*: most populous Arab state at 95m; NE corner of Africa; ancient history of Pharaonic, Ptolemaic-Hellenistic & Roman rule; C7th Arab invasion; Abbasid & Fatimid dynasties followed; c1250 Mamelukes, originally Turko-Circassian slaves (Mameluke means slave), took control; 1517–1798 Ottoman rule with Mamelukes as ruling class; 1798 Napoleon invades but occupation not sustainable; 1805-67 Ottomans resume control through Mehmet Ali Pasha (Mohammed Ali) who led Albanian detachment; declared himself Khedive; his family ruled until 1952; 1867 Ottomans recognise Egypt as autonomous vassal state; 1869 Suez Canal completed in partnership with French; 1875 Khedive Ismail, facing bankruptcy, sold his shares to British; 1882 rebellion v European control by Ahmad Urabi; suppressed by British-French bombardment of Alexandria & defeat at Tel el-Kabir; 1882-1914 British occupation with Khedive remaining nominally in power; 1914-1952 British protectorate; 1919 rebellion v British rule; 1922 British granted nominal independence; Fuad made king; 1952 revolution, Fuad's son, King Farukh, overthrown; June 1956 Gamal Abdul Nasser becomes President; Soviet support; July 1956 Suez Canal nationalised; consequent abortive occupation of Suez Canal by British & French; 1967 Israel defeats Arab coalition & occupies Egyptian-governed Gaza; 1970 Nasser dies; succeeded by Anwar el-Sadat who sought US support; 1973 Egypt attacks Israeli-occupied Sinai, but repulsed; 1979 peace treaty with Israel; 1981 Sadat assassinated as reprisal for peace treaty by members of Egyptian Islamic Jihad; fatwa approving this action issued by cleric Omar Abdel-Rahman, later convicted in US for role in 1993 World Trade Centre bombing; succeeded by Hosni Mubarak; 2005 election, Muslim Brotherhood win 88 seats; 2011 revolution & Mubarak deposed; MB's Freedom & Justice Party becomes largest in parliament; 2012 MB's Mohammed Morsi elected President; 2013 army under General Abdel Fattah el-Sisi ousted Morsi & cracked down on MB; 800 killed in MB protest camp. See also Muslim Brotherhood.
Ekeus, Rolf: *147 149*: Swedish diplomat; 1991-97 director of UNSCOM.
EKO: *9*: UK coy making radios & televisions.

Elba House: *131*: Palestinian trading coy in Amman.
Elections: *Iraq – 81 177 194 200 202 307-08; UK – 103fn 146fn 233; US – 202+fn*.
Elf-Total. See Total.
Emergency Committee for Iraq: *217*: formed 2005; aim to ensure top Ba'athists tried fairly; Chair shared by Mahathir Mohamed, Ramsay Clark, Roland Dumas & Ahmad Ben Bella – qv all.
Emigration. See Arab emigration.
Engineering manuals: *55*.
Enrica: *208*.
Epigraphic clay tablets: *221*.
Erbil: *61 205*: capital Kurdish region; 350 km N of Baghdad, pop 850,000.
Ernst and Young: *33*: international professional services firm.
Escape from Iraq in 1970: *18-19*:
Escrow account: *136 177 273*: in principle, neutrally managed a/c receiving & disbursing money on agreed terms.
Ethics: *93 117 127 135 296 306*.
Euphrates, R: *3fn 12 96 137 342*: 2800 km long; rises in E Turkey, flows through Iraq to confluence with Tigris at Qurna.
Eurofighter Typhoon combat jets: *254*.
European Union (EU): *38-39 102 110 171 199fn 242*: in 2018 27 countries.
Expatriate Iraqis in Britain: *80 121 206-07*.
Expulsion of Iraqis & Palestinians from Kuwait: *57fn*: 1991.
Extremism: *84 157 242 308 317 341 351*.
Exxon: *2 15 211*: US multinational oil & gas corp; was Standard Oil; 1999 merged with Mobil.

Fadhil: *5 10 13*: 3rd eldest brother of author.
Fadhil Ali Othan: *210*.
Fadhil Othman: *8-9*.
Fahed Abdul-Karim al-Dulaimi, Dr: *229*.
Falah al-Jibouri: *205 265*: Iraqi-American; helped US pre-Iraq war. See Falah Aljibury & Falah al-Jubbari who may be same person.
Falah Aljibury: *205fn 206*. See Falah al-Jibouri & Falah al-Jubbari who may be same person.
Falah al-Jubbari: *209*. See Falah al-Jibouri & Falah Aljibury who may be same person.
Falah Khawaja: *208*.
Falih al-Khayat: *31 74fn 131 207-08*: Deputy Minister of Oil.
Falluja: *58 185 190 202*: city 69 km W of Baghdad on the Euphrates.
Famine: *188*.
Farmer: *114-19*.
Farming: *36-39 65; after 78 image 3; 114-122; after 130 images 1-7*.
Farouk al-Kasim: *209*.
Fatchett, Derek: *102 104*: Lab MP; d 1999.
Father of author. See Hamza el-Taher.
Faupin, Mathieu: *344*: French lawyer of Tariq Aziz qv.

Faw: *3+fn*: small port on Al-Faw Peninsula nr Shatt al-Arab; 103 km SE of Basrah.
Fawzia: *5*: eldest sister of author.
Federal Reserve: *177 248*: US.
Feipco Amatco Petroleum for Oil Services: *208*.
Feith, Douglas: *147-48; after 173 image 3; 183+fn 184 237+fn*: 2001-05 US Rep Under Sec of Defence for Policy.
Fenchurch Street Station: *7*: London terminal of Tilbury & Southend lines.
Ferguson, Niall: *71fn*: historian known for challenging views on international history.
Fertiliser: *118 330*.
Fianna Fáil: *81*: centre-right liberal conservative political party in Ireland.
Filoni, Fernando: *90fn*: Apostolic Papal Nuncio to Iraq; succeeded Giuseppe Lazzarotto.
Finast: *208*.
Finnish Government Commission of Inquiry in Cambodian war: *247*.
First Gulf War: *xv xvii 40 57fn 69 71 74 112 150fn 348*: 1991; followed Iraq's 1990 invasion & annexation of Kuwait; UN coalition force retook emirate.
First World War. See WWI.
Fisk, Robert: *81 149fn*: ME correspondent; since 1989 for *The Independent*; based in Beirut qv.
Fluor: *35 209*: American-based multinational engineering & construction coy.
Flying hospital: *87 90*: proposal floated by Canon White qv.
Flynn, Paul: *xxiv 104*: Lab MP; voted v Iraq war; following Chilcot report called for prosecution of Blair; held all those who voted for Iraq war culpable.
Foot, Michael: *169*: 1980-83 Lab leader; uncle of Paul Foot, co-founder of *Private Eye* qv.
Ford, Gerald: *127*: 1974-77 Rep US President.
Ford Open Prison: *282 287-90; after 291 image 4*: category D men's prison nr Arundel; 1960 founded on old RAF station.
Foreign and Commonwealth Office (FCO): *103 111-13 136 157 189 190fn 222 225 234 235fn 318*: UK govnt.
Fouad Ajami: *148*: Lebanese American; Shia; supporter of Iraq war; Prof Stanford Uni.
Foundation for Relief & Reconciliation in the Middle East: *88*: 2005 founded by Andrew White qv.
Fox, Roland: *134*.
France: *60 93 135 170 196 217 251 338*.
Freedman, Sir Lawrence: *234 236 238*: historian, member of Independent Inquiry qv.
Friends House, Euston: *161; after 173 image 1*: where Stop the War Coalition was founded in 2001.
Friendship Across Frontiers (FAF): *chapters 7, 13 & 14 plus 78 80 92 121 139 146 147fn 162 165-66 172-73 225fn 229fn 238 248 260 264 306 311-14*: campaigning organisation of author; founded 1993, wound up 2011.
Frigg field: *30+fn*: off Norwegian coast; named after Norse goddess.
Frontline: *148*: US investigative tv programme on Public Broadcasting Service (PBS); began 1983.

Fuad al-Rikabi: *18fn*: 1951 founded Arab Socialist Ba'ath Party, Iraq Region.
Full spectrum dominance: *153 166 191*: military control over all dimensions of battlespace, incl globally.

Gaddafi, Muammar. See Muammar Gaddafi.
Galloway, George: *xv 63-68 75-76 77+fn; after 78 images 7&8; 82+fn 95 123 149+fn 161 162fn 168-69 248-49 251 271 303*: Lab & after 2005 twice Respect MP; campaigned v Iraq sanctions through Mariam Appeal; 1994 & 2002 met Saddam; 2004 backed Impeach Blair campaign; 2009-10 Viva Palestina convoys to Gaza.
Gamal Abdul Nasser: *50 329*: led 1952 overthrow of monarchy; 1956-70 President of Egypt; d in office; widely revered in ME.
Gandhi International Peace Award: *301 302+fn*.
Garda: *292-93*: police service in the Republic of Ireland.
Garden of Eden: *4*: said to have been at Qurna, 74 km NW of Basrah.
Garner, Jay: *176-77 181-82 184*.
Gavron, Robert, Lord Gavron: *241*: printing millionaire; Lab benefactor; life peer.
Gaza Strip and City: *45 89*: 6-12 km wide & 41 km long; under 1947 partitions area was larger but reduced during 1948 war; 1948-67 ruled by Egypt; 1967 to present occupied by Israel, despite 2005 disengagement which removed troops & settlements on the ground; pop of whole strip nearly 2m, half registered refugees; Gaza City (pop ½m has ancient history incl Philistine & Phoenician rule.
General Electric Company (GEC): *40*: UK, 1886-1999; not to be confused with US General Electric.
General Synod: *92*: deliberative & legislative body of CofE; founded 1970.
Geneva conventions. See Geneva.
Geneva: *6 206-08 212 219 222-23 302*: Swiss city; 1863 Red Cross founded; 1864 onwards Geneva conventions protecting non-combatants in armed conflict; 1920-46 seat of League of Nations at Palais des Nations; now occupied by UN as one of its four major office sites.
Genocide: *110 347-50*.
German, Lindsey: *161*.
Germany: *60 79 158 170 181+fn 183+fn 338*: state in N Central Europe created 1871 following Franco-Prussian war; 1903 launch of project to complete German financed Berlin-Baghdad Railway by extending Anatolian Railway to Baghdad & Persian Gulf (completed 1940); planned as alternative route via allied Ottoman empire to Germany's African & other possessions; also oil exploitation plans along route in Iraq; one of causes of tension leading to WWI; after WWI & WWII borders changed & extent reduced; post 1945 US & UK policy to reduce Germany to a pastoral society; state divided between Soviet-occupied communist E & allied-occupied W; 1945-46 Nuremberg trials of war crimes; pastoralisation & denazification policies abandoned in view of Soviet threat; 1990 unification as Soviet Union dissolves; pop 83m. See also Morgenthau Plan.
Ghada Karmi: *44*: doctor, activist & academic; b 1939 in Jerusalem; her family fled in 1948; settled in Golders Green, London.
Ghazi Haider: *208*:
Gilad Atzmon: *241*: jazz musician, activist, writer, ex-Israeli.

Gilbert, Sir Martin: *234+fn 236 238*: historian, member of Independent Inquiry qv.
Gillanders, Roddy: *255 258*: senior investigating lawyer at SFO.
Gilligan, Andrew: *156*: BBC correspondent; 2003 correctly claimed govt 'sexed up' reports on WMDs; lost his job as a result.
Glancey, Jonathan: *71fn*: PPE at Oxford; wide interests esp architecture.
Glasgow: *64 73-74 169*.
Glasgow Hillhead: *64*: 1918-97 constituency after which abolished; 1987-97 represented for Lab by George Galloway qv.
Glaspie, April: *47*: 1988-90 US Iraq Ambassador.
Glaxosmithkline: *249*: major pharmaceutical coy.
Glendevon Farm: *65*: Winchburgh, W Lothian.
Global Research: *111fn 191 192fn*: Centre for Research on Globalisation founded 2001 by Michael Chossudovsky.
Goldsmith, Peter Henry, Lord Goldsmith: *156-58 244; after 246 image 4; 252-53 254-55*: 1999 created Lab peer; 2001-07 Attorney General.
Goldstone, Richard: *248*: S African Justice, served on Independent Committee.
Governor of Baghdad. See Jasim Nesaif.
Governor of Basrah. See Latif Mahal Hamoud.
Governorate(s): *15 99 210*.
Grand Avenue, Hove: *297*.
Gray Mackenzie: *3 13*: London-based trading coy.
Great Iraqi Revolution: *71fn*: 1920; v British occupation; crushed at great human cost.
Great Manmade River Project: *49*: Libya; scheme transferring water from aquifers in S of country to N.
Greek delegation: *76-77*: 1994.
Green Zone: *2 194 213 243*: estab 2003 in Karkh district of central Baghdad; aka International Zone; deemed safe c/f Red Zone, the remainder of the city & beyond.
Green, David: *258*: 2012-present Director SFO; 2016 extended by two years.
Griffin, Bill: *81*.
Grimsley, Mr: *13*: GM at BPC; friend of Mr Walker qv.
Growth hormones: *37*.
Guardian, The: *71fn 128fn 154+fn 215 223fn 244fn 249 255fn 256+fn 302fn*: Liberal UK newspaper founded 1821 as Manchester Guardian; 1959 adopted present name in recognition of being nationally read.
Gulf, The. Refers, as noun & adjective, to all states bordering Arab/Persian Gulf; Iran, Iraq, Kuwait, Saudi Arabia, Bahrain, Qatar, UAE & Oman; 1981 these, minus Iran & Iraq, formed political & economic union called The Gulf Cooperation Council (GCC). See entries for Arab/Persian Gulf & countries mentioned (except Oman because no entry).
Gulf of Mexico: *26-27*.

Habbaniya airbase: *5 15*: in al-Anbar governorate, 89 km W of Baghdad.
Hadfield, Greg: *298*: Sec of Hove Lab Party branch; member of Momentum.
Hafez al-Assad: *342*: 1971-2000 President of Syria; succeeded by his son Bashar.

Hague conventions: *212 302*: 1899 & 1907, laws of war & definition of war crimes.
Hague, William: *343*: Con MP; 1997-2001 Leader of the Opposition; voted for Iraq war & for investigation.
Haifa: *after 14 image 5*: author's niece.
Hain, Peter: *109 111-13 349-50*: b 1950 in Nairobi to S African anti-apartheid parents; 1951 moved to S Africa; soon joined parents' campaigning; 1966 emigrated with parents to UK; 1968 joined Lib Party; 1971 elected Chair; 1975 elected President of Young Libs; 1977 joined Lab Party & founded Anti-Nazi League; 1991 elected Lab MP for Neath; 1999-2001 Foreign Sec followed by other positions in Lab govnt incl 2005-07 N Ireland Sec; 2000 set up secret war avoidance channel to Tariq Aziz qv using William Morris, Burhan Chalabi (Iraqi-born but not known relation of Ahmad) & Nasser al-Khalifa (Qatari Ambassador to UK); 2003 voted for Iraq war but later called it a 'disaster'.
Halabja: *84 113 127*: city in Kurdish part of Iraq; 240 km NE of Baghdad; 1988 death by gassing of large number of civilians during Iran–Iraq war.
Halliburton: *50+fn*: US corporation, one of the world's largest oil field service companies.
Halliday, Denis: *86 109 113 136 202 225 226fn 230 270 281 301 302+fn 315 349-50*: 1997-98 UN Humanitarian Coordinator in Iraq.
Hamas: *309*: founded 1987; offshoot of Gaza branch of Muslim Brotherhood which Israel had actively encouraged as counterweight to PLO; mixture of hard line & pragmatism.
Hamid, Lieutenant: *18*.
Hamid al-Bayati: *170*: opponent of Saddam; 2006-13 Iraqi rep at UN.
Hamid Yussef Hamadi: *120 230 322*: Minister of Culture in Ba'athist regime; 2012 released from jail & left Iraq.
Hamida Na'ana: *249-51*: Syrian journalist rewarded with oil allocations by Tariq Aziz qv.
Hammam: *116*: aka Turkish bath; similar to sauna.
Hammersmith: *35*: London borough 7 km W of centre.
Hampton Court Palace: *267*: C16th Royal residence 19 km SW of Central London on R Thames; founded by Cardinal Wolsey who gifted it to Henry VIII.
Hamza el-Taher: *3-5 11-13; after 14 image 4; 19*: father of author; d 1973.
Hamza/Hamza ibn Abdul-Muttalib: *26*: companion & uncle of the Prophet Mohammed.
Hancock, Mike: *xxiv 104*: 1984-87 SDP MP; 1997-2014 Lib Dem MP; 2014-15 Independent MP; rep Portsmouth S; voted v Iraq war & for investigation.
Handford, The Rt Rev Clive: *89*: Bishop of Cyprus & the Gulf.
Hani: *after 14 image 5*: author's nephew.
Hansard: *96fn 97+fn 100fn 111fn 112 113fn 171fn 221fn 232fn*: publication containing parliamentary debate transcripts in UK; similar publications, also called Hansard, in many Commonwealth states; named after 1st official printer to Westminster parliament.
Haram Al-Sharif (the Noble Sanctuary): *125*: E Jerusalem; incl al-Aqsa mosque; regarded by Sunni Muslims as 3rd holiest site of Islam.
Harris, Robert: *108*: journalist & author; former political editor of *The Observer*.

Harvard Medical School report: *xv 63*: 1991; on effect of sanctions on children.
Hasan, Aftab: *270 272 274*: Pakistani oil trader linked with author's case.
Hashim al-Khursan, Dr: *30 59 209-10*.
Hayes police station: *260 274*: Hayes is a suburb 21 km W of Central London.
Heathrow: *7 66 167*: largest airport in Britain; 25 km W of Central London.
Hijaz Railway: *67.*
Hezbollah (Party of God): *309 351*: Shia Islamic political & militant group, Lebanon; founded 1985.
Hijab: *60*: women's clothing usually covering head & chest worn in presence of men.
Hijaz, liberation of: *48*: 1916-17 Arab Revolt v Turkish rule declared by Hussein bin Ali, Sharif of Mecca; supported by British; Col TE Lawrence sent to assist. See Lawrence of Arabia.
Hillier, Mark: *109*: oil & gas extraction equipment specialist.
Hinchley Wood: *27; after 78 images 2; 261 267 290 292*: suburb 20 km SW of Central London.
Hiroshima: *303 346*: Japanese city; suffered first attack by atomic bomb; killed c100,000.
Hislop, Ian: *297*: journalist, satirist & since 1986 editor of *Private Eye*.
Historical narrative, control of: *xvii 193*.
Hitchens, Peter: *68*: journalist/author, Anglican, Burkean conservative-cum-social democrat.
Hitler, Adolf: *86fn 181*: founder of National Socialist Party; 1933-45 Chancellor of Germany. See WWII.
Hodge, Margaret: *258*: Lab MP, various ministerial positions; voted for Iraq war & v investigation; 2010-15 Chair Public Accounts Committee which 2013 investigated SFO.
Hogg, Douglas: *xxiv 104*: 1990-95 Con Minister of State for Foreign Affairs; 1995-97 Minister of Agriculture; 2004 backed Impeach Blair campaign.
Holborn: *262*: area of Central London.
Holiday work: *9.*
Hollande, François: *346 350*: 2012-17 French President.
Holocaust: *70 378*.
Holy See: *90fn 92*: apostolic episcopal jurisdiction of the bishop of Rome, i.e. the Pope.
Home Detention: *186-87 290-91*: referred to colloquially as tagging.
Hoon, Geoff: *109*: 1999-2005 Defence Minister.
Hosan al-Musali, Dr: *229.*
Hoshyar Zebari: *176*: Kurd; 2003-14 Iraqi Foreign Minister; UK citizen; lived Crockford's Casino.
Hoskins, Dr Eric: *69*: Canadian epidemiologist; commissioned by UNICEF qv.
Hosni Mubarak: *309*: 1981-2011 President of Egypt; 2011 stood down during Egyptian uprising; put on trial for murder of protesters; 2017 acquitted.
House of Commons: *xxiv 63-64 68 96 97+fn 110 150 154 170 174 221 233 253*: one of two Houses of Parliament; other House of Lords.
House of Lords: *135*: upper house of parliament in UK; members unelected by popular vote.

Houses of Parliament: *after 78 image 5; 96*: comprises Houses of Commons (elected) & Lord (unelected).
Hove Constituency Labour Party: *after 291 image 5; 295*.
Howell, Alan: *270*: author's accountant for over 35 years.
Howells, Kim: *348*: 2001-03 Lab Under-Sec of State; 2005-08 Foreign Sec; voted for Iraq war & v investigation.
Huda: *after 14 image 5*: author's niece.
Human Rights Watch: *219*: 1978 founded as Helsinki Watch; NY-based NGO.
Human rights: *xv xvii 44 65 152 169 180 187 196 215 217 219-20 223 238-39 296 302 312 316 344*.
Hume, Cardinal Basil: *87 299-300*: 1976-99 RC Archbishop of Westminster.
Hunter, Betty: *199*: officer of Palestine Solidarity Campaign.
Hurd, Douglas: *77 104*: 1989-95 Con Foreign Sec.
Hussan Shahristani: *170*: 2006-10; Minister of Oil.
Hussein bin Ali: *48*: Sharif/Emir of Mecca; 1916 Arab Revolt; collaborated with Col Lawrence. See Lawrence of Arabia.
Hydrocarbon law: *179 210-11*.

Ibrahim al-Jaafari: *200-01*: 2006 17 days PM of Iraq; 2014-present Foreign Minister.
Ibrahim al-Marashi: *154+fn*: US graduate student, prob Iraqi, from whom dodgy dossier text lifted.
Ibrahim Bahr al-Ullum: *265*: son of Ayatollah Mohammed Bahr al-Ullum qv; oil minister 2003-04.
Idi Amin: *25*: 1971-79 Ugandan President, groomed by West incl Israel to replace leftist Obote; 1972 expelled Ugandan Asians; switched allegiance to Gaddafi & Soviets; c1980 exile in Jeddah, Saudi Arabia, where he d 2003.
Illiteracy: *5 11 52 55 94 123 308*.
Imad Hage: *163*.
Imam Ali Mosque, Najaf: *186*.
Iman Omar Abdul-Aziz, Dr: *229*.
Imperial College, London: *72 209*.
Imperial legacy: *45-56*.
Imran Khan. See Khan, Imran
Independent Committee into the Oil-for-Food Programme (Volcker Committee & Report): *216fn 246-53 268+fn 271 275*.
Independent, The* + *The Independent on Sunday: *xxiv 76fn 85fn 222 235fn 237+fn 238fn 341 345fn*: Liberal UK newspaper founded 1986; 1990 sister *Independent on Sunday* launched; 2016 went exclusively online.
India: *22fn 71 339*: large state in S Asia, pop 1.3bl, 80% Hindu, 14% Muslim; 1858-1947 direct British rule; British occupation of Iraq managed from British India; 1947 partition from Pakistan (incl E. Bengal, now Bangladesh) & independence.
Inequality in Iraq: *79*.
Infant mortality: *137*: deaths per 1,000 live births of children under one.
Information Clearing House: *178fn*: daily news headlines digest.
Information Commissioners Office: *257fn*: public body, UK.

Ingrams, Richard: *237 238fn 241*: journalist, co-founder & 2nd editor of *Private Eye* qv.
Institute of Electrical Engineers: *10*.
Intellectual cleansing: *153 193 226-30 309 318*: process of removing intellectual potential of a country.
Intermarriage: *author's parents xx-xxi 3 5; 347*.
International Advisory and Monitoring Board (IAMB): *177 179*.
International Anti-Occupation Network, The: *202*: appears to have arisen out of paper 'US Genocide in Iraq' by Douglas, I., Abdul Ilah Albayaty & Hana Al Bayaty, 2007, possibly produced as University of Nablus study; online.
International Emergency Committee for Iraq. See Emergency Committee for Iraq.
International Federation of Human Rights: *219*: founded 1922; fed of 178 organizations.
International law: *86 157-58 166 179 212 222-23 240 302 335 338*: rules re relations between states; roots in 1648 Peace of Westphalia.
International Ministry at Coventry Cathedral: *87*: realised until 2008 through 1940 founded International Centre for Reconciliation; 1998-2004 Andrew White & 2002-04 Justin Welby co-directors; 2008 superseded by Coventry Cathedral Reconciliation Ministry.
IMF (International Monetary Fund): *177 195*: works 'to foster global monetary cooperation, secure financial stability, facilitate international trade, promote high employment and sustainable economic growth, and reduce poverty around the world'; 1944 formed at the Bretton Woods Conference; criticised for being ignorant &/or insensitive to local conditions, imposing a Western template, & making harmful demands. See World Bank.
International Zone. See Green Zone.
Interview of Saddam Hussein by Tony Benn: *xxiv 168 Appendix 3*: 2003.
Intifada, First: *51*: 1987-93 Palestinian uprising v Israeli occupation.
Intifada, Second: *125-26*: aka Al-Aqsa Intifada, 2000-05; followed Sharon's visit to Haram al-Sharif.
Invasion of Kuwait by Iraq: *23 41 43 46 131 167*: 1990.
Investigation of author: *247-52 259-61 266-74*.
Iran: *xix 31-32 36 40-41 46 49 53 54+fn 55 59 69 73 80 84 85 88 119 127-28 133 151-52 157 178 192 200-01 227 257fn 309-10 330-31 343 351*: large state E of Iraq & Persian Gulf, W of Pakistan & Afghanistan; Islamic republic (Shia); pop 80m.
Iran-Contra scandal: *53-54*.
Iran-Iraq War: *31-32 36 40-41 46 53 55 59 69 73 84-85 119 127-28 330 343*: 1980-88; prompted by Iraq fears of Iran's fundamentalist Shia regime; 1m+ killed; UN brokered ceasefire.
Iraq: *c700 hits*: state N of Saudi Arabia, E of greater Syria, W of Iran; ancient history; created following collapse of Ottoman Empire during WWI; 1917-21 British occupation; 1921-32 League of Nations endorsed British mandate; British appoint as king Faisal I (son of Hussein bin Ali, Sharif of Mecca qv, & brother of Abdullah, Emir of Transjordan 1921-46, & King of Jordan 1946 until his assassination in 1951); 1932-58 semi-independent kingdom protected by British; 1933-39 King Ghazi succeeds Faisal I; 1939-58 Faisal II; Britain retained military

bases; 1955 British sponsored Baghdad Pact consisting of Iran, Iraq, Pakistan, Turkey & UK; aim, like NATO, to contain Soviet expansion; 1958 monarchy overthrown; new govnt withdraws from Baghdad Pact; British bases taken over; Iraq's main income from oil; pop. 37m, majority Shia, minority Sunni; N of country Kurdish (largely Sunni). See also Babylon.

Iraq (United Nations Sanctions) Order, 2000: *266*: incorporated sanctions into UK law.

Iraq Inquiry: *xix 157 158fn 203fn 231-44; after 246 image 6; 264; What Chilcot didn't say 316-21*: aka Chilcot Inquiry; re UK involvement in 2nd Gulf War; estab 2009, reported 2016.

Iraq Liberation Act: *106 148*: US, 1998.

Iraq National Oil Company: *209*: founded 1966; 1987 merged with Oil Ministry; operations then split into regional companies.

Iraq Survey Group: *172*: set up after 2003 war; multinational. See Duelfer Report.

Iraqi Council of Representatives: *193*.

Iraqi Governing Council: *177 180 186*: 2003-04; provisional govnt.

Iraqi Interim Government: *177 201 217*: June 2004 – Jan 2005.

Iraqi Mission at UN: *165*.

Iraqi National Congress (INC): *106 146*: 1992 founded in Vienna by Ahmed Chalabi with CIA finance & pressure.

Iraqi Petroleum Company (IPC): *11 13 15 26 30-31 55 211 264*: 1912 Turkish Petroleum Coy set up by Deutsche Bank, Anglo Saxon Oil Coy, British owned Nat Bank of Turkey & Armenian Calouste Gulbenkian; 50% of shares British by 1914; 1920 San Remo conf transferred German share to French; 1925 1st concession with royalties to British mandated Iraq; 1928-29 US involvement agreed & renamed IPC; 1938 Mosul & Basrah subsidiaries formed; 1970s nationalisation, N & S Oil Coys replace Mosul & Basrah subsidiaries; 2003 onwards, privatisation with US dominant.

Iraqi Police Academy: *5*: still exists, unlike many other Ba'athist institutions.

Iraqi Police Force: *201*.

Iraqi Transitional Government: *177*: May 2005 - May 2006.

Iraqisation: *13 15-16 21 24 33*: Ba'athist programme to replace foreign workers with Iraqis.

Ireland: *101 135 169 181fn 253 292 313 350*: large island W of Great Britain incl in UK until 1921; then partition into Republic of Ireland (Eire aka Irish Free State) in S & W (largely RC), & N Ireland (Ulster; dwindling Protestant majority); latter continued under devolved or direct UK admin.

Irish parliament. See Dail.

Irish Radio: *45*.

Irish Times: *86fn*: founded 1859.

ISIS: *88 307 Endpece*: Islamic State of Iraq & Syria/the Levant (ISIL) aka Daesh & Islamic State; fundamentalist Sunni resistance to Western presence & influence.

Islamic State. See ISIS.

Islamic Da'wa Party: *200-01*: Islamic Call Party; Shia; founded 1957 to counter Arab nationalist secularism; backed Iranian Revolution & Khomeini during Iran-Iraq War; with Supreme Islamic Iraqi Council one of two main parties in United

Iraqi Alliance which won 2005 elections; led by Haider al-Abadi, since 2014 PM; Tehran supports financially.
Israel: *11 110 189 192 237-38 241 338 351*. See also Zionist entity & Palestine.
Israel Policy Forum: *241*: USA.
Israeli National Security Research Centre: *129*.
Issam al-Chalabi: *208*.
Istanbul: *6 9*: mainly on European side of Bosporus; pop 15m; old Ottoman capital; previously known as Constantinople.

Jaber al-Ahmad al-Jaber al-Sabah, Sheikh: *23*: Crown Prince of Kuwait till 1977; then Emir; d 2006.
Jaber Amin al-Bawi, Dr: *229*.
Jabotinsky, Zeev: *147*.
Jackson, Glenda: *xxiv 104*: Lab MP; actress; voted v Iraq war & for investigation.
Jackson, Jesse: *169*: Baptist minister; US civil rights campaigner; twice Dem presidential candidate.
Jagger, Bianca: *169*: Nicaraguan human rights advocate; ex of Mick Jagger of Rolling Stones.
Jalal Talabani: *177 192 242 314*: Kurdish warlord; 2006-14 President of Iraq.
Japan: *128 332 338*.
Jasim al-Khaldi, Dr: *229*.
Jasim Nesaif: *70*: Governor of Baghdad.
Jeish Mohammed: *185 202 205*: aka Mohammed's Army of Ansar; Sunni resistance organisation.
Jerusalem/Al-Quds: *45 62 77fn 125*: Arabic; city in centre of Palestine; holy to Christians, Jews & Muslims; 620 Muslims believe Mohammed travelled on a night journey from Jerusalem to view heaven & hell; 1948 city divided between old walled city & adjoining area called E Jerusalem – annexed by Jordan with rest of W Bank – & W Jerusalem, annexed by Israel; 1967 E Jerusalem captured by Israel & in 1980 annexed.
Jewish Community, Baghdad: *95fn 342*.
Jews: *11 51 128 197+fn 226 237fn 241 321*: a people deriving their religion/identity from the Judaeans (hence the name) of Palestine; racial element debated.
Jews for Justice for Palestinians: *197+fn*.
Jihad: *219 347*: literally striving, now generally used to mean holy war, i.e. striving v enemies of Islam.
Joffé, George: *109*: Visiting Prof, King's College London Uni; international relations.
John Paul II, Pope: *86*.
John, Sir Elton: *216fn*: UK singer, pianist & composer.
Johnstone, Brendon: *101*: Chair of the Kuwait-Ireland Trade Association.
Joint Intelligence Committee: *154 156*: UK; founded 1936; supported by Joint Intelligence Organisation under Cabinet Office.
Jones, Hope: *88+fn*. See also *By the Rivers of Babylon*.
Jordan/Hashemite Kingdom of Jordan: *62 79 82 114 131-32 140 143 180 194 270*: Apart from its port at Aqaba, landlocked country between Palestine on W,

Iraq on E & Syria to N; ancient history of habitation; 169 BC Nabateans, nomadic Arabs, estab kingdom with capital at Petra qv; Romans & Ottomans also ruled; 1921 following Arab Revolt British protectorate called Transjordan with Hashemite Emir, Abdullah I, 2nd son of Hussein bin Ali qv, Sharif of Mecca q; 1946 became independent state with Emir promoted to King; 1949 renamed Hashemite Kingdom of Jordan following annexation of W Bank incl E Jerusalem; 1951 King Abdullah assassinated by Palestinian at Al-Aqsa Mosque in Jerusalem because rumoured he planned to sign peace treaty with Israel; 1967 military pact with Egypt; Israel launches pre-emptive strike on Egypt; Arab forces defeated & Jordan lost W Bank; 1970 'Black September' attack by Jordanian army on Palestinian fedayeen; PLO forced to move to Lebanon; 1988 signed a peace treaty with Israel & renounced claim to W Bank; 1994 founding member of the Arab League & Organisation of Islamic Co-operation; pop 10m, 90% Sunni Muslims; incl est 2.1m Pals, 1.4m Syrian refugees & many Iraqi Christians refugees.
Jordanian Oil Ministry: *57*.

Kadhimiya: *70 90*: neighbourhood of N Baghdad, 5 km from centre; considered holy city by Shias.
Kamal Majid: *162fn*: founding member of Stalin Society; patron of Stop the War Coalition.
Kamil: *5; after 14 image 5*: eldest brother of author.
Karbala: *xvi 70*: also spelt Kerbala; holy Shia city; 113 km SW of Baghdad; pop 690,000.
Karkh: *194*: Central Baghdad W of Tigris, where Green Zone is situated.
Kaupthing Bank: *257fn*: Icelandic; 2008 crashed.
Kellogg Brown Root (KBR): *50fn 207*: US engineering, procurement, & construction coy.
Kelly, Dr David: *156+fn 232 315+fn*: MOD biological weapons expert.
Kennedy, Charles: *169*: 1999-2006 Leader of Lib Dems; voted v Iraq war & for investigation.
Kennedy, Helena, Baroness Kennedy of The Shaws: *103*: 1997 created Life Peer; 1998-2004 Chair, British Council; barrister, broadcaster, Lab member of HofL.
Kensington: *35 113*: district of London beyond W End; many embassies.
Kent: *296*: county in extreme SE of England closest to France.
Kerbala. See Karbala.
Khadouri, Victor & Violet: *257fn*: Iraqi-Jewish parents of Tschenguiz brothers.
Khalid al-Duwaisan: *44fn 102*: 1993-present Kuwaiti ambassador to Britain.
Khamis al-Obeidi: *217*: represented Saddam during his trial; murdered during proceedings.
Khan, Imran: *243+fn 244 306*.
Khayam Hotel: *6*: Baghdad.
Khmer Rouge: *246-48*: followers of Communist Party of Kampuchea (Cambodia).
Khomeini, Ayatollah. See Ayatollah Ruhollah Khomeini.
Khor Az Zubbayr: *330*: Iraq's only deep-water navigable outlet to Gulf, avoiding Shatt al-Arab.

Khorramshar: *331*: Iranian city on Shatt al-Arab; held by Iraq for 7 months in 1980; pop 130,000.
Khouri brothers: *131*.
Kindergarten: *5*.
King Olav V: *30fn*: 1957-91 ruled Norway until his death.
King, Oona: *103*: Lab MP; 2005 defeated by Galloway; 2011 created Baroness King of Bow; voted for Iraq war & v investigation.
Kingston-on-Thames: *40 43 89 92 132*; Royal borough 17 km SW of central London.
Kirkuk: *30 61 109 175 264*: oil-rich city 240 km N of Baghdad; pop 850,000, part-Kurdish.
Kissinger, Henry: *346-47 351-52*: 1973-77 US Sec of State under Nixon & Ford.
KLM: *6*: Dutch airline founded 1919; now part of Air France-KLM.
Kork: *314*: mobile phone network post-2003.
Kosovo: *236*: partially recognised landlocked state in Balkans; 2008 declared independence from Serbia; Pop c2m, c95% Albanian Muslims.
Kurdish enclave: *140 143*: 1991 UNSCR 688 estab 'safe haven' in part of Kurdish area.
Kurdish warlords: *140 242*. See also Masoud Barzani & Jalal Talabani.
Kurdistan: *205 210 332*: Kurdish region incl parts of Iraq, Syria, Iran & Turkey; national aspirations.
Kut/Kut al-Imara: *71fn 134*: 160 km SE of Baghdad on Tigris.
Kuwait: *19-21 23-26 28 31 40-41 43-46 48-49 51 56 57+fn 65 71-73 75-77 101 112 122 128 131-32 167 180 215 314 329 331-32 343*: oil-rich emirate at head of Arab/Persian Gulf; al-Sabah ruling family; 1899 becomes British protectorate to ensure independence from Ottomans; 1961 independence from UK; 1990 invasion & annexation as 19th province by Iraq; 1991 al-Sabah rule restored by UN coalition force; pop 4.2m, 1.3m Kuwaitis, 2.9m expatriates.
Kuwait Oil Company (KOC): *20-24*: founded 1934 by Anglo-Persian & Gulf Oil; HQ Ahmadi qv, Kuwait.
Kuwaiti Embassy in London: *101*: located in Knightsbridge.
Kuwaiti senior supervisors: *20 22*.
Kuwait-Ireland Trade Association: *101*.
Kyle, Peter: *after 291 image 5 (of constituency office); 296*: 2015 elected Lab Progress MP for Hove.
Kyoll: *209*.

Labour Left Briefing: *161*: 1980 founded as *London Labour Briefing*; founders were members of Chartist Minority Tendency, former Trotskyist part of Chartist Collective; later changed to *Labour Briefing*; 1995-2008 *Labour Left Briefing*; then reverted to *Labour Briefing*; monthly magazine; supported by Ken Livingstone & Tony Benn.
Labour Party: *68 102-03 106 108 169 172 197 233 241 253 293-95 298 349*. UK; socialist political party founded 1900; 1997-2010 in govnt.
Lake District: *257-58*: area c370 km NNW of London; popular for its spectacular mountains & lakes.
Lancet, The: *186 187fn*: weekly peer-reviewed general medical journal; founded 1823; offices now in London, New York & Beijing.

Laos: *352*.
Latif Jorephani: *7*.
Latif Mahal Hamoud, General: *72*:, Governor of Basrah.
Law No 80: *15*: after 1958 coup; restricted British oil concessions to 5% of Iraqi territory.
Lawrence of Arabia, Col TE Lawrence: *48 67fn*: British archaeologist, military officer, diplomat, writer; 1916 sent from Cairo to Hijaz on intelligence mission; with other British officers, liaised with Emir Faisal, a leader of Arab Revolt v Ottoman rule; 1918 Damascus taken; disillusioned by British policy in ME after WWI.
Lawrence, Stephen: *243fn*: black UK teenager; 1993 murdered in London in a racially motivated attack.
Lazzarotto, Giuseppe: *90+fn*: Apostolic Papal Nuncio to Iraq.
LBC (Leading Britain's Conversation): *45+fn*: radio station; 1973 founded as London Broadcasting Coy; 1st licensed commercial radio station in UK.
Le Pen, Jany: *93-94 163*: French; 2nd wife of Jean-Marie Le Pen; 1995 founded SOS Enfants d'Irak.
Le Pen, Jean-Marie: *93*: French; 1972-11 founder & leader Front Nationale.
Lebanon: *62 79 110 202*: state estab as French mandate by 1920 Treaty of Sèvres; intended to be Christian; independence achieved by late 1945; 54% of 6m pop now Muslim resulting from differential birth rate & ½m Palestinian refugees; diverse Christian & Muslim sects; 1975-90 civil war; 1976 Arab League agree Syrian Arab Deterrent Force; 1982 Israeli invasion & siege of Beirut; PLO forced to move base from Beirut to Tunis; by 1985 Israel had withdrawn from all but S Lebanon; 2000 Israel completes withdrawal from S; followed by 2005 Syrian withdrawal; 2006 34-day war between Israel & Hizbollah.
Leeds University: *68*.
Legal Aid: *262 292*: UK; state financial assistance to people unable to pay for legal representation.
Leigh, David: *155fn 256+fn*: UK journalist.
Lenin, Vladimir: *95*: 1917-24 communist leader of Russia/Soviet Union; d in office; phrase 'useful idiots' attributed to him but no evidence he coined it.
Leslie: *27-28*: friend of Sudanese friend, Yahya, & husband of Pauline.
Levantine politics: *246-47*.
Levy, Michael, Lord Levy: *108 157 165 241*: 1998-2007 Blair's Personal Envoy to ME.
Libby, Lewis 'Scooter': *155*: Chief of Staff to Vice-President Dick Cheney.
Liberal Democrats (Lib Dems): *104 174 305*: formed 1988 by merging of Lib & short-lived Social Democratic Parties.
LIBOR-rigging: *257+fn*: UK; interest rate manipulation by bankers.
Libya: *25-26 28 30 35 49 56 79 97-98 180 190fn 237fn 242 307 309 347 352*: state in N Africa, bordered on E by Egypt, & on W by Tunisia & Algeria; ancient history; 1551-1911 Ottoman Tripolitania; 1911-1943 Italian rule; 1943-1951 British military admin except French admin Fezzan in SW; 1951-69 King Idris; 1969 Muammar Gaddafi qv overthrows king; Feb 2011 uprising; UNSC authorised intervention; Gaddafi killed; unstable since; pop 7m.
Libya's Revolution Day: *263*.

Lindauer, Susan: *163fn 165 315*: American peace activist working for UN.
Linking of author's case. See Consolidation of hearings.
Linlithgow: *xvi 63 97 110 113*: royal burgh & county town, W Lothian, Scotland; 5 km from Dalyell's The Binns.
Linwood: *36*: New Forest qv, Hampshire.
Lisbon: *27*: capital of Portugal, on the Atlantic coast, pop ½ m.
Livingstone, Ken: *169*: 2000-08 Lab mayor of London.
Llewellyn, Tim: *xv 63-64 73+fn; after 78 image 9; 305 Appendix 2*: ex-BBC reporter, free-lance journalist.
Lloyd George, David: *71fn*: 1916-22 Lib PM; 1919 major player in Paris Peace Conf which produced Versailles, St German, Sévres, Neuilly & Trianon treaties & launched League of Nations.
Lloyd-Roberts, Sue: *79 81+fn 133*: tv journalist contributing to ITV & BBC; focus on human rights.
London: *3 7-8 19-20 22 28 32 35-36 47 55 59 63 66 68 72 80 96 134 166 169 172 176 180 199 201 236 244 257+fn 277 299 302 322 347-48 350-51*: pop 9m.
London Review of Books: *69+fn*: UK fortnightly journal of literary et al essays.
London School of Economics (LSE): 68.
London: *numerous*: pop 9m.
Longfellow, Henry Wadsworth: *120*: lived 1807-1882; American poet.
Looting: *59-60 61 185 188*.
Loraine-Smith, Judge Nicholas: *271 274 292*.
Loughborough University: *68*.
LPC: *351*: French tv channel.
Lucas, Caroline, Dr: *xxiv 104 162fn*: 2008 to present Co-Leader of Green Party; 2010 to present Green MP for Brighton Pavilion; supportive of Palestinians.
Ludot, Emile: *344*: French lawyer of Tariq Aziz.
Luxor: *63*: town on Nile in Upper Egypt; Pharaonic remains; Valley of the Kings; pop ½ m.
Lyne, Sir Roderic: *234-35*: retired diplomat, member of Independent Inquiry qv.

M.W. Kellogg: *50*: UK contractor serving hydrocarbon market; 2010 taken over by Kellogg Brown Root (KBR) qv.
Machiavelli, Nicolo: *178+fn 204+fn*: lived 1469-1527; author of *The Prince* & *The Art of War*.
Madoff, Bernie: *257 +fn*: US stockbroker; 2009 pleaded guilty to fraud estimated at $64.8bl.
Mahathir Mohammed: *217*: 1981-2003 & from May 2018 Malaysian PM; joint-chair of Emergency Cttee qv.
Mahdi Army: *186 200*: Iranian based Shia militia.
Mahmud Ahmadinejad: *200*: 2005-13 President of Iran.
Mahon, Alice: *xxiv 104 107 162fn 164 169*: Lab MP; voted v Iraq war & for investigation.
Maia: *322-23*: aka Khaton, yoga teacher.
Majnoon oilfield: 208.
Major, John: *78fn 97*: 1990-97 Con PM.
Malaria: *69*: tropical disease, potentially fatal if undiagnosed; caused by mosquito-borne parasite.

Malnutrition: *332*.
Malta: *2 25*: Mediterranean island state 80 km S of Sicily; 1814-1964 British rule.
Manal Younis, Dr: *60*: 1979 appointed head of Women's Fed; 2003 fled country.
Mandelson, Peter, now Lord Mandelson: *313*: Lab MP; various ministerial posts under Blair & Brown; voted for Iraq war & v investigation; 2008 created life peer.
Mansfield, Michael, QC: *243+fn 244 263*: barrister.
Marina Club: *32*: Abu Dhabi.
Marquil: *13*: partly British-built quarter of Basrah where author & Doreen lived nr power-station.
Marr, Andrew: *171*: British political commentator & tv presenter.
Marriages: *11; after 14 image 3; 33*. See also Saunders, Doreen, & Pauline.
Marsden, Paul: *xxiv 104*: 1997-2005 MP for Shrewsbury & Atcham; until 2001 Lab, then Lib Dem; Nov 2001 a leader of Stop the War demo v war in Afghanistan; shortly after switched parties; 2003 speaking tour in US opposing war in Iraq; major voice calling for vote on war; 2004 backed Impeach Blair campaign & announced not standing at following election; switched back to Lab 2005 to improve chances of his parliamentary Lab supporters who were restanding.
Marsh Arabs: *3 73-74 185 305*: c½m inhabitants of Tigris-Euphrates marshlands in SE Iraq; largely Shia.
Marshall-Andrews: *xxiv 104 221*: Robert, Lab MP; voted v Iraq war & for investigation.
Martin, Michael: *154*: 2000-09 Speaker of House of Commons; d 2018.
Martindall, Stewart: *36*.
Mary Rose: *92 115; after 130 image 4*: wife of Sabah Kamal.
Marx, Groucho: *341*.
Masoud Barzani: *61 192 205 242 314*: Kurdish warlord.
Massacre of British Forces in WWI: *71+fn*: 1915-16 siege of Kut qv.
Mattis, General James 'Mad Dog': *191fn*:
McCann, Daniel: *285*.
McDermott Engineering Inc: *26 30-31 33 55 132*: North Sea project TCP2.
McDonnell, John: *xxiv 104*: Lab MP; voted v Iraq war & for investigation; Sept 2015 following election of Jeremy Corbyn as Lab leader appointed Shadow Chancellor of Exchequer.
McGurk, Gerard: *138 269*.
McKiernan, General: *184*: 2003 led coalition & U.S. ground forces in attack on Iraq; 2008-09 Commander, International Security Assistance Force (ISAF) Afghanistan.
Media: *xxv 71 101-02 135 148 150 162 187 236 303-04 306 317 348*.
Medical care: *52 123 224 306 308 310*.
Medicines/drugs: *59 63 69-70 73 77 94 96 99 133 137 336 348*.
Mentality, Iraqi: *118 120*.
Mercenaries: *194 243*.
Mesopotamia: *46 71fn 84 118 329*: means 'between the rivers', i.e. the Tigris & Euphrates basin.
Messenger of God, The: *26*: film shot in Tripoli. See Quinn, Anthony.

MI5: *347*: British domestic counter-intelligence & security agency; now Security Service.
MI6 (SIS): *149 150fn 347 351*: British foreign intelligence service; now Secret Intelligence Service.
Michel Aflaq: *18*: Syrian philosopher/sociologist; pioneer of Arab nationalism/ Ba'athism in 1940s.
Middle East Group at FCO: *225.*
Middle East war, 1967: *62 388*: aka six-day war.
Milan: *21*: N Italian city, in Lombardy region, pop 1.3m.
Miles, Oliver: *xxiv 189 190+fn 234 235+fn 236 237fn 238 241+fn 347*: retired diplomat; 1984 appointed Ambassador to Libya very shortly before murder of WPC Yvonne Fletcher outside Libya's London embassy; Tripoli embassy therefore closed (reopened in 1999); 1985-88 Ambassador to Luxemburg; 1993-96 Ambassador to Greece.
Militias: *185 213 227 314 318*: Iraq post-2003.
Military service: *18.*
Mill, John Stuart: *108*: lived 1806-73; UK philosopher, political economist, & civil servant.
Ministers in Saddam's regime: *xxiv 14 30 60 70 74-75 82-83 85 87 90-91 120 123-24 131-32 134 144 164 192 204 220 222 227 230 322; T Aziz Appendix 4.*
Ministry of Agriculture, UK: *37.*
Ministry of Defence (MOD), UK: *92 156.*
Ministry of Information, Iraq: *8.*
Ministry of Oil, Iraq: *9 16 28 40 55-56 59 131 133-34 143 163 185 188 206 248.*
Ministry of Trade, Iraq: *188.*
Mishaal bint Fahd, Princess: *96fn*: Saudi, executed for affair; subject of film *Death of a Princess.*
Missing persons in Iraq: *314.*
Missouri: *172.*
Mitcham: *26*: suburb 12 km SW of Central London.
Mobil: *2 15 26 211*: major American oil coy; 1999 merged with Exxon.
Mobile phone networks: *191 314*: Iraq post-2003.
Mohammad Al-Adhami: *67*: British Iraqi Friendship Society.
Mohammed Bahr al-Ullum. See Ayatollah Mohammed Bahr al-Ullum.
Mohammed Bouazizi: *308*: Tunisian street vendor; 2010 burnt himself to death in Sidi Bouzid, town 270 km S of Tunis, inaugurating 'Arab Spring.'
Mohammed ElBaradei: *335*: Egyptian; law scholar & diplomat; 1997-2009 DG of International Atomic Energy Agency (IAEA); 2012 formed Constitution Party; 2012-13 leader of opposition to Mohammed Morsi's govnt.
Mohammed Qimaishi: *114*: Petcon rep in Iraq.
Mohammed Saleh Mahdi: *70 230*: Saddam's Minister of Trade; arrested 2003.
Mohammed's Army of Ansar. See Jeish Mohammed.
Momentum: *295-96 298*: pro-Corbyn grass-roots campaigning faction of Lab Party formed 2015.
Mongomery, General Bernard: *309*: British WWII soldier.

Morgenthau Plan: *183+fn*: 1944 presented at 2nd Quebec Conf by Henry Morgenthau qv; aim to reduce Germany to pastoral society; Churchill, after hesitation, endorses it.
Morgenthau, Henry: *183+fn*: 1934-45 US Treasury Sec under Roosevelt; central role in financing US engagement in WWII; 1944 devised plan to disempower Germany. See Morgenthau Plan.
Morocco: *49 50*: N African Arab-speaking state/kingdom. W of Algeria; Atlantic & Mediterranean seaboards; name comes from 'maghreb' meaning 'west'.
Morris, Benny: *126+fn*: one of self-described 'new historians' in Israel.
Moses, Lord Justice Alan: *256*.
Mossad: *178 204*: Israeli intelligence agency; estab 1949.
Mosul: *2 15 30 203 218*: major city 400 km N of Baghdad; 2014 occupied by ISIS; 2016-17 retaken at great cost by govnt forces supported by US-led Coalition; pop 600,000.
Mother of author. See Rifaat Wahaib.
Mowaffak Al-Rubaie: *44 61 88; after 173 image 9; 218 305*: National Security Advisor to Coalition Provisional Authority qv; 1979-2003 lived in London; 1979-91 head of Da'wa party's international section; studied at Baghdad Medical School & King's College Medical School.
Mowlam, Mo (Marjorie): *169*: Lab MP; 1997-99 N Ireland minister; 1999-2001 Cabinet Office minister; d 2005.
Ms Dynamite/Niomi Arleen McLean-Daley: *169*: English rapper, singer, songwriter.
Muammar Gaddafi: *25 49 52 56 85 128 296*: 1969-2011 'Brotherly Leader & Guide of the Revolution of Libya'; 1975 published *The Green Book* outlining political philosophy; rejects capitalism, communism & representative democracy & promotes direct democracy overseen by General People's Committee; 1984-99 break in diplomatic relations with UK; 1999 embassy reopened; 2003 renounced WMDs & relations with the US/UK improved; 2004 Blair visited Gaddafi & developed rapport; US reopened embassy; c2006 Richard Perle advised Gaddafi professionally; Feb 2011 uprising on Tunisian & Egyptian model, but regime resisted; counterattacked along coast towards Benghazi; UN authorised NATO intervention; Oct 2011 battle at Sirte where rebel forces captured & killed him. See also Libya; Miles, Oliver.
Mudiff/Guest house: *74*.
Mun'im Samerahi: *124*: Saddam's Deputy Oil Minister in eighties.
Muqtada al-Sadr: *186 200*: Shia cleric, politician, militia leader; led Mahdi Army.
Musab al-Zarqawi. See Abu Musab al-Zarqawi.
Muslim Association of Britain: *162 169*: founded 1997; prominent in opposing Iraq war.
Muslim Brotherhood: *309*: formed 1928 in Ismailia, Egypt, by schoolteacher Sheikh Hassan al-Banna & 6 workers of Suez Canal Coy; anti-Western cultural, economic & political imperialism; social services outreach; branches across Arab world (incl Iraqi Islamic Party, formed 1960, banned 1961; still exists); played roles in 1948 Arab-Israeli war, 1952 overthrow of monarchy; banned by Nasser after which operated from a Munich mosque; in 70s invited back by Sadat, though remained technically illegal; 2005 election MB candidates stood as independents;

won 88 seats c/f 14 other opposition seats; Mubarak answered MB's 'charm offensive' with liberal measures to please West; 2011 revolution & election; MB legalised, formed Freedom & Justice Party which became by far largest in parliament; 2012 1st free presidential election in Egypt; MB's Mohammed Morsi elected with small margin; increasing opposition by liberal Muslims & Christians; 2013 army under General Abdel Fattah el-Sisi ousted Morsi & cracked down on MB; 800 killed in MB protest camp.

Muslims: *50 52 204 289 304 317 321 342 347*: followers of teaching of Mohammed in C7th; c1.8bl worldwide, 24% of global pop; majority of pop in 50 countries; Sunni Muslims (at least 75%) believe 1st 4 caliphs were rightful successors to Muhammad; Shia Muslima (10-20%) believe Muhammad appointed son-in-law, Ali ibn Abi Talib, as successor & only certain descendants of Ali could be Imams; most Iranians & majority of Iraqis Shia.

Mustard gas: *72fn 113*.

Myers, Air Force Gen Richard: *152 184*: US; 2001-05 Chair Joint Chiefs of Staff.

Mylvaganam, Paul: *263*: barrister. See de Silva, Desmond.

Nabataean remains: *62; after 78 image 4*: at Petra qv, Jordan, dating from 312 BC; capital city of Nabataeans; similar remains at Mada'in Saleh in Saudi Arabia, on route of defunct Hijaz Railway, less well-known.

Nabeel Mohammed al-Obaidi, Dr: *229*.

Nabieha: *after 14 image 5*: author's sister-in-law.

Najaf: *116+fn 186 200*: city 160 km S of Baghdad; 3rd holiest city of Shia Islam; nr Euphrates; pop 1.4 m.

Nash, Steve: *25 30*.

Nasir al-Tikrity, Dr: *229*.

Nasiriyah: *175 201*: city on Euphrates; 248 km W of Basrah & 370 km SE of Baghdad; nr ruins of ancient city of Ur; pop 860,000.

Nasser, Gamal Abdul. See Gamal Abdul Nasser.

National Assembly. See Parliament/National Assembly, Iraq.

National Executive Committee (NEC): *293-97*: Lab Party governing body.

National Petroleum Construction Company: *33*: Abu Dhabi.

Nationalisation of oil industry: *21 31 55*.

Nationality & naturalisation: *18 328*: 1980 author naturalised as UK citizen.

Natiq al-Bayati: *208*.

NATO (North Atlantic Treaty Organisation): *171*: 1949 N Atlantic Treaty founded military alliance of 29 N American & European countries; aimed to contain Soviet expansion.

Neoconservatives (Neocons): *183 187fn 201 237-38*: US; started as group of liberals in 1960s who questioned their own liberalism; context was anti-Vietnam war protests & pacifist foreign policy of Dem Party, growth of New Left & counterculture; significant Jewish contribution; prominent in Bush Jr's admin; pro Iraq war.

Nepal: *350*.

New Forest: *xviii 36*: unenclosed pasture, heathland & forest W of Southampton, inwards from S coast.

New Scientist: *63*: weekly international science magazine, founded in 1956.

New York Times: *106 107fn 148 154 155fn 163fn 219fn*: widely read daily paper; considered liberal in US terms; founded 1851.
New York: *62 83 145 163 215 272 177*: E coast US city; many skyscrapers; seat of UN; pop 8.5 m.
New Zealand: *170.*
Newsnight: *44+fn 45 182+fn 349*: UK; in depth tv news programme on BBC2.
Newspapers: *314*: Iraq post-2003.
Nicaragua: *54 127 169.*
Nicholson, Emma, Baroness: *100 305*: 1987-95 Con MP; 1995 defected to Lib Dems; 1997 created Baroness Nicholson of Winterbourne; 1999-2009 Lib Dem MEP & joined Committee on Foreign Affairs; focus on human rights & democracy; 2016 returned to Con party.
Niger: *155+fn.*
Nile, R: *49*: 6,853 km long; sources in Central Africa & Ethiopia; flows into Mediterranean.
Nixon, Richard: *346-47 351*: 1969-74 Rep US President.
Nobel Peace Prize: *346*: created 1901 by Swedish arms manufacturer Alfred Nobel; annual awards.
No-fly zones: *61 126*: 1991 imposed in Kurdish region; 1992 in S below 32rd, later 33rd parallel.
Noori Juwair: *13.*
North Africa, date cultivation in: *4.*
North Oil Company: *30*: formed after 1970 nationalisation from MPC incl Kirkuk, where HQ was now based.
North Sea oil: *25 30.*
North, Oliver: *54.*
Norwegian Ministry of Oil: *28 209.*
Nouri al-Maliki: *177*: 2006-2014 PM; 2007 became leader of the Islamic Da'wa Party.
Novak, Robert: *155+fn*: aka The Prince of Darkness, conservative US journalist.
Nuclear Non-Proliferation Treaty: *44*: 1970; Israel is not party.
Nuremberg trials: *244*: allied forces military tribunals held in Nuremberg following WWII.

O'Brien, Mike: *190*: 2002-03 Minister of State at FCO.
O'Keefe, Ken: *165-66.*
O'Neill, Sean: *281.*
OAPEC: *32-34 295*: Organisation of Arab Petroleum Exporting Countries.
Obama, Barack: *346 350*: Dem US President, 2009-17.
Observer, The: *108*: UK; 1791 founded; world's oldest Sunday paper; 1993 acquired by Guardian Media Group; social/liberal/social dem.
Occupation: *2 5 10 44-46 48 50 71fn 101 119 176 180 181 190-91 194-204 207 211-12 215 244 247-48 266 273 298 309 311-12 318 331.*
OECD (Organisation for Economic Co-operation and Development): *256*: 36-member intergovernmental organisation; 1961 founded to stimulate economic progress & world trade; committed to democracy & market economy.
Office of Special Plans: *183*: US.
Office of Strategic Influence: *148*: US.

Official sale price (OSP): *139*.
Oil & oil industry: *xvii xxiii 2 9 13-18 20-22 25-26 28 30-31 37 40 44 46 50 53-56 57fn 59 61 64+fn 75; after 78 image 1; 79 81 99 117 123-24 131-36 138-40 142-44 152 163 170 175-79 185 187-88 194 201-02 206-09 210+fn 211-12 215 216fn 230-31 240 242 247-49 250+fn 251 254fn 265 267 269-73 275 281+fn 292 295 307-10 312 316-19*.
Oil conferences: *79 133 207-10*.
Oil reserves: *54 338*.
Oilfields: *27 56 79 109 133-34 175 182 206-08 304fn 319 331 339*.
Oil-for-Food Progamme: *xvii 82 111 113 133-37 139-40 176 215 240 248+fn 250fn 252 259 267-68 271 273 275 301 303 348*.
Omaar, Rageh: *xviii 140+fn*: BBC world affairs correspondent; reported from Baghdad during 2nd Gulf War.
Omeid Mubarak: *70 75; after 78 image 8; 87 90*: Saddam's Minister of Health.
OPEC (Organisation of Petroleum Exporting Countries): *53-54 210 295*: 1960 founded in Baghdad by Iran, Iraq, Kuwait, Saudi Arabia & Venezuela; from 1965 HQ in Vienna.
Operation Iraqi Freedom: *175*: US strategic plan for 2nd Gulf War.
Operation Mass Appeal: *140*: British SIS campaign aimed at raising support for 2nd Gulf War. See also MI6.
Operation Menu: *346*: 1969-70 secret US bombing campaign v Cambodia as part of Vietnam war & Cambodian civil war.
Opposition, The: *xvii 44+fn 61 71 80 106 119 146-47 161 170 187 243 265 299-300 304-05 311 331*: in context of this book, largely anti-Ba'athists, usually living abroad.
Ordinary National Diploma (OND): *9*: UK Further Education qualification equivalent to A level.
Organisation of Arab Petroleum Exporting Countries. See OAPEC.
Orphans in Iraq: *314*.
Osama bin Laden: *145 342 351*: Yemeni-Saudi; 1988 co-founded al-Qaeda (qv) with Abdullah Azzam & Ayman al-Zawahiri to fight Russians in Afghanistan; 2002 letter calling on Americans to convert to Islam & 'reject the immoral acts of fornication, homosexuality, intoxicants, gambling, and usury;' claimed Western govnts & society dominated by Jews.
Oslo accords: *51*: 1993-95 agreements between Israel & PLO initiated in Norway.
Ottoman Empire: *15 46 84 203 329*: 1299-1922; incl Balkans, Anatolia, Levant, N Africa & beyond; capital Istanbul; founded by Osmanli Turks; 'Ottoman' & 'Turkish' often used interchangeably when referring to history of the empire.
Ouseley, Sir Duncan Brian Walter: *244*: High Court judge.
Overstaffing by foreign companies: *16 21*.

Pace, Peter: *184*.
Pack of cards representing wanted Ba'athists: *175*.
Pakistan, Islamic Republic of: *22+fn 243 262-63 270 272-73 286*: a Commonwealth state created 1947 by partition of British India into Muslim & Hindu states; until 1971 incl E Bengal, now Bangladesh; 96 % Muslim; official languages Urdu & English; pop 193m.

Palast, Greg: *182 205 206+fn 265*: author & freelance journalist often working for BBC & Guardian.
Palestine: *4fn 5 11 45 51-53 62+fn 101 125 126+fn 129 180 196 199+fn 203-04 226-27 240-41 308 311 316-17 338 351*: country bounded by the Mediterranean, R Jordan, Lebanon & Egypt; until 1917 Ottoman rule; 1917 occupied by British; also in 1917 Balfour Declaration to Lord Rothschild, a leader of the British Jewish community, saying Britain favoured creation of Jewish homeland in Palestine; 1920 League of Nations granted Britain mandate to rule; Jewish immigration accelerated; Arab resistance to this resulted in restrictions in late 30s; Jewish terrorism to achieve statehood; 1945 Arab League formed in Alexandria, with Palestine permitted a delegate; 1947 UNGAR 181 ruled Palestine should be divided between Jewish state (56% of land) & Arab state; rejected by Arabs; 1948 British withdrew & Israeli state declared; Arab armies attempted unsuccessfully to prevent implementation; ethnic cleansing of areas designated for Israel; 1949 armistice giving Israel 68% of Palestine; 1959 group of diaspora Palestinians incl Yasser Arafat formed Fatah with a self-help nationalist ideology; Jan 1964 Arab League held its 1st summit in Cairo; Ahmad al-Shuqayri mandated to establish a Palestinian entity; May 1964 Palestinian National Council convened in Jerusalem & formed Palestine Liberation Organisation with Shuqayri as Chair; 1967 war, W Bank, E Jerusalem & Gaza occupied; Fatah joined PLO & became majority faction; 1969 Yasser Arafat elected Chair; 1980 E Jerusalem annexed; 1987-93 1st intifada (uprising) v occupation; 1993-95 Oslo accords attempt to resolve conflict; 2000-2005 2nd intifada; 2012 granted non-member observer status at UN. See also Zionist entity & Yasser Arafat.
Palestine Liberation Organisation (PLO): *128*. See also Palestine.
Palestinian refugees: *226, 338.*
Panama hat, Lock & Co: *121 332.*
Papal Nuncio in Baghdad: *90+fn*: Pope's representative in Iraq. See Vatican.
Paris: *xxv 28 105 157 207 347 351.*
Parliament/National Assembly, Iraq: *75 123-24 193 210.*
Parliamentary immunity, UK: *68*:
Parliamentary Labour Party Foreign Affairs Group: *xv.*
Parsons Corporation: *25*: American construction coy.
Patriotism: *xvii 3 125 205 207 211 213 225 228 230 273.*
Pauline: *27 28 32-33 25 43*: author's 2nd wife.
Paxman, Jeremy: *44*: British broadcaster, journalist, author & quizmaster.
Paying the Price: Killing the Children of Iraq: *111+fn 112 191fn*: 2000 documentary by John Pilger on ITV.
PC2 (Petro-Chemical 2): *40-41*: joint project in late eighties between Bechtel & Ministry of Oil.
Peace Envoy to ME for the Quartet qv: *306*: 2007-15 Tony Blair qv.
Peace movement: *61-62 66 165-67 169-70 339.*
Pentagon: *88 106 145 172*: HQ US Dept of Defence qv; across Potomac from Washington, DC.
Pentlands Constituency (Edinburgh): *100*: 1974-97 Con MP Malcolm Rifkind; 1995-97 he was Foreign Sec.
Perenco: *133-36 138-39 142-43 207 247 251 292 297*: French oil coy.

Perle, Richard: *163 183 237fn*: US; 2001-03 Chair Defence Policy Board; c2006 professional advisor to Gaddafi.
Perrodo, Hubert: *133*: French businessman; 1975 founded Perenco.
Persian Gulf. See Arab/Persian Gulf.
Personal Envoy to ME: *108 241*: 1998-2007 Lord Levy; appointed by Blair.
Peshmerga: *175*: Kurdish guerrilla organisation/military forces in federal region of Iraqi Kurdistan.
Petcon: *30-32 40-43 57fn 114 131-33 210fn 259 316* : engineering coy founded by author in 1976.
Petra: *62; after 78 image 4*: Jordan, 236 km S of Amman, Nabataean remains.
Petrochemicals: *330*.
Petrodollar: *52 159*: notional unit of currency earned by a country from export of oil.
Pfiffner, James P: *181fn*: US; prof of public policy at George Mason Uni, Arlington VA.
Philippines: *22fn*.
Pieth, Mark: *248*: Swiss prof of criminal law; served on Independent Committee qv.
Pilger, John: *xxiv 111+fn 112+fn 191fn Endpiece*: Australian journalist & award-winning documentary film maker; since 1962 based mainly in UK.
Pillar, Paul: *184*:
Pinter, Harold: *161 169*: Nobel Prize-winning English playwright; founder member of Stop the War Coalition qv.
Placenta Bay, Newfoundland: *158*.
Plame, Valerie: *155*: CIA operative specialising in WDMs; wife of Joseph Wilson qv.
Poindexter, John: *54*.
Pol Pot: *346-348*. Cambodian politician; 1963-98 General Sec of communist Khmer Rouge.
Poland: *175*.
Political Parties: *314+fn*: Iraq post-2003.
Political Prisoners: *196 Chapter 14*.
Pollination of date palms: *4*.
Portugal: *27-28 158*.
Poverty in Iraq: *314*.
Powell, Colin: *148 160 184 235 300*: 2001-05 US Sec of State; retired General; Jamaican descent.
Powell, Enoch: *120fn*: 1950-74 Con MP for Wolverhampton W; 1960-63 Minister of Health; 1974-87 Ulster Unionist MP for S Down, N Ireland; 1968 speech opposing immigration.
Prague Spring: *309*.
Prashar, Baroness Usha: *234-35*: b in Kenya, came to UK in 60s; crossbench member of HofL; served on Independent Inquiry qv, & appointed Privy Counsellor (qv) for the purpose.
Prescott, John: *106*: Lab MP, 1997-2007 Deputy PM; told Chilcot he doubted legality & intelligence re WMDs; after publication of report said invasion was illegal, based on inadequate documentation; 2010 made a life peer as Baron Prescott.

Presidential election, Iraq, 2002: *81*: Saddam reportedly elected with 100% support.
Presidential palace: *175*.
Press Complaints Commission, UK: *237fn*:
Price, The Rt Rev Peter: *89 92*: Suffragan Bishop of Kingston.
Primakov, Yevgeni: *343*: Gorbachev's special envoy to Iraq; 1996-98 Russian Foreign Minister.
Primary school: *6*.
Primordial view of post-2003 conflict: *203*: term used by Dr Toby Dodge to describe approach which 'starts with an *a priori* assertion of a society deeply divided by ethnic and sectarian tensions;' this promoted by Leslie Gelb & Peter Galbraith, retired US diplomats; accordingly conflict seen as inevitable.
Prince Bandar bin Sultan: *255+fn*.
Prince, The: *178+fn*: a polemic by Nicolo Machiavelli published posthumously in 1532.
Princess Diana, Diana Princess of Wales, Lady Di: *xxv 105*: née Diana Spencer; 1981 mar Prince Charles, heir to British throne; active campaigner on HIV & landmines; 1996 divorced; 31st Aug 1997 killed in car crash in Paris.
Private Eye: *296-97*: satirical fortnightly current affairs magazine; originated mid-50s as Shrewsbury School magazine edited by Richard Ingrams, Willie Rushton, Christopher Booker & Paul Foot (nephew of Michael Foot qv); 1986-present Ian Hislop editor.
Privatisation: *159 182 209 210+fn*.
Privy Counsellor/Councillor: *232-33*: member of privy council, a body advising head of state, esp, as in UK, monarch.
Production share agreements: *210*.
Project for the New American Century: *166fn 187+fn*: estab 1997; neocon think tank.
Prosecution Substantive Submission, 5th Nov 2010; states prosecution's position on the defence's argument of abuse of process.
Prosecutions for paying surcharge: *138fn 269+fn 271+fn*: worldwide 3 cases: US Oscar Wyatt qv, UK Aftab Hasan & author.
Pubic Accounts Committee: *258*: 2013 investigates SFO.

Qatar: *89 309*: independent emirate in Arab/Persian Gulf; al-Thani dynasty; Al Udeid Air Base nr capital, Doha, hosts US Central Command HQ & other coalition air-forces; used in 2003 invasion of Iraq; pop 2.6m.
Quartet, The: *199fn*: body founded 2002 consisting of UN, EU, US & Russian reps aimed at mediating in the Israel-Palestine conflict.
Quebec Conference, 2nd: *183fn*: 1944; Churchill, Roosevelt, Morgenthau et al. The 1st conf was in 1943. See Morgenthau Plan.
Queen Elizabeth II Centre, Westminster: *239*.
Queen's Counsel (QC): *157 243 263*: eminent lawyer (usually barrister or advocate) appointed by monarch as an advisor on matters of law; during reign of king, title is King's Counsel (KC). Desmond de Silva was a QC.
Quinn, Anthony: *26*: Mexican-American actor; shooting of *The Messenger of God* in Tripoli.

Qurna: *3fn 4*: 74 km NW of Basrah at Tigris/Euphrates confluence; said to have been Garden of Eden.
Qusay Hussein: *175*: 2nd son of Saddam Hussein; heir apparent; July 2003 killed in Mosul with brother Uday & possibly Uday's 14-year-old son Mustapha in shoot-out with US forces.

Race Relations Coordinator at Wandsworth prison: *282.*
Radio interviews: *45+fn 63 189 196.*
Radio stations in Iraq: *314*: post-2003.
Radwan al-Saadi, Dr: *134*: Saddam's DG of Exploration.
RAF: *71+fn*: UK; Royal Airforce.
Rafid: *after 14 image 5*: author's nephew.
Rafid Ahmad Alwan al-Janabi: *299-300+fn*: German Iraqi; known by US Defence Intelligence Agency as 'Curveball'; Iraqi informant.
Rafid Mohammed al-Omar, Dr: *229.*
Rafidain oil field: *133-34 207*: nr Kut.
Raghad: *217-18*: Saddam's eldest daughter; lives with mother, Sajida Talfah, under royal protection in Jordan.
Railway electrification programme: *40-41.*
Raiser, Dr Konrad: *86*: General Sec of the World Council of Churches qv.
Ramadi: *13*: beside Euphrates; 110 km W of Baghdad, 50 km W of Falluja; pop 375,000.
Rammel, Bill: *221-22*: Lab MP; various ministerial positions incl 2002–2005 Parliamentary Under Sec of State at FCO & 2008–2009 Foreign Sec; voted for Iraq war & v investigation.
Rape: *188*:
Rasheed Hotel. See Al-Rasheed Hotel.
Reagan, Ronald: *54 127*: 1981-89 Rep US President; 1983 secret order to support Iraq v Iran by all means.
Re-categorisation: *286-88.*
Reed, Oliver: *7*: 1980s star in *Clash of Loyalties* produced by Latif Jorephani; known for upper-middle class, macho image; other film roles in *The Trap* (1966), *Oliver!* (1968), *Women in Love* (1969), *Hannibal Brooks* (1969), *The Devils* (1971), *The Three Musketeers* (1973), *Tommy* (1975), *Lion of the Desert* (1981), *Castaway* (1986), *The Adventures of Baron Munchausen* (1988) and *Funny Bones* (1995); alcoholic, drinking partner The Who drummer Keith Moon; d aged 61 in 1999.
Referendum on constitution: *211 217.*
Refineries and Gas Industry Administration: *210.*
Refrigeration: *115*:
Refugees from Iraq: *304 314.*
Regan, Carol: *199*: officer of Palestine Solidarity Campaign.
Regime change: *52 56 148 152 157 223 238 240 319.*
Rehabilitation of Offenders Act: *298.*
Release from prison: *290-91*: 27th April 2011; 2 days later wedding of Prince William and Catherine Middleton at Westminster Abbey.
Release of British citizens held in Iraq: *75-76*: 1993 arranged between Dalyell & Heath.

Religion: *118 316*. See also Christians & churches; Muslims; Jews.
Renouf, Lady Michèle: *262-63*: Australian-born advertising model-turned-political-activist.
Reparations: *43 77 99*.
Republican Guard: *40 44*: elite troops of Iraqi army directly reporting to Saddam.
Republican Palace: *194*: Saddam's venue for high-profile mtgs; not bombed in 2003; became HQ of coalition forces; in Green Zone.
Resistance: *52 119 126 151 153 175 181 185 190 198-200 202 205 209 216 321 339*.
Reynolds, Albert: *xv 81-85 86fn 135 181 293 341 343*: 1992-94 Taoiseach (qv) of Eire; 1999 became Chair of Bula; d 2014.
Riadh Habboush: *209*.
Rifaat Wahaib: *5 11-12*: mother of author; d 1961.
Ricciardone, Francis (Frank) J Jr: *80*: US Arabist diplomat; now President of AUC.
Rice, Condoleezza: *184 202*: 2001-05 US Rep National Security Advisor; 2005-09 Sec of State.
Rickets: *73*: deficiency disease caused by lack of vitamin D or calcium.
Ride, Paul: *75*.
Ritter, Scott, Col: *149 150fn 315*: US; 1991-98 UNSCOM inspector; rejected linking bin Laden & Saddam.
Road Map: *199fn*: proposed plan for resolution of Israel-Palestine conflict by the Quartet qv.
Robertson, George, now Lord Robertson of Ellen: *102 104-05*: Lab MP.
Roman Catholic Church: *87 91-92 115 287 300*.
Rome: *124 169*.
Roosevelt, Franklin D: *127 158 183fn 236*: 1933-45 Dem US President.
Roskill, Eustace, Lord Roskill: *253*: 1980-86 Lord of Appeal in Ordinary; 1986 chaired Fraud Trials Committee, leading to Criminal Justice Act 1987 which estab SFO.
Ross, Carne: *272 315fn 349*: Deputy 1st Sec at UK Mission to UN; 2004 testified to Butler Review qv; resigned from Civil Service; formed 'Independent Diplomat' advisory group.
Roston, Aram: *106+fn 148+fn 152fn 178fn 183fn 193+fn*: US investigative journalist; author of *The Man Who Pushed America to War*.
Royal Flying Corps: *71fn*: formed 1912, merged with Royal Naval Air Service to form RAF 1918.
Royal Jordanian Airlines: *66*.
Royal Naval Air Service: *71fn*: 1912 founded by Churchill; 1918 became part of newly formed RAF.
Royal Tank Regiment: *121*.
Ruddock, Joan: *xxiv 104*: Lab MP; voted v Iraq war & v investigation.
Rumsfeld, Donald: *127 128fn 146 176*: 2001-06 US Rep Sec of Defence; 1983 visited Iraq; following year diplomatic ties resumed.
Russell, Bertrand, 3rd Earl Russell: *198+fn*: b 1872 d 1970; British philosopher, logician, mathematician, historian, writer, social critic, political activist & Nobel laureate; 1st President of CND qv.

Russia, the Russian Federation: *13 36 54 60 153 199fn 251 282 338 344 351*: world's largest state, stretching from Pacific to Baltic & bordering Arctic; reduced in global power since 1991collapse of Soviet Union qv, but continues significant player, incl in ME; pop 145m.

Saad al-Hayani, Dr: *229.*
Saadalla al-Fathi: *210.*
Sabah family. See Al-Sabah; Kuwait.
Sabah Juma: *210.*
Sabah Kamal: *92 115; after 130 image 4; 168*: wife Mary Rose.
Sabians: *192*: aka Mandaeans; revere Adam, Abel, Seth, Enos, Noah, Shem, Aram, & John the Baptist; speak E Aramaic dialect.
Sabra and Shatila: *125*: 1982 massacres of Palestinians et al by militias allied to Israel.
Sabri al-Qaysi, Dr: *229*:
Saddam Children's Hospital: *68-69.*
Saddam goes to Hollywood: *7*: tv programme on UK Channel 4, re production of *Clash of Loyalties* qv.
Saddam Hussein Abd al-Majid al-Tikriti: *xv xvii xviii xix xxiv xxv 7-8 23 44fn 47 49 51-53 61-62 65+fn 68-69 72fn 73-75 76+fn 77+fn 80 82+fn 83-85 93 95 99-103 105-12 114: author's encounter with, & assessment of 120-30: after 130 image 8; 132 140-44 147-48 149+fn 151-53 155 158-59 161 163 165 167 168+fn 170 173 175 177 188 190 192 201 204 214-15: trial & execution 216-20: 223fn 227 234 237 239 240 242-43 247 261 271 296-97 299 300+fn 301 304-05 317 330-32: Benn's interview Appendix 3: 341-44 345+fn 348-49*: b 1937 d 2006; 1979-2003 President of Iraq; after school studied law; 1957 dropped out to join Ba'athist party; strongly influenced by Nasser; 1958 General Abd al-Karim Qasim qv overthrew Faisal II; 1959 involved in failed attempt to assassinate Qasim because of his refusal to join Nasser's United Arab Republic & his alliance with communist party which opposed pan-Arabism; fled to Syria where he met Michel Aflaq qv; 1960-63 lived in Egypt; 1963 Qasim overthrown & Abdul Salam Arif became president; Saddam returned to Iraq; 1964-66 in prison following crackdown on Ba'athists by Arif; after escaping Ahmed Hassan al-Bakr (qv), his cousin, appointed him deputy leader of underground Ba'ath cell; 1968 participates in bloodless coup which brought Ba'athists to power; Al-Bakr became president, Saddam his deputy & deputy chair of Ba'athist Revolutionary Command Council which 1968 to 2003 was ultimate decision-making body of Iraq; by 1969 Saddam leading force in party; promoted stability in divided country using stick of repression & carrot of higher living standards; 1972 nationalised oil industry & signed 15-year cooperation treaty with Soviets; promoted social, health & educational services; UNESCO gave him award in recognition; 1976 promoted to general; 1978 expelled Khomeini qv, who had lived in Al-Najaf since 1964; 1979 purged Ba'ath party to prevent union with Syria; many executed; same year Khomeini returned from France to Iran & overthrew Shah; 1980-88 Iran-Iraq war; 1981 nuclear enrichment plant (built with French assistance) bombed by Israel; 1990 invaded & occupied Kuwait following disputes over money & oil; believed US would not intervene; UN sanctions imposed; 1991 coalition led by US evict Iraqi forces from Kuwait &

UN sets up UNSCOM to ensure Iraq destroys WMDs; 2003 coalition forces invade Iraq; Saddam captured; 2004-06 tried & executed.
Saddam Children's Hospital: *68-69*: located at Saddam Medical City, Baghdad.
Saddam Zebin Hassan: *139*: DG of SOMO.
Saddam's man: *xxv 102-03 105 271.*
Said, Edward: *61*: Palestinian-US citizen; father was US Army veteran in WWI; Greek Orthodox (non-practising); Prof of lit at Columbia Uni; a founder of postcolonial studies; in *Orientalism* (1978) he describes Western tradition of prejudiced interpretations of the East; author also of several books on Palestine.
Salah al-Din al-Bitar: *18fn*: collaborator with Michel Aflaq in founding Arab nationalism/Ba'athism.
Salah al-Shaikhly: *101 209*: opponent of Saddam; 2004-08 Ambassador to UK.
Salah, Khalid Khadom, Dr: *229.*
Salahuddin/Saladin: *53 109*: Sunni Kurd; 1174-1193 1st Sultan of Egypt & Syria; founded Ayyubid dynasty; 1187 took Jerusalem from Crusaders.
Salam Mukhus al-Hayati, Dr: *229.*
Salisbury: *76*: city 137 km WSW of London.
Salmond, Alex: *xxiv 104*: MP, 2004-14 Leader of SNP; 2007-14 1st Minister of Scotland; strong opponent of Iraq war; usually voted for investigation; 2004 support for impeachment of Blair.
Saltburn: *20*: seaside town in Cleveland, N Yorkshire; 19 km SE of Middlesbrough.
Samarra: *116+fn*: 125 km N of Baghdad on Tigris; Abbasid capital; distinctive architecture.
Samuels, David: *162-65*: US; 1996-2018 Contributing Editor at Harper's Magazine.
San Diego: *176*: Californian coastal town, 37 km N of Tijuana in Mexico.
Sanctions, UN, on Iraq: *xv xvii xviii xxv 1 2 44-45 56 59 63 64fn 65-69 72-73 75 77-79 85-86 87+fn 90-92 95-103 107 109-12 117-19 123 125-26 131-35 137-38 140-41 143 159 167 170 176 189 195 197 205 213 223 225 240 242-43 247 250 252-53 255 259 261 264 265-66 269-70 273 275 281+fn 293 295 297-98 301 303-04 307 311-13 315 317 332 341 348-49*: imposed 1990, lifted 2003.
Sandinistas: *54*: National Liberation Front in Nicaragua; Marxist; 1979 overthrew Somoza regime; 1990 Contras, heavily supported by US, ousted Sandinistas. See Iran-Contra scandal.
Sands, Phillipe QC: *157-58+fn.*
Sarah, Rabbi Elizabeth Tikvah: *197fn*: 2000 appointed to Brighton & Hove Progressive Synagogue; 2006 she mar Jess Wood Sarah in 1st public same-sex wedding in synagogue following 2004 Civil Partnership Act.
Sassifon: *114*: ancient remains. See Suwaira.
Saudi Arabia: *23 26 53-54 95 153 168 190 252 254+fn 255+fn 256 301 310 329*: kingdom covering most of Arabian peninsular; 1744 1st Saudi regime formed by pact between Muhammad bin Saud & Ibn Abd al-Wahab, founder of puritanical Sunni movement; expanded from area around Riyadh; 1802 sacked Karbala, 1803 captured Mecca; 1818 Ottomans repossess Mecca; 1824 2nd Saudi regime, mainly around Riyadh; 1891 ousted by al-Rashid family; exile in Kuwait; 1902 Abdul-Aziz ibn Saud retook Riyadh; 1913 took Hofuf; 1924-25 took Hijaz; 1932 Kingdom of Saudi Arabia declared; 1938 large oil reserves discovered;

1941 production begins by US-controlled ARAMCO; 1953 Abdul Aziz dies & succeeded by Saud; 1964 replaced by Faisal; 1973 Saudis led oil boycott of countries supporting Israel in 1973 war; 1975 Faisal assassinated & succeeded by Khalid; 1978 Saudis acquire 100% interest in ARAMCO; 1979 uprising in Shia town of Qatif following Iranian revolution; same year short-lived occupation of Grand Mosque in Mecca in attempt to overthrow Saud family; 1982 Fahd succeeds Khalid; in 80s Saudis spend $25bl supporting Iraq v Iran; 1990 following Iraq's invasion of Kuwait Saudis fear they'll be next; ask US to intervene; allowed stationing of US forces, foreign women to drive etc; collaborated militarily in action v Iraq; during 90s & beyond increasing unrest re Western presence; bombings & violence in Riyadh, Jeddah, Yanbu & al-Khobar (19 USAF personnel killed in last); 1994 bin Ladin's citizenship revoked; 1998-2000 al-Qaeda claims responsibility for bombing of 2 U.S. embassies in E Africa & of USS Cole nr Aden; 2001 15 of 19 identified as involved in 9/11 were Saudi; 2003 Saudis ambivalent re US action fearing destabilising aftermath, incl pro-Iranian regime on its border; however did not deny use of its bases for attack; 2005 Abdullah succeeded Fahd; 2015 Salman succeeded Abdullah, but Crown Prince & Deputy PM Mohammed bin Salman increasingly influential & introduces reforms.

Saunders, Doreen: *11-12 17-18 21 27 326*: first wife of author.
Saut al-Jamaheer **(Voice of the Masses)**: *242*: monthly newspaper of Iraq-backed Arab Liberation Front qv; Chief Editor Tariq Aziz.
Sawers, John: *189*.
Scarlett, John: *154+fn*: 2001-04 Chair of UK Joint Intelligence Committee.
Scientists: *77 178fn 228+fn 229*.
SCIRI. See Supreme Council for the Islamic Revolution in Iraq.
Scotland: *100 254*.
Scottish National Party (SNP): *104 197*: founded 1934 to campaign for Scottish independence from UK.
Scud missiles: *51 159*: series of tactical ballistic missiles developed by Soviet Union.
Second Gulf War: *54fn 151 172 174-76 233*: 2003; invasion & occupation by UN coalition force, principally US/UK.
Secondary school: *6-8 30*.
Second World War. See WWII.
Secret Intelligence Service. See MI6.
Sectarian relations: *61 122 182 188 192 200 218 223 306 308 347*.
Security companies post 2013: *314*.
Security Council (& General Assembly), UN: *43-44 54 98 128 133 136 149-50 160 171 176 226 240 266 301 331 335-36 348*: 15 members, 5 with veto; resolutions binding on UN members. **General Assembly**: unlike Security Council equal representation for all member states; may recommend on all matters except peace & security under Security Council consideration; 2/3 majority required on important matters; e.g. 1947 UNGAR 181, partition plan for Palestine. See also United Nations Organisation; entries beginning UNSCR; Palestine; Zionist Entity.
Security Service. See MI5.
Sentence: *xxv 246 274-76 281 286 288 291-92 294 299*.

Serious Fraud Office (SFO): *138 142+fn 215 247 249 252-55 256+fn 257+fn 258+fn 259 261-62 264 267 269 271 275*: UK; founded in 1987.
Severance packages at SFO: *258.*
Shadow cabinet: *95 103*: British govnt; the opposition's govnt-in-waiting.
Shahada: *218fn 219+fn.*
Shaibah: *15*: military base in Basrah governorate; 1932-58 retained by British following independence.
Shakespeare, William: *121.*
Sharon, Ariel: *125*: Israeli General, blamed for Sabra & Shatila qv; 2001-06 PM.
Sharq al-Awsat: *168*: Saudi-financed newspaper.
Shatt Al-Arab: *3+fn 140 270 330*: 200 km waterway from confluence of Tigris & Euphrates at Qurna out to Gulf.
Shawkya: *5*: 3rd elder sister of author.
Shejeera: *after 130 images 1-7; 115.*
Shell: *2 19-21 211*: officially Royal Dutch Shell plc; 1907 created by amalgamation of Royal Dutch Petroleum Coy & Shell Transport & Trading Coy Limited of UK; aim to compete with Standard Oil; one of the 6 top oil & gas coys in the world.
Shimesiani: *57*: quarter in Amman.
Shepherd Market: *263*: Mayfair.
Sheraton Hotel, Baghdad: *40.*
Shi'a Islam. See Muslims.
Shin Bet: *129*: Israel's internal security service; 2000-05 led by Avi Dichter.
Shock and Awe: *347*: US military tactic of overwhelming power & spectacular displays of force to paralyze enemy; used in 2003 war.
Shoja al-Hashawi, Dr: *229.*
Short, Clare: *102-05 171 225 234-35*: Lab MP, 1997-2003 International Development Minister; 9 March 2003 called Blair reckless in BBC radio interview & threatened to resign if Iraq war declared without clear UN mandate; however 18 March voted for war; 12 May resigned; Nov 2004 published *An Honourable Deception?: New Labour, Iraq, and the Misuse of Power*; Sept 2006, announced not standing at next election; ashamed of Tony Blair's govnt; Oct 2006 after censure by Lab whip resigned from party continuing as Independent Lab MP; 2007 accused EU & Britain of colluding in building of new apartheid regime in Israel-Palestine & supported boycott of Israel on S African model; 2010 in evidence to Chilcot criticised Blair, Goldsmith & others for deception.
Siena, Portugal: *27*: not to be confused with the city in Tuscany, Italy.
Silva, Desmond de. See de Silva, Desmond.
Simpson, Alan: *xxiv 104 164 303*: left-wing Lab MP; in response to events following 9/11 founded 'Labour Against the War' group; opposed Afghan war & occupation of Iraq; 31 October 2006 among 12 Lab MPs backing Plaid Cymru & SNP's call for inquiry into Iraq War; stood down 2007.
Simpson, Dominic: *209.*
SIS. See MI6.
Skinner, Dennis: *xxiv 104*: left-wing Lab MP; voted v Iraq war; 2015 nominated Corbyn for leadership.
Sky: *45*: UK telecommunications & broadcasting coy.
Smith, John: *102-104*: MP, Leader of Lab Party; 1994 d at 55 of heart attack.

Smuggling: *79 140 240 252 270.*
Sneh, Ephraim: *126*: 1999-2001 Israeli Deputy Defence Minister.
Social Democrats, Iraq: *5.*
Social mobility: *123.*
Socialist Workers Party (SWP): *161*: UK; radical-left political party; 1950 founded as Socialist Review Group by supporters of Tony Cliff (b Yigael Gluckstein in 1917 in Palestine);1933 became Trotskyist & anti-Zionist, 1947 emigrated to Britain); 1962 party became International Socialists; 1977 became SWP.
Solidarity, Friendship and Peace Organisation: *66*: Iraq; prob ceased to exist post-2003.
Somerset: *63*: county in SW England.
SOMO. See State Oil Marketing Organisation.
Somoza, Anastasio: *127*: 1967-72 & 1974-79 Nicaraguan President.
Sonnet, Keith: *162fn.*
Sookhdeo, Canon Patrick: *89*: Barnabas Fund.
Sophocles: *120fn*: Greek playwright, c496-406 BC.
Souad: *5*: 2nd eldest sister of author.
Souq: *116*: Arab for marketplace or market quarter.
South Africa: *198 248 255-56*: 1948-94 policy of racial separation called Apartheid; comparisons made with Israeli rule in Palestine.
South Oil Company: *30-31 209*: replaced BPC following nationalisation of oil industry.
Southend-on-Sea: 6-11 13; *after 14 image 2; 92* : 64 km E of London at mouth of Thames estuary into N Sea; pop 182,000.
Southend Technical College: *7-8*: later S Essex College.
Southwark Crown Court: *after 246 image 5; 267 274.*
Soviet Union: *50 243*: communist state in Eurasia that existed from 1922 to 1991.
Spain, date cultivation in: *4.*
Speaker, The: *75(Iraq) 97fn 154 169 221*: presiding officer in UK House of Commons & Iraq National Assembly.
Spectator, The: *73fn 87fn 88 333fn*: weekly conservative magazine.
Spink, Paddy: *134.*
Sport: *16 32*:
Sri Lanka: *262-63*: formerly Ceylon, island state in Indian Ocean S of India; pop 21m.
St George's Church, Baghdad: *91-92.*
Stahl, Lesley: *303*: US journalist.
Stalin, Joseph: *305*: 1922-52 General Sec of Soviet Union's Communist Party; 1941-53 Chairman of Soviet Union's Council of Ministers; d in office.
Stark, Freya: *342*: b in Paris 1893 d in Italy 1993; Anglo-Italian explorer & travel writer; numerous books on travels in ME & Afghanistan; one of first non-Arabs to travel through Empty Quarter.
State of the Union Address 2003: *155.*
State Oil Marketing Organisation (SOMO): *9 133 139 142 231 250 274*: still exists.
Steel, David, Lord Steel of Aikwood: *98*: Lib Dem MP, 1976-88 party leader, 1999-2003 Presiding Officer of Scottish Parliament; visited Iraq.

Stop the War Coalition: *161-62+fn 169 196-97 199 248 298 312.*
Strathclyde University: *68.*
Straw, Jack: *235 244*: 2001-06 Lab Foreign Sec; told Chilcot decision to go to war with Iraq had haunted him; voted for war & v investigation.
Stuttgart: *12*: town in S. Germany.
Subjugation of Arab/Islamic world by the West: *36*:
Sudan: *27 48 180 310*: large African state S of Egypt; pop 40m, 70% native Arab speakers.
Suez Canal: *10 50*: Mediterranean to Red Sea; 193 km; built by French; opened 1869; nationalised 1956.
Suez crisis: *9-10*: 1956; immediate cause nationalisation of Suez Canal by Nasser qv. See also Egypt; Eden, Sir Anthony.
Suicide bombing: *126 317.*
Sulaymaniyah: *61 70 210*: Kurdish city 263 km N of Baghdad, in Kurdish Autonomous Region; pop 656,000.
Suleiman Adil al-Dulaimi, Dr: *229.*
Sullivan, Justice Jeremy: *256*: High Court of Justice, ruled with Moses in BAE case.
Sunglasses, Carrera: *121.*
Sunni Islam. See Muslims.
Supreme Council for the Islamic Revolution in Iraq (SCIRI): *151-52 178 200 204-05*: 2007 name changed to less provocative Islamic Supreme Council of Iraq.
Surbiton: *27 36 22*: suburb 25 km SW from Central London.
Surcharge: *xvii 124; surcharge crisis 137-44; 215-16 231 246+fn: Volcker 247-52: 259 261: hearings 266-74: 292 297.*
Sussex: *282 296*: historic English county 76 km S of London on S coast; 1974 divided into two counties, E & W Sussex; Brighton & Hove largest city of whole county.
Suwaira: *114+fn 115*: town on Tigris 105 km SE of Baghdad; 1920-26 Abdul-Karim Qasim (who was of Kurdish-Sunni & Shia descent), leader of 1958 coup, lived here; ancient remains as at nearby Sassifon.
Sykes-Picot agreement: *48*: secret 1916 carve up of ME by UK & France (Tsarist Russia assented).
Syria: *12 18fn 34 48 79 137 143 180 190 194 202 242 250 309 342 346-47 350-52*: state at E end of Mediterranean, S of Turkey, N of Jordan, partly E of Lebanon; Mediterranean seaboard N of Lebanon; former French protectorate; 1958-61 union with Egypt called United Arab Republic; 1963 Ba'athist coup d'état; 1967 Israel captured & later unilaterally annexed 2/3 of Golan Heights in SW of country; 2011 uprising started in Deraa, leading to civil war; ISIS has joined rebels who are backed by West; Hizbollah supports govnt which is backed by Russia; pop 17m; land now occupied by Israel-Palestine, Jordan, Lebanon & Syria called Greater Syria, or Esh-Sham in Arabic.

Taha Hamoud: *134*: Saddam's Deputy Oil Minister.
Taha Yassin Ramadan: *217*: 1991-2003 joint Vice-President of Iraq; executed 2007.
Taif: *13fn*: Saudi town, 200/106 km E of Jeddah/Mecca resp; alt 1,879 metres, summer resort; pop 1m.

Talib Naji Talib: *209.*
Taoiseach: *xv 81 293*: name of PM, chief executive & head of govnt of Irish Republic.
Tariq Ali: *161 162fn*: UK-Pakistani activist, founder member, Stop the War.
Tariq al-Mashhadami, Dr: *229.*
Tariq Aziz: *xv xxiv 64 74-75; after 78 image 10; 81-84 85+fn 87 90-91 95fn 124 128 140 144 164 167-68 175 181 214-15 220-27 250 Appendix 4*: 1979-2003 Deputy Iraqi PM; 1983-91 Foreign Minister; 1957 joined Ba'ath party; 1974-77 member of Regional Command Council; 1977 became member of Revolutionary Command Council; condemned those Arab states which were subservient to US & supported sanctions; 2000 UK Jr Minister for Foreign Affairs, Peter Hain qv, set up secret war-avoidance team, but after initial cooperation, Aziz refused to meet delegations, no doubt distrusting those sent.
Tawfiq Saddi, Dr: *229.*
Taylor, Ian: *xxiv 104 212*: backbench Con MP, voted v Iraq war with 14 of his Con colleagues; stood down as MP in 2010.
Taylor, Sir Teddy: *xxiv 104*: Con MP; d Sept 2007; voted for Iraq war; absent for vote on amendment saying case for war not estab; after war voted 5 times for investigation.
Tchenguiz, Robert: *257+fn*: brother of Vincent; Iraqi of Jewish descent; SFO paid £1.5m compensation.
Tchenguiz, Vincent: *257+fn*: brother of Robert, Iraqi of Jewish descent; SFO paid £3m compensation.
TCNs. See Third Country Nationals.
TCP2: *28+fn*: oil rig platform in Norwegian waters.
Technology transfer: *52 55*: process of transferring technological know-how to those without it.
Teesside: *19-21*:
Telemetering: *14 17.*
Television interviews: *45 63 196.*
Tenet, George: *184*:
Terrorism: *54 146 159 190 215 218 309 Endpiece.*
Thailand: *137.*
Thamir al-Ghadban: *207-09*: part of opposition; later Minister of Oil.
Thamir Ogali, Dr: *163 210*: DG of Ministry of Oil in Ba'athist regime.
Thatcher, Margaret: *166 254fn 343*: 1979-90 Con PM; negotiated Al-Yamamah qv weapons deals with Saudis.
Third Country Nationals (TCNs): *22fn 211.*
Thomas, John, Lord Thomas of Cwmgiedd, QC: *244*: 2013-17 Lord Chief Justice.
Threadneedle Street: *13*: in the City of London qv.
Tickell, Sir Crispin: *190*: 1987-90 UK ambassador to UN; signed Oliver Miles' (qv) open letter.
Tigris, R: *3fn 46fn; after 130 images 1&5; 83 96 114-15 117 137 342*: 1850 km long; rises in SE Turkey; flows through Iraq to confluence with Euphrates at Qurna.

Tikrit & Tikriti clan: *64 124 175 185 192 204 216-17 219 342*: 140 km NW of Baghdad, home of Tikriti clan, ie members of Hussein/Tulfah family bearing surname al-Tikriti.
Times, The: *xxiv 5 77fn 236 237fn 281+fn; after 291 image 3*: right of centre newspaper with establishment status; founded 1785.
Tonge, Dr Jenny, Baroness Tonge: *xxiv 104*: 1997-2005 Lib Dem MP; 2005 made life peer; 2003 voted v Iraq war & for investigation; after visit to Gaza compared it to Warsaw Ghetto; Jan 2004 sacked as Lib Dem children's spokeswoman for saying that if she were to live in the circumstances experienced by Palestinians she 'might just consider' becoming a suicide bomber (see Blair, Cherie); Nov 2004 backed Impeach Blair campaign; 2006 heavily criticised for saying 'The pro-Israeli lobby has got its grips on the western world, its financial grips. I think they've probably got a grip on our party;' 2010 removed as Lib Dem health spokeswoman in HofL following her call for investigation into allegations IDF was harvesting organs in Haiti; 2012 given ultimatum by Nick Clegg, leader of Lib Dems & Deputy PM in Con-Lib Dem coalition, to apologise for saying 'Beware Israel. Israel is not going to be there forever in its present form' et al; responded by resigning the whip (cutting her ties with the party, but remaining a member); 2016, called on British Jews to condemn Israel; Campaign Against Antisemitism demanded her expulsion from Lib Dems; thereupon suspended; she responded by resigning from party; expressed interest in joining Lab party now Jeremy Corbyn was leader.
Tooks Chambers: *263.*
Total S.A.: *28*: French oil coy; 2000 merged with Elf Aquitaine (which Saddam had awarded exclusive contract to Iraqi oilfields in 1993); name briefly changed to TotalFinaElf; 2003 present name adopted.
Tower Bridge: *167*: London.
Townsend, General Charles Vere Ferrers: *71fn.*
Trade unions in Britain: *9 20 169.*
Trafalgar Square: *10*: London.
Transjordan. See Jordan.
Trebil: *67; after 78 image 11; 93*: Iraq, village nr Karameh/Trebil Border Crossing with Jordan.
Tribalism: *24 52 118 179 191fn 192 304.* See also Tikrit & Tikriti clan.
Tripoli, Libya: *25-26*: capital, Roman remains in city & at Leptis Magna nearby; pop 2.5m.
Truman Library of Independence Missouri: *172.*
Truth, Justice and Peace: *165-66.*
Tulkaram: *5*: Palestinian town; now on border between Israel & occupied territories; E of Israel's security barrier; 'depth barrier' nearer to town cutting it off from hinterland & refugee camp; pop 51,300, refugee camp 11,000.
Tunisia: *26 35 49-50 54 210 308 310*: N. African Arab state between Libya & Algeria; pop 11.4m.
Turkey: *6 12 48-49 71fn 75 84 110 140 143 166 242 270 347 351*: state formed from remainder of Ottoman empire qv after WWI; 1908 Young Turks, a group incl Mustafa Kamal (later named Atatürk, meaning father of the Turks), forced Sultan Abdul Hamid to restore 1876 constitution; 1914 they favoured alliance with Germany & Austria-Hungary; Ottoman empire was already crumbing; 1920

Treaty of Sévres carved it up, incl Turkish speaking Anatolia; 1919-23 Turkish War of Independence led by Mustafa Kamal; 1923-38 (when he d) Turkey's 1st President; modern secular state; 1952 joined NATO; 1974 invaded Cyprus following decade of unrest & coup replacing Archbishop Makarios with Nikos Sampson who favoured union with Greece; 1983 estab Turkish Republic of Northern Cyprus, only recognised by Turkey; 1984 Kurdistan Workers' Party (PKK) began separatist insurgency; 40,000 casualties to date; Tayyip Erdogan (2003-14 PM, 2014-present President) with his Justice & Development Party, has pursued socially/religiously conservative & economically liberal policies; 2011 lifted ban on wearing of Hijab in universities; 2013 ditto public buildings; 2016 unsuccessful coup, answered by a purge of opponents of the govnt; pop 81m.
Turkomans: *180 192*.
TV stations: *314*: Iraq post-2003.
Two Peoples, One Future: *197*: statement by Jews for Justice for Palestinians.
Two-state solution: *199fn*: a proposal to end Jewish-Arab conflict by creating two states alongside each other, one Jewish, the other Palestinian; since 1967 Palestinian state envisaged as being in the occupied territories of W Bank, E Jerusalem & Gaza.

UAE. See United Arab Emirates.
Uday Hussein: *83 175*: eldest son of Saddam Hussein; July 2003 killed in Mosul with brother Qusay & possibly his 14-year-old son Mustapha in shoot-out with US forces.
UK, United Kingdom: *(includes Britain) xiv xvii xviii 1 6 8 10 13-14 16-17 22 24-26 32 35 39 41 43 45fn 49-50 57fn 60-61 64 66 70 73-78 83 85 87 91-92 94-95 97-99 101-03 108-09 111-12 119 122 129 131 134 136 138 140 143 147 150 154 157-59 161-63 165 167 169 171 173 175 178 190+fn 191 193 196 198 201 207-08 210fn 212 231 234 239-40 242-43 245 247-51 254+fn 257 265-71 273 275 299 302-04 306-07 310 313 315 317 319-21 329-30 337-39 344 347-51*: 1707 Act of Union joined kingdoms of England & Scotland.
Umm Qasr: *72-73 Appendix 2*: port city S of Iraq nr Kuwait border; 63 km S of Basrah; naval base estab after 1958 revolution; pop 108,000.
United Nations/United Nations Organisation (UN): *xviii 1 2 43-44 59 69 72-73 77 82-83 86 87fn 91 97-99 109-10 131 134 136-39 143 147 149 150+fn 151 156 158 160 165 170-71 177 180 190 199fn 225-26 240 244 247-48 248fn 251-52 259 261 263-66 268-69 273 275 300-03 313 315-16 318 331-32 337-38 348-49*: international body to promote co-operation & create global order; founded 1945; raised ME hopes of justice in the region; replaced League of Nations (1920-46); League required unanimous decisions, lacked representation for ½ world's pop under colonial control & membership inadequate (US never joined, USSR, Germany & Japan members for only part of its existence); 1942 'Declaration of United Nations' by WWII Allies; 1945 51 states joined, now 193 members; HQ extraterritorial site in NY; 5 principal organs General Assembly, Security Council qv (for binding resolutions on peace & security), Economic & Social Council, Secretariat & International Court of Justice; UN agencies incl World Bank qv, World Health Organization, World Food Programme qv, UNESCO & UNICEF qv; 5 permanent members of Security Council (China, France, Russia, UK & US) have veto power; 1948 Universal Declaration of Human Rights.

UN Convention on the Rights of the Child: *69*.
UNICEF (United Nations Children's Fund) reported 1991-98 ½m. 'excess' deaths of under 5s.
United Arab Emirates (UAE): *31 180 194*: fed in E Arabia of 7 emirates, Abu Dhabi (the capital) qv, Ajman, Dubai qv, Fujairah, Ras al-Khaimah, Sharjah & Umm al-Quwain; formed 1971; ruled by Britain as Trucial States before that; pop 9.2m of which 1.4 Emirati citizens, 7.8m expatriates.
United Nations Act: *266*: UK, 1946; enabled govt to enact non-military SC resolutions by orders in council; no need for parliamentary approval.
United Nations Associations (UNA): *248fn*: worldwide group of independent associations 'dedicated to inform, inspire, and mobilize' people 'to support the ideals and vital work' of the UN; 1945 UNA UK & 1946 UNA USA founded; while supportive of UN, UNAs also provide criticism, e.g. on veto.
United Nations Boundary Commission: *331*.
United Nations Monitoring, Verification and Inspection Commission (UNMOVIC): *150+fn 170*: 1999-2007 replacement for UNSCOM.
United Nations Security Council Resolutions (UNSCRs): *43-44 98-99 133 138 171 176 336*. See also UNSCR 661, 687, 986, 1330, 1441 & 1483.
United Nations Special Commission (UNSCOM): *44 147-150 150fn 156*: 1991-1999 inspects Iraq's compliance on WDMs; replaced by UNMOVIC.
UNMOVIC. See United Nations Monitoring, Verification and Inspection Commission.
UNSCOM. See United Nations Special Commission.
UNSCR 661: *43 59 125 133 136 138-39 143 247 268 270 273*: 1990; imposed sanctions on Iraq; admin by 661 Committee.
UNSCR 687: *44*: 1991; extension of 661 following First Gulf War.
UNSCR 986: *98-99*: 1995; oil-for-food resolution.
UNSCR 1330: *138*: extended oil-for-food programme.
UNSCR 1441: *336-37*: 2002; offering Saddam 'a final opportunity to comply with its disarmament obligations'.
UNSCR 1483: *176 180*: lifted sanctions & started wind-up of oil-for-food.
Uranium: *155*.
Uranium tipped weapons: *69 112 195 348*.
US military's ties with Andrew White: *88*.
US, United States of America: *(includes America) xviii xix 1 2 6 13 20 22 45 47 49-50 53-54 56 61-62 79-80 83-85 88 91 95 97 105-06 108 111-12 119 122 127-29 131 136 138 140 142-43 145-51 153 155 158-59 162 164-65 167 169-70 172-80 82 185-89 191 193 196 198-205 207-10 212 215-17 221-24 226 235 237-38 242 246-48 251 255-56 265 270 273 275 293 298 300 302-04 309-10 312-14 316-17 337-39 343-44 348-50*. 1776 founded on Enlightenment principles after declaring independence from British rule; now a union of 50 states; despite rise of other economies, still world's most powerful state economically & militarily; though less dependent on ME oil since 1970s (now c13% of imports) long-term reserves in the ME remain attractive; aim to keep options open; pop 326m.
USS Abraham Lincoln: *176*.

Vanity Fair: *148*: monthly magazine of popular culture, fashion & current affairs; ran 1913-36; revived 1983.

Vatican: *109 217 226*: city-state surrounded by Rome; residence of RC pope.
Vicar of Baghdad. See White, Canon Andrew.
Victory Arch: *after 291 image 6*: or Swords of Qadisiyah; a monument of outstretched hands holding crossed swords in central Baghdad; built to commemorate Iran–Iraq War; 2007 new Iraqi govnt under Nouri al-Maliki started removal, but challenged by US Ambassador Zalmay Khalilzad, who blocked the demolition; 2011 restoration work began.
Vietnam: *128 352*.
Vision for Iraq and the Iraqi People, A: *158*: 2003; part of outcome of Atlantic Summit qv, Azores.
Vitol: *249-51*: global energy/commodity trading coy founded Rotterdam 1966.
Voice of America: *45*: U.S. govnt-funded international news source.
Volcker report. See Independent Committee.
Volcker, Paul: *after 246 image 3; 246-53 268+fn 271 275*: Chair of the Independent Committee qv; 1979-87 Chair of Federal Reserve.
von der Goltz, Baron Colmar: *71fn*: German Field Marshall.
von Sponeck, Hans-Christof: *86+fn 91 113 136 208 225 230 270 302 315 348-50*: aka Hans von Sponeck; 1998-2000 UN Humanitarian Coordinator in Iraq; resigned, as had his predecessor, Denis Halliday; 1957 among 1st conscientious objectors in W Germany; 2005 served as expert on World Tribunal on Iraq.
von Sponeck Hans Graf: *86fn*: Hans-Christof's father.

Wadi Rum: *62*: Jordan; protected desert wilderness 100 km S of Petra.
Wainwright, Michael: *75*.
Wakefield, Mary: *87fn 88fn*: journalist; commissioning editor, *The Spectator*.
Waleed al-Jubori, Dr: *229*.
Walker, Mr: *35*: GM of the shipping coy Gray Mackenzie.
Wall Street Journal: *84*: founded 1889; US business international daily based in NY City; largest circulation in US.
Wandsworth jail/gaol/prison: *xvi xxiii; after 291 images 1&2; 275-89 323*: built 1851, category B (moderate security).
War on terror: *148 161 236*.
Wardle, Robert: *254-56*: 2003-08 Director of SFO.
Washington DC: *47-48 88 145 149 152 187fn 189 299 302 347*: Capital of the US.
Washington Post: *151fn 155+fn* : US; widely read daily paper; aims to be middle of the road.
Waterborne diseases: *137*.
Weapon sales: *254fn 310 332*.
Weapons of mass destruction (WMDs): *43-44 110-11 147-52 154-56 159 162-64 170-73 176 188 233 239 281 300fn 320 334-36*.
Webber, Andrew Lloyd, Lord Lloyd-Webber: *216*.
Wembley Park: *26 27 31*: district of London 12 km NW from centre.
West Bank: *4fn 45*: Palestine.
West Lothian: *65-73*: Scottish lowland county; aka Linlithgowshire.
Westminster: *87 239*: area of central London on N bank of Thames; incl Palace of Westminster, Buckingham Palace, Westminster Abbey & Westminster Cathedral (RC).

Whisky: *26 83 121*.
White, Andrew, Canon: *86-90*: 1998-2004 co-director International Centre for Reconciliation at Coventry Cathedral, from 2002 with Justin Welby; 2005 became vicar of St George's, Baghdad; 2013 recalled by Archbishop Welby citing security concerns.
Whyte, David: *212+fn*: now Prof of Socio-legal Studies, Uni of Liverpool.
Widows in Iraq: *59 314*.
Willcocks, Sir William: *46fn 342*.
Williamson, Phillipa: *257*: 2008-12 CEO of SFO.
Wilmshurst, Elizabeth: *157+fn*: legal advisor, FCO.
Wilson, Joseph: *155+fn*: sent by CIA to investigate Niger story; husband of Valerie Plame; 1992-95 Ambassador to Gabon & São Tomé & Príncipe.
Wiltshire: *63*: county is S central England.
Winchburgh: *65*: W Lothian.
Wolfgang, Walter: *162fn*.
Wolfowitz, Paul: *150 183-84 237+fn*: 2001-05 US Deputy Sec of Defence.
Women in Iraq: *59-60 79 118 123-24 180-81 228fn*.
Women's Federation: *60 79*.
Women's liberation movement in the West: *60*.
Wood, Mike: *xxiv 104 313*: backbench Lab MP, 1997-2015; voted v Iraq war; 2006 one of 12 Lab MPs backing call by Plaid Cymru & SNP for inquiry into war.
World Bank: *177 195*: created 1944 at Bretton Woods Conference; provides loans to countries for capital projects; criticised for being ignorant &/or insensitive to local conditions, imposing a Western template, & making harmful demands. See IMF.
World community: *196 301*.
World Council of Churches: *86*: founded 1948; RC Church not incl though it sends observers.
World Food Programme: *86 302 315*: UN; world's largest organization addressing hunger.
Wright, Rosalind: *254+fn:*, 1997-2003 Director of SFO.
WWI cemeteries in Iraq: *92*.
WWI: *60 71fn92 203*: 1914-18; simply put conflict between, on one side, the German Empire, the Austro-Hungarian Empire & the Ottoman Empire; & on the other side, the British Empire, the French Empire, the Russian (Tsarist) Empire & from 1917 the US; the first side was defeated.
WWII: *58 198 340*: 1939-45; simply put conflict between on the one side Germany, Italy & the Japanese Empire; & on the other the British Empire with Commonwealth countries, the French Empire (Metropolitan France overrun in 1940), & from 1941 both the Soviet Union & the US; the first side was defeated.
Wyatt, Oscar: *215 216+fn*: Texas oilman, friend of Saddam; 2007 sole US conviction for paying surcharge.
Wyoming: *152*: state in mountain region of W US.

Yahya: *27*. Sudanese colleague at Coppas.
Yasser Arafat: *51-52 128*: Palestinian leader; 1959 founding member, together with other diaspora Palestinians, of Fatah, with a self-help nationalist ideology;

Arafat then head of General Union of Palestinian Students (GUPS) at Cairo Uni; 1969-2004 Chairman of Palestine Liberation Organisation (PLO); d 2004 in suspicious circumstances. See Palestine.
Yellow fever: *348*: acute viral disease causing bleeding; transmitted by infected mosquitoes.
Yemen: *180 242 309 310*: Arab state in SW of Arabian peninsular, pop 28 m.
Yoga: *xviii 267 284-85 289 291 315 321-25*.
Young, Canon Ian: *89*.
Yousif al-Kubaisi, Dr: *229*.
Yugoslavia: *12*: 1918-92 state in Balkan peninsular formed out of Serbia & parts of dissolved Austria-Hungary; 1953-80 Josip Broz Tito was PM; 1992 disintegrated.

Zain: *314*: mobile phone network post-2003.
Zarqa: *67*: Jordan.
Zarqawi. See Abu Musab al-Zarqawi.
Zawiyya: *25*: Libya.
Zena Haddad: *xxv 263 273 286*.
Zermatt: *11*.
Zhako: *332*:, city nr Turkish border in Iraqi Kurdistan.
Ziad Aziz: *124 224-25*: son of Tariq Aziz; 2001 imprisoned for corruption; now lives in Jordan.
Zionist: *51-53 107-08 125-28 147 157 178 183fn 187 199 203-04 226-27 236-37 238+fn 241 296 317 320-21*: as a noun a believer in development & protection of a Jewish national state; originally location debated; since at latest 1917 Balfour Declaration Palestine was the objective; 1948 state achieved; some say Zionism no longer applicable term & Israel qv is a post-Zionist state, its citizens & supporters post-Zionists; this perception not common in Arab & Muslim world; 'Zionist' used also as adjective. See Zionist entity.
Zionist entity: *36 44 49-51 53 80 89 105 126 128-29 147-48 152 159 164 178 180-81 191 199fn 227 240-41 309-10 321 338*: term used to refer to Israel by those opposed to its existence, or at least its policies; 1896 Theodor Herzl, Jewish-Hungarian journalist, published *The Jewish State*; backed every horse by negotiating with all the contemporary great powers in furtherance of his plan; acknowledged indigenous pop would need to be displaced; E European Jews would only support Jewish state in Palestine; Herzl d 1904, but his blueprint was followed in many respects; 1917 Balfour Declaration that Britain favoured Jewish homeland in Palestine; 1920-48 League of Nations British mandate, of which UN inherited responsibility in 1945; 1947 after filibustering by the Zionist delegation which won invaluable 3-day delay, UNGAR endorses partition plan with small margin over required 2/3[rds]; Jerusalem to become international city; 1948 Israeli State declared in 56% of land; by 1949 armistice Israel occupied 68% incl W Jerusalem; 1967 remainder of Palestine occupied; 1980 E Jerusalem annexed; pop incl Israeli settlers 8.5m; 21% Palestinian. See also Palestine.
Zuheir Ibrahim: *66 74*: pre-2003 Iraqi Chargé d'Affairs, London.

Additional abbreviations used in this index which are not listed on pages xii to xiv

a/c=account
admin=administration
aka=also known as
alt=altitude,
AUC= American University of Cairo
b=born
bl=billion
C=century
c=approximately
cap=caption of illustration
CofE=Church of England
Con=Conservative
conf=conference
corp=corporation
coy=company
d=died
dept=department
dtr=daughter
E=east
esp=especially
estab=established
fed=federation
fn=footnote;
g=great
gdtr=granddaughter
govnt=government
HofL=House of Lords
HQ=headquarters
INC=Iraqi National Congress
incl=including/includes/included
Jr=junior
km=kilometre(s)

Lab=Labour
Lib Dem=Liberal Democrat
lit=literature
m=million
mar=married
MB=Muslim Brotherhood
ME=Middle East/Eastern
mtg=meeting
N=north
nat=national
neocon=neoconservative
nr=near
NY=New York
prob=probably
Prof=Professor
pop=population
PPE=Philosophy/Politics/Economics
qv=refer to index entry with the preceding word/phrase
R=River
RC=Roman Catholic
re=concerning
rep=representative/representing
resp=respectively
S=south/southern
sec=secretary
snr=senior
uni=university
USAF=US Airforce
v=against
W=west/western

Lightning Source UK Ltd.
Milton Keynes UK
UKHW021822211218
334403UK00001B/6/P